NAPOLEON III
AND
MEXICO

NAPOLEON III

AND

MEXICO

American Triumph over Monarchy

by
ALFRED JACKSON HANNA
and
KATHRYN ABBEY HANNA

THE UNIVERSITY OF NORTH CAROLINA PRESS · CHAPEL HILL

Library of Congress Catalog Card Number 72–156761
ISBN 0–8078–1171–8
Manufactured in the United States of America
Printed by The TJM Corporation

CONTENTS

———◄◆►———

MAPS

———◄◆►———

Prepared by K. Richard Robinson

ILLUSTRATIONS

————◆————

The political caricature was the most powerful editorial weapon of the nineteenth century. This art form, in distorting the salient features of leading personages and graphically and grotesquely exaggerating events, created humor, satire, and ridicule.

Leading publications of caricatures in the era of Napoleon III were, in France, the daily *Charivari*; in England, the weekly *Punch*, and in the United States, *Harper's Weekly*. Among the cleverest caricaturists of this period were Henri Daumier, Gustave Doré, George Cruikshank, Thomas Nast, and Sir John Tenniel, whose illustrations in *Alice's Adventures in Wonderland* (1866) gained him fame and immortality.

The following caricatures are representative of the hundreds drawn to interpret and clarify actions included in this volume.

ACKNOWLEDGMENTS

---◀◆▶---

The authors started this project in 1944 in Mexico. On a research trip to Mexico in 1946 the authors located the long lost
Maximilian archives that had not been sent to Austria, and
marked them for the guidance of other scholars. For a description of these papers of the Maximilian empire, see the bibliography, "Official Records, Mexico." Search for other materials
was continued in South America, in Canada, in England, a large
part of a year in France, and in many of the leading depositories
and libraries of the United States.

The investigation of materials pertinent to an undertaking
which occurred more than a century ago was so extensive and
complicated that it was necessary for the two authors to devote
the major part of a quarter of a century to its research and writing. Throughout this quarter of a century innumerable courtesies were extended the authors as they traveled thousands of
miles and consulted with hundreds of investigators.

Generous grants were given the authors by the American
Philosophical Society and the Social Science Research Council.

See the bibliography for courtesies extended by those in charge
of historical materials in archival depositories, libraries, colleges
and universities, and historical organizations and by individuals
in many parts of the United States, Latin America, England,
France, and other areas.

Seven friends—Ernest A. Brunoehler, Jr., Elizabeth E. Hamer,
Velma O. Jerkins, Irving A. Leonard, Julian Nally, Emmett
Peter, Jr., and Richard F. Trismen—rendered incalculable serv-

ices in consultations, editing, and preparation of this manuscript.

Others who gave similar services were Alan Abele, Angela Palomo Campbell, Margaret D. Duer, Jane F. Fletcher, Roberta Hamilton, Anne B. Hicks, Edith G. Knepper, Emilia Eulalia Knight, John Large, Jr., George E. Larsen, Katharine Lewis Lehman, Michael Lever, Flora L. Magoun, Olive Mahony, Carolyn McFarland, Robert Ryal Miller, Helen Pratt, Jean O. Phillips, James Gamble Rogers II, Lenore S. Roland, William Shelton, Eleanor Sreb, Ann Hall Tennis, and Gerard Walker.

PROLOGUE: AN OVERVIEW

————◆————

A classic synonym for catastrophe was coined when Napoleon Bonaparte lost both army and empire at Waterloo. Half a century later, an American Waterloo was to befall another Bonaparte, Napoleon III. But it has been obscured by a curious myth of ardent friendship between France and the United States.

The link of amity forged by the French alliance enabling the thirteen English colonies to gain independence was profoundly emotionalized by the filial devotion of Lafayette to Washington. When the twenty-year-old Frenchman joined Washington's staff, his virtual adoption ineradicably symbolized an attachment between the two countries. Indeed, American gratitude to France in the tense days of her struggle for freedom was so deep as to create one of the strongest of international traditions.

Not even the grim imminence of a war between France and the United States in the 1860s penetrated this pervasive myth. Only the good sense of President Lincoln and the diplomacy of Secretary of State Seward prevented military strife over French violation of the sovereignty of Mexico.

The crisis between Lincoln and the French emperor grew out of a sharply divided ideology—whether republics or monarchies would prevail in the Western Hemisphere. European monarchs, in particular Napoleon III, feared American republican ideas would subvert their systems and tradition.

Napoleon III undertook to establish on the southern frontier of the United States a strong monarchy as a barrier against further U.S. expansion. He also proposed to convert the other

[xiii]

Spanish American republics into monarchies similar to the Second Empire of France. The historian Dexter Perkins, who characterized the French emperor as half genius and half scheming politician, asserted this fantastic scheme was the most "sinister project, in terms of American interest, American influence and American ideas . . . ever . . . conceived in the history of the Monroe Doctrine."

Monarchs had governed the New World since its European colonization. On July 4, 1776, some two-thirds of the Anglo-Americans in the colonies established by England in North America proclaimed their freedom from what they regarded as the decadent rule of kings. One-third of the colonists remained loyal to King George III. Some Loyalists fought with the British army against their fellow Americans. In retaliation the Patriots jailed some Loyalists, put others on parole or in detention camps, and occasionally tarred and feathered them. When the thirteen English colonies became free, probably 200,000 Loyalists had died, had been exiled, or had migrated to Canada, the Bahamas, and other parts of the British Empire.

Later, when the Spanish American colonies achieved independence, they were divided over whether to establish monarchies or republics. Mexico was freed by General Iturbide, who assumed the title of emperor. Described by historian Hubert Herring as "one of America's most spectacular rascals," he was executed after a reign of less than a year. Mexico then became a republic. A brief, grotesque experiment in monarchy occurred in Haiti. A Brazilian monarchy, established after the separation of that country from Portugal, ended as late as 1889, when Brazil too became a republic.

Spanish colonies in the Americas, influenced by Rousseau and other philosophers, established republics similar in form to the United States. However, their advancement was seriously retarded by high illiteracy and by the sharply different heritage between native Indians and European immigrants.

New World improvements on democratic processes were regarded by the ruling classes of Europe as insidious to their governments and traditions. Fear by monarchs for their system increased in the 1820s through the 1850s as the United States grew phenomenally in population, literacy, wealth, and military power. The United States from the days of its founding had determined to improve on the classic Greek ideal of democracy.

Its extraordinary advancement was attributed to such democratic innovations as free distribution of land by homestead, free public schools, and freedom of religion. In less than half a century, its national domain spanned the continent from the Floridas to the Pacific. Even Great Britain became apprehensive over the almost 4,000-mile boundary Canada shared with the United States.

Many Americans did little to allay the mistrust of U.S. republicanism. George Bancroft, widely recognized in Europe as a statesman, proclaimed, "The world is growing weary of that most costly of all luxuries, hereditary kings." On a mission to Europe when Bancroft was asked why he and his fellow diplomats appeared at European courts dressed in black like so many undertakers, he is said to have responded prophetically that Americans represented the burial of monarchy.

The violation by Napoleon III of the sovereignty of the Republic of Mexico initiated his "Grand Design for the Americas." Mexico and the other Spanish American republics were to be "regenerated" into stable, prosperous, enlightened monarchies. With the then vast empire of Brazil, they would gradually increase Latin influence in the Americas. France, as the dominant Latin empire, would draw these monarchies into her economic orbit and in time this alliance would make her the most powerful force in the world. The Latins would surpass the political power of England and the United States; Paris would be the supreme cultural center; and the church at Rome would again hold the scepter of religious imperialism.

Much of the writing on the French emperor's scheme for the Americas has been by Europeans who, not understanding basic American convictions, ignored the facts stressed by Dexter Perkins. The Bonaparte dream for New World achievements was designed to exert a profound influence on the world. The French scholar Albert Guérard maintained that this project formed the "deepest thought of the Second Empire." A revised tracing of factors out of which it was created provides ample evidence that the emperor's mentor was Michel Chevalier. The official relationship of Chevalier to Napoleon III in the 1850s and 1860s and Chevalier's interpretation of the Mexican project confirm this influence. Chevalier's investigations of and writings on the democratic processes of the United States preceded the more famous observations and writings of Tocqueville.

The principal architect of Napoleon III's "deepest thought" was the young Marquis de Radepont, soldier and diplomat. A record of Radepont's influence on Napoleon III was largely overlooked in the French archives until its inclusion in these pages.

Publications on the French in Mexico, 1861–67, have not stressed the full meaning of the expedition as a plot against the United States.

Because the noted Count Corti was the first historian to use the valuable Maximilian archives in Austria, his work has long been regarded as one of the most authentic interpretations of the French Intervention in Mexico. However, its authenticity was primarily limited to a biographical study of Maximilian and Charlotte. The empire over which these sovereigns ruled never developed beyond the embryonic concept. Charming and romantic as these young rulers were, they were pathetically incompetent, indecisive, ambitious, and stubborn. The chief defect of Corti's work was his neglect of American sources. By ignoring these sources, Corti failed to grasp the American reactions which finally dominated the outcome.

The exhaustive investigation by the scholarly Carl H. Bock is an indispensable account of the Tripartite (English, French, Spanish) Treaty signed in London, the military expedition to Veracruz and the futile conferences there of commissioners representing the three invading empires. But as its title, *Prelude to Tragedy*, indicates, his study treats only the first three years of the undertaking.

Only by tracing the roles of leading American participants can there be an accurate, comprehensive, and balanced conclusion of Napoleon III's invasion of Mexico. Foremost was the leadership of Abraham Lincoln and his creation of a new Latin American policy. He and other New World statesmen attempted to unify the Americas against European monarchs and to a considerable degree succeeded.

Another American head of state, Benito Juárez of Mexico, demonstrated the extraordinary heritage of American Indian endurance and immovable adherence to convictions.

He possessed an alter ego in the Mexican diplomat Matías Romero. Both natives of Oaxaca, they made heroic contributions in defense of Mexico and of the Americas. Romero, appointed envoy to the United States at twenty-three, was a diplomat possibly as able as any European counterpart. He possessed a shrewd understanding of both European and U.S. conditions. As Harvard scholar George Parker Winship explained, Romero was the preeminent Spanish American builder of Lincoln's Latin American policy.

Romero's strongest ally, asserted the *Washington Star*, in "welding the bonds of union" between Mexico and the United States, was his wife, the former Lucretia Allen of Philadelphia. "She was a great favorite in the Mexican capital," reported the *Star*, because of her fluency in the Spanish language, her wit, and her beauty. In Washington, she saw more visitors every day than all the other ladies of the diplomatic corps combined; her public receptions were almost as well attended as similar events at the White House.

Confederate aspirations were strongly favored by the French and Mexican emperors. On the Rio Grande was the Confederate agent, the bilingual José Quintero. He broke through the U.S. blockade by shipping cotton across the river to the Mexican port of Matamoros and bringing in arms on the return trip. He succeeded in this phenomenal task under such varying and sometimes conflicting conditions as were imposed by Santiago Vidaurre, tyrannical caudillo of northeastern Mexico, by President Benito Juárez, and by military commanders under the French. The so-called Duke of Sonora, Senator William M. Gwin, once a congressman from Mississippi and later a U.S. senator from California, worked out a project with Napoleon III whereby 30,000 Southern refugees would develop gold and silver mines in northwest Mexico. Commodore Matthew Fontaine Maury, who, prior to 1861, had a worldwide reputation as an oceanographer in the U.S. Navy, and whose birthday is celebrated in the schools of Virginia, was appointed Imperial Commissioner of Immigration by Maximilian in an attempt to create a "New Virginia" in Mexico. He established small Confederate refugee settlements in the majority of Mexican states.

Almost unnoticed by European writers was U.S. diplomat General Henry Shelton Sanford, who operated confidentially as the Belgian-based roving political observer for Lincoln. Skilled as a linguist and with an extensive acquaintance with leaders in European centers over a long period, Sanford kept Lincoln and Seward exhaustively informed of trends. His commentaries on French relations and his evaluation of leading personages strengthened the hand of his government.

Also neglected has been the brief but important service of Carl Schurz, one of the great statesmen of the 1860s. He and another highly educated refugee revolutionist from Germany, who knew European conditions at first hand, served consecutively as U.S. ministers to Spain. Schurz, to whom Lincoln wrote, "to the extent of our limited acquaintance no man stands nearer my heart than yourself," sent Lincoln in 1861 an astute evaluation of a powerful participant in the Tripartite Treaty negotiations drawn from his interviews with General Juan Prim and other high Spanish officials. Schurz and his successor at Madrid, Gustav Koerner, as delegates to the Republican Convention of 1860, were active in nominating Lincoln for the presidency. The delicacy of Koerner's diplomacy and understanding of the Spanish character and culture are obvious in his book, *Aus Spanien*.

Lincoln and Seward drastically changed the U.S. policy toward Latin America. They exercised rigid discrimination in sending there as ministers and other representatives of the United States only those who could convince the Latins that the United States no longer condoned slavery, had abandoned the ambition to expand its territory and henceforth would extend the utmost respect and courtesies to the Latins, especially in the settlement of claims.

Among these able statesmen was the brilliant lawyer, wit, and noted orator, Thomas Corwin. His ardent defense of Mexico in the U.S. Senate when the United States made war upon her gave him an instant welcome when Lincoln sent him as minister to that country to help initiate the new Latin American policy.

In Guatemala, adjoining Mexico on the south, was Elisha O. Crosby of California, who undertook to solve problems complicated by Maximilian.

In the extremely difficult post of minister to reactionary and promonarchical Ecuador was Austrian-born Friedrich Hassaurek. He possessed such a crusading spirit for the expansion of human freedom that in his earlier career in Ohio he had become known as "the beer hall Demosthenes."

These and the other unsung defenders of New World independence and democracy are here extended recognition.

In the treatment of Latin American nations as in the creation of other constructive policies, the most active official was Secretary of State William H. Seward. Former governor and two-term senator of New York, he had been the strongest contender for the presidential nomination that was captured by Lincoln. As a senator he gained fame in the slave issue by proclaiming a "higher law than the Constitution." Another household phrase originated by Seward was the "irrepressible conflict," based on Lincoln's "house divided" speech.

Few statesmen ever faced problems more confused and involved internationally than did Seward in the early 1860s. Possibly no secretary of state ever committed more outrageous blunders than he did upon assuming that high office. An astonishing lack of judgment during his early tenure provoked such criticism as that attributed to Lord Palmerston who described him as a vaporing, blustering, ignorant man. He not only virtually suggested that the president abdicate his power to him but also proposed waging war on France and Spain to reunite the Union and the Confederacy.

Seward did indeed have much to learn about human nature and foreign relations but he possessed the rare ability to learn from his mistakes and to act wisely on what he had learned. He grappled with one crisis after another and, as the most intimate continuous associate of Lincoln, grew in discernment and stature.

Seward's voluminous state papers raised national morale, informed the electorate, and clarified the significant issues in this resoundingly important international conflict. His writing also elicited from abroad a profound respect for the independent spirit of the United States and her sister American republics. Nowhere in his career did Seward demonstrate more fully the quality of his mind and the exercise of genius than in arranging the forces that brought about in Mexico the American Waterloo of Napoleon III.

ABBREVIATIONS

---◆---

AG	Archivo General de la Nación
AHR	*American Historical Review*
AMG	Archives du Ministère de la Guerre
AN	Archives Nationales
Arch. Max.	Archiv Kaiser Maximilians von Mexiko
Auessern	Politisches Archiv des k. k. Ministerium des Auessern
BFO	British Foreign Office Papers
BFSP	*British and Foreign State Papers*
Corres. mexicana	*Correspondencia de la legación mexicana en Washington durante la intervención extranjera, 1860–1868*
CP	Correspondance Politique des Consuls, Archives du Ministère des Affaires Etrangères
DB	Dossiers Biographiques
G and P	Genaro García and Carlos Pareyra, eds., *Colección de documentos inéditos ó muy raros para la historia de México*
HAHR	*Hispanic American Historical Review*
JSH	*Journal of Southern History*

LC	Library of Congress
M et D	Mémoires et Documents, Archives du Ministère des Affaires Etrangères
NA	National Archives
NYPL	New York Public Library
ORA	*Official Records of the Union and Confederate Armies*
ORN	*Official Records of the Union and Confederate Navies*
SHQ	*Southwestern Historical Quarterly*

NAPOLEON III
AND
MEXICO

1

Napoleon III's Grand Design
for the Americas
1840s–1850s

Of all European schemes to exploit America the sinister plot of Napoleon III in the 1860s is the least understood because it ended in disaster before it could be achieved. The designation it has carried for the past century, the "French Intervention in Mexico," was the beginning only of the Bonaparte dream. It was indeed an intervention, but intervention describes only a first step and not the concept behind the action. Potentially it was dangerously explosive to the United States and other American republics. The war it brought about involved primarily France and Mexico. On the periphery were Austria, Belgium, England, and Spain. Men who did the fighting were, in the order of importance, Mexicans, Frenchmen, Austrians, Belgians, Egyptians, Sudanese, and a negligible number of Union veterans for the Mexican republic and Confederate veterans for the Mexican Empire.

The battleground was Mexico; the villain, Napoleon III, emperor of the French; the figurehead, Maximilian, emperor of Mexico, impressive, but a sham and utterly incompetent; two persevering and inspiring heads of American states, Benito Juárez of Mexico, and Abraham Lincoln of the United States of America. As stalwart defenders of American republics were two geniuses of diplomacy, Matías Romero, Mexican minister to the

[3]

United States, and William H. Seward, U.S. secretary of state.

One of the more authoritative biographers of Napoleon III, Albert Guérard, contended that this plot for the Americas was the "deepest thought," the most significant concept, and the most arresting undertaking of the Second Empire of France.

A prediction of this Bonaparte dream by a British scholar was published in July, 1864, in the prestigious *Blackwood's Edinburgh Magazine*, entitled "The Napoleonic Idea in Mexico." This scholar, Robert Hogarth Patterson, in 1860 had written *The New Revolution; or, The Napoleonic Policy in Europe*. Some of the predictions in Patterson's book were fulfilled, some were not. Nevertheless, his thinking and even some of his rhetoric were so close to that of the French emperor that his article in *Blackwood's* four years later should not be ignored.

"It is a task as novel as it is honourable," wrote Patterson, "for a monarch to attempt the regeneration of a country other than his own, to carry civilization and prosperity into a region of the globe where they have fallen into decay,—even though he undertook the task primarily with a view to his own interests. To raise a country thrice as large as France from a state of chronic desolation—to pierce it with railways, to reconstruct the old watercourses of irrigation, to reopen the rich mines, and to make the waste places blossom with flowers and fruits and useful plants, is certainly a noble design. And still nobler is it to rescue a population of eight millions from anarchy, demoralisation, and suffering.... Napoleon ... has placed the Mexicans on a vantage-ground which they could not have obtained for themselves, and he gives to them a Government temporarily aided by his troops, recognised by the Powers of Europe, and possessing a fair amount of credit in other countries, by which the work of regenerating the moral and material condition of Mexico may be carried out."

The sinister motive of this proposal—from the U.S. point of view—was to change Spanish American republics into monarchies. If such monarchies could be developed in America as the Second Empire of France had been created, then Napoleon III believed the growth and resultant power of the United States would be so curtailed that its expansion would be stopped.

If Napoleon III's Grand Design were to be his greatest achievement, it must so affect the course of the New World as to eclipse even the American dream of the first Napoleon. When he, in 1803, ceded the extensive Louisiana domain to President Thomas

Jefferson, he and Talleyrand abandoned the French aspiration for a colonial empire in the heart of the Americas. Unable to establish the power of France in the New World, the first Napoleon decided to help indirectly the United States become a transatlantic power which in time would surpass his detested rival, England. His comment on the sale of Louisiana was: "I have just given England a maritime rival that sooner or later will lay low her pride."[1]

Napoleon III (1808–73), nephew of Napoleon I, was the son of King Louis Bonaparte of Holland. In exile much of his early life, Louis Napoleon, the future Napoleon III, was educated by tutors, selected by his mother. In advanced studies a scholar possessed of genius supervised his intellectual development. The devotion of the student prince to his tutor ever kept before him the adventures of intellectual curiosity.

After his dismal failure, in 1836, to inspire the French army to an uprising at Strasbourg to return the Bonapartes to power, Louis Napoleon was shipped off by France to the Americas on the frigate, *Andromède.* Forced to remain at sea four months, he was finally allowed to land in the United States. In New York he studied social, economic, and political conditions. After spending less than three months there, he returned to Switzerland because of the serious illness of his mother, Hortense, daughter of the Empress Josephine and her first husband, the Vicomte de Beauharnais. Following her death he was a refugee in England until 1840. In August of that year Louis Napoleon chartered a small steamer and with some fifty followers landed at the French port of Boulogne. His second attempt to rouse the French army to support him under the imperial eagle ended in failure and imprisonment.

True to the habits he acquired from his tutor, he continued to study in the fifteenth-century prison on the river Somme where Joan of Arc had once been confined. Here, isolated in unhealthful quarters at the base of a grim 100-foot tower, he devoted some five years to intellectual pursuits. His consuming ambition for future power impelled him to acquire a comprehensive grasp of world affairs. One of his fields of concentration was the small, strategically located, republic of Nicaragua. The government of that country provided him with original and extensive source

1. E. W. Lyon, *Louisiana in French Diplomacy, 1759–1894* (Norman, Okla., 1934), p. 206.

materials about the significance to the Western Hemisphere of a proposed trans-isthmian canal. Nicaraguans invited him to direct their proposed undertaking of connecting the Atlantic with the Pacific.

So genuinely impressed was Louis Napoleon by the possibilities of a waterway across Central America that he induced his long-time British friend, Lord Malmesbury, to visit him in prison. Malmesbury was asked to persuade Sir Robert Peel, the prime minister, to support Louis Napoleon's proposal to accept the invitation of Nicaraguan statesmen to help them "establish a stable political situation." An important proviso was that Louis Napoleon "felt capable of undertaking the task only if he were assured beforehand of the foreign support which alone could provide the necessary protection and credit for the new regime." Obviously, the future emperor had to gain his freedom to accept such an offer; to achieve this, he requested British intercession with King Louis Philippe of France for release from prison on condition that he never return to Europe.[2]

The English government was unmoved by Malmesbury's intercession, and nothing came of this Bonaparte New World dream.

In 1846, the year after Louis Napoleon escaped to England, he completed and published in that country a pamphlet embodying his extensive research on the New World and advocating support of the proposed Bonaparte canal. Entitled *Canal of Nicaragua; or, A Project to Connect the Atlantic and Pacific Oceans by Means of a Canal*, by N. L. B., it revealed that its author had become widely knowledgeable about economic conditions in the New World and world trade there.[3] The creative thinking devoted to canal projects by the young Louis Napoleon was to be given enduring expression by his important role as emperor in the success of the Suez Canal. Its builder, Ferdinand de Lesseps, a cousin of the Empress Eugénie, declared that Eugénie was to the union of the Mediterranean and the Red Sea what Isabel of Spain had been to the discovery of America.

Louis Napoleon's stay in England as a refugee was terminated by the rapid succession of events: (1) the abdication of King

2. Edward W. Richards, "Louis Napoleon and Central America," *Journal of Modern History*, XXXIV (June 1962), 179.

3. Michel Chevalier, *L'Isthme de Panama* (Paris, 1844). This pamphlet undoubtedly provided much of the essential information used by "N. L. B."

Louis Philippe of France; (2) the establishment of the Second Republic; and (3) Louis Napoleon's election in 1848 by more than five million votes to the presidency of his native France.

Four years after this election, he assumed the title Napoleon III and gained the acceptance of European monarchs by overthrowing the Second French Republic and establishing the Second Empire. This was at a time when the rising power of U.S. democracy was resented and even feared by monarchs. The political Frankenstein obliquely created by the first Napoleon had thus in time become a threat to the monarchy of France, as well as to the sea power of England. Consequently, Napoleon III sought ways of halting its creeping potential menace.

Reversing his uncle's policy, Napoleon III made of England an ally instead of an enemy, and of its queen a friend. When the French emperor visited Victoria in England, she conferred upon him the Order of the Garter. With England Napoleon III defeated Russia in the Crimean War, preserved the integrity of Turkey, consolidated his power in Europe, and advanced his personal prestige. Thereafter, the policy of the Second French Empire was developed largely in harmony with that of Great Britain, and eventually Napoleon III became the dominant ruler in Europe.

Even before he made an intensive study of conditions in the New World, Louis Napoleon appears to have been fascinated by his family's connections with the Americas, including his own brief visit to the United States. His grandmother, the Empress Josephine, an American, was a native of the French island of Martinique in the Caribbean. There his mother, Queen Hortense, spent three years as a young girl. The first wife of his youngest uncle, Jerome, was Elizabeth Patterson of Baltimore. (Their grandson was to be Theodore Roosevelt's secretary of the navy.) At the age of twenty-three Louis Napoleon received firsthand information about the republic of the United States and its frontier from his first cousin, "Colonel" Achille Murat. Murat, crown prince of Naples, was the son of Caroline Bonaparte and of the great cavalry leader of Napoleon I's armies. This nephew of Napoleon I emigrated from exile in Austria to the United States in 1823, became a citizen, married a great grandniece of George Washington, and became a planter and lawyer in Florida, then partly populated by Indians. He loved the raw life of pioneers on the American frontier and served as a county judge near Tallahassee. He expressed his admiration for the democracy of the United States and life in America in several books written in French, and translated into English, German, Dutch, and Swedish.[4]

The Bonaparte first cousins—Achille Murat and Louis Napoleon—met in London in 1831 at a Bonaparte reunion and also there on at least one other occasion. Murat's godmother, Louis Napoleon's mother, the former Queen of Holland, was shocked by Murat's democratic ideas, noting that life in a "little American hut" severely limited his horizon.[5]

When he became emperor of the French and a world leader, Napoleon III began dreaming of an adventure in the New World, involving the United States. The wealth and power of this republic had risen in part through its acquisition from Napoleon I of the vast Louisiana area from the Mississippi to the farthest western reaches of the Rocky Mountains. As this republic continued its phenomenal expansion by encompassing the Spanish Floridas and the Mexican domain of Texas, New Mexico, and California, numerous French observers speculated on the nature of its position as a world power and its threat to monarchies.

One of the most discerning commentators on the emerging power and importance of the United States was Alexis de Tocqueville. As early as 1835 Tocqueville, in his *La Démocratie en Amérique*, prophesied that the Americans and the Russians seemed "to be marked out by the will of Heaven to sway the destinies of half the globe." These two enormous nations were, he wrote, entirely self-sufficient and possessed of "seemingly limitless natural resources and promise of huge population growth."

Journalist Clement Duvernois believed France to be menaced by "the prodigious development of the American power." He was convinced that France should "create a counterweight to the Republic of the United States."

A French leader who strongly advocated that his country should aid Mexico in halting the expansion of the United States was Hippolyte Dommartin, author of *Les Etats-Unis et le Mexique: L'Intérêt européen dans L'Amérique du Nord* (1852). He predicted that for Europeans Mexico was the key to the Western Hemisphere. Writings such as these encouraged Napoleon III

---

4. A. J. Hanna, *A Prince in Their Midst* (Norman, Okla., 1946), pp. 247, 248.
5. Ibid., p. 170.

to strike out boldly with the "deepest thought of the Second Empire."

Its dismal Waterloo in 1867 was followed so swiftly by the collapse of the Second Empire that Napoleon III's Grand Design for the Americas was all but lost in the calamitous confusion of France following its defeat in 1870 by Prussia. A complete understanding of the Mexican catastrophe was further obscured by the universal vilification of Napoleon III. A torrent of defamation by Victor Hugo consigned him to the depths of ridicule. Bismarck contemptuously characterized him as "a great unfathomed incapacity." Horace Greeley, and other defenders of American republics, believed that "no plot so gigantic ever before perished so swiftly and so utterly" as did the dream of Napoleon III for monarchy in the Americas. Yet for a period much longer than the reign of his uncle he was the virtual arbiter of Europe.

The startling and inglorious defeat of the French by the Prussians so crushed Napoleon III and overwhelmed France that interest in the grandiose scheme in the New World was replaced by rapidly rising concern over more imminent and multiplying crises in Europe. Since then, whenever the French people have recalled the disastrous Grand Design of Napoleon III in Mexico, it has been with resentment and anguish over the cruel loss of life and callous expenditures thousands of miles across the ocean. The world turned to other matters and for the time forgot Napoleon III and disregarded what he did in the building of the Suez Canal. Therefore, efforts to understand and describe the "deepest thought of the Second Empire" have had to await evaluation.

A more balanced judgment is emerging. It was Guérard's judgment that "Napoleon III has won the respect and sympathy of practically every critical historian."

Creator of the Second Empire, he developed it along the lines of social and economic progress. In contrast to his serious weaknesses and failures, he was a humanitarian in outlook, raised the level of living conditions in France, and refashioned Paris as a world center, the magnificence of which has remained preeminent.

2

Mexico
A New World Crimea
1847–1857

It was with the utmost relief the young Marquis de Radepont in 1847 quitted the French Legation in Washington for a special mission to Mexico. An officer in the French army and a diplomat, he had been sent to the United States to observe conditions there. His special mission was to safeguard the rights of French citizens in the areas through which the U.S. invaders were fighting their way from Veracruz to Mexico City in the war the United States was waging against Mexico.

Of his experience as he accompanied the U.S. Army, Radepont caustically reported: ". . . about 300 bandits named the Texas Rangers disembarked at Veracruz. . . . They left with a convoy commanded by General Patterson and I had the honor of being included in this convoy, but having been robbed three times by these dangerous volunteers, I preferred . . . to go by myself to Mexico City among all the dangers along the road which happily I avoided."[1]

The rough experiences of this French observer with the rowdy Texans heightened his dislike of U.S. expansionists and intensified his fear of their republican system of government.

Radepont's impressions reflected the deep concern of François

1. Memoir Concerning the Military Operations of the Americans and Mexicans, 1859, M et D, Mexique, IX.

EXPANSION OF UNITED STATES: 1803 - 1856

Guizot, master spirit of French policy toward the United States under King Louis Philippe. Defender of Latin nations in the New World, Guizot was opposed to the rapid expansion of the Anglo-Saxon United States. In 1846 he publicly challenged President Polk's reinterpretation of the Monroe Doctrine. In Washington Radepont was repelled by the conduct of the boisterous lawmakers whose advocacy of expansion had alarmed Guizot. Radepont observed that many of them advocated "the right of our Manifest Destiny to spread over this whole continent."

The aristocratic Frenchman was startled to learn that the arch expansionist was the president himself, James K. Polk, whose revival of the dormant Monroe Doctrine gave it new strength and significance.

Menacing symbols of U.S. expansion in Mexico were the Texas Rangers, with whom Radepont had traveled. When they arrived in Mexico City, they were regarded as a "sort of semicivilized, half man, half devil, with a slight mixture of lion and the snapping turtle."[2] Their old-fashioned maple stock rifles lay across their saddles, the butts of two large pistols stuck out of their

2. Jacob F. Wolters, "The First Texas Ranger," *Texas Reader* (1947), p. 176.

holsters, and around the waist of each was belted a pair of Colt's six-shooters. They wore, not uniforms, but frontier garb. Some wore broad-brimmed Texas hats and others, caps of skins of animals.[3]

As the Texas Rangers rode through the Mexican capital, the streets were lined with spectators. When a Mexican threw a rock at one of the horsemen, "a flash was seen, a report was heard, and the offender fell dead. . . . Ere long another stone was thrown and another Mexican launched into eternity."[4]

When Mexico was virtually forced to cede California and New Mexico to its northern neighbor, the Marquis de Radepont was convinced that the United States was a menace. After the U.S. armies returned home, Radepont remained in Mexico. He made friends among Mexican conservatives and the diplomatic corps. His nephew, a banker, was secretary of the French Legation, headed by Vicomte Jean Alexis de Gabriac. No longer officially associated with the French government, Radepont became interested in the development of a French settlement, El Uvero, in the state of Veracruz. In time he was connected with the large hacienda of the Mackintosh family.

The Spanish American republic in which Radepont remained possessed a government similar in form to that of the United States, but in operation it was semifeudal. He observed in Mexico appalling illiteracy. Power and privilege were vested in the military, the clergy, and the owners of large haciendas. They were drawn almost exclusively from the whites, less than a million of the approximately 8,000,000 population. Fully 5,000,000 were of unmixed Indian blood. Laboring under serf-like conditions, they were set apart from, and often indifferent to, or resentful of, the upper classes. A third group, the mestizos, of mixed blood, occasionally rose to the status of the whites, but their environment was basically Indian. Hence, Mexico was predominantly a land of Indians ruled by relatively few whites.

Independence from Spain in 1821 increased the power of the three privileged groups. Officers of the army acquired a virtual mastery of the country. They precipitately abandoned any political leader who failed to produce pay and promotion and any government which threatened their privileges. Consequently, they formed the backbone of the ever-recurring revolts and opened

3. Ibid.
4. Ibid., p. 177.

the door for the entry of such tyrants as the "spectacular rascal," "Emperor" Iturbide, and the wily general Antonio López de Santa Anna.

Independence canceled the crown's restraint on the clergy. The Church, which owned virtually half the taxable property of the country, paid no taxes and churchmen enjoyed the privilege of being tried only in clerical law courts. Mutual interest led the Church to ally itself with Conservatives. At times church financial aid went to support political partisans. Whenever the future looked ominous for its privileges, the Church, whose form of government was monarchical, favorably regarded proposals for monarchy for the nation. United by kinship to the more influential clergy and to the higher echelons of the army were the wealthy landowners. These *hacendados*, although not outside the civil law, barely acknowledged its restrictions. They kept pace with the Church in acquiring more land during the wars of independence and the frequent domestic uprisings.

During the forty years after independence Mexican presidents, almost without exception military chieftains, gained power by violence. They retained it only so long as they controlled the country by superior physical force. They succeeded each other with a savage loss of life, wanton destruction of property, and disregard for obligations, domestic and foreign. These presidents, beholden to the power groups, the Church and the owners of large haciendas, did not enforce tax regulations. When other revenues failed to stretch to meet the demand, the dictators expediently floated loans in foreign countries. As scant effort was made to meet these obligations, even the interest was seldom paid.

Regardless of the amount of money borrowed abroad, Mexico continued to overspend its income. To lay hands on ready cash the hard-driven governments at times exacted funds by confiscating foreign properties or by forcing loans from both Mexicans and foreigners. When foreigners could obtain no compensation or relief from oppression, they appealed to their respective governments for protection. Aid usually came in the form of warships to bombard Veracruz or to seize its customs house. Under such pressure Mexico would agree to a new convention, pledging a system of payments on both private claims and loans from foreign governments. Invariably another default would shortly follow. Foreigners soon learned to capitalize on this repeated drama. They padded their claims for damages so that fact and fancy became inseparable.

Political resurgence, born out of the chaos that followed war with the United States, began to pursue a tortuous course. Neither Liberals nor Conservatives, but Moderates headed the Mexican government in the late 1840s and early 1850s. They drastically reduced the army budget and made an agreement with English bondholders to set aside a percentage of customs duties toward the payment of the nation's largest foreign debt. The government likewise undertook to reduce the domestic debt by drawing on the $15,000,000 paid by the United States for the cession of half the national domain of Mexico at the close of the war between the two countries. Improvements in conditions generated hope for further reforms among Liberals.

Young intellectuals, disciples of Rousseau and Jefferson, struggled to liberate Mexico from the rigid control of the army and the church. As the Liberals grew more articulate, Conservatives rose to the defense of their convictions and special privileges. They were alarmed by the demands for democratic processes. The Marquis de Radepont, strongly sympathetic to the Conservatives, denounced the liberal philosophy for Mexico as a threat to order and a means of prolonging domestic civil strife. He feared it would open the door to further aggression from the United States.

Radepont witnessed violent reaction in 1853. So apprehensive were Conservatives over the growing condemnation of special privileges that they seized the government by force and again recalled to power the tarnished dictator Santa Anna. His coup seemed to be only a prelude to the establishment of a monarchy, an intent revealed to Paris by the French minister, Vicomte de Gabriac. Long an advocate of monarchy in Mexico, he reported that Mexican Conservatives would seek aid from European monarchies. They had faith in the willingness and ability of Napoleon III to induce England and Spain to arrange a tripartite intervention.[5] Radepont believed that Napoleon III was the only monarch whose leadership the Mexicans would accept. José María Gutiérrez de Estrada, an exile because of his outspoken advocacy of monarchy, was authorized by the Mexican monarch-

5. French minister to Mexico André Levasseur to Walewski, April 30, 1854, CP, Mexique, LXI.

ists to quit his Roman palace for Paris, Madrid, and London in search of a candidate for the proposed Mexican throne.[6]

No response came from the European monarchs. In 1854 England and France were sending armies to the Crimea to block Russia's advance toward Turkey. As the struggle continued in Mexico, Radepont saw a significant parallel between Mexico's perilous location bordering the United States and Turkey's age-long vulnerable position on Russia's frontier. He was convinced that the European monarchies could halt U.S. aggression against Mexico just as they were endeavoring to protect Turkey from Russian encroachment. Radepont conceived a design as Mexican conditions worsened.

Radepont was affronted by still another aggression from the United States. An area known as the Gadsden Purchase, now southern New Mexico and Arizona, was acquired for $10,000,000. This cession negotiated by Santa Anna to pay off his henchmen so enraged liberal and moderate Mexicans that he was for the last time forced out of office. With his ouster the Liberals assumed power and immediately undertook to abolish the special privileges of the clergy and the military, and prepared to write a new constitution to safeguard these reforms. No compromise was possible with the adamant Conservatives; thus the way was paved for the War of the Reform, a social and political upheaval comparable to that which had rocked France during the preceding century.

To the Marquis de Radepont and Minister de Gabriac, the success of the Liberals in 1855 was a catastrophe. In late 1856 Gabriac assured his superiors in France that a plan was under way to strike "a mortal blow against demagoguery and especially American demagoguery."[7] This was Radepont's "design." The time seemed propitious; the Crimean War was over and the existence of the Turkish Empire was no longer threatened. France and England were presumably freed for fresh enterprises. With the financial assistance of a Mexican friend, Radepont embarked for France.

While Radepont was crossing the ocean, Gabriac dared to ap-

---

6. *Circulares y otras publicaciones hechas por la legación mexicana en Washington durante la guerra de intervención en 1862–67*, 2 vols. (Mexico City, 1868), I, 232.

7. Gabriac to Walewski, September 1, 1856, CP, Mexique, LXI.

proach his opposite in the British Legation. Stressing the fact that he was acting without instructions from Paris, he spoke cryptically of "the pressing need for European intervention in Mexico." Mexicans were incapable of governing themselves, Gabriac alleged. Left to their own devices they would fall victims to the rapacity of the United States. Such a disaster could be prevented, provided monarchy under a European prince was substituted for the republican form of government. Vociferous objection might be expected from Washington, but, were the situation handled prudently, the Yankees would be "unaware of what was happening until it was too late for interference."[8]

Realizing that something specific lay behind Gabriac's vague warnings, the British minister reported promptly to Foreign Secretary Lord Clarendon, who refused to consider any part of the scheme. He doubted that Gabriac acted on his own initiative. Clarendon instructed his ambassador at Paris to find out what Napoleon III was promoting.

English suspicion of Napoleon III reflected the general attitude that accompanied the return of the Bonaparte dynasty. But gradually throughout Europe derision and contempt were being replaced by new respect for the French emperor. Meanwhile, early in October 1856, Radepont presented his "Design for Mexican Regeneration" to the French foreign minister, Count Alexandre Walewski, illegitimate son of Napoleon I. Radepont petitioned for an audience with the emperor in order to explain his "design."[9]

In the document he left at the Quai d'Orsay, Radepont argued that Europe must wake up and assess the role of the Americas and their impact on national interests of the Old World. The Americas, especially the United States, sheltered the lost sons of monarchy; not only sheltered them but used them as a means of spreading disorder in neighboring countries against stable society. As Radepont analyzed the facts, the policy of the United States in the Western Hemisphere paralleled that of Russia in Europe. Just as Russia protected the Greek Orthodox Church, the United States was protecting democratic institutions. The United States did not maintain a large army but instead used "pirates and filibusters" whom the government could disavow

---

8. Lettsom, British minister to Mexico, to Clarendon, September 19, 1856, quoted in Daniel Dawson, *The Mexican Adventure* (London, 1935), pp. 50–51.

9. Radepont to Walewski, October 4, 1856, CP, Mexique, LXVI.

if they failed. "The Republicans of North America," asserted Radepont, "are neither less firm nor less clever than the czars." Consequently, the motives which had led France and England to stop Russian expansion in Europe ought to impel them to halt further territorial acquisitions. Unless this was done, Europe would one day learn that the United States had occupied Havana and was ready to absorb French and English possessions in the Caribbean.

Radepont further explained that Mexico was a land which had never had a chance to develop its potential strength and wealth because the right kind of leadership had never existed. The "best minds of the country" had admitted they could not save themselves; therefore, they had asked for foreign assistance, but the obstacles attendant to European intervention were "nearly impossible" to overcome. "The solution I propose is easier," Radepont argued. It would have the advantages of an intervention without its dangers. Mexico saved by her own hands would retain her own nationality; a few years of wise government would give her a place among the richest states.

Salvation by Mexican hands "without foreign bayonets," the marquis contended, would confound the United States by using that country's own techniques. This salvation, he argued, was nothing less than the establishment of monarchy in such a way that it would appear an act of the national will of Mexico and thus conform to the stern 1845 dictum of President Polk that peoples of the Americas should decide their own destiny. This task was more important and more economical than building up Greece or Turkey to block Russia. Because the French met with great friendliness in Mexico, they should take the lead, Radepont counseled. Napoleon should name the lucky prince who would see "opening to him the best future that was ever offered to any man." Once word of the choice leaked back to Mexico, two months would suffice to manage the election of the proposed ruler. Rallying the majority of Mexicans around him, the new monarch would then mount his throne and the regeneration of Mexico would commence. Even if the United States frowned upon expanding the monarchical system, how could she flout so open an expression of the Mexican will? The value to the new monarchy would not end with Mexico. Mexico cooperating with the Brazilian Empire would make it possible for other Latin American states to be rescued from the anarchy of republicanism. Thus would be formed a Latin bloc with Rome as its spiritual head and Paris as its cultural and economic arbiter.

Aside from moral backing, the support Radepont sought for Mexico was outlined in detail. Fifty officers and five hundred or six hundred men would be enough to indicate more potential aid if the United States moved menacingly, but not enough to impress Mexicans as a foreign expedition.[10]

Although Radepont's plan tactfully deferred to Napoleon III in the selection of a candidate for ruler, he had in mind the Orleanist prince, the Duc d'Aumale, son of Louis Philippe. Indeed, he had already composed a letter to be sent at the proper time to the Duke. "I arrive from Mexico, my lord," read this letter, "to offer you a crown; say the word and before six months you will be Emperor of the most beautiful country in the world, arbiter of the New World, and possessed of the finest destiny which could fall to the lot of man."[11]

While waiting to be received by Napoleon III, a favor the emperor did not hasten to grant, Radepont perfected his modus operandi. A provisional government of five might be established; its function would be to convoke a council of notables. This august body would proclaim the monarchy and call the monarch. On sober second thought, Radepont increased the proposed monarch's retinue of foreign soldiers from 500 or 600 to 7,000, to be supported by Mexico.[12]

Late in October Napoleon left for Compiègne. Somewhat discouraged over the delay, Radepont decided to approach England, his second choice for a backer. The British foreign secretary was more accessible than the French emperor and granted the coveted appointment early in November 1856. Lord Clarendon was courteous yet determined not to interfere in the domestic affairs of any country. He was frank to say he would be glad to see the Mexicans "do something sensible."[13] This was the utmost satisfaction Radepont could draw from him. Clarendon was more candid to a high English official, General Charles Fox, to whom he wrote: "M. de Radepont is a gentleman, entirely, and I wish he were not engaged in such a wild goose chase

10. Plan for the Regeneration of Mexico, ibid.
11. Radepont to Duc d'Aumale, January 2, 1857, Marquis de Radepont Papers, Houghton Library, Harvard University, Cambridge, Mass.
12. Plan for Mexico, November 1856, ibid.
13. Radepont to Gabriac, November 26, 1856, ibid.

as finding a king for that nation of unredeemable ruffians, but he could kill two birds with one stone if he induced *L'Enceinte* [Queen Isabel II of Spain] to transfer herself there. It would do good to Spain and it would not make Mexico worse."[14]

Eventually on November 24, 1856, Radepont found himself face to face with Napoleon III. They discussed at length Radepont's design for Mexico. Radepont urged immediate action. Intoxicated over the spread of their boundaries across the North American continent within less than one-half century, U.S. expansionists, declared Radepont, dreamed of acquiring more lands from their neighbors. Demanding better transportation facilities to the Pacific, they had already constructed a railroad across the Isthmus of Panama and were advocating a canal through Nicaragua or across the Mexican Isthmus of Tehuantepec. The emperor somewhat casually commented that no name for the proposed prince for Mexico's throne had been mentioned, whereupon Radepont confided his suggestion of the Duc d'Aumale, under whom he had served in Algeria. Fourth son of Louis Philippe, the Duc d'Aumale had distinguished himself in that campaign. Napoleon III appeared to be impressed and told Radepont, rather offhandedly, that he would sanction the raising of French soldiers for such an undertaking in Mexico. Within a few months of Radepont's audience with Napoleon III, the French emperor mentioned to Benjamin Disraeli, English prime minister, his "wish and willingness to assist in establishing a European dynasty in Mexico," and said that "for his part he would make no opposition to the accession of the Duc d'Aumale to such a throne."[15]

Radepont's independently conceived design for Mexico was basically similar to the project Napoleon III, when a prisoner in the 1840s, had worked out with Latin Americans for the building of the proposed Bonaparte canal between the Atlantic and the Pacific. This early Bonaparte blueprint called for the political and financial support of England to stabilize Central America and make of it a world center of trade.

With this encouragement Radepont set out for Gibraltar to interview the Duc d'Aumale.[16] There Mexican regeneration re-

14. Clarendon to Fox, November 28, 1856, ibid.

15. James M. Thompson, *Louis Napoleon and the Second Empire* (Oxford, 1954), p. 216.

16. Radepont to Gabriac, November 26, 1856, Radepont Papers.

ceived a swift setback. The Duke was appreciative, interested, and wished to be kept informed of events; beyond that he was much too prudent to commit himself.

Radepont lingered in Europe until March 1857, without seemingly having made any progress toward his goal. Actually he had planted a concrete idea in the mind of Napoleon III that would become the so-called most significant concept of the Second Empire of France.

3

The Impending Crisis
1857-1859

In 1857, the Marquis de Radepont returned to Mexico from his interview with Napoleon III. In his absence the reformers had been making progress in attempts to eliminate special privileges of the Church and the army. President Ignacio Comonfort harbored the naïve illusion that Conservatives could be induced to accept these reforms.

Early in 1858 Comonfort, outmaneuvered by his opponents, resigned and fled to the United States. His successor, Benito Juárez, supported uncompromisingly the reforms of the new constitution. A Zapotec Indian, he had been an able, honest governor of Oaxaca. The inevitable conflict between his reform government and the Conservative forces brought on the War of the Reform. Unable to hold Mexico City, Juárez hurriedly moved the Liberal government to Querétaro.

Pursued by Conservative military forces from Querétaro to the Pacific coast, Juárez took ship for Panama, crossed the isthmus and made his way to the Liberal stronghold, Veracruz. Here he set up his government and increased its resources by siphoning off the customs receipts of the country's only important port. In addition to Veracruz, large areas of Mexico remained loyal to the Liberals.

Although the Conservatives maintained their grip on Mexico City, they were not able to win control of the entire nation.

Their leader, twenty-seven-year-old Miguel Miramón, was recognized president of Mexico by European powers and the United States in accordance with the custom of regarding as the official government that faction in possession of the national capital. Desperate financial straits soon sucked both Conservatives and Liberals down to the subterranean level of forced loans and confiscations alienating foreign creditors and residents alike.[1]

John Forsyth, U.S. minister to Mexico, later a prominent Confederate, anxiously watched the worsening situation. Fearing the British fleet might appear off Veracruz to enforce payment of debts, he hurriedly and, without authority, negotiated a treaty for extending to the Conservatives a loan of $15,000,000. He confidentially described the proposed treaty as a "floating mortgage upon the territory of a poor neighbor."[2] Forsyth warned President James Buchanan that if the United States did not aid Mexico, some other nation would. "What if it comes in the form of a French prince supported by 10,000 French bayonets" he asked, "or of British gold?"[3]

Disapproving the proposed treaty, the administration in Washington instructed Forsyth to offer a maximum of $5,000,000 for Baja California and a maximum of $10,000,000 for the major portion of Sonora and a part of Chihuahua,[4] both in northwest Mexico on the United States border. The Conservatives did not respond to this overture; whereupon Forsyth went home incensed by Miramón's hostility to the United States.

In his annual message to Congress of 1858, President Buchanan listed claims against Mexico at more than $10,000,000. "The most reprehensible means have been employed to extort money from foreigners" to carry on the War of the Reform destined to reduce Mexico "to a condition of almost hopeless anarchy and imbecility." Buchanan "earnestly" recommended a "temporary protectorate" over the northern portion of Chihua-

---

1. For a comprehensive analysis of Mexican finances by a French economist, see Michel Chevalier, *Le Mexique, ancien et moderne*, trans. Thomas Alpass, 2 vols. (London, 1864), II, 248–59.

2. Forsyth to Cass, April 4, 1857, quoted in Dexter Perkins, *The Monroe Doctrine, 1826–1867* (Baltimore, 1933), p. 335; James M. Callahan, *American Foreign Policy in Mexican Relations* (New York, 1932), pp. 240–41.

3. Forsyth to Cass, April 4, 1857, quoted in Perkins, *Monroe Doctrine, 1826–1867*, p. 334.

4. Callahan, *American Foreign Policy in Mexican Relations*, p. 248.

hua and Sonora to check Indian depredations preventing the settlement of the American Southwest.[5]

Shortly thereafter Buchanan's emissary Robert M. McLane went to Veracruz, authorized to recognize Juárez as president of Mexico. Considering it unwise and probably impossible to conclude a cession of territory while Mexico was so divided, McLane proposed an entirely different arrangement. After months of diplomatic attack and counterattack, his final proposal to Melchior Ocampo, minister of foreign affairs of the Juárez government, would grant the United States a perpetual right-of-way across the 130-mile Isthmus of Tehuantepec where Americans were eager to construct a canal or railroad; two railroad routes across northern Mexico with free ports; the right to protect transits with troops; the right to intervene on occasions of extreme danger; and the right to exercise a general power of police protection over all Mexico. For such unprecedented concessions the Juárez government was to receive a loan of $4,000,000.[6] Six months later, tragically torn by the divisive slavery issue, the United States summarily rejected the proposed McLane-Ocampo Treaty.[7] Yet it exerted a heavy influence on Juárez who bore until his death a burden of censure for having agreed to terms that would have placed the United States in virtual control of Mexico. The Conservatives criticized Washington for attempting to recognize Juárez to gain more territory and privileges.[8] This unmasking of the aggressive designs of the "perfidious Yankee" left the Conservatives in the position of defenders of the national domain, whether they deserved it or not. It likewise made them more receptive to the idea of European aid and pressed home to Great Britain and France the belief that a policy of drifting was untenable.

Meanwhile, in 1858, the British minister to Mexico had assessed the situation. The Americans would do nothing, he thought, "beyond their favorite warfare of blustering and bullying. Foreign intervention, or even conquest would be a matter of very easy accomplishment" since "the great body of the Na-

5. James D. Richardson, *A Compilation of the Messages and Papers of the Presidents, 1789–1897*, 10 vols. (Washington, D.C., 1896–1900), V, 512, 514.

6. Callahan, *American Foreign Policy in Mexican Relations*, pp. 268–69; Samuel F. Bemis, *Diplomatic History of the United States* (New York, 1955), p. 391n.

7. Callahan, *American Foreign Policy in Mexican Relations*, p. 271.

8. Ibid., p. 270.

tion, including all the wealthy classes, is favorably inclined to such a change, and a British or Anglo-French Intervention would be preferred to any other." The Briton opposed an expedition that included Spain because "the Spanish element would spoil all."[9]

The hint that Mexico might pass under British protection was promptly denounced by London as a "future embarrassment if not . . . an actual misfortune." However, the British admitted that change in Mexican administration was essential, "disfigured and disgraced" as it then was by "a system which is a mere mockery of government."[10]

Coincident with the proposal of British intervention was an attempt by Conservatives to secure aid from Napoleon III and Queen Victoria. French Minister Gabriac reported to Paris that the Conservative government hoped to obtain funds by mortgaging church property, using the proceeds to obtain a loan with which to import a corps of French soldiers, four or five warships, and a French general in command.[11] To the Conservatives' plea, based on the desire to vanquish the Liberals and prevent conquest on the part of the United States, the British response was negative; the French, vague.[12]

The next year Victoria received a petition from Conservatives imploring aid from England, France, and Spain to forestall the impending victory of the "demagogic" Liberals.[13] Juan Nepomuceno Almonte, Mexican minister to Paris, who also looked after affairs in Madrid and London, found the British foreign secretary sensitive to Mexico's predicament but reluctant to interfere. His Lordship mentioned a concerted move by England, France, Spain, and the United States for the restoration of order.[14] However, he did not regard 1859 as the propitious year inasmuch as Napoleon III was about to make war upon Austria to break her control of Italy and advance unification of that country.

9. British minister to Mexico Otway to Foreign Secretary Malmesbury, August 2, 1858, quoted in Daniel Dawson, *The Mexican Adventure* (London, 1935), p. 6.

10. Malmesbury to Otway, November 10, 1858, ibid.

11. Gabriac to Walewski, August 1, 1858, CP, Mexique, XLIX. Statistics of funds and French forces are listed here.

12. Walewski to Gabriac, September 30, 1858, ibid.

13. Otway to Malmesbury, January 2, 1859, BFO, Mexico, quoted in Dawson, *Mexican Adventure*, pp. 9–10.

14. Malmesbury to Otway, January 7, 1859, BFO, Mexico, quoted in Dawson, *Mexican Adventure*, p. 11.

When the Italian war ended without having plunged Europe into the expected general conflict, England and France, whose legations were accredited to the Conservatives under Miramón, still hesitated to take action. If the McLane-Ocampo Treaty should be ratified by the U.S. Senate, they reasoned, the Liberals would replenish their war chest and a Liberal victory become more likely.

This prospect panicked the Marquis de Radepont. Consequently, in 1859, he carried a second memorial to the Quai d'Orsay, repeating his plan of regeneration and emphasizing that France alone could save Mexico.

"Why this exaggerated fear of intervening in the internal affairs of Mexico?" Radepont asked. The Americans were constantly interfering "always to the prejudice of Europe." He disapproved of what he described as the prevailing impulse of Europe to yield to the insolent demands of Americans; he was convinced the United States would be tractable if Europe would only speak "loud and firm."[15]

Changes in foreign ministries in Great Britain and France had brought into power Lord John Russell and Edouard Thouvenel. Thouvenel looked upon his office as a mirror of his emperor's mind and his policy reflected the thinking of his ruler more faithfully than that of his predecessor, Count Walewski.[16] Neither Russell nor Thouvenel accepted Radepont's advice to adopt a firmer attitude but both believed the time had arrived to do something. Russell took the initiative. He suggested a joint Anglo-French call for an armistice of six months or a year. In this cease-fire interim a provisional regime would be set up and an assembly called, under the benign influence of the mediators, to establish a new government. Exerting moral pressure, England and France, in the interests of order, would ensnare the dove of peace, according to the Russell formula. Without waiting for French concurrence Russell instructed the British chargé d'affaires in Mexico to approach both Miramón and Juárez concerning the first steps in the contemplated reconciliation.[17]

Lord Cowley, British ambassador to France, interpreted the

15. Memoir Concerning the Military Operations of the Americans and Mexicans, 1859, M et D, Mexique, IX.

16. Christian Schéfer, *La Grande Pensée de Napoléon III* (Paris, 1939), pp. 13, 52.

17. Russell to Mathew, January 26, 1860, *BFSP*, L.

Russell formula to Thouvenel in February 1860. He made no mention of monarchy but assumed that, exhausted by anarchy, neither Conservatives nor Liberals were capable of restoring domestic tranquillity. To one who had the Radepont design tucked away in his pocket, the British proposal seemed rather flabby but still a step in the right direction. Thouvenel informed the French representative at the Court of St. James's that while he doubted the proposal's success he welcomed its trial. The attitude of the United States was a question mark, but it was assumed she would be hostile, certainly if not informed in advance.[18] Gabriac was instructed to cooperate with his British counterpart to conclude an armistice.

Accordingly, the two diplomats in Mexico each proposed an armistice to Miramón and Juárez even though disagreeing on its terms. The Protestant Englishman advocated freedom of worship and clerical reform. The French minister believed these controversial questions which in large part had been responsible for the War of the Reform should await later solution.[19] Probably strategy rather than proclericalism dictated the French opinion. Radepont had already suggested that this delicate problem be compromised;[20] and if the armistice resulted in a new government, ecclesiastical specifics, so to speak, might properly be left to its determination. Both Miramón and Juárez received the Anglo-French efforts with coolness.

While parleys for the armistice were being initiated by British and French representatives, Miramón made a last desperate attempt to capture Veracruz; previously he had been repelled by Liberal strength combined with a dreaded ally, yellow fever, which prevailed at times in the low country about the seaport. For this campaign Miramón employed a new technique, a naval attack. Temporarily on satisfactory terms with Spain, he had two vessels fitted out in Havana, one a warship, the *General Miramón*, the other a cargo vessel, the *Marquis de la Havana*. Significantly flying no national flag, these vessels arrived in the vicinity of Veracruz March 6, 1860. South of Veracruz was a United States squadron under the command of Captain Joseph R. Jarvis. He had learned through Havana that General Tomás

18. Thouvenel to Persigny, February 21, 1860, CP, Angleterre, DCCXVII.
19. Gabriac to Thouvenel, March 29, 1860, CP, Mexique, LIII.
20. Note for the Minister on Memoir of Radepont, March 1860, ibid.

Marin was preparing a sea approach to aid Miramón's attack by land. When the two flagless ships resisted all hints to identify themselves, Jarvis sent the corvette *Saratoga* to investigate. The *General Miramón* made ready to escape and opened fire. The *Saratoga* shot away the *General Miramón*'s smokestack. After one-half hour's engagement the *General Miramón* grounded. Meanwhile, the *Marquis de la Havana,* less brash than her companion, ran up the Spanish flag. Both vessels were captured along with General Marin.

In reply to violent protests from the French and Spanish squadrons off Veracruz, Jarvis maintained that the *General Miramón* had fired the first shot and that the *Marquis de la Havana* was obviously her confederate. Spain had committed a breach of neutrality in allowing the Miramón government to outfit the two vessels at Havana.[21]

Discouraged by the failure to capture Veracruz, for which he blamed the United States naval squadron, Miramón accepted on April 12, 1860, the mediation proposed by England and France. He even suggested increasing the mediation group to include other powers. Nine days later, Juárez, confident of ultimate victory, made it clear he wanted no foreign interference and refused to participate in any armistice. For his independence Juárez was labeled "insolent" by French Minister Gabriac.[22]

After they were unable to mediate, neither England nor France was inclined to resume the initiative in solving the Mexican crisis.[23] However, the issue continued to preoccupy their foreign offices. Spain's attitude necessarily required consideration. Although Mexico had thrown off Spanish control in 1821, Spain refused for fifteen years to acknowledge her independence. In the intervening period she had more than once contemplated reconquest. Beneath the surface irritation Spain longed to seat a Spanish prince on a Mexican throne. Spain's truculence always disturbed England and France; they believed intervention by

21. Gabriac to Thouvenel, April 11, 1860; note on the ships, April 28, 1860, ibid.; Radepont to Napoleon III, May 10, 1860, Marquis de Radepont Papers, Houghton Library, Harvard University, Cambridge, Mass.; Turner to Jarvis, March 8, 1860, Jarvis to Yancey, March 11, 1860, Captain's Letters, January–March, 1860, vol. I, Records of the Home Squadron, 1860–61, Dept. of the Navy, NA.

22. Gabriac to Thouvenel, April 24, 1860, CP, Mexique, LIII.

23. Note for the Minister, April 1860, ibid.

Spain would give the United States precisely the excuse she sought to annex not merely Mexico but also Central America and Cuba.[24]

Nevertheless, France wanted to include Spain in any project she might undertake in Mexico. It would be almost impossible to exclude her, and besides Napoleon III had adopted a policy of favoring Spain because she was a Latin nation. Rather reluctantly Russell conceded the inclusion of other powers because he wished to draw the United States into the circle.[25] For her part, France wanted no tight commitment on Mexico. For the time being she preferred to observe events and urged that both English and French legations in Mexico, then about to receive new ministers, work together. It would be even better, suggested Thouvenel, if both ministers could arrive at their posts at the same time and jointly make a fresh start.[26] The British did not reject this idea; they merely ignored it.

As the tragic War of the Reform (1857–60) continued, infuriating and shocking disregard for international responsibilities by both Conservatives and Liberals occurred. The Miramón faction seized a mule train transporting $6,000,000 worth of silver belonging to British and French nationals; the Juaristas captured a silver convoy amounting to some $400,000.[27] That Juárez disclaimed responsibility for this act and promised restitution made no difference. Miramón grew so unfriendly to the British representative in Mexico City that the diplomat was authorized to retire to Jalapa and "keep aloof from both parties."[28] Shortly afterward a "crowning act of violence" took place: agents of the Miramón government broke into the British Legation and made off with $1,000,000 belonging to British bondholders.

24. Clarendon to Lettsom, July 1, 1856; Cowley to Clarendon, June 6, 1856, quoted in Dawson, *Mexican Adventure*, p. 37; Schéfer, *La Grande Pensée de Napoléon III*, pp. 9–12.
25. Russell to Mathew, June 28, 1860, *BFSP*, LI.
26. Thouvenel to Persigny, June 21, 1860, CP, Angleterre, DCCXVII.
27. Mathew to Russell, September 28 and September 29, 1860, *BFSP*, LI.
28. Russell to Mathew, August 24, 1860, ibid.

4

A "Mistletoe Sprig" on the French Nobility 1859–1861

As the summer of 1860 passed, conditions in Mexico grew chaotic.[1] Enormous thefts of silver by both the Juárez Liberals and the Miramón Conservatives would likely produce punitive action from France and England. Moreover, in the United States sectional strife was on the verge of erupting. The French minister in Mexico, Vicomte de Gabriac, with whom the Marquis de Radepont had been closely associated in working out plans for a European intervention in Mexico, was replaced.

This delicate diplomatic post was entrusted by the French emperor to Count Pierre Elizodor Alphonso Dubois de Saligny. His thirty years in the foreign service included assignments as attaché in two European legations and six years as secretary of legation in Washington. Saligny's first impressions and observations of the Americas were made while Andrew Jackson, one of the most determined presidents prior to the Civil War, "reigned" in the White House. Saligny and his superiors were incensed over "Old Hickory's" firm and uncompromising dealings with France, which forced the payment of sizeable debts owed since the time of Napoleon I. Throughout the six years he was in Washington Saligny's antipathy and that of his government for United States penetration into the Mexican domain continued to increase.

1. Rapport à l'Empereur, March 15, 1860, CP, Mexique, LIII.

From Washington Saligny was sent to the newly established Republic of Texas on a secret mission to make recommendations regarding its recognition. His favorable report led to the opening of a French Legation, the first from Europe, and his appointment as chargé d'affaires in that new republic.

Welcomed at Houston in January 1840, amid pomp and the booming of cannon, he traveled to the capital, Austin, then a small frontier town. He made his headquarters at the Bullock Hotel, a two-story log building, the best in Austin. He paid what he later admitted to be counterfeit money to the teamster transporting his personal effects. When he refused to make redress, members of the Texas cabinet reimbursed the drayman to quiet the commotion. Although a representative of the French court, so devoid of diplomatic grace and suavity was Saligny that a former president of the Texas republic described him as a parasite, a "sort of mistletoe sprig on the French Noblesse."

Seemingly, Saligny's chief interest in accepting the Texas assignment centered about efforts to advance his own personal gain. He attempted to influence the Texas Congress to pass legislation which would have awarded some three million acres of unsettled land in west Texas to a French immigration company. This flagrant interference in the domestic affairs of a foreign nation involved him in Texas politics to such an extent that he finally left Texas, claiming he did so because of indignities he was forced to suffer. He returned to Texas in 1842 and again in 1844, serving as chargé d'affaires until Texas was annexed to the United States.[2]

Following Saligny's deplorable and far from diplomatic conduct in the Republic of Texas, he was a member of the Turko-Russian Commission at the conclusion of the Crimean War. Saligny's appointment in 1860, as minister to war-torn Mexico, was attributed to his friendship with the powerful Duc de Morny. Illegitimate half-brother of the Emperor Napoleon III, Morny had highly questionable speculative investments in Mexico.[3]

Controversy over Saligny's role may never entirely cease. To

2. For further information about Saligny in Texas and the amazing incident of his fight with Bullock over Bullock's pigs, see J. W. Schmitz, *Texan Statecraft, 1836–1845* (San Antonio, 1941), pp. 71, 72, 74, 155–59, 228–34; Bernice B. Denton, "Count Alphonso de Saligny and the Franco-Texienne Bill," *SHQ*, XLIV (1941), 137.

3. Henry B. Parkes, *A History of Mexico* (Boston, 1950), pp. 254–55; *New York Times*, April 25, 1862, p. 4.

some he was a veritable Prince of Darkness, to others, a devoted servant of the emperor. Mexican Liberals loathed him; so did the French army. His British and Spanish colleagues had scant respect for him. On the other hand, those Mexicans and Frenchmen dedicated to the creation of a monarchy in Mexico believed wholeheartedly that Saligny's leadership was indispensable. For almost three years Napoleon III, disregarding all criticism, appeared to repose full confidence in him.

Whether Saligny's actions exceeded the emperor's intentions may be judged by comments of his contemporaries. The secretary of the French Legation in Mexico and nephew of the Marquis de Radepont believed Saligny's "secret" instructions were to provoke a rupture by any means possible between France and President Juárez of the Mexican republic in such a way that coercive measures would be necessary.[4] Lord Russell assumed "Saligny had no reason to doubt that he was acting in strict conformity with the wishes and intention of the French Government."[5] To the paymaster of the French Expeditionary Corps in Mexico, Saligny wrote: "My only merit consists in having understood that the Emperor intended to intervene and in having made that intervention indispensable."[6]

Saligny's conduct in Mexico was truculent, ruthless, and violent, characteristics his adversaries believed he assumed to create discord. Saligny was the "evil genius of France at the beginning of the Mexican 'question,' " declared Gustave Cluseret, one-time French minister of war who won distinction as a brigadier general in the Union army. It was Saligny, wrote Cluseret, "who furnished combustibles for the fire, grouped them, placed them, ignited them, and continually stirred their flames to fury." It was the conviction of this contemporary that Saligny had one of the clearest minds it was "possible to meet with; and, as neither his conscience nor his sensibility ever interposed between his mind and his aim, he often attained it."[7]

4. De la Londe Collection, Paris.

5. Russell to Wyke, March 15, 1862, *BFSP*, LIII.

6. Paul Gaulot, *La Vérité sur l'expédition du Mexique*, 3 vols. (Paris, 1889–90), I, 33.

7. Gustave P. Cluseret, *Mexico and the Solidarity of Nations* (New York, 1866), p. 86. Cluseret's amazingly tempestuous career included membership in the French Corps Législatif; he fought in the Crimean War, commanded the French Legion in Garibaldi's Italian forces, and won distinction as a brigadier general in the Union army.

French Foreign Minister Thouvenel meticulously briefed Saligny on his responsibilities. He was told that, since Juárez was willing to purchase United States support with concessions, Miramón's government appeared more likely to preserve Mexico's territorial integrity. Nevertheless, the real solution for Mexico's anarchy was a new government to succeed both warring factions. Great Britain had previously suggested an armistice for that purpose; the proposal had failed. A fresh approach to the problem must be made, and Saligny was to work for this end with the British minister and probably with the minister from Spain.[8]

Saligny studied the data available, conferring with the Quai d'Orsay and the emperor. On June 7, 1860, he formulated his views on Mexico for the Foreign Office. Renewed efforts for peace along lines already rejected were not possible. The Conservatives under Miramón were in a precarious position. If they fell, little could be expected from the Liberals under Juárez. Saligny contended that European powers had small chance of successful efforts for peace but time might work in their behalf. Most of Mexico's troubles were derived from the United States, he charged, for without aid from above the Rio Grande, Juárez could not have held out against Miramón. The approaching United States presidential election, he believed, would throw the Yankees into dissensions with unpredictable results. While watching these desirable complications mature, England and France should avoid any course compromising their dignity and prestige. Should Juárez win over Miramón, it might even be necessary to recognize the Liberal government. In conclusion, Saligny urged that, to assure the desired outcome, the French and British ministers should act in close harmony.[9]

A "Note," in the French foreign archives, presumably the record of a conference between the emperor and Thouvenel, expressed the emperor's judgment that mediation between Miramón and Juárez was no longer practical. The declaration favored by England, that no intervention was intended, was disapproved. There was one way only to clear up the Mexican imbroglio, and of this it was unnecessary to speak further; the outcome would rest "solely on the impulse . . . [the Emperor's] agent [Saligny] gives it." No further instructions would be given Saligny, and

8. Thouvenel to Saligny, May 30, 1860, CP, Mexique, LIII.
9. Saligny to Thouvenel, June 9, 1860, ibid.

England would be urged to send her minister to Mexico as soon as possible. France, England, and Spain trusted one another's intentions, concluded the "Note," but not those of the United States.[10]

Saligny arrived at Veracruz the middle of November 1860. With Juaristas in control of that port he did not tarry but continued his journey toward the capital. At Jalapa he met the Prussian representative and the British chargé d'affaires, who agreed that Miramón was lost; this Saligny reported to Paris. By the end of December 1860, the Juaristas had triumphed over Miramón's Conservatives, and the War of the Reform was over, though thousands of Conservatives were to remain in arms, terrorizing the countryside.

Early in January 1861, Juárez reestablished his government in the national capital, and according to Saligny, committed more follies than a stronger government would risk.[11] From the start, Saligny saw the worst in the Juárez regime. Possibly it was the "impulse" Napoleon III expected of him.

The Quai d'Orsay, disappointed and disturbed by the overthrow of Miramón, reminded Saligny that a new situation was being faced about which the emperor wanted specific information at once, especially concerning the satisfaction of claims against Mexico.[12]

Even more aroused were Mexican Conservatives abroad who, having served the Miramón government, found themselves political exiles. Among the jobless were Juan Almonte, minister to France, and José Hidalgo, who as Legation secretary had been moved from Madrid to Paris to capitalize on an acquaintance with the Empress Eugénie. Paris became headquarters for these exiles over whose plots for monarchy Gutiérrez de Estrada presided.[13] They hovered about the Tuileries, described their country as they wanted it to appear, and took good care that no one of different persuasion received a hearing at court.

As soon as the Juárez cabinet was reorganized in Mexico City,

10. Note to the Minister, September 1860, ibid.
11. Saligny to Thouvenel, January 26, 1861, ibid., LIV.
12. Thouvenel to Saligny, January 30, 1861, ibid.
13. José M. Hidalgo, *Apuntes para escribir la historia de los proyectos de monarquía en México desde el reinado de Carlos III hasta la instalación del emperador Maximiliano* (Mexico City, 1869), p. 50; see also his *Un hombre del mundo escribe sus impresiones: Cartas*, ed. Sofía Verea de Bernal (Mexico City, 1960), pp. 17–56

the new minister of foreign affairs, Francisco Zarco, approached Saligny. He said Mexico wanted, above all, to be a friend of France and would neglect nothing to accomplish it. Flattered by such deference to his country and himself, Saligny replied that recognition of Juárez depended on the adjustment of French claims. "For the moment," he exulted, "I am entirely master of the situation."[14]

On March 11, 1861, Saligny and Mexican Foreign Minister Zarco drew up an agreement whereupon the French diplomat presented his credentials and five days later was received by President Juárez. Saligny contended it was the best settlement of claims the French had ever made.[15]

The English chargé d'affaires had returned to the British Legation in Mexico City. His Foreign Office had informed him that the Juárez government would be recognized if it were inclined to arrange for the settlement of British claims, but that actual negotiations for damages would await the arrival of the new minister, Sir Charles Lennox Wyke. The chargé d'affaires precipitately recognized Juárez February 24, 1861, upon the Liberal government's expressed willingness to enter into negotiations for the settlement of British claims.[16] Thus, when Wyke arrived in Mexico he discovered the reward he, as the new minister to Mexico, was to have given Juárez, for satisfactory agreement had already been granted.

Wyke had served Britain in Guatemala throughout the preceding eight years and had been knighted for the title claims, since disputed, enabling London to rule a portion of that country as a crown colony. He had visited Paris, where he conferred with Thouvenel and Napoleon III. He appeared to share their conviction that interference in Mexico was inevitable and that the establishment of a monarchy would be a proper panacea for Mexico's political ills. On the strength of this interview Thouvenel advised Saligny that a "useful understanding" was possible between him and the Englishman.[17]

Wyke's instructions, of which Thouvenel received a copy, laid British policy on the line. Of major importance was the question

14. Saligny to Thouvenel, February 4, 1861, CP, Mexique, LIV.
15. Saligny to Thouvenel, March 28, 1861, ibid.
16. Daniel Dawson, *The Mexican Adventure* (London, 1935), p. 60. The chargé d'affaires was George Mathew.
17. Thouvenel to Saligny, March 7, 1861, CP, Mexique, LIV.

of damages. Wyke was reminded that Great Britain was non-interventionist, even though she wished to see Mexico stable and independent. He was specifically cautioned against seeking to influence the Mexican government and "still more against entering into any contract with the representative of any other power for exclusive influence over the councils of the Government." He was to take no part in political questions between Mexican factions. Should differences arise between Mexico and any foreign power, he was to use his best efforts to avoid a rupture without assuming the role of mediator. Nothing was said specifically about cooperating with the French minister.[18]

British appraisal of Mexican conditions in the early months of 1861 resembled that made by France. The retiring British chargé d'affaires spoke well of Juárez as an individual while admitting demoralization of his government and predicting its inevitable bankruptcy. In the upper classes he found an "utter want of patriotism," with some talk of a military dictator. Peace was desperately needed yet "native and foreign elements are at work to disturb the existing state of things." New convulsions could be expected unless the Juárez government was "avowedly upheld" by England or by the United States.[19]

Similar pessimism filled Wyke's letters after his arrival in May 1861. Funds from sales of church lands were being spent rather than applied to Mexico's financial obligations, leaving small chance of compensation for foreign claims. The Conservatives still held four to six thousand men under arms, led by such commanders as General Leonardo Márquez, who had held up the British silver train. "The only hope of improvement I can see is to be found in a small moderate party who may step in before all is lost," concluded the British minister. But barring coercive measures from outside, Moderates would remain cowed by the other two factions and thus, immobilized.[20]

The seeming harmony between the English and French points of view was severely jolted when Wyke learned Saligny had espoused the cause of the banking house of J. B. Jecker, established in Mexico since 1835, and that among its heavy investors was the Duc de Morny. From then on the two legations drifted

18. Instructions to Wyke, March 30, 1861; Russell to Wyke, March 30, 1861, *BFSP*, LII.
19. Mathew to Russell, May 12, 1861, ibid.
20. Wyke to Russell, May 27, 1861, ibid.

apart and the ministers became suspicious of each other.

Jecker's bank had contracted with the Miramón government for the partial conversion of the public debt. From the transaction, which had a face value of $15,000,000, the Conservatives actually received only $7,500,000. Jecker stood to profit by some 25 to 30 percent. New bonds also carried inducements for their investors. Merchants attracted by such terms requested the French minister to urge Miramón to guarantee this privilege for five years; accordingly, the French Legation was involved in a second decree of the Miramón Conservative government, proclaimed January 30, 1860.[21]

The disintegration of Miramón's fortunes paralleled the weakening of the banking house of Jecker. By the time Miramón was defeated in December 1860, Jecker was in the hands of creditors. Among his assets was the unsold portion of bonds. A Juárez proclamation in 1859 had warned that those who lent money to anti-Juárez factions would find their claims worthless; nevertheless, holders of Jecker bonds professed to believe that Miramón, recognized as he was by European nations, had headed a de facto, and therefore, legitimate government. In line with this assumption Jecker bondholders were incensed when, in January 1861, Juárez declared, as he had warned he would, that the Jecker bonds were void.

Appeals from losing bondholders were received by both the French Foreign Office and the French Legation in Mexico. Saligny was instructed to sustain the demand for compensation made by the bondholders of the "honorable house of Commerce of Paris having interests in Mexico." Already he had entered the lists in their behalf. Such good will as was generated from the Zarco-Saligny Claims Treaty was thrown overboard by the attempt to force the Juárez government to validate the Jecker bonds. Certainly Saligny knew this; probably, he recognized the issue as a useful tool for the "impulse" he was instructed to give the emperor's design. Supporting this assumption was the peremptory communication to the Juárez government of the French position, stated in purposely tactless words.[22] Obviously, claims payments to France, plus recompense to the House of Jecker,

21. Jean B. Jecker, "La Créance Jecker," *Revue Contemporaine*, LXI (January 15, 1868), pp. 128–49; Pierre de la Gorce, *Histoire du Second Empire*, 7 vols. (Paris, 1894–1905), IV, 37 ff; Wyke to Russell, January 19, 1862, *BFSP*, LIII.

22. Saligny to Thouvenel, May 9, 1861, CP, Mexique, LIV.

and payment of legitimate damages owed other nations would more than deplete the Mexican treasury.

Saligny offered to scale down the claim and force its acceptance on Jecker. He proposed reducing the capital to $10,000,000, and a 20 percent rebate on treasury debts to 15 percent. "This transaction which I take it on myself to propose seems to me to be the only means of avoiding a rupture which would lead to the ruin of your government and your country,"[23] he warned Zarco. Reluctantly, Zarco admitted that Mexico did not plan to write a new international agreement, but he wished to postpone adjustment. Congress would meet in a few days and he needed advice.[24]

The Mexican Congress, called to order on May 9, 1861, argued the Jecker bond question in two secret sessions. When the negotiations undertaken with Saligny were not approved, Zarco resigned. Congress was ready to slam the door on all further consideration when one sober-minded representative hinted that such a step might mean war with France. In this predicament, the legislative body fell back on a favorite device of those in a tight spot; it appointed a commission of three to study the problem. Before this commission could act, Mexico, the United States, and France were embroiled in cataclysms beyond their control.

23. Saligny to Zarco, May 2, 1861, Confidential, ibid.
24. Zarco to Saligny, May 4, 1861, ibid.

5

"Prelude to Tragedy"
1861–1862

━━━━━━◄◆►━━━━━━

As the War of the Reform in Mexico was ending, an equally tragic domestic struggle was beginning to divide the republic to the north. There, after the election of Abraham Lincoln to the presidency, the Southern states seceded and created the Confederacy. These events precipitated the exchange of shots at Fort Sumter, South Carolina, and opened a four-year war which ended in 1865.

Below the Rio Grande events were likewise moving rapidly. When in July 1861, the Mexican Congress voted to discontinue interest payments on debts and claims, the French Minister Saligny and the British Minister Wyke reacted at once. Saligny demanded repeal of the offending decree in twenty-four hours. To the plea that nothing could be accomplished in so short a time, he was deaf. Before the twenty-four hours had expired, he sent a note breaking off all relations between France and Mexico. British conservatism was slower. Wyke offered a forty-eight hour ultimatum and then suspended relations. It was a slight distinction, but significant.

Three months later, on October 31, special ambassadors from England, France, and Spain signed a treaty in London to coerce Mexico into paying long accumulated debts and claims covering the lives and property of citizens of the signatory powers.[1] Be-

1. For an analysis of diplomatic negotiations of England, France, and Spain leading up to the signing of the London Convention, October 31, 1861, see Carl H.

hind this action were secret intentions, conflicting policies, and imperial aspirations of the three participating empires. The British were determined not to involve themselves in the internal affairs of Mexico. To France and Spain the resurgence of monarchy in Mexico was the underlying aim of the expedition, yet neither dared admit it to England; her cooperation, or at least her acquiescence, was needed. The motive of Napoleon III was to develop a design for the Americas he had vaguely worked out in prison.

Meanwhile, two able and influential statesmen in the Americas, Matías Romero, Mexican representative at Washington, and William H. Seward, Lincoln's secretary of state, were discussing the imminence of a violation of the Monroe Doctrine by Napoleon III of France, Victoria of England, and Isabel II of Spain to collect from Mexico long-due claims. Romero insisted that Napoleon III intended to change the Mexican government from a republic to a monarchy and also that the French Empire was entirely hostile to the United States. Seward then did not believe European interference would extend beyond sending ships to occupy Veracruz. Romero pressed the issue more strongly, alleging that Mexico would not be offended if the United States accepted an invitation from the three monarchies to collect claims owed the United States; in that case she would have a voice and a vote in the threatened violation of the Monroe Doctrine. Seward was thoughtful: "It is very hard to have to declare war on a friend to contribute to saving her," he mused. Furthermore, the United States did not wish to break her tradition of avoiding foreign alliances, and she was too much the friend of Mexico to resort to force.[2] Romero replied that circumstances frequently caused anomalies.[3]

Because the Civil War in the United States prevented her from protecting Mexico from European invasion, the tripartite em-

---

Bock, *Prelude to Tragedy: The Negotiation and Breakdown of the Tripartite Convention of London, October 31, 1861* (Philadelphia, 1966), pp. 122–215. Dr. Bock's exhaustive study of the beginning of the French interference in America is a scholarly and detailed compilation of diplomatic correspondence, a tracing of the policies of England, France, and Spain, and a narrative of the tripartite expedition to Mexico. Yet this 799-page volume covers only the year 1861 and a part of 1862.

2. Seward to García y Tassar, December 4, 1861, Papers prepared for the Cabinet, BFO 115/286.

3. Romero to minister of foreign affairs, November 23 and November 30, 1861, *Corres. mexicana,* I.

VERACRUZ: THE MOST IMPORTANT MEXICAN PORT

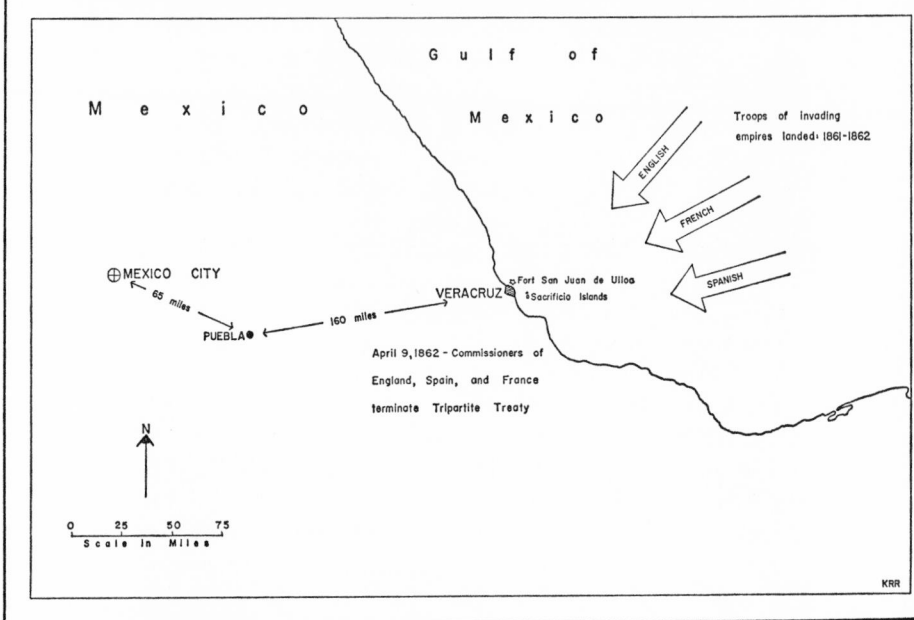

pires were forced to move quickly. Few, if any, in Paris, London, or Madrid contemplated or desired a restored Union.

On December 8, a Spanish squadron of twenty-six ships and six thousand troops began arriving off Veracruz. Within nine days the Spanish flag flew over the ancient fort and without resistance Veracruz was occupied. In his proclamation, the invading commander assured Mexicans that Spain had "no mission of conquest" but was "solely . . . demanding satisfaction for the non-fulfillment of treaties."[4]

Between January 6 and 8, 1862, the British and French arrived, the British with seven hundred marines and the French with two thousand troops and five hundred Zouaves.[5]

Five commissioners from the invading governments were authorized to determine procedures for collecting the debts and claims demanded by the tripartite alliance. Commissioners for

4. For the proclamation of General Gasset, the Spanish Commander, see Bock, *Prelude to Tragedy,* p. 275.

5. Ibid., p. 279.

PRIM

This interpretation of Prim was by the French artist André Gill, known for his caricatures of Notables under the Second Empire. Prim dominated the Tripartite Conference at Veracruz and by exposing the Machiavellian scheme of Napoleon III he broke up the treaty and caused the withdrawal from Mexico of all Spanish and English troops. He was the only Spanish statesman to make a notable contribution to the New World in the nineteenth century.

Illustration from Charles Fontane,
Un Maître de la Caricature: André Gill, 1840–85 (Paris, 1927).
(Library of Congress)

[41]

France were Vice Admiral Jean de la Gravière Jurien and Count Dubois de Saligny; and those for England were Sir Charles Lennox Wyke and Commodore Hugh Dunlop. Chairman of these commissioners was the Spanish General Juan Prim, Count of Reus and Marquis de los Castillejos. The tact of commissioners Wyke and Prim lessened Mexican resentment to the presence of almost 10,000 foreign troops.

Assembling at Veracruz on January 9, 1862, for a series of conferences that was to last until April 9, these five commissioners concluded amicably the first question discussed: they agreed on the propriety of explaining to the Mexicans why they were at Veracruz. This vague, general proclamation, previously prepared by Prim,[6] assured Mexicans that the allies wanted to "stretch out a friendly hand" and "preside at the good spectacle of your regeneration." The Mexican people, "without the intervention of foreigners," were to reorganize themselves "in a solid and permanent manner."

In spite of this auspicious beginning, the commissioners almost immediately encountered serious barriers to a common understanding of their joint mission. During the next three months the atmosphere was tense, the proceedings were invariably argumentative and occasionally insulting. The French emperor had counted heavily on support from Spain, whereas Spanish Commissioner Prim, almost from the beginning, saw eye to eye with England. Mexican exiles in Europe, strongly promonarchical, had convinced Napoleon III that, upon the landing of European troops, their compatriots would rise as one and support the establishment of a monarchy. Wyke, the English commissioner, discovered no adherents to a monarchy in Mexico, and Prim, commissioner for Spain, whose uncle by marriage was in the Juárez cabinet, was convinced that the Mexicans were definitely not promonarchists.

On February 19, General Prim, as chairman of the allied commissioners, and Mexican Foreign Minister Manuel Doblado had a personal meeting at La Soledad, perched high on the banks of the river Jampa, twenty-five miles west of Veracruz. Prim convinced Doblado "that the rumors he had heard of our coming here with the intention of upsetting the present government and establishing a monarchy in its stead are entirely false."[7] The

6. Ibid., pp. 293–94.
7. Wyke to Russell, February 22, 1862, *BFSP*, LIII.

Tripartite Treaty of London, October 31, 1861, not only restricted action to the collection of claims and grievances but disavowed intervention in domestic affairs. In response to Prim's explanation Doblado replied that, if the Juárez government were recognized and the allies would meet to negotiate claims, they might move their troops from the disease-infested coast to healthier locations. Prim and Doblado drew up an agreement for the negotiation of claims.

When the Spanish commissioner returned from La Soledad to Veracruz and presented this agreement, the English commissioners accepted. Even Saligny agreed, although under protest and after vigorous disagreement with his colleagues. Never fear, he reported to Paris, the Mexicans would soon give the commissioners an opportunity to break the convention.[8]

By the first of March French and Spanish troops were on the move to more healthful locations of some 2,500 feet elevation; the French at Tehuacán, the Spanish at Córdoba. The English marines were to have gone to Orizaba, but they were ordered to reembark. After the last detachment of European troops moved from the Gulf coast, the flag of the Mexican republic again waved over Veracruz. Some three hundred men from the invaders' fleets held the city, and in rotation, about fifty occupied the fort.

While these troop movements were in progress, the commissioners continued wrangling in a long series of almost continuous conferences.[9] Acrimonious exchanges grew in volume and intensity. Inevitable delays occurred when the commissioners referred their questions to their respective governments for instructions. At this juncture Secretary of State Seward notified England, France, and Spain that the United States disapproved of monarchy in Mexico supported by foreign intervention.[10]

Finally, the commissioners of the three invading nations acknowledged their inability to agree. They, therefore, at Orizaba, on April 9, 1862, resolved, subject to the approval of their respective governments, to discontinue the tripartite expedition. Not one goal of the London Convention had been realized. Each government in time accepted and approved the recommenda-

8. Saligny to Thouvenel, March 11, 1862, CP, Mexique, LVIII.
9. These conferences were analyzed by Bock, *Prelude to Tragedy*, pp. 293–336, 404–29.
10. Seward to Adams, March 3, 1862, Instructions, Great Britain, Dept. of State, NA, XVIII.

tions of the allied commissioners. Queen Victoria's reaction, when informed of the disagreement at Orizaba, was: "The conduct of the French is everywhere disgraceful. Let us . . . have nothing to do with them in the future in any proceedings in other countries."[11] Meanwhile, General Prim reembarked his troops, and both the Spanish and English forces sailed from Veracruz. Thus ended the first act of the tripartite invasion. In it had been laid the groundwork, not for peace, but for renewed conflict and final rupture among the allies.

The underlying causes of the breakup of the expedition were:

1. French insistence—chiefly through Saligny—on demands for payments to France so excessive as to provoke a war. Behind these demands was the secret scheme for the establishment of a monarchy.

2. British objection to inclusion of the Jecker bond debt in the French claims.

3. Spanish and British refusal to support the French intention of "regenerating" Mexico.

4. Spanish and English exasperation over the arrival in Veracruz of Juan Nepomuceno Almonte, illegitimate son of one of the three liberators of Mexico, José Morelos. Almonte, Mexican general second in command under Santa Anna at the Battle of San Jacinto, where Texas won its independence, was educated in the United States and had been minister of Mexico to the United States and France. It was to France that he fled after Juárez and the Liberals triumphed in the War of the Reform. Almonte and other émigrés in Europe met secretly with Napoleon III, and later with Maximilian, to draft preliminary plans for the overthrow of Juárez and the substitution for the republic of a monarchy. Almonte had been sent to Veracruz by Napoleon III to rally promonarchists in Mexico to the support of the invading French.[12]

From the outset, Saligny had a concrete program of action: the allies would land, issue a proclamation to the Mexican people, and present the joint ultimatum to Juárez on a take-it-or-leave-it basis. Of course, it would be refused; Saligny had seen to it that no self-respecting government would accept the

11. From "The Queen's Letters, 1862," May 17, 1862, quoted by Bock, *Prelude to Tragedy*, p. 431.

12. Ibid., pp. 404–52.

French demands. Thereupon, the march to Mexico City would begin and by January's end or early February at the latest, the allies would be in the capital. Probably Saligny expected little enthusiasm for monarchy in Veracruz because of the influence there of Liberals; in Puebla and Mexico City the temper would be different. Always a political realist, he believed the allies should accept support from any source and welcome any individual who endorsed monarchy, regardless of his affiliations, past or present. He was not one to be offended if his supporters served private ends, provided they also served his.

Vice Admiral Jurien and his officers became the target of Saligny's harangues about what could be done with a display of sufficient courage. The vice admiral struggled to get along with him; but his good resolutions were severely taxed when Saligny insisted he could march to Mexico City with five hundred men because the French were so loved that no one wanted to resist them. Jurien had no illusions. "They detest us here, only less than the Spaniards, that is all," he wrote his superiors in Paris, adding sagely, "The foreigner in arms is always odious."[13] There was love of France in Mexico Jurien later admitted, but it was the love of revolutionary France, not France as the ally of Spain or the imposer of order. The treatment Saligny received from the Mexicans was an example of how much the Paris ideal of monarchy appealed to the Mexicans; his person had been outraged and his character attacked. Jurien further wrote, "If there is anyone more odious to the liberal party than Spain I fear it is the French Minister."[14]

On the night of April 9, 1862, after the withdrawal of the British and Spanish commissioners from the Orizaba conference, the French commissioners notified the Mexican republic that they would immediately begin hostilities. On April 16, they issued a proclamation intended to convince the Mexican people how much France yearned for their welfare.[15] Almonte had already proclaimed himself the supreme power of Mexico; this was indisputable evidence that his protectors, the French, expected to overthrow Juárez. By his wholehearted backing of Almonte and the other Mexican exiles, Saligny disregarded the warnings from Thouvenel that Napoleon III did not propose to support

13. Jurien to Thouvenel, February 1, 1862, Papiers de Thouvenel, DB, AN, X.
14. Jurien to Thouvenel, February 10, 1862, ibid.
15. Proclamation of Saligny and Jurien to the Mexicans, CP, Mexique, LIX.

any *one* party.[16] Saligny rationalized his position by arguing that the "Party of the Intervention" was a designation so general as to obviate the necessity of inquiring into the antecedents of its adherents.

At last the time had come for Saligny's long-awaited "impulse"—military action in Mexico. No longer were there English and Spanish barriers to the French march from Veracruz to the capital.

Such a *coup de théâtre*, Saligny was convinced, would succeed by moving too rapidly for President Juárez to marshal a defense. Other Frenchmen agreed with him,[17] and the Marquis de Radepont, architect of the Grand Design, after he joined the French camp, shared Saligny's views. Even so, a dash of several hundred miles through unknown country and fortified mountain passes to an equally unfamiliar destination could not have failed to horrify Vice Admiral Jurien and others trained in orthodox warfare. Furthermore, demonstrations in favor of the expedition and of monarchical government had not materialized.

In this way the prelude to tragedy was to be followed swiftly by the unfolding of the tragedy itself.

16. Thouvenel to Saligny, April 30, 1862; May 31, 1862, ibid., LVIII.
17. Diary of the Comte de la Londe, de la Londe Collection, Paris.

6

Lincoln's Latin American Policy
1861–1863

————◄•►————

"Mexican affairs have suddenly come to be very interesting to the Black [Lincoln's] Administration," was the confidential comment John Forsyth, former U.S. minister to Mexico, sent from a peace conference in Washington to his Confederate colleagues late in March of 1861.[1] Earlier that month Lincoln, while considering ministers for England, France, Mexico, and Spain, had written, "We need to have these points guarded as strongly and quickly as possible."[2] Mexico might become the most important foreign post, editorialized the *New York Tribune*, since it would counteract "the filibustering projects of the Southern Confederacy."[3] Thomas Corwin, rabid antiexpansionist, was selected as minister to Mexico and informed by Secretary of State Seward that the post was "perhaps the most interesting and important one within the whole circle of our international relations."[4]

The mission to Mexico climaxed Corwin's long, distinguished career. For a dozen years he had served as a member of Congress and had also been governor of Ohio, United States senator and, in Fillmore's cabinet, secretary of the treasury. He was a great orator at a time when oratory shaped public sentiment. So powerful was his opposition to the United States' making war

1. Forsyth to Davis, March 20, 1861, Pickett Papers, LC.
2. Lincoln to Seward, March 11, 1861, Lincoln Papers, LC, XXXVI.
3. *New York Tribune*, editorial, March 13, 1861.
4. Seward to Corwin, April 6, 1861, Instructions, Mexico, Dept. of State, NA, XVII.

The "Rail Splitter" at Work Repairing the Union

LINCOLN

Lincoln's early respect for Latin America was demonstrated when, as a congressman from Illinois, he strongly opposed the U.S. war of aggression against Mexico. As president his new Latin American policy made friends below the border by denouncing U.S. territorial expansion, abolishing slavery, and amicably adjusting claims.

Lithograph by Joseph E. Baker, 1865
(Library of Congress)

against Mexico as to declare in the U.S. Senate his hope that the Mexicans would receive the invading armies "with bloody hands and hospitable graves."[5] For this utterance he was hanged in effigy even by members of his own party.

Corwin was described by an American girl who knew him in Mexico as "tall, stout and somewhat awkward in his gait; his double chin was lost between the exaggerated points of the stiff white collar so characteristic of our American statesmen of that time. His kindly smile and natural charm of voice and manner, however, soon attracted and held those who at first found him unengaging."[6] She compared his very large sparkling brown eyes to those of a chihuahua.

The new minister's instructions from Washington were to combat Confederate influence in Mexico. His task was to convince the Juárez government that continuance of the U.S. Civil War was inimical to the welfare of all republican governments in the Western Hemisphere. He was to block Confederate attempts to gain recognition from Mexico, warning against aggressive designs of the Confederacy, especially attacks from California and Texas. This he accomplished within a few months and with little difficulty. His second purpose, to initiate Lincoln's new Latin American policy, was designed primarily to correct previous mistakes, namely, acquisition of territory and overinsistence in assessing claims for loss of lives and property of United States citizens. In view of the threatened intervention of European monarchies, Corwin was to give assurances to President Juárez that the United States desired Mexico to "retain its complete integrity and independence,"[7] and form of government (republic).

En route to his post Corwin traveled from Veracruz to Mexico City with Sir Charles Wyke, the British minister, with whom he maintained cordial relations as long as Wyke stayed in Mexico. At the capital he readily made friends with Mexican officials for whose problems he had both understanding and sympathy as is clear from the following dispatch to Seward: "In the last forty years Mexico has passed through thirty-six different forms of government, has had . . . seventy-three Presidents. Still I do not despair of the final triumph of free government. . . . The signs of

5. Frank L. Owsley, *King Cotton Diplomacy* (Chicago, 1959), p. 110.
6. Sara Yorke Stevenson, *Maximilian in Mexico* (New York, 1899), p. 147.
7. Seward to Corwin, April 6, 1861, Instructions, Mexico, Dept. of State, NA, XVII.

regeneration, though few, are still visible. Had the present liberal party enough money at its command to pay an army of 10,000 men, I am satisfied it could suppress the present opposition, restore order and preserve internal peace. . . . I am persuaded the pecuniary resources to effect these objects at this time must come from abroad. This country is exhausted . . . by forty years of almost uninterrupted civil war."[8]

Arguments charging the Confederacy with nefarious designs south of the Rio Grande received support from the Mexican Legation in Washington even before Lincoln's inauguration. The youthful Matías Romero was there studying with the utmost diligence and observing movements and plans of both the Union and the Confederacy. His contacts in Washington extended far beyond the executive and the state departments. He had access to both houses of Congress, especially to the Senate through Charles Sumner of the Foreign Relations Committee, and in time to the cabinet through a close friendship with Postmaster General Montgomery Blair, who passed on tidbits from cabinet meetings.[9] Except for a few months, Romero remained in Washington for the entire French occupation of his country.

Although Romero never wholly exonerated the United States from expansionist tendencies, he believed a successful Confederacy would expand aggressively and warned Juárez accordingly, adding that Southerners had referred to the Gulf of Mexico as a Confederate lake. Secession was merely a first step in the long-range policy to extend slavery, and designs were already afoot to grab Mexican territory by negotiation or by filibustering from Texas.[10]

Romero's warnings, combined with Corwin's own highly effective propaganda, soon tipped the scales against the Confederacy. By July 1861, Corwin received "positive assurance . . . that . . . the [Juárez government] will not entertain any proposition" leading to recognition of the Confederacy. He added that "well-informed Mexicans in and out of the Government seem to be well aware that the independence of a Southern Confederacy would be the signal for a war of conquest with a view to establish-

8. Corwin to Seward, June 29, 1861, Dispatches, Mexico, ibid., XXVIII.

9. Robert W. Frazer, "Matías Romero and the French Intervention in Mexico" (Ph.D. diss., University of California, 1941).

10. Romero to minister of foreign affairs, Confidential, February 9, 1861; February 21, 1861; March 25, 1861, Corres. mexicana, vol. I, pt. 2.

ing slavery in each of the twenty-two states of this Republic."[11] Corwin had been actively at work only thirty-five days before John T. Pickett, the Confederacy's agent, landed at Veracruz.

Plans for Pickett's mission took shape in March of 1861 while he was in Washington serving as secretary to the Confederate Peace Commissioners. One of the commissioners, John Forsyth, recommended Pickett as one possessing a "thorough knowledge of Mexican character," who knew the leaders and was "eminently suitable for a position so delicate and important."[12] This eulogy was erroneous. Fiery, adventurous, and loving excitement, Pickett was tactless and far from exemplary in his conduct, alternating between threatening language and unauthorized hints of bestowing favors.

To advance his fortunes as agent to Mexico, Pickett reported to the Confederate government that, in his opinion, there would be no permanence in the government of Mexico so long as the country was governed by Mexicans, that nothing less than foreign intervention would bring about peace.[13] Pickett was instructed not to ask for recognition of the Confederacy but to promise a ready response if Mexico wished to grant it, and to be receptive to the formation of an alliance. The Confederacy expected Mexico to observe the strictest neutrality in the U.S. Civil War. Pickett was to use all means at his disposal "to match the proceedings of . . . and to counteract"[14] the Union Minister Thomas Corwin.

Upon arriving at Veracruz, Pickett filled his dispatches with assurances that the prevailing sympathy "appears to be with our cause," and that the policy of the governor of the state of Veracruz would preserve strict neutrality in coastal waters and accord belligerent rights to the Confederacy. On reaching the capital, confidence made Pickett more demanding. He told Manuel Zamacona, minister of foreign affairs, that the Confederacy "demanded" rather than "expected" neutrality from Mexico.[15]

A later communication enumerated Confederate virtues; slavery was similar to Mexican peonage, and the South was sincere in comparison with Northern hypocrisy. Such was the sympathy

11. Corwin to Seward, July 29, 1861, Dispatches, Mexico, Dept. of State, NA, XXVIII.
12. Forsyth to Davis, March 20, 1861, Pickett Papers, LC.
13. Forsyth to Davis, March 20, 1861, with enclosure by Pickett, ibid.
14. Confederate Secretary of State Toombs to Pickett, May 17, 1861, ibid.
15. Pickett to Toombs, June 15, 1861; June 27, 1861; July 26, 1861, ibid.

between Southerners and Mexicans that, if secession did not result in the independence of the South, "hundreds of thousands" of her sons would emigrate "with their goods and chattels (as did the children of Israel) to some convenient and attractive Promised Land."[16] Zamacona could not have been enthusiastic about Mexico's becoming a "promised land" for Confederates but he recognized Pickett as a confidential agent and assured him that Mexico's policy was one of neutrality.[17]

The situation changed dramatically when Pickett learned that the Juárez government had given the Union permission to march troops from Guaymas, on the Gulf of California, to Arizona,[18] in order to protect Arizona from a suspected Confederate advance.[19] Zamacona explained to Pickett that the Mexicans did not understand that Arizona was part of the Confederacy, an obvious hint that the Confederacy might be already expanding.[20] Pickett retorted that prior to secession the South had favored "extension" (the word he used for expansion) to balance the political power of the North, but, after secession, the "policy . . . ceased to exist; in fact, died a natural death." In a shrewd move to undercut Corwin, he then volunteered to transmit to the Confederate government "proposals for the retrocession to Mexico of a large portion of the territory hitherto acquired from her by the United States"[21] (Texas, New Mexico, and California).

By the middle of September 1861, Mexico regarded the Confederacy with undisguised suspicion. Pickett blamed Corwin for fomenting this distrust. But Corwin does not deserve sole credit for Mexico's preference for the Union. Mexico's immediate dangers were her empty treasury, the continued attacks of undefeated Conservatives, and the demands of European powers. Money was the lifeline of the Juárez government, and Washington was the only place where there was a prospect of getting it. As a South Carolinian wrote from Mexico to the Confederate government in Richmond, the Mexicans believed that men,

16. Pickett to Zamacona, August 3, 1861, Expediente H/310 (72:73) /3, Legajo 6-1-2, 1861, AG.

17. Zamacona to Pickett, August 16, 1861, ibid.

18. Pickett to Zamacona, August 26, 1861, ibid.

19. Seward to Corwin, May 9, 1861, Instructions, Mexico, Dept. of State, NA, XVII.

20. Zamacona to Pickett, August 26, 1861, Expediente H/310 (72:73) /3, Legajo 6-1-2, 1861, AG.

21. Pickett to Zamacona, September 16, 1861, ibid.

money, and arms would be "lavishly supplied" by the United States in vindication of the national integrity of Mexico and of the Monroe Doctrine.[22]

By November Pickett reluctantly conceded the obvious fact that the Confederacy had "few or no friends" in Mexico. The Mexican government was ignoring him and his mission had come to an end.[23] He had been arrested for disorderly conduct in a bar and his "confidential" reports to Richmond with many uncomplimentary comments about Mexico had been intercepted in New Orleans and shared with the Juárez government. Yet, Pickett's failure had some bearing on the developing international situation. When the Juárez government rejected the Confederacy, the Juárez regime in turn became expendable to the Richmond government. Richmond, in an effort to win recognition from France, had previously accepted monarchy in Mexico and hoped for an alliance with it. In fact, Confederate agents argued in Paris that success of the French Mexican enterprise depended on a successful Confederacy. When Pickett left Mexico in December 1861, he knew that French intervention was a certainty.

As danger from the Confederacy declined, Corwin immersed himself in the greater problem of European coercion of Mexico. He knew his country could not prevent the obviously imminent intervention. Because no military assistance could be spared with domestic war clouds getting blacker, no diplomatic demands could be made which might be answered by aid to the Confederacy. The final remedy was money from loans, which would be effective only if England, France, and Spain agreed to settle peacefully their claims on Mexico.

To forestall consequences as unwelcome to the United States as to Mexico, Corwin proposed a loan, not exceeding $10,000,000 to $12,000,000, payable in installments. In return the United States might receive Baja California, thought to be in danger of seizure by the Confederates, or a tariff reduction on imports, say 50 percent less than the rate accorded other nations. Such an arrangement would be unpopular in both countries, he admitted ruefully, remembering his own opposition to the acquisition of Mexican territory.[24] Corwin also made a second suggestion to

22. Cripps to Confederate Secretary of State, April 22, 1862, Pickett Papers, LC.
23. Pickett to Toombs, November 29, 1861, ibid.
24. Corwin to Seward, June 29, 1861, Dispatches, Mexico, Dept. of State, NA, XXVIII.

Secretary Seward. He thought England and France intended to frighten Mexico into submission to their will or to create a pretext for something even worse—intervention by arms. "Europe is quite willing to see us humbled," Corwin wrote, "and will not fail to take advantage of our embarrassment to execute purposes of which she would not have dreamed had we remained at peace."[25] He regarded President Juárez and his republican government, if given financial aid, competent to save their country from foreign intervention. Only from the United States could such aid come. While Corwin was endeavoring to work out a plan helpful to Mexico, that country's Congress was incautious enough to suspend interest payments on debts and claims owed England, France, and Spain. Thereupon Corwin proposed that the United States pay Mexico's suspended interest obligations, taking as security the mineral rights of the northern states of Mexico. This loan would be specifically pegged to the debt settlement. For the United States to pay debts other than her own was a radical departure from any previous U.S. policy. For England and France to permit the "aggressive Yankee" to pay Mexican debts and thereby gain further influence in that country was also a radical departure from everything thought and talked about in European courts.

In Washington Romero at the Mexican Legation argued vainly in behalf of a loan to his country. Zamacona, minister of foreign affairs, refused to consider the price: "It is inconceivable," he declared, "that this government would make agreement about the sale of territory . . . or mortgage the wealth of undeveloped lands . . . which would foreshadow any danger to our nationality."[26] Repeated conferences with Seward forced Romero to conclude that a loan to Mexico would be approved by neither the Department of State nor the Senate if the money were used to make war on other powers.[27] This would risk international involvement and the Union could not take on an enemy from the outside.

But as the door closed on a general loan to Mexico, it opened on an earmarked loan to meet the interest payments on the Mexican debts. On August 24, 1861, Seward gave Corwin permission to attempt negotiations for such an agreement. Corwin was au-

25. Ibid., July 25, 1861.
26. Zamacona to Romero, September 8, 1861, Confidential, *Corres. mexicana*, I.
27. Romero to Zamacona, September 12, 1861, ibid.

thorized to frame a treaty by which the United States would pay, over a period of five years, the interest of 3 percent on Mexico's funded foreign debt. Repayment would bear 6 percent interest and the loan would be secured by public lands and mineral rights in the northern states of Mexico. Negotiations were not to be concluded unless Britain, France, and Spain agreed not to make reprisals.[28] In September 1861, the gist of the proposed U.S. treaty with Mexico that Corwin proposed to Seward was known to London and Paris; its provision whereby the United States would undertake the suspended interest payments of Mexico was first revealed to the British and French legations in Washington with the information that American ministers to the governments concerned were instructed to discuss the issue further. Charles Francis Adams, U.S. minister to London, brought the question to the attention of Lord Russell during a visit to Abergeldie Castle. He told Russell the United States was disturbed by rumors of interference in Mexico and the possibility of imposition of a new government by foreign arms. A European intervention in Mexico might involve the United States, to protect her own interests, in the various struggles of Europe. It would be much better if the threatened use of force by the European powers were forestalled by agreement whereby the United States guaranteed, for a specified period, interest payments on Mexican debts.

Despite his reluctance Seward saw in Corwin's proposal to underwrite interest payments an advisably calculated risk. Washington regarded European interference in Mexico as only a shade less ominous than rebellion at home. Britain, France, and Spain might start a war of reprisal which could result in the subjugation of Mexico. If that took place and the South made good its secession, the end must be a return "of the American continent under European domination." The summer of 1861 passed in grim uncertainty awaiting Seward's reply.

Mexico was indeed becoming one of the most important of the Lincoln legations, just as Seward had predicted, and focal point of the Latin American policy of the Union. Corwin was rapidly developing into an extremely valuable foreign representative in this critical period. The new Latin American policy initiated in Mexico by Lincoln, continued by President Andrew

28. Seward to Corwin, August 24, 1861, Instructions, Mexico, Dept. of State, NA, XVII.

Johnson, and administered throughout both administrations by
Secretary of State Seward, was gradually carried over into the
other Spanish American republics.

As in Mexico, advocates of monarchy in most of these countries
were from conservative and clerical groups. They represented
entrenched position, power, and wealth which had suffered disastrously from abuses under the republican form of government.
This condition, as reported to Washington by Friedrich Hassaurek, minister to Ecuador, was in general as follows: "We must
either . . . be swallowed up in the end by the Anglo-Saxon race
or follow the example of the French in Mexico. . . . Bad . . . as
foreign intervention may be, it is our last and our only hope."[29]

Prior to the Lincoln administration, the State Department had
pushed the chronic question of U.S. claims—not always honestly
assessed—so long and so aggressively as to embitter the Latin
Americans against the United States. As irresponsible expansionists recklessly expressed their faith in the manifest destiny of
Anglo-Americans to impose their political and social institutions
on the peoples to the south,[30] resentment, fear, and hatred were
engendered.

The immediate need for a friendlier attitude toward the
"Colossus of the North" in the crisis of European intervention
was expounded by Matías Romero, remarkably perceptive Mexican diplomat. "Before the [U.S.] Civil War commenced," he
explained, "it appeared that . . . [the United States] was the only
enemy . . . Mexico had . . . because [its] usurping policy had de-
prived us of half our territory and [was] a constant menace. . . .
Nothing, therefore, was more natural than to see with pleasure . . . a division which . . . would render almost impotent
against us each one of the . . . [two sections of that country, the
North and the South]. . . . We [now] find ourselves [facing] the
hard alternative of sacrificing our territory and our nationality
at the hands of . . . [the United States] or our liberty and our
independence before the despotic thrones of Europe. The second
danger is immediate and more imminent. . . ."[31]

29. Friedrich Hassaurek, *Four Years Among Spanish-Americans* (London, 1868),
p. 244.

30. A. Curtis Wilgus, "Official Expressions of Manifest Destiny Sentiments Concerning Hispanic America, 1848–1871," *Louisiana Historical Quarterly*, XVI
(July 1932), 486–506.

31. J. Fred Rippy, *Latin America in World Politics* (New York, 1938), pp.
238–39.

The heart of Lincoln's Latin American policy was to amend the unfortunate aspects of U.S. relations with Latin America and to substitute for undue pressure on claims a policy of mutual understanding and self-respect founded on a sounder basis. The need for this change was stressed by Matías Romero who was one of the ablest Spanish American statesmen of the 1860s. Lincoln's instructions to U.S. ministers and other officials in Spanish America constituted an emotionally earnest crusade for the survival of free institutions; slavery, long abolished in free Spanish America, was severely condemned, and human rights were vigorously defended. Confederates were castigated as filibusters and expansionists, intent on the extension of slavery southward and the overthrow of legally constituted government; Confederate policies were also closely allied with the depredations of French and Spanish imperialism. In short, Lincoln and his Secretary of State Seward emphasized to all United States officials accredited to the Spanish American republics the desirability of presenting the Union as the one powerful defender of republicanism against monarchy and Old World interference and, therefore, the protector of all sovereignty in the Western Hemisphere.

7

The Sinister Design Revealed
1861–1863

Operating in secrecy as was his habit, Napoleon III gradually drew back the veil concealing his sinister conspiracy against the United States. The first official information reaching the people of France was an imperial decree of November 20, 1861, in the *Documents diplomatiques* proclaiming the London Convention of the preceding October 31 and the tripartite expedition of England, France, and Spain to collect debts and damages from Mexico. Early in January 1862, a few weeks after this announcement was made in Paris, English, French, and Spanish commissioners began holding a series of conferences in Veracruz to carry out the purpose of the London Convention. Toward the end of January the official and semiofficial press of France began advocating a monarchy in Mexico.[1]

Six months later, on July 3, 1862, Napoleon III revealed an outline of his American operations in a secret letter to Major General Elie Frédéric Forey, who was about to leave France for Mexico to assume command of forces there.

Four months after Napoleon III had given these instructions to Forey, his announcement in *Le Moniteur* gave the French nation the emperor's justification for the Mexican expedition.

Two months later, in January 1863, the *Documents diplo-*

1. Daniel Dawson, *The Mexican Adventure* (London, 1935), pp. 215–16; Carl H. Bock, *Prelude to Tragedy: The Negotiation and Breakdown of the Tripartite Convention of London, October 31, 1861* (Philadelphia, 1966), p. 364.

NAPOLEON III

Grandson of the American-born Empress Josephine, the future Napoleon III, after escaping from a medieval prison, was elected president of France by five million votes. He created the Second Empire and became emperor. With Queen Victoria he defeated Russia to protect Turkey.

Frank Leslie's Illustrated Newspaper, 10 January 1863
(Library of Congress)

matiques carried a further announcement of the beginning of the Grand Design. In that year was also published in Paris an elaboration of the secret scheme in an anonymous pamphlet, *La France, le Mexique et les Etats-Confédérés.* This was a surprisingly frank indictment and severe denunciation of the American Union; it enthusiastically advocated the independence of the Confederacy and described the proposals for regenerating Spanish America.

Shortly after the Confederacy suffered two of its severest calamities, Gettysburg and Vicksburg, the *New York Times*, in reproducing a translation of the anonymous pamphlet, editorialized that it "has caused some stir both in Europe and this country, from the fact that . . . it was currently reported to have been 'inspired' by the Emperor Napoleon, and to be indicative of his policy on this continent. The fact of 'inspiration' has been semiofficially denied in Paris, and ostentatiously denied in this country from [the French Legation in] Washington; but those who fully comprehend all the mysteries of Imperial 'inspiration' are still of the opinion that the brochure has some degree of it and that it was thrown out with the Emperor's sanction, to subserve a purpose. . . ."[2]

Ten days after the *New York Times* reproduced the pamphlet attributed to Napoleon III's "inspiration," another translation of the pamphlet was published as a separate brochure in New York City. Its translator, William Henry Hurlbert, internationally noted journalist, one-time editorial writer on the *New York Times,* and later editor of the *New York World,* claimed in the preface of the separate brochure that the original pamphlet in French "obtained world-wide notoriety as embodying the first coherent view which has been made public of the designs of Napoleon III in the New World."[3] If indeed the anonymous pamphlet had the blessings of Napoleon III, here is what it revealed of French plans for America:

2. *New York Times*, September 25, 1863, pp. 4–5.
3. Michel Chevalier, *France, Mexico and the Confederate States,* trans. William Henry Hurlbert (New York: C. B. Richardson Co., 1863). The original *La France, le Mexique et les Etats-Confédérés* (Paris: E. Dentu, 1863), was attributed to Michel Chevalier, as spokesman for Napoleon III. A long review of *La France, le Mexique et les Etats-Confédérés* was also published by C. B. Richardson in New York in 1863. It was by Vine Wright Kingsley and included Napoleon III's July 3, 1862, letter to Forey and General Prim's letter to Napoleon III of March 17, 1862.

JUSTIFICATION OF THE FRENCH IN MEXICO

. . . The origin of the actual war in Mexico is more than justified by the wrongs which France is bent upon redressing. The object of that war is to aid the Mexicans in establishing, according to their own free will and choice, a government which may have some chance of stability. . . .

[After the debacle at Puebla, May 5, 1862] it was then decided that a complete army corps, armed with formidable artillery and adequate means of transportation should be embarked for Mexico as soon as the season would allow. The money expenditures required by this considerable movement of troops and warlike material was simply an advance made upon the enterprise. Where so many people insisted upon seeing nothing but a little glory to win, Napoleon III had already laid the foundations of a completely new system of policy. While for everybody else the Mexican war was a mere military question, he was limiting and determining the part to be played by our soldiers, our seamen, and our diplomatists, in this enterprise which is to give to France the commercial rank she has a right to hold. . . .

TO PROTECT LATINS

France must oppose the absorption of Southern America by Northern America; she must in like manner oppose the degradation of the Latin race on the other side of the ocean; she must establish the integrity and security of our West Indian colonies. It is the interests which compel France to sympathize with the Confederate States which have led our banners up to the walls of Mexico.

TO HELP CONFEDERATES

The recognition of the Southern States will be the consequence of our intervention, or rather our intervention has prepared, facilitated, and made possible a diplomatic act which will consecrate the final separation and secession of those states from the American Union.

TO ADVANCE COMMERCE

The thirty thousand Frenchmen who today [1863] occupy Mexico or are pursuing Juárez to San Luis Potosí, are the advanced guard of an immense commercial army, and their bayonets will open to our commerce harbors which have been too long closed upon it. Let us then hear no more of these mendacious outcries over the emptiness of our projects in Mexico. What Napoleon III means he means distinctly, he has long meant it, he will continue to mean and to will it until it is achieved. . . . He means to regenerate our trans-Atlantic commerce, to restore to it or to create for it profitable avenues and outlets: he means that our national industry in all time to come shall be able to provide itself with the materials indispensable to its success. This is his meaning, and he will pursue this purpose until he has accomplished it. . . .

To Eradicate Governmental Inequities

When one runs over the catalogue of the riches of Mexico, its wealth in grain and gold—those two vital forces of nations—one is tempted to ask how it is that its inhabitants make no more of their advantages? Why is it that notwithstanding European aid the movement of industry in that country has never been orderly and regular? It is hardly possible that anarchy should have taken root in the needs and aspirations of a population too sparse for the country it inhabits. In Mexico disorder has never arisen from the lower ranks of society, it descends from the upper and governmental regions. The people are not the agitators, and brigandage itself has been most commonly undertaken by persons of property, generals, even by the aides-de-camp of presidents. The Indians, not naturally industrious, live on the plantations or factories of Europeans, whilst the mixed race seeks in tyranny, exactions, and robbery, the facile existence which it does not care to ask from labor. . . . In short, although there is an actual want of population in Mexico, there is more idleness there than industry; and this unfortunate state of things, this destruction of agriculture and industry by the depredations of indolence, will continue to exist till European emigration shall modify the relations of the three races which barely people these immense regions.

Mexico waits for—invites—demands emigration; not the unhealthy foolish emigration which transports from one latitude to another, creatures without industry or intelligence which find no room in our social system. . . .

Regeneration of the Latins

Let the certainty of protection lead this population to Mexico, and the age of its regeneration will not be long in coming to that country, thenceforth filled with new inhabitants, ready for all progress, familiar with the newest discoveries of modern industry, and supported by the intelligent liberalism of the flag of France. It is beginning to be seen that our national interest, much more than the desire of adding a new name to the long list of our military victories, has led France into Mexico. Let us not be troubled, then, with regard to the future of this expedition. Whether Maximilian accept or refuse the throne of Mexico; whether any other prince accept that throne or not; or whether beneath the wings of our eagles some as yet nameless government be established there, the influence of France will remain in Mexico.

"THE WONDERS OF FRANCE"

The French soldier takes his country with him. Our army, made up of workmen and laborers who all look forward to their return to the workshop or the plough, is an army of creators, and not of destroyers. It takes into Mexico all that Mexico needs: 1st. Cohesion; because it is the most complete and sincere expression of modern democracy; 2nd. Order; because it permits all citizens of that unfortunate nation to develop their own interests; 3rd. Industry; because it furnishes to languishing enterprise, workmen, foremen, artisans, managers, because it familiarizes the Mexican people with the wonders of France and of French industry; 4th. An army; by its example and its instruction.

Thus, then, and naturally, by a diffusion and profusion of interests and of labor, the desire and need of firmness in the political system will be fortified. In the great movement of our country, industrial and financial interests control and conduct society. Questions of politics disappear before social questions. Twenty years ago the opposition was republican—today it is social. And the theory of human equality no longer assumes to reduce the great to the condition of the lowly, but to raise the lowly to the level of the great. The problems of general prosperity, of the increase of wages, of cheap production, of public hygiene, can be much more easily solved under a powerful government. The [French] empire has disciplined socialism, and put it to use. The empire has conquered and decapitated anarchy. This it is that the empire is to do in Mexico, and this it cannot do securely and properly until the Confederate States have been recognized.

THE U.S. DANGER TO EUROPE

If war had not broken out between the Northern and Southern States of America, Europe would not yet have been impressed with the dangers which threaten her from the power of the Union.

Although she had become tributary to the new world, Europe had taken no precaution to prevent the consummation of a crisis which

she had never foreseen, and which for two years she has been enduring. It has cost us something to learn how precarious is the fortune
of an industry compelled to seek its raw materials in a single market,
to all the exactions and all the vicissitudes of which it must necessarily submit. . . .

MINNESOTA PAYS $25 FOR INDIAN SCALP

Honest and intelligent men are no longer to be duped by these
coarse devices, and Mr. Lincoln's abolition cry finds no echo.

If there be sceptics on this point, let me remind them of the Lynch
law which prevails in the North; of the way in which the Indians are
still hunted down; of the decree published but the other day by the
Governor of Minnesota, offering a reward of twenty-five dollars for
every Indian scalp. These are disagreeable things to happen among
a people who profess to be fighting for the abolition of slavery; and
were that people to triumph, the poor negroes would find their way
to liberty a path of thorns.

But the first European power which shall recognize the Confederate States will have a right to obtain much more for the negro than
the Federals could secure for him through their "Union by victory."
This first power being France, we may be sure that the cause of
civilization, humanity, and progress, will not be forgotten by her.
All that is difficult, even impossible, while the conflict rages, will become easy with the return of peace. The emancipation of the blacks,
the complete abolition of slavery, can only be the work of peace and
of time; and an alliance with the South will effect that great social
renovation which England, with her "right of search," has so vainly
sought to bring about.

"MONROE DOCTRINE NOTHING MORE NOR LESS THAN INSURANCE AGAINST CIVILIZATION"

. . . Slavery cannot possibly be made a serious argument against
the recognition of the South. France and England live on good terms
with Spain and Brazil; they even protect Egypt and Turkey, and these
countries maintain slavery with no show of a disposition to abolish it.
France will use her influence to secure the gradual emancipation of
the slaves without making slavery a ground for refusing recognition.

The North, made keen-eyed by selfishness, has certainly foreseen
this; and the famous Monroe doctrine is nothing more nor less than
a policy of insurance against civilization. . . .

AN INDEPENDENT CONFEDERACY

The American war, from which France has suffered more than

England, can be useful to us only if the North and South part company definitively; and for these reasons:

1. The Confederate States will be our allies, and will guarantee us against attack by the North.

2. Mexico, developed by our efforts, and sheltered from the attacks of the North, will reward all our hopes.

3. Our factories will be insured the supplies which they absolutely require.

Were the American war to end otherwise, all the adventurers whom peace would let loose would simply fling themselves into Mexico, and all that we have gone so far to secure would be gathered in by the men of the North.

The North, whether in the domain of arms, of ideas, or of production, cannot and will not absorb the South.

We see, then, that neither peace nor absorption nor conquest is possible. There is nothing left but secession at the end of the war.

While the Americans of the North could make Europe believe they were fighting against rebels it was the duty of Europe to let them go on, despite the sufferings to which Europe was exposed by the contest; but the states of the South have set forth their policy, their purposes, their rights; they desire separation; they refuse to enrich the North; they are tired of always giving and never receiving; they have determined to live their own life. The North American exaggeration of commercial interests has borne its fruits, and the South proposes to reconstitute its national system with an eye to its own interests. Now, since those interests conform to those of France; since the cause of the South is not only just, but logical; France does not hesitate to declare her sympathies, and her first act of sympathy naturally must be the recognition of the Confederate States.

Recognized by France, the strength of those states is quintupled at once; and their adversaries lose all that they gain. For other states are waiting to follow the example of France; among the commercial powers of the second rank many desire the establishment of a Confederate republic as a means to decentralization of the Union. These powers, hitherto kept aloof by the phantom of slavery, will follow France, because the whole world knows that France lends her aid only to works of social progress.

These powers will naturally be joined by Spain, which possesses Havana. Austria, which will be more directly involved in the affairs of the new world if she accepts the Mexican throne for Maximilian, must likewise recognize the Confederate States.

And England will then do what we have done. She will recognize the South.

The Northern States will no longer persevere in a strife thenceforth become hopeless and useless.

The Navy of France is an argument which, in case of necessity, would support her diplomatic action.

This exposé at a crucial period in the history of the United States was attributed by William Henry Hurlbert to Michel Chevalier. Whether or not Chevalier wrote the anonymous pamphlet, he had expressed identical political convictions and undoubtedly exerted a profound influence on some of the policies of Napoleon III. Chevalier had supported Louis Napoleon's coup d'etat of December 2, 1851, when control of the government was seized, was a member of the Council of State and a senator of the Second Empire. Early in his career Chevalier was an ardent follower of the socialistic philosopher, Henri de Rouvroy, Comte de Saint-Simon, who fought with Lafayette at the Battle of Yorktown in Virginia. For two years Chevalier edited the *Globe*, official publication of the Saint-Simonians.

The statesman and historian, Adolphe Thiers, sent Chevalier to the United States in 1833 to study canals and railroads. After the extension of the scope and length of time of his mission, Chevalier visited nearly every part of the United States, and Mexico and Cuba as well. His observations in all these areas were extensive and penetrating. His first-hand interpretations of the United States, published in the *Journal des débats*, preceded the monumental Tocqueville work, *La Démocratie en Amérique* (1835), and were regarded by some critics as more profound and systematic. Albert Gallatin, scholar, statesman, and U.S. minister to France, lauded Chevalier's description of the United States as "the most graphic and truest tableau of the social state of America." Chevalier's writings on the United States appeared in book form in 1836 under the title, *Lettres sur l'Amérique du Nord*. In 1844 he published a valuable pamphlet on the Isthmus of Panama.

A study of these early writings of Chevalier and Louis Napoleon's serious reflections on an American canal to connect the Atlantic with the Pacific would appear to provide irrefutable evidence in tracing the origin of Napoleon III's Grand Design. This evidence, combined with two articles by Chevalier in the *Revue des deux mondes* in 1862 describing conditions in Mexico provided additional proof. Conclusive evidence of Chevalier's influence is confirmed in his 1863 interpretation of the French expedition to Mexico, *Le Mexique, ancien et moderne*. Basic proposals covering the period from the early 1840s were (1) fear of the expansion of the United States; (2) the critical need of stabilizing governments in Spanish America by transforming them into monarchies; and (3) the superimposing of superior European immigration in Spanish America. Briefly, such reforms would provide raw materials for Europe while opening American markets for European products.

That Chevalier was the imperial spokesman is made even more evident by a comparison of the anonymous pamphlet published in Paris in 1863 with Chevalier's two-volume 1863 work. In this work Chevalier asserted that Napoleon III was the protector of the Latin peoples on the Spanish and Italian peninsulas contiguous to France as well as the Latins overseas. He insisted France would not tolerate "the absorption of Southern America by Northern America" and would not allow "the degradation of the Latin race on the other side of the ocean." Chevalier asserted that French support of the Confederacy had caused France to undertake the expedition to Mexico. He boldly declared that French recognition of the Confederacy would lead to the "final separation" of the Southern states from the North American Union.

Chevalier explained that France intended to develop wealth in Spanish America by selected immigration. "Instead of drawing immigrants of independent political and religious convictions who had populated the United States, France would direct to Mexico immigrants who, conditioned by the disciplined socialism of France, were familiar with the newest discoveries of modern industry." A parallel made by Chevalier was that Mexico would emerge from anarchy with the establishment of a strong monarchy just as anarchy had disappeared in France when the Second Empire succeeded the Second Republic.

Chevalier concluded his embellishment of Napoleon III's intervention in New World affairs by expressing the fervent hope for a Confederate victory. "It would," he claimed, "assure France that (1) the Confederate States will be our allies, and will guarantee us against attacks of the North; (2) Mexico, developed by our efforts, and sheltered from attacks of the North, will reward all our hope; and (3) our factories will be insured the supplies which they absolutely require."

Other evidence that Chevalier was a close associate of Napoleon III is available in the negotiations between England and France over the Anglo-French Treaty of Commerce in 1860. According to the leading authority on this treaty, Dr. Arthur Louis Dunham, the negotiators were Michel Chevalier and Richard Cobden, English economist and "apostle of free trade." Dr. Dunham maintains that as the French author of the treaty, Chevalier "was the statesman who was primarily responsible for the commercial policy of France."[4]

4. Arthur Louis Dunham, "Chevalier's Plan of 1859: The Basis of the New Commercial Policy of Napoleon III," *AHR*, XXX, no. 1 (October 1924), 76; see also Dunham's *Anglo-French Treaty of Commerce in 1860 and the Progress of the Industrial Revolution in France* (Ann Arbor, 1930).

8

Unfolding of the Tragedy
1862

Less than one month after the Spanish and English troops had withdrawn in May of 1862, the French army began the march to Puebla from which they expected to proceed to the capital. Meanwhile, Juárez had decreed martial law and declared all areas occupied by the French in a state of siege. New instructions from Paris had placed Brigadier General Charles Latrille, Comte de Lorencez, in charge of the land forces. Highly connected, he was married to the daughter of a *maréchal* of France and had been a part of the first Napoleon's command. Lorencez had recently arrived in Veracruz with reinforcements of more than 4,500 men. Saligny had promised that the inhabitants of the old and famous city of Puebla about 200 miles west of Veracruz would be waiting, flower laden, to greet their "regenerators" and that priests would celebrate "Te Deum." Whether or not General Lorencez believed these tales, he displayed no genius in deploying his soldiers. Early on the morning of May 5, 1862, the invading columns assaulted the Cerro de Guadalupe guarding the access to a fortified and strongly garrisoned Puebla. By nightfall the wide, deep ditch obstructing the passage was filled with dead and dying French soldiers—upwards of 1,000; and the wall of the city, defended by Juarista General Ignacio Zaragoza, remained unscaled. Lorencez and his troops retreated to Orizaba.

Saligny then urged Lorencez to bypass Puebla and proceed to Mexico City as the U.S. forces had done in 1847. The commander and his officers refused to consider such unconventional tactics.

Saligny was furious, as was Napoleon III, when news of the disaster reached Paris. After expressing his mortification over this blot on French glory, the emperor wrote his defeated commander, Lorencez, that although he understood the conditions, the world would not.[1]

The summer of 1862 brought stagnation and discord, a combination disastrous to the morale of any army. Seemingly, everyone in the French camp wrote home complaining of everyone else. Radepont, who had persuaded Napoleon III to undertake the scheme, carried on voluminous correspondence, not only with the emperor but with various notables at court. Lorencez wrote the minister of war, Saligny wrote Thouvenel, and officers and soldiers were equally busy scratching their pens. All told essentially the same tale; it was not possible to describe the disaster at Puebla in terms other than that the allegedly best-trained troops in the world—veterans of French campaigns in Crimea and Italy—had been defeated by the allegedly worst.

Optimism gradually oozed away from Lorencez. "I continue to regret that I do not meet a single partisan of monarchy in Mexico," he wrote the minister of war. "However, I hope that I am in error and I think that by a French occupation of several years we could reach that objective. But we should not announce it beforehand and not have an Almonte in the bottom of our luggage who says he is the Mexican nation." It was the understanding of Lorencez that the emperor had not planned to use Almonte in that way but rather as a member of the allied armies who, at the right moment, would exert his influence to organize a provisional government. Saligny had pushed Almonte ahead with excessive zeal as one under the protection of Napoleon III. Lorencez concluded, "I am sure that nothing will be possible in Mexico with Almonte and M. S. [Monsieur de Saligny]."[2]

Following the humiliating French defeat before Puebla, Juárez held out the olive branch. Wounded French captives were returned to Orizaba, and decorations and medals found on the dead were sent to Lorencez for delivery to their bereaved families. The Mexican generals offered to negotiate with Lorencez. The French general's response, more brusque than he may have intended, was that the French Minister Saligny, alone, held dip-

1. Napoleon III to Lorencez, June 15, 1862, CP, Mexique, LIX.
2. Lorencez to minister of war, July 22, 1862, AMG, Mexique.

lomatic powers.[3] At this juncture the Juárez structure of expectations began to crumble.

Early in 1862 the Lincoln administration displayed toward events in Mexico a seeming indifference most disturbing to the persevering Romero, Mexican representative in Washington.[4] Henri Mercier, French minister there, conceded that America was indifferent. So did the representatives of England and Spain. The deceptive reserve of the State Department rested on necessity rather than on choice. Washington thought that Union aid to Juárez must not lead France or England to transform into concrete support their disquieting predilection for the Confederacy. Until the strength of the Union was demonstrated on the battlefield, its diplomacy was obliged to play a cautious game.

Late in December 1861, President Lincoln had submitted to the Senate for advice only the draft of the treaty Minister Corwin had negotiated with Juárez. Despite the president's prodding, it was February before the Senate considered it in executive session. Meanwhile Corwin had sent home another suggestion. Under stress of the menacing arrival at Veracruz of the European invaders, Corwin had worked out a basis for full payment in ten years of the entire long-accumulating Mexican debt, estimated by him as $90,000,000. The proposed U.S. loan was to be secured by a mortgage on unsold lands of the national domain and 25 percent of the customs.[5] That Corwin seriously contemplated underwriting this colossal obligation whereby control of Mexican finance by the United States would inevitably be assumed staggers credulity.

When the U.S. Senate finally considered Mexico's crisis, the chairman of its Foreign Relations Committee advocated a loan of $15,000,000 provided the invading powers accepted a settlement of their claims, but Senator John Sherman abruptly terminated discussions on February 25, 1862, by introducing a resolution opposing assumption of any of Mexico's debt or payments dependent on the concurrence of foreign powers. The vote on the Sherman resolution, passed by 29 to 9, combined three points of view: (1) opposition to entangling the United States in foreign

3. Léon de Montluc, ed., *Correspondance de Montluc et Juárez* (Paris, 1885), p. 84.
4. Romero to minister of foreign affairs, January 6, 1862, *Corres. mexicana*, II.
5. Basis for Mexican debt statement, undated and unsigned, received by State Dept., February 4, 1862, Dispatches, Mexico, Dept. of State, NA, XXIX.

agreements, (2) opposition to new accessions of territory, and (3) belief that public credit could not sustain the loan in wartime.[6] Had the Senate favored a Mexican loan, Seward expected to offer England, France, and Spain the mediation of the United States.[7]

On the arrival of the second Corwin Treaty of April 6, 1862, Lincoln was inclined to pocket the document quietly until a more favorable moment. But Corwin frantically defended his handiwork. He contended the French could never conquer Mexico and that, if Mexican lands were mortgaged to the United States, they would pay off the loan without question. Later, he made the fantastic proposal of arranging for freed Negroes of the South to settle on the Mexican lands as security for the loan. Corwin estimated that 5,000,000 former slaves could be accommodated in the hot coastal lands alone. He argued that if the United States did not use these lands the British might.[8] By June Corwin was afraid of Almonte's maneuvers for monarchy. To ratify the proposed Corwin Treaty of April 6 was the "obvious interest of the United States as well as its duty."[9] In August, however, Corwin urged that ratification be delayed to await the outcome of the Virginia campaign. Request for postponement had also been made by Mexico. As long as ratification was pending, "she will seem to have one friend," wrote Corwin.[10] By this time the issue was already dead. Yielding to Corwin's insistence, Lincoln had sent the treaty with supporting correspondence to the Senate, but without recommendation. A few weeks later, on July 12, it was tabled indefinitely.

Pressed by dire need, the Juárez government had prepared to draw on the hoped-for loan from the United States. Romero was instructed to establish a credit of $30,000 or $40,000 for the benefit of a confidential agent en route to Paris and London by way of Washington, and to supply funds to a member of the Mexican

6. U.S., Senate, *Journal of Executive Proceedings of the United States Senate* (Washington, D.C., 1828–1919), XII, February 25, 1862; Seward to Corwin, June 24, 1862, Instructions, Mexico, Dept. of State, NA, XVII.

7. Romero to minister of foreign affairs, January 24 and February 24, 1862, *Corres. mexicana*, II.

8. Corwin to Seward, May 5, 1862, and May 20, 1862, Dispatches, Mexico, Dept. of State, NA, XXIX.

9. Corwin to Seward, June 3, 1862, ibid.

10. Corwin to Seward, August 28, 1862, ibid.

Congress who came to the United States to purchase arms and military supplies.

When the two agents arrived in Washington during the summer of 1862, they received the disheartening verdict that no money would be available from the U.S. treasury. The secretary of state offered a small sum from private means but preferred no involvement in further contributions. In the course of a luncheon at Seward's house, U.S. policy became even more discouragingly clear to the Mexicans; all that the United States was willing to do was to inform France that her Mexican policy was a mistake. If U.S. nationals in Mexico found themselves in danger, they must return home.[11]

Forlornly, Romero informed his government that Seward would take no risks. "There is no doubt," he wrote, "that in the present circumstances the United States would sacrifice Mexico if she thought it would save her from French intervention in the U.S. Civil War which hangs over her."[12] French recognition of the Confederacy would not help Mexico a bit, and the prospect of such a calamity only made Washington more reluctant to antagonize Napoleon III.[13]

Romero underestimated Seward's alarm over French designs and especially his concern over the repeated mention of Maximilian as the future ruler of Mexico. The secretary of state had already made known his views to the European courts concerned, not as a protest or as a direct request for explanations, but in a prudent communication bearing the date March 3, 1862. This document, distributed by U.S. representatives at London, Madrid, and Paris, presented a strong case in support of republican institutions in the New World and the desire of American nations to keep them free from interference. Strong faith was expressed in their enduring value. Attempts by European powers to change them would surely fail, predicted Seward, and in failing, increase rather than decrease disorder and revolt. Monarchy in Mexico would be unstable if the throne were "assigned to any person not of Mexican nationality." Only armed support could assure an imposed monarchy. President Lincoln did not doubt the good faith of the European monarchs; nevertheless,

11. Romero to minister of foreign affairs, July 21, 1862, *Corres. mexicana*, II.
12. Romero to minister of foreign affairs, July 26, 1862, ibid.
13. Romero to Fuente, September 18, 1862, ibid.

he would be pleased to receive from them further explanations of their plans in view of the growing opinion abroad that a monarchical government under a foreign prince was about to be introduced into Mexico. Regardless of its own domestic crisis, the United States entertained "cordial good wishes for the safety, welfare, and stability" of the Mexican republic.[14]

Summing up the policy of the United States, Seward wrote: "We do not feel at liberty to reject the [French] explanations or to anticipate a violation of the assurances they convey."[15] Seward was far too astute and well-informed by the mounting evidence on his desk to feel the bland trustfulness which he assumed and decreed for his ministers in foreign capitals. In 1862, the United States could be no arsenal of democracy.

While door after door was closing against hapless Mexico, her friends in Paris made a futile effort to influence the Tuileries.[16] Napoleon III would see none of them or let himself be influenced by go-betweens, however highly placed.

These repeated rebuffs led Juárez and his colleagues to instruct intermediaries to cease working for the republican cause. In a personal note of appreciation, Juárez informed one of them prophetically that the Mexican republic was assembling troops: they were not as well equipped as French soldiers but "come what may, they will defend with honor the cause of their autonomy and Liberty." There would be the question of a king and a protectorate; "really the war will only have begun, even after the occupation of Mexico."[17] Later, Juárez elaborated his thought with clarity and courage: "I must say—and God grant that I am wrong—it appears useless and entirely sterile . . . to make the government [of France] understand the justice of our cause. We must not delude ourselves, . . . the mind of the imperial government has decided to humiliate Mexico and impose her will on it. . . . There is no help but in defense. But I can assure you . . . the imperial government will not succeed in sub-

14. Seward to Adams, March 3, 1862, Instructions, Great Britain, Dept. of State, NA, XVIII.

15. Seward to Corwin, June 24, 1862, Instructions, Mexico, ibid., XVII.

16. Efforts of these Mexican friends, one of whom (Hersaut) had been a strong adherent of the Bonaparte cult, are detailed in Montluc to Napoleon III, July 15, 1862, Dossier de Montluc, Papiers de Tuileries, AN; Hersaut to Montluc, July 25, 1862, in Montluc, Correspondance, p. 109; Montluc to Napoleon III, August 7, 1862, Dossier de Montluc, Papiers de Tuileries, AN; and Montluc to Juárez, August 15, 1862, in Montluc, Correspondance, p. 118.

17. Juárez to Montluc, August 27, 1862, in Montluc, Correspondance, p. 120.

duing the Mexicans, and its armies will not have a single day of peace."[18]

French nationals resident in Mexico likewise worked to persuade Napoleon III to change his Mexican policy. On June 2, 1862, Romero in Washington sent Seward a copy of a "Declaration of Impartial French Democrats" resident in Mexico; it declared the French had always helped liberal Mexicans and, as a result, Mexico had a high respect for France. Juárez had been elected as honestly as Napoleon III, it claimed. What the French commissioners had stated "with imperturbable coolness . . . is as false as false can be and well does M. de Saligny know this." The role of Almonte had been infamous, and charges of violence against French nationals exaggerated. "What we comprehend very well is that we are playing an ignoble part—the part of the wolf—and that we desire Mexico to take that of the lamb,"[19] was the conviction of these French nationals living in Mexico.

Probably the severest blow Mexico suffered as she readied herself for the French invasion was the refusal by the United States of permission to buy arms and munitions. By August 1862, an agent had contracted with private parties in New York to ship munitions on credit to Matamoros, where payment would be made. Clearance papers for exports were under the supervision of the treasury whose Secretary Salmon P. Chase asserted that the cargo was excessively large: 36,000 guns, 4,000 sabers, 1,000 pistols and munitions to match. Romero countered by explaining that the munitions were not types used by U.S. forces and, therefore, would not diminish U.S. Civil War supplies. Chase then insisted that both the secretary of the navy and the secretary of war concur in the export before clearance papers were given. Here the project stalled permanently; Secretary of War Stanton refused to allow any export of arms. Romero was outraged; he even contemplated a direct appeal to Lincoln. Mexico had no munitions factories, and unless she bought arms abroad she could not defend herself.[20]

Meanwhile, Juan Bustamente, a Mexican congressman, was steering a smaller consignment of munitions toward Canada en route to Matamoros. It was stopped at the Canadian border;

18. Juárez to Montluc, August 28, 1862, p. 123, ibid.

19. Romero to Seward, June 2, 1862, enclosure, Notes, Mexico, Dept. of State, NA, X.

20. Romero to minister of foreign affairs, June 17, 1862, and August 28, 1862, *Corres. mexicana*, II.

export of munitions was against regulations, officials declared. They might fall into Southern hands.[21] An embargo on all shipment of arms was proclaimed by Lincoln on November 21, 1862.

Possibly Romero could have borne this disappointment with better grace if France had not made purchases in the United States. By November 1862, the Mexican consul at New York reported large shipments of mules, wagons, and provisions for Veracruz, obviously intended for a French push into the interior of Mexico. What was contraband anyway, Romero demanded of the State Department, if not mules and wagons without which the French army could not move inland?[22] If the United States would not lend money or sell arms to Juárez for fear of breaking neutrality, how could she trade in contraband with France? Seward protested rather weakly that traffic in arms was forbidden only because the United States needed them herself. Romero charged this was "only the ostensible reason."[23] His resentment at being unable to prevent the strangulation of his country by a European invader almost exceeded his endurance. "I think," he wrote home, "the conduct of . . . [the United States] justifies me in breaking off relations and asking for my passport."[24] Eventually, President Juárez permitted him to return to join the army.

One by one, the nations whose interests lay in Mexico stood aside during the summer of 1862. The United States fought for a restored Union. Spain, too weak to lead France and too proud to follow her, took refuge in neutrality. England's position was more puzzling. Its government played a dangerous game, according to the U.S. Minister Charles Francis Adams in London, by discarding policies in force for years. It would profit Britain nothing if France succeeded in Mexico.[25] Possibly Adams never grasped the belief of Lord Russell that the French enterprise would not succeed, or that advantages could be drawn from keeping Napoleon III occupied outside Europe. Perhaps there was another factor: the United States should never be allowed to play England and France against each other.[26]

21. Romero to minister of foreign affairs, November 20, 1862, ibid.

22. De la Fuente to Romero, October 27, 1862, ibid.

23. Romero to minister of foreign affairs, November 6, 1862, ibid.

24. Romero to minister of foreign affairs, January 19, 1863, ibid., III.

25. Adams to Seward, November 1, 1863, Dispatches, Great Britain, Dept. of State, NA, LXXVII.

26. British minister to U.S., Lyons to Russell, August 3 and August 14, 1863, BFO 5/892.

As French vessels loaded with reinforcements steamed into the harbor of Veracruz, truly, there was, as Juárez had declared, "no help but in defense."

In dealing French pride a savage blow at Puebla, victorious Juaristas forced France into making the honor and glory of her flag the paramount issue. Frenchmen, who had begun to doubt the wisdom of the Mexican venture and had cast dubious glances at its cost, did not now question the necessity of demonstrating French superiority by a victory on the battlefield. Few of them knew enough about Mexico—its yellow fever areas, its high mountains and its hot country—to assess the price of that victory. Even those to whom such knowledge brought apprehension did not foresee that Mexico would start Napoleon III's downfall as Spain had been the cause of a similar fate for his uncle, Napoleon I.

To guard against an American Waterloo, France must not only reorganize and reinforce the expedition, but also must add enormous funds to the already rapidly mounting expenditures. When asked for supplementary credits, the Corps Législatif voted them as routine business. The few opponents of the emperor joining with his supporters erased the Puebla defeat. Yet the issue was not allowed to pass without argument. In the course of discussion questions were raised about the purposes of the expedition. The insinuation was made that a foreign monarch would be forced upon free Mexicans to collect tainted money by which a person of great political significance [Morny] profited.

By debates in the Corps Législatif the Mexican question was aired before the nation since, by a decree of the previous November 24, 1861, the press was given the right to publicize parliamentary proceedings. Heretofore uninformed and indifferent to the Mexican problem, the French public now began pricking up its ears. Village philosophers talked knowingly of Maximilian and of Jecker's financial deals, and a subtle distrust of Napoleon III's motives began to permeate the nation.

This crisis the French emperor attempted to meet by dispatching his friend, General Elie Frédéric Forey, to succeed where Vice Admiral Jurien, General Lorencez, and Minister Saligny had failed. No longer was there to be any division of authority. Forey who had fought the Russians in the Crimean War and the Austrians in Italy, arrived in Mexico September 25, 1862, with a large body of reinforcements.

In addition to whatever verbal advice may have been given Forey, his basic instructions were incorporated in the famous secret letter of July 3, 1862, signed by the emperor. In January 1863, an expunged and edited version of the Forey letter was published in the *Documents diplomatiques* (Yellow Book) for public circulation. This revised document has since been reproduced in numerous writings. In the archives of the Quai d'Orsay is the original with revisions in the same handwriting as letters signed by Napoleon III and marked "corrected for the Yellow Book."[27]

The original and the revision reveal instructive differences. The original letter opened with military matters. The emperor then spoke about Saligny of whose personal traits he knew nothing but whose dispatches had been full of sense and dignity. "I do not doubt that if his advice had been followed, our flag would now float over Mexico City. They say that he has misled the government on the true state of affairs in Mexico; on the contrary, I like to recognize that he has always told the truth."

General Forey's procedure upon arriving in Mexico was specifically spelled out. Once more Mexicans were to be presented with a proclamation setting forth the aims of the Grand Design in noble phrases. All Mexicans who associated themselves with the French were to be welcomed, and Mexican auxiliary forces were to be paid, clothed, and fed; no party cause was to be espoused. Forey must insist that everything be provisional until the Mexican people should have spoken. Religion was to be protected but the sale of church lands sustained.

Upon reaching Mexico City, he was to call an assembly of all those who had embraced the French cause to decide the form of government. The purpose of the expedition was not to force a government on the Mexicans, emphasized the emperor, but to make sure of political stability. If Mexicans desired monarchy, France would support it and the general might suggest the Archduke Maximilian of Austria as France's candidate.

"As for the prince who may mount the Mexican throne," continued Napoleon III, in the original Forey letter, "he will always be forced to act in the interests of France, not only by gratitude but especially because those of his new country will be in accordance with ours and he will not be able to sustain himself without our influence."

About debts, claims, and damages to French nationals, Napo-

27. Napoleon III to Forey, July 3, 1862, M et D, Mexique, X.

leon III's letter to Forey was silent. When the almost hysterical devotion to French "griefs," so much a part of earlier policies, is recalled, this omission is revealing. The emperor had regarded indemnities as secondary, and now that they were no longer needed to mislead England and France, they were not even mentioned.

Some months later, when the emperor's letter to General Forey was prepared for publication, modifications in wording as well as phrases omitted and retained were conspicuous. Naturally enough, the first paragraphs dealing with military matters and the job of getting along with Saligny were omitted. Deleted also was all reference to Maximilian and the French influence over "the prince who may mount the Mexican throne." The emperor's almost brutal candor to his general was no proper reading for the Austrian. It would never have done to inform the archduke so rudely of the manner in which Napoleon III viewed their prospective relationship, a view very similar to that Maximilian had guessed in his letter of April 8 to Metternich. Other reasons for being cautious about monarchy and Maximilian had developed by the time the letter was to be published. Conditions in Mexico by the end of 1862 were far too uncertain for France to expose her hand. In July of that year the emperor was still planning to make Maximilian an emperor, despite rumors about the court and among the ministers to the contrary. He had told Metternich to urge the archduke to "trust" him.[28]

There was one design Napoleon III took no pains to conceal while editing the Forey letter for publication. He did not hesitate to state openly that the object of his Mexican expedition was the containment of the United States. He had not always expressed himself so frankly nor was such candor to be continued. For years European monarchs had talked among themselves about the necessity of stopping the expansion of the United States but invariably they had been prudent in their public utterances. By 1865, the emperor would claim innocence of anti-Americanism in his Mexican venture. Only for a brief period did he remove the mask that had hidden his hostility toward the United States. This was in his letter of July 3, 1862, to Forey:

There will not be lacking people who will ask why we are going to spend men and money in this enterprise.

28. Egon Caesar Corti, *Maximilian and Charlotte in Mexico*, trans. Catherine Alison Phillips, 2 vols. (New York, 1928), I, 183.

In the actual state of the civilization of the world, the prosperity of America is not indifferent to Europe, for it nourishes our industry and gives life to our commerce. We are interested in seeing the United States powerful and prosperous, but we have no interest in seeing that republic acquire the whole of the Gulf of Mexico, dominate from this vantage-point the Antilles and South America, and become the sole dispenser of the products of the New World. Mistress of Mexico, and consequently, of Central America and of the passage between the two seas, there would be henceforth no other power in America than the United States. If, on the contrary, Mexico conquers its independence and maintains the integrity of its territory, if a stable government is constituted there by the arms of France, we shall have opposed an insuperable barrier to the encroachments of the United States, we shall have maintained the independence of our colonies in the Antilles, and of those of ungrateful Spain, and this influence will radiate northward as well as southward, will create immense markets for our commerce, and will procure the materials indispensable to our industry.

Even here, frankness paid tribute to other ends. Napoleon III retained, in the edited draft, "no desire" that the United States spread herself over Central and South America whence she "would be the sole dispenser" of the New World commerce. Nevertheless, he dropped all reference to the "insuperable barrier," which his proposed new government in Mexico would build "against the encroachments of the United States," in favor of a bit of flattery for the Latins. "We shall," read the new version, "have given back to the Latin race on the other side of the ocean its force and its prestige."[29] In former pronouncements the emperor had not inclined his thoughts to the Latin race which he proposed to advance through the medium of an Austrian prince. Two contemporaries of Napoleon III held opposite views on the significance of his reference to the Latin race. Ollivier, statesman and historian, believed it was an afterthought borrowed from the parlance of the Mexican émigrés. Chevalier, economist and author, asserted that one of the main motives of French policy was to nurture and advance the Spanish branch of Latin civilization in the New World.[30]

General Henry M. Sanford, U.S. minister to Belgium and eyes

29. Napoleon III to Forey, July 3, 1862, M et D, Mexique, X; succeeding quotations are from the same source.

30. Emile Ollivier, *L'Empire libéral: Etudes, récits, souvenirs,* 17 vols. (Paris, 1895–1915), V, 258.

and ears of Seward in western Europe, heard versions of the same theme; Napoleon III dreamed of fulfilling his uncle's ambitions of French preeminence in the Western Hemisphere; the Civil War in the United States was really a struggle between Franco-Latin and Anglo-Saxon races although only about 1 percent of the Confederates had French lineage.[31] When Sanford sent Seward the Yellow Book version of the Forey letter, he drew attention to the phrases about the "Latin Race." This was the kind of talk, he remarked, "which I have heard *ad nauseum* in Parisian Salons."[32]

To Seward the contents of the Forey letter could not have been a surprise in spite of his insistence as late as November 1862 that the French designs were not directed against the United States. The Confederates, hopeful of tangible friendship with France, were somewhat abashed to learn of her antipathy to Anglo-Saxon expansion. The *Richmond Inquirer* wondered whether Napoleon III fathered the letter or whether it was more Yankee propaganda.[33] Whatever interpretation North or South wished to believe, the frank threat against the United States lay exposed. According to the historian Dexter Perkins, "A franker expression of hostility than this could hardly be looked for. The irritation at American jingoism, the suspicion of American purposes based upon Buchanan's messages and the McLane-Ocampo Treaty, these may help to explain such a view as that expressed above, but they cannot alter its fundamental character, or shake in any manner the clearly established thesis that one of the principal objects of the Mexican intervention was to checkmate the United States."[34]

While Forey was receiving instructions, Thouvenel informed Saligny that he was now riding in the back seat, so to speak, whence, it was hoped, he would not attempt too much driving. Saligny took the demotion with grace. Thouvenel was adroit but he penned three notes clarifying his instructions to Saligny. Saligny's role would be effaced during military operations but his knowledge of Mexico was still valuable. Thouvenel had no doubt that Saligny's relations with Forey would be cordial; in

31. Sanford to Seward, August 13, 1862, and September 2, 1862, private, Henry Shelton Sanford Papers, Sanford Memorial Library, Sanford, Florida, reel 95, box 140, folder 10.

32. Sanford to Seward, January 20, 1863, private, ibid., folder 11.

33. *Richmond Inquirer*, February 6, 1863.

34. Dexter Perkins, *A History of the Monroe Doctrine* (Boston, 1955), p. 118.

fact—and here was a bit of a thrust—his cooperation had already been pledged to the new commander. Saligny's post would be comparable to "chief of mission." All dispatches were to pass through Forey's hands and all action was to be initiated by him. A second thought seems to have prompted Thouvenel to provide Saligny with something to do. He was instructed to work on a treaty to be eventually negotiated with Mexico. Should the Juárez republic survive, the question of claims must still be settled. A new government would not eliminate such negotiation but France might be more generous. Saligny must study both possibilities.[35]

After he had learned of Forey's appointment, Saligny wrote Thouvenel he had never wanted to influence military affairs; he had only "ventured some advice."[36] He accepted the chief of mission post although he admitted it was a minor role. This amiability did Saligny no harm at court. In November 1862, Radepont was informed that Napoleon III had conferred on Saligny the Cross of the Grand Officer of the Legion of Honor, to be presented by Forey.[37]

Thouvenel had reminded Saligny frequently that the emperor did not wish to support one party alone. Gutiérrez de Estrada and the Bishop of Puebla, arch reactionaries and ultra clericals, found themselves more and more out of favor at the Tuileries. The Spanish-born, strongly proclerical Empress Eugénie thought Gutiérrez de Estrada's views resembled the fanaticism of Philip II of Spain.[38] An outright statement of this pious deception had been sent to Lorencez by the emperor on June 15, 1862, as follows: "It is contrary to my interest, my principles, or my origin to impose any kind of government whatsoever on the Mexican people."[39]

In these statements and sentiments lay one of the tragic inconsistencies of Napoleon III's Grand Design. It ran through the entire period of occupation. Napoleon III either did not grasp it or would not resolve it. What the emperor apparently wanted to bring about in Mexico, and in the other Spanish areas of

35. Thouvenel to Saligny, July 8, 1862; July 23, 1862, nos. 12 and 13, CP, Mexique, LIX.
36. Saligny to Thouvenel, August 26, 1862, ibid.
37. Saligny to Thouvenel, September 17, 1862, ibid.
38. Daniel Dawson, *The Mexican Adventure* (London, 1935), p. 230.
39. Napoleon III to Lorencez, June 15, 1862, CP, Mexique, LIX.

America which, in his dreams, he saw gravitating within the French orbit, was the same goal sought by Juárez and the Liberals. Yet France initiated her scheme of regeneration for Mexico by attempting the overthrow of the republican government and alienating the Liberal group. Eugénie was indisputably pro-clerical; yet there is no convincing evidence that Napoleon III intended to restore privileges to landowners and clergy. Only the Conservative defenders of these two factions urged him to intervene and supported his troops in their advance on Mexico City. His recognized objective, monarchy, was achieved by denying the principles for which he had always stood.

9

Creating an Empire in America
1862–1863

————◆————

Retreating from the May 5, 1862, defeat at Puebla, the French army, dejected, resumed camp at Orizaba. Enthusiasm for the task of reattacking Puebla and marching to the Mexican capital was noticeably diminished. The Marquis de Radepont reported the intrigues, desertions, false moves, mistakes, and all the other ills which had plagued the expedition. His letters contained so many "cruel truths" that his correspondents hesitated to show them to the emperor.[1] To French deserters Juárez offered aid until they could provide for themselves.[2]

Apprehensively Mexico City awaited the approach of the French. Members of Congress quarreled among themselves and continued amateurish experiments with government.

General Forey's early proclamations promising acceptance of the will of the Mexican people led them to hope for negotiations. Once the prestige of French arms had been restored by seizing the capital, Mexicans hoped for a settlement of claims, leaving Juárez as president. The U.S. minister Corwin also belonged to this school of thought.

Of the handful of diplomats still at Mexico City the most popular was the recently arrived thirty-two-year-old Manuel Nicolás

1. Radepont to General Rolin, May 2, 1863, Marquis de Radepont Papers, Houghton Library, Harvard University, Cambridge, Mass.
2. Corwin to Seward, September 28, 1862, Dispatches, Mexico, Dept. of State, NA, XXIX.

Corpancho of Peru. His mission was to urge Mexico to join a movement already endorsed by Chile and Ecuador, to form an American Union. Mexican Liberals welcomed this friendly gesture from a sister republic. A subscription banquet was given April 21, 1862, in Corpancho's honor at the Teatro Nacional at which Juárez presided. More than two hundred men of prominence in politics, journalism, and letters attended. Some two months later Mexico signed the Corpancho Treaty to defend and preserve New World independence.[3]

The Peruvian's efforts, although representing friendship rather than military and financial assistance, raised the morale of the beleaguered republic. His articles in Mexican newspapers received enthusiastic praise. He was wined, dined, and, for the moment, strongly identified with the Juarista cause.

No one in France, or for that matter at Forey's headquarters, could understand the delay of many months at Orizaba in view of the creative energy which characterized Forey's earlier career. Historians, likewise seeking an explanation for this delay, have missed the main point by stressing the unfamiliar and forbidding terrain and the difficulties of transportation and supply. Probably the most potent influence on Forey was the awareness, ever before him, that his predecessors had failed. He well knew Napoleon III would not tolerate a second tragedy at Puebla. Consequently, he refused to begin his campaign until all preparations were such as to assure victory.

When in March 1863, the second siege of Puebla was finally begun by more than 30,000 French veterans, its defense by General Gonzales Ortega surpassed all expectations. Then Mexican hope came alive for a repetition of the Cinco de Mayo triumph at Puebla the year before. At the end of two months, however, the Juaristas were forced to surrender Puebla. The flowers and "Te Deums" promised by Saligny were still not noticeable, but something more important was, namely, the open road to the capital. The taking of Puebla had involved preparations of more than a year by a vice admiral and two generals. As there was little possibility of defending Mexico City, no more military opposition impeded the invasion of Mexico by the French.

In the capital, with much oratory, Congress at its last session on May 31, 1863, granted President Juárez extraordinary powers

3. For the mission of Corpancho see Emilia Romero, *Corpancho: Un amigo de México* (Mexico City, 1949).

TEMPORARY LOCATIONS OF
JUÁREZ GOVERNMENT: 1863-1867

for the duration of the French occupation. That evening the president of the republic accompanied by advisers, ministers, and congressmen, left the city he was not to see again for four years and set up his government at San Luis Potosí. The Diplomatic Corps, consisting only of representatives of Peru, Ecuador, Venezuela, and the United States, was invited to accompany, under safe escort, the now itinerant legitimate government of Mexico. The four envoys met at the U.S. Legation on June 1, where, after a short discussion, they decided to decline the Juárez invitation. Communication from Mexico City with their respective countries was safer and less subject to delays; the early days of French occupation might be dangerous for their nationals.[4]

On June 7, 1863, General Achille François Bazaine with an advance guard entered Mexico City. The main body of the army arrived three days later. General Forey, with Almonte at his right and Saligny at his left, rode at the head of the French columns; they dismounted at the cathedral and, led by the clergy, entered for a "Te Deum." If newspaper accounts are to be believed, about 100,000 Mexicans watched the invaders with emotions of pleasure or prudence or mere curiosity.

The capital had surrendered to Forey, but Forey had surrendered to Saligny. Radepont wrote that Forey was "letting himself be entirely guided" by Saligny who "used all his talents for the organization of a provisional government."[5]

Churchmen, assuming that they occupied a favored position again, took the opportunity to restore the outlawed religious processions under the guise of celebrating deliverance by the French. By this act Napoleon's Grand Design again became bound to the Conservatives as, inevitably, it had to be, for they were the only group which supported it. Forey seemed not to have realized the evolution of his policy since the preceding September. "I am organizing with Saligny and Almonte a provisional government," he reported to Paris, June 14, 1863, "which according to the instructions of the Emperor, must be composed of moderate men of all parties."[6] The paradox of using Saligny, Almonte, and company to attract "moderate men of all parties" failed to register in Forey's mind or, if it did, he continued to try to make extremes meet, with the inevitable lack of success. His interviews with Father Francisco Xavier Miranda were examples.

Miranda, powerful leader of the arch conservatives, had left Mexico in 1862 until events looked more auspicious. On his return he was taken to see Forey by Radepont. The sparks began to fly when Forey told him that as an ultraconservative he must state his principles so that his presence would not conflict with the policies of the emperor. Miranda asked what were the prin-

---

4. Corwin to Seward, June 26, 1863, Dispatches, Mexico, Dept. of State, NA, XXX.
5. Charles Blanchot, *Mémoires: L'Intervention française au mexique*, 3 vols. (Paris, 1911), II, 4.
6. Radepont to General Rolin, June 24, 1863, Radepont Papers.

ciples of ultraconservatism that he was presumed to represent.
If his presence were an obstacle, it was because he stood for monarchy and was against "social radicalism." Of course he might be
an obstacle, because usurpers of church lands would have no rest
while Miranda had influence; Forey had accepted the sale of
church properties on instructions from Napoleon III. Forey required Miranda to state, "I am not a monarchist and the French
Intervention does not come seeking monarchy." A manifesto was
drawn up that Miranda refused to sign, threatening to leave
Mexico. Here Saligny took over; the manifesto, he soothed, was
merely for the consumption of European liberals. Father Miranda pondered: would he save his pride or sacrifice it in order
to raise a cry of alarm that would stop the prospects of the do-
gooders? He decided on the latter course. An edited manifesto
was prepared for Europe but attracted little notice in Mexico.
This ordeal surmounted, Miranda retired, devoting his time to
lamenting the evils he saw. Forey had turned Almonte into an
errand boy; speculators in church lands were running wild and
General Leonardo Márquez, who had stolen $600,000 from the
British silver train, and his followers plundered for the neces-
sities of life when Forey was not looking.[7]

Forey and Saligny proceeded pell-mell with the political reorganization. Saligny assumed the lead on the false assumption
that, so far, developments had proved his theories to be correct.
He asserted that it was impossible to call a general congress on
the European pattern; representatives of distant cities could not
be reached, and the Indians never shared in the government. The
capital, he claimed, adequately represented all Mexico.[8] According to this assumption, the 200,000 inhabitants of Mexico City
spoke for 8,000,000 citizens of the country; Liberal strongholds
elsewhere were ignored.

Following Saligny's plan, Forey nominated on June 16, 1863,
a committee of thirty-five Notables to initiate the provisional
government. This committee appointed a triumvirate of execu-
tives consisting of Almonte, General Mariano Salas, and the
archbishop-elect of Mexico, Pelazio Antonio Labastida, who was

7. Miranda to Rafael Rafael, June 12, 1863, G and P, vol. XIII, *Correspondencia secreta* . . . , pt. 3.
8. Saligny to Forey, June 16, 1863, copy, enclosed in Romero to Seward, February 20, 1864, Notes, Mexico, Dept. of State, NA, XVII.

still in Europe. The committee of 35 later enlarged its membership to 250 and then declared itself a constituent assembly. At a meeting held July 10, all but two of the 250 voted for the establishment of a monarchy. The crown was offered to Maximilian or, in the case of his refusal, to any prince selected by Napoleon III. The assembly also designated Almonte, General Salas, and Archbishop-elect Labastida as the Regency to rule Mexico until the sovereign arrived.

Events were at last transpiring as they had so long been planned, rejoiced Radepont. He was gratified that the regeneration he had been advocating for seven years was finally about to begin.[9] Forey, Saligny, and Almonte were likewise satisfied. Unfortunately for them Napoleon III was not.

The emperor's indignation was directed against a modus operandi, reversing the instructions he had repeated over and over in letters to the commander. Napoleon III, in his letter of July 3, 1862, to Forey, had named Maximilian as a likely candidate for the Mexican throne, but in his subsequent instructions the emperor had not mentioned the archduke. The emperor had written Forey that men and not opinions must govern his estimate of adherents. Forey had been told to accept the support of "all honorable men" without binding the expedition to any one group or making commitments prior to establishing the provisional government.[10] In other words, cautioned the emperor, "You must be master in Mexico without seeming to be."[11]

Napoleon III's instructions had been to set up at once a provisional government firmly controlled by France. General Forey had been urged to act quickly to restore French prestige which had been dimmed by the delay in his march from Orizaba. Key towns were to be occupied, order was to be restored to the customs; in short, a foretaste was to be given of what Mexico could become under French guidance. When the people had been sufficiently impressed, a "vote," preferably on the basis of general suffrage, could be taken on the nature of a permanent government.[12] "Our object, you know, is not to impose a government

9. Radepont to General Rolin, July 11, 1863, Radepont Papers.
10. Napoleon III to Forey, November 30, 1862, G and P, vol. XIV, *La intervención francesa en México*, pt. 2.
11. Napoleon III to Forey, February 14, 1863, ibid.
12. Napoleon III to Forey, April 14, 1863, ibid.

on the Mexicans against their will or make our success contribute
to the triumph of any party whatsoever."[13]

The overthrow of the republican government, which the emperor euphemistically called "regeneration," initiated the Grand
Design for the Americas. The establishment of monarchies in
the Western Hemisphere was only a means to that end and Maximilian was one of the agents for monarchy. Added insight into
the emperor's thinking is provided by the fantastic proposal in
which he reorganized the Union, Confederacy, and Mexico into
geographic divisions forming a confederation similar to that of
the German states.

In the spring of 1863 the general European situation and
French domestic problems forced themselves on the emperor's
attention. In the judgment of General Sanford, Lincoln's confidential agent, there was "not a state [in Europe] that has not
cause for serious preoccupation close at home," and amid the international uneasiness there was always that "perpetual night-
mare, the Emperor." Even Great Britain with whom Napoleon
III was friendly, found the amiability of the nephew almost as
trying as the hostility of the uncle. Domestic affairs in France
developed their own problems. An 1863 election of members of
the Corps Législatif, Sanford observed, increased the opposition
to about twenty-five with an additional twenty-five members who
were not genuine imperialists. Forey's taking of Puebla caused
rejoicing throughout France, spurring the hope in many that the
"regeneration" of Mexico was over. This hope soon dimmed,
especially when Forey asked for more reinforcements. "All in
all," wrote Sanford, "how the Emperor must wish just now that
he had that incubus of Mexico off his shoulders."[14]

The pattern of events in Mexico soon became set beyond the
power of change. Because he was under the tutelage of Saligny,
Radepont, and the Mexican Conservatives, Forey may not have
sensed any change in policy by the Quai d'Orsay from 1862 to
1863. The 1863 instructions did not state that monarchy had
been discarded; they merely indicated a readiness on the part of
Napoleon III to consider alternatives.

The emperor had not foreseen that Forey, Saligny, and Al-

13. Napoleon III to Forey, June 13, 1863, ibid.
14. Sanford to Seward, May 19, June 5, August 13, 1863, private, Henry Shelton Sanford Papers, Sanford Memorial Library, Sanford, Fla., reel 95, box 14a,
folder 11.

monte would run a political marathon from June 10 to July 10, 1863. On the contrary, prior to their arrival in Mexico City, Napoleon III had decided that neither Forey nor Saligny would guide Mexican steps to the "stability and order" of which he talked so constantly. Marked first for removal was Saligny. A few days after Paris learned of Forey's capture of Puebla, Thouvenel's successor as foreign minister, Drouyn de Lhuys, invited Saligny back to France with the comment, "The Emperor considers as accomplished the aid you were to render General Forey." Assuming the French were about to enter Mexico City, the foreign minister explained: "To appreciate and complete the result of these events, His Majesty wishes to receive from your own lips information which could contribute to clarifying his decisions."[15] Saligny was to leave as soon as possible, but a confidential letter to Forey of the same date permitted the departure to be postponed if Forey thought it necessary.[16]

Shortly after Paris learned that Mexico City was in the hands of the French, Forey was removed from his command and ordered home to receive a *maréchal's* baton. It was explained that this high distinction would be too great for a commander in Mexico. If Saligny had not left, the two could travel together. General Bazaine, whose energy and ingenuity had already attracted the emperor's notice, became the fourth commander of the expedition. He was made responsible for both military and diplomatic relations until Marquis Charles François Frédéric de Montholon, successor to Saligny, could arrive and assume the post of minister accredited "to the new government which will be constituted in Mexico."[17]

In a confidential dispatch to Bazaine outlining procedures, the emperor wanted Mexicans conciliated and encouraged to realize what "generous thought of regeneration" had inspired the French. Bazaine was informed he must guard against allowing Mexicans to think France would be influenced by any one of the factions dividing the country. First, he must rally around himself men who had the sympathy of the people and, through them, form a provisional government. The people must be won to France through complete freedom of action as well as the benefits they could see emerging from the new security. Bazaine, the

15. Drouyn de Lhuys to Saligny, June 15, 1863, CP, Mexique, LX.
16. Drouyn de Lhuys to Forey, June 25, 1863, ibid.
17. Drouyn de Lhuys to Bazaine, July 15, 1863, ibid.

instructions went on, was to search for new resources with which to pay the expenses of the army and to settle the claims. This would require a study of unexploited riches. The establishment of order must precede action on the nature of a new government.

Bazaine was cautioned not to "engage in any enterprises which may take you away from your base of operations and necessitate the sending of more troops" to Mexico. Juárez, it was assumed, would retire into inaccessible regions and collect partisans around him, but "it will not be wise to undertake their pursuit." After a provisional government was organized, Bazaine was to induce occupants of those areas not held by Juaristas to adhere to the new regime.[18]

Napoleon III was understandably dismayed when, at the end of July 1863, reports came that the Regency was already in operation, that Maximilian had been called to the throne, and that a delegation en route to Miramar Palace would stop in Paris to thank the emperor for his services. Once more, as in the winter of 1862, distance and slow communication presenting the emperor with a fait accompli forced him to meet a situation he had not expected to arise. Just as he had had to accept a rupture of the allied expedition, he now tried to make the most of the newly organized government in Mexico and tie it as closely as possible to his Grand Design. He urged Maximilian to leave Europe as soon as preparations could be made: "the soldiers of France are at their posts; he should go to his" was the advice of the French Foreign Office.[19] Napoleon III sought not only to shorten the period of Regency but also to broaden the base of the new throne. It is not clear whether he thought a government patched together by 250 Conservatives and clericals would not contribute to his dream of regeneration, or that he feared objections to the methods of electing the archduke; possibly it was a combination of both.

At any rate, before Napoleon III heard from Miramar, his foreign minister further instructed Bazaine. His Majesty welcomed the action of the Notables, wrote Drouyn de Lhuys with more tact than truth, but it must be followed by an endorsement of the people.[20] The day following the forwarding of this dis-

18. Drouyn de Lhuys to Bazaine, Confidential, ibid.

19. Gutiérrez de Estrada to Baron de Pont, July 30, 1863, in Daniel Dawson, *The Mexican Adventure* (London, 1935), p. 291.

20. Drouyn de Lhuys to Bazaine, August 14, 1863, CP, Mexique, LX.

patch, August 16, 1863, Maximilian's secretary sent a letter to José Manuel Hidalgo, Mexican exile in Paris, written, obviously, for the perusal of Napoleon III. The archduke had the impression that Almonte had acted precipitately and without full consideration of the will of the Mexican people. It was not possible to conclude, without more evidence, that Mexicans really wanted a monarchy.[21]

Simultaneously, Drouyn de Lhuys sent Bazaine additional instructions, this time quite specific. Bazaine was informed that "the Emperor's highest expression of policy" was his manifesto of a Grand Design for America defined in his letter to Forey of July 3, 1862, and "it is always to this memorable document that we must return." France did not seek colonies, colonial establishments, or political and commercial advantages to the exclusion of other nations, Bazaine was informed. The meeting of the Mexican Notables was a favorable symptom, but France accepted it "only as a first indication of the will of the country; the assembly recommends to its citizens the adoption of the institution of monarchy and designates a Prince for their votes." The provisional government must now be submitted to the voice of the people.[22] The foreign minister shrewdly refrained from indicating how this "vote" would be taken in a large mass of illiterates, but the emperor insisted that Bazaine seek a method that blended with Mexican customs.

From the theme of suffrage, Drouyn de Lhuys passed on to other problems which had irritated his sovereign. France could not undertake tutelage over the Mexicans and regretted acts of Forey, such as confiscation of property; this smacked of permanent government. Such action should be temporary only.

By the end of August 1863, a dispatch from Saligny arrived in Paris saying that he declined the trip home because Forey had indicated his services were still needed in Mexico. But the day of Saligny's ascendancy had passed. He was ordered home. Forey was also reminded that Paris awaited his arrival. Each resented the recall.

It was September 30, 1863, before Forey turned over his command to Bazaine. Saligny delayed even longer, hoping against hope that he would be restored to office, or be permitted to re-

21. Baron de Pont to Hidalgo, August 15, 1863, quoted in Dawson, *Mexican Adventure*, p. 291.
22. Drouyn de Lhuys to Bazaine, August 17, 1863, CP, Mexique, LX.

main in Mexico to practice law as a private citizen. He was about to marry into a prominent Mexican family; this and other considerations of fortune tied him to Mexico. Indeed, gossip around the Tuileries already assigned him personal gain from his ministerial post. It was ruinous to leave just as Mexico was supposed to flower economically under French protection. Saligny had been the principal obstacle to the fusion of political parties, in Bazaine's judgment. "The Mexican government, if there is a Mexican government, offers resistance to the instructions of His Majesty because it is helped by Saligny who declares, everywhere, 'in Paris they know neither the men nor the situation in this country and they will end by doing what I wish.' "[23] The Foreign Office wrote twice more to Saligny, ordering him to leave; finally, Bazaine was instructed to force him out, and set January 2, 1864, as the date for his departure.[24] Saligny's friends were equally reluctant to see him go. Almonte considered it a disaster and Radepont poured out his disapproval. The recall of a man, who, in spite of everything, had carried out the policy of the emperor was almost a "public calamity."[25] Later, when hope of Saligny's restoration to favor had vanished, Radepont wrote a friend at court. The Mexican expedition was not a European war, he explained, at the end of which diplomats of combatants were changed. Saligny's recall was regarded as a disavowal of his policies; it had done much harm to the Conservatives and encouraged the Liberals. And then Radepont began to excuse himself for endorsing Saligny. The fact was, he stated, he had frequently supported what he did not approve because the attacks on Saligny had been so absurd.[26]

Radepont was informed that the recall of Saligny was the result of pressure; the army hated him.[27] The explanation was that there was severe criticism of his connection with the Jecker enterprises and of his too close identification with Conservatives. That Napoleon III must have known for a long time of Saligny's espousal of the Conservative cause leads to some speculation as to why he was recalled at this particular time. Was Saligny favored earlier because Napoleon III accepted his opinions in spite

23. Bazaine to Randon, September 27, 1863, AMG, 1862–64.
24. Bazaine to Randon, December 4, 1863, ibid.
25. Radepont to Clermont-Tonnerre, September 11, 1863, Radepont Papers.
26. Radepont to Clermont-Tonnerre, September 25, 1863, ibid.
27. Clermont-Tonnerre to Radepont, November 12, 1863, ibid.

of counterevidence, or because of his single-minded determination to deposit the French army in Mexico City? It took no time at all for the emperor to dispose of Saligny after he knew his army would take the Mexican capital. He then became sensitive to the complaints of soldiers and court gossip although for over a year both had been unheeded.

When the new minister, the Marquis de Montholon, arrived in Veracruz in January of 1864, he met Saligny and his bride just down from the capital. He saw no evidence of wealth, he reported, and could not believe his predecessor had made money from his position.[28] The correctness of Montholon's judgment was borne out by Saligny's situation in the ensuing years. Whatever he might have hoped to gain from Mexican regeneration was apparently never received for the excellent reason that Mexico did not regenerate. Two years later, Saligny's application for a pension was denied.[29]

Forey and Saligny probably never grasped the extent of their ruler's "deviationism" or understood the decisive changes he contemplated making. No matter how impetuously Forey, Saligny, Almonte, and the Mexican Notables had acted, the emperor could not deny his own creation. But in the readjustment he made, there was frank rejection of Conservative-clericalism. France did not intend to restore the old order. Apologists for the Grand Design pointed out that, in the early days, it took a wrong turn and never recovered its direction; they argued that Forey was to blame for the blunder, that he should have dissolved the Regency, defied Conservatives and clericals, and initiated a fresh start.[30]

28. Montholon to Drouyn de Lhuys, January 1, 1864, CP, Mexique, LXI.
29. Saligny to Napoleon III, July 8, 1867, Dossier of Saligny, Papiers de Tuileries, Mexique, AN.
30. Blanchot, *Mémoires*, II, 2 ff.

10

Candidate for the Mexican Throne
1861–1864

The people of Mexico have been ruled by heads of state ranking from indigenous chieftains to European emperors. Rulers of the most advanced early civilization, the Mayan, were hereditary. The Aztec emperor, Montezuma II, was dethroned by Hernando Cortez and his European barbarians in 1519 when they despoiled prehistoric Tenochtitlán, which later became Mexico City. During the next three centuries the kings of Spain ruled Mexico through viceroys. When, in 1821, Mexicans under General Agustín de Iturbide gained independence from Spain, their liberator proclaimed himself emperor. This empire lasted less than two years. From 1823 until the Juárez regime, Mexico, except for brief periods, was under the ruinous caudillo system of government, misnamed a republic. The empire imposed by France extended from 1864 to 1867.

In 1861 Archduke Ferdinand Maximilian of Austria was twenty-nine and jobless when he learned of the occupational opening for a monarch in Mexico. In 1857 he had married the seventeen-year-old Princess Charlotte, daughter of King Leopold of Belgium, uncle of Queen Victoria of England. Maximilian found in Charlotte a mentor as well as a wife. Her intellect was superior to that of her husband and she was more ambitious. Childless, she centered her attention entirely on the fortunes of her husband.

Shortly after his marriage Maximilian received his first public appointment, governor general of the Austrian possession of Lombardy-Venetia, where his liberalism was frowned upon by conservative Austria and rejected by Italians who would be satisfied with nothing short of national independence. When the alliance between Napoleon III and the King of Sardinia made Austria's hold over northeastern Italy tenuous, Maximilian was replaced by a more seasoned official.

Frustrated by his first venture in politics and dubious about another opportunity, Maximilian settled at Miramar, an elaborate palace that he built on a promontory near Trieste overlooking the Adriatic. Here he indulged his taste for beauty in architecture and landscaping and learned that both were exceedingly expensive. An observer from the British Embassy in Vienna wrote that the archduke was "a continual embarrassment" to the Austrian emperor and his government. "He is very extravagant and speculative, but he certainly has more cleverness than any of the others and might do well if means were found of keeping him under control."[1]

Time has dealt gently with Maximilian by enveloping his three-year career in the New World with a romantic glow his contemporaries would not have considered justifiable. More liberally educated than most princes, he tasted and found intellectually delectable languages, literature, the arts, and the natural sciences just then coming into vogue. Gentle, kind, and tenderhearted by nature, he was a liberal by persuasion, all of which led him to plan great deeds for human advancement. Pride in the Hapsburgs and a sense of obligation to the imperial family were pronounced; they eventually led him into needless executions. His judgment was frequently clouded by an incredible capacity for self-deception. Slow to reach decisions, he occasionally displayed that stubbornness sometimes associated with weakness. When reality confused Maximilian, he developed illnesses modern medicine would probably diagnose as psychosomatic. His extravagance made debt an inseparable companion. Because of mediocre judgment he was apt in time of crisis to be deceived and subject to undue influence. These liabilities were partially offset by charm and good intentions.

Emile Ollivier, one of the five famous opponents of Napoleon III in the Corps Législatif, believed that uppermost in the French

---

1. Bloomfield to Russell, January 30, 1862, private, Bloomfield Papers, BFO.

emperor's mind was the desire to cultivate Maximilian's brother, the Emperor Franz Joseph, sufficiently to induce him to relinquish Venetia.[2] Franz Joseph may have sensed this possibility; it may have accounted for Austria's reiteration that she had no interests in Mexico.

Early in November 1861, following the signing of the Tripartite Treaty in London by England, France, and Spain, Napoleon III was full of confidence over his determination to place Maximilian on the throne of Mexico, according to Prince Metternich, Austrian ambassador to Paris. The French emperor outlined to Metternich the steps by which the Austrian archduke would be called to Mexico and even indicated how the new monarch would lay the foundation for his state. A council of notable Mexicans would establish the throne, he indicated, since it would not be fitting for a Hapsburg to submit to general suffrage.[3] Strange words, these, from a sovereign who owed his own power to popular vote. (Here Napoleon III was inconsistent both in describing his own rise to power through popular vote and with his previous and subsequent advocacy of the democratic process.)

In response to such Bonaparte enthusiasm, the Austrian emperor and the Archduke Maximilian agreed to receive Gutiérrez de Estrada, whose long-time advocacy of a monarchy in Mexico had forced him to live in Europe as an exile. Through Metternich, Franz Joseph suggested that prominent ecclesiastics and Conservative exiles be returned to Mexico to do their bit. To Metternich's surprise Napoleon concurred in these views which were by no means consistent with his own record of liberalism. Finally, Maximilian wrote Napoleon III directly, expressing for the first time his appreciation of the honor extended and mentioning conditions of acceptance he believed must be met.

Almonte, the Mexican exile who had represented the Conservative government in France and England, was introduced by the French ambassador in Vienna. It was explained that Almonte might go to Mexico as Maximilian's advance agent to advertise, as it were, to his prospective subjects the qualities of the prospective emperor.

As a preliminary Almonte and the arch-reactionary bishop of

2. Emile Ollivier, *L'Empire libéral: Etudes, récits, souvenirs,* 17 vols. (Paris, 1895–1915), V, 260.

3. Metternich to Rechberg, November 16, 1861, France, Auessern, IX.

Puebla Labastida visited Maximilian's Miramar palace simultaneously. Conversations between Maximilian and the bishop were amiable but inconclusive. On the other hand Almonte and Maximilian succeeded in drawing up a protocol each signed January 22, 1862.[4] This surprising procedure occurred less than one month after troops of the tripartite empires landed in Veracruz. An amazing document, it covered thoroughly the whole subject of monarchical organization and was composed before any news had reached Europe of the arrival of the tripartite expedition in Mexico. For many of the protocol provisions, such as the final disposal of French troops, neither signatory had the slightest authority. One of its incredible provisions was the assigning of funds to Almonte for bribing important Mexicans. He was also to nominate candidates for titles of nobility.

Rumors that Maximilian was being groomed for an American destiny were circulated by the grapevine and even appeared in the press in various capitals. Such rumors were so numerous by the opening of 1862 that Lord Russell, the British foreign secretary, felt impelled to investigate. Breaking a heretofore consistent silence about Mexico, he asked the Austrian ambassador at London if it were true that the archduke had accepted the offer of a Mexican throne. Maximilian had neither accepted nor refused was the reply, since various conditions had to be met. Russell was puzzled that the archduke was attracted by so difficult a task, a monarchy among so many republics. Brazil was a successful monarchy, countered the Austrian. "But their emperor Pedro is Portuguese," replied Russell. "The idea comes from France," the Austrian concluded, and it would remain to be seen what Napoleon III would accomplish.[5]

In the weeks that followed, Russell made his country's position unpleasantly clear. The British had not been interested in Napoleon III's monarchical design. The Foreign Office, which had believed the project for monarchy had "fallen in the water," discovered it was regarded as the real purpose of the tripartite expedition and had been the subject of negotiations with Austria. "We are decided to associate with the plan in no way,"[6] Russell informed the Austrian ambassador. Thouvenel had known this

4. This document is reproduced in Daniel Dawson, *The Mexican Adventure* (London, 1935), pp. 197–98.
5. Apponyi to Rechberg, January 20, 1862, Angleterre, Auessern, VIII.
6. Apponyi to Rechberg, February 28, 1862, ibid.

for a long time; as for Guitiérrez de Estrada, he had never had any communication whatever with England.

Disconcerted, the Viennese diplomat retreated before the bald truths of British policy. He hastened to the French ambassador, who confirmed his fears by explaining that England could not have justified the Mexican expedition before Parliament if it bore any association with Maximilian. As soon as Napoleon III's ambassador to London had realized that his emperor's secret design was unwelcome to England he did not open his mouth on that subject. The archduke would have a hard time getting any aid from England, the Austrian ambassador wrote Vienna. The entire situation described by France did not coincide with actual conditions. He added that England must be made to understand that Vienna had no interest in Mexico and that the conversations already held were not official.[7]

Lord Russell instructed his representatives in Vienna and Madrid to feel the pulse of those capitals. In Vienna, the opinion was that Mexican émigrés in Paris appeared to have initiated the candidacy of Maximilian. Russell demolished this suggestion by saying that the Mexican exiles were notorious "for unfounded calculations of the strength of their partisans in their native country."[8] England would have none of their work although she wanted stable government in Mexico as strongly as any nation.

Such interest in the Mexican throne as Vienna may have harbored in July 1861 was badly shaken in the early months of 1862 by the revelation of Britain's stern opposition. The reverse was true of Maximilian. He and his wife looked upon the mission from across the sea with growing fascination. Correspondence increased between them and the Tuileries: Charlotte declared to the Empress Eugénie that they were "called by Providence" to promote a "holy work" in the New World:[9] she envisioned herself as starting a crusade to rescue the benighted, God-forsaken Mexicans. Maximilian's fervor led him to forget the low opinion he had formerly held of Napoleon III and to write, with fulsome flattery, to the man who was creating a destiny overseas.

Until an intermediary was selected to act as the liaison between Miramar and the Tuileries, these letters passed through

7. Rechberg to Apponyi, February 25, 1862, ibid.

8. Russell to Bloomfield, February 13, 1862, *BFSP*, LIII.

9. Charlotte to Eugénie, January 22, 1862, in Henry Salomon, *L'Ambassade de Richard de Metternich à Paris* (Paris, 1931), p. 152.

the Austrian Embassy in Paris. To the Austrian ambassador Metternich, who considered the Mexican design as "one of those fancies which the happy optimism of the Emperor thinks up, one does not know how," Maximilian's rhetoric was embarrassing. Metternich's cup of mortification overflowed when the archduke requested the two-volume work on Julius Caesar by Napoleon III and wrote that "apart from the interest in the judgment of one great man about another, the noble and generous thoughts of the august historian will become an abundant source of great learning for me." Could the Austrian emperor do anything about these letters, Metternich implored; they were so lacking in dignity.[10]

Spain's reaction to the candidacy of Maximilian was more important than the British Foreign Office realized. The British did not know about a secret understanding between France and Spain to turn the expedition into the means of creating a monarchy. Spain explained that, although she had heard of the interest in Maximilian, she had had no part in proposing him as ruler. Explicit and prophetic were the Spanish minister's remarks on the subject: "A Monarchy under a European prince, if not guaranteed by Europe, would not last a year."[11]

Notwithstanding Spain's official ignorance about the Hapsburg candidacy, she had been far from blind to what was going on. For months, signs of Spanish restiveness and disapproval had multiplied. On the day signatures to the Tripartite Treaty were exchanged, the Spanish representative was circulating rumors embellished with his own criticisms of Napoleon III's interest in Maximilian. By mid-December 1861, however, Madrid informed her ambassadors at the allied courts that if Mexicans desired a monarch, Spain was not unmindful of her "historic rights."[12] Later that month, the Spanish Senate was informed that Spain had no official candidate for the Mexican throne, nor had there been official communications among the allied powers on the subject.

The English attitude was that she took the Tripartite Treaty seriously but would not object if the Mexicans chose Maximilian. The Spanish concurred but stated that they would not promote

---

10. Metternich to Rechberg, June 30, 1862, ibid., pp. 150–52.
11. Crampton to Russell, January 30, 1862, *BFSP*, LIII.
12. Calderon Collantes to Mon, December 9, 1861, *Diario de las sesiones de Cortes* (Madrid, 1861–62); also Christian Schéfer, *La Grande Pensée de Napoléon III* (Paris, 1939), p. 172.

Maximilian themselves. If Mexicans desired a monarch, Spain would accept the Count of Flanders, younger son of Leopold of Belgium, who would marry the ten-year-old Infanta. General Prim could prepare for this accession by assuming a temporary dictatorship over Mexico. Rather than support Maximilian as ruler of Mexico, Queen Isabel II would endorse the republic.[13]

The U.S. chargé d'affaires in Madrid assessed the situation shrewdly: to relinquish the dream of a Spanish dynasty wounded Spain. He believed the sacrifice had been accepted "perhaps with the scarcely avowed hope that the course of events in Mexico will itself defeat the plan."[14] To offset the initiative of Napoleon III there was a tendency by Spain to draw closer to England and to spread the rumor that the Spanish General Prim with the sanction of England might maintain the Mexican republic.

Whether Napoleon III allowed his volatile mind to note the cracks beginning to appear in the facade of his Grand Design cannot be known with certainty. Before long, however, the breaks were too large to be ignored.

13. Arrangoiz to Miranda, March 27, 1862, G and P, vol. IV, *Correspondencia secreta* . . . , pt. 2.

14. Perry to Seward, March 13, 1862, Dispatches, Spain, Dept. of State, NA, XLIII.

11

Regeneration by the Sword
1863–1864

———————◄◆►———————

Vexations confronting Napoleon III mounted increasingly throughout the year of the Regency. That year, from the middle of 1863, was filled with both domestic and international frustrations, premature actions of Saligny and General Forey in preparing for a Mexican monarchy as well as with the vacillations of Maximilian. Circumstances considered as assets or ignored entirely in 1861 were viewed as liabilities two years later.

Possibly the gravest liability was the drain on the French treasury. The minister of finance disclosed the disquieting fact that up to September 9, 1863, France had spent 172,000,000 francs and it was time the investment began to pay off. He urged that the minister to Mexico, Marquis de Montholon, be instructed to propose a convention with the Regency for the reimbursement to France.[1] Strict economy was asked of General Bazaine, successor to Forey as French commander, so that "reassurances" could be given to the French people. Above all, he must manage the occupation of Mexico in such a way as to require no reinforcements.[2] French financial agents were dispatched from Paris to try to straighten out Mexican fiscal confusion.

Now that he had no Saligny to tell him what he wanted to hear, Napoleon III was frankly worried about the occupation of

1. Fould to Drouyn de Lhuys, September 9, 1863, CP, Mexique, LX.
2. Randon to Bazaine, October 15, 1863, reproduced in Paul Gaulot, *La Vérité sur l'expédition du Mexique*, 3 vols. (Paris, 1889–90), I, 255–59.

Mexico. In addition to gratuitous information coming to the court, he received from Bazaine bimonthly reports containing serious discrepancies on military and political conditions.[3] While praising his soldiers and promising control of Mexico in three months, Bazaine complained loudly of difficulties and setbacks in administration. The emperor admitted ruefully that news from Mexico was so contradictory he did not know what to believe. Rather pathetically he reiterated that he had never intended to favor reaction; he had always proposed to organize the country with men of good will irrespective of party.[4] To hasten stability, he gave Bazaine both political and military powers while Montholon would handle only financial negotiations with the Regency.[5]

Even before Forey was replaced, the French had noticed a growing coolness toward French regeneration of Mexico. On June 29, 1863, the Teatro Nacional in Mexico City was the scene of the first ball of the new regime. Attended by some 3,000 persons, this function was eulogized as "an eloquent protest against the past" and the "expression of resolute hope for the future."[6] But many prominent persons were noticeably absent.

Auspicious as the ball had appeared to be, it failed to initiate an era of good feeling. Individual Frenchmen who wished to remain alive found it safer to remain within the confines of the capital. Forey ordered all Mexicans who entered Mexico City to appear before the authorities and swear to keep the peace. Thereafter, the nearby village of San Angel provided Liberals with a rallying point. In August 1863, three French soldiers were assassinated at suburban Tlalpam, whereupon Forey seized hostages as security and decreed that the municipality pay a heavy fine. The decree warned that if violence broke out again the hostages would pay with their heads and, if that did not bring order, the town would be destroyed.[7]

All foreign envoys were suspect, most of all Corpancho of Peru. The Peruvian flag flew over four dwellings where Juárez Liberals often received refuge. Not content with this, Corpancho passed messages from Mexico City to Juárez's government at San

3. These bimonthly reports are in the AMG, 1862–64.
4. Napoleon III to Bazaine, September 12, 1863, G and P, vol. XVI, *La intervención francesa en México*, pt. 2.
5. Drouyn de Lhuys to Montholon, December 15, 1863, CP, Mexique, LX.
6. *La Sociedad*, July 1, 1863.
7. Ibid., August 24, 1863.

Luis Potosí. By August 20, both Forey and the Regency lost patience and ordered members of the Peruvian legation to leave the capital in three days and the country in eight.[8] Other legations were uneasy; along with them Corwin, the U.S. minister, was far from certain of his own fate.

The Liberal party, continuing to hold aloof from the new order, was "not nearly so weak as those who do not fight against it pretend," lamented Forey.[9] Members of the Regency were far too reactionary since they favored reprisals against their foes and demanded prominence for themselves hardly in keeping with their subservience to the French army. After Bazaine assumed command, the Regency became increasingly difficult to control.

Most serious of the mounting quarrels was that with the Church. As explained by Chevalier, the French policy was for the new Mexican government to "adopt the mass of liberal and progressive ideas to which all civilized states have successively rallied," and not to "run in the fated track of those antiquated maxims, according to which all liberty—religious, political, or economic—is a curse." The aim of France should be to make "the relations of the Church in Mexico what they are at home; to insist that liberty of worship should be recognized: that the clergy should not form a State within the State . . . that the clergy should cease to be proprietors of the best portion of the territory; and, consequently, that the laws formerly passed for the sale of the church lands should remain in force."[10] This kind of thought was diametrically opposed to the Conservative conviction. It was one thing for European countries to tamper with religious freedom, wrote Miranda "but in our country, where there is no other foundation, to reject [the Church's position] . . . is the same as to leave society without a base." He would not tolerate "what is called the spirit of the century."[11]

Napoleon III ordered an investigation of fraudulent sales of church lands and confirmation of bona fide transactions. As General Bazaine proceeded to carry out the order, he encountered

8. Arrago to Corpancho, August 20, 1863, reproduced in Emilia Romero, *Corpancho: Un amigo de México* (Mexico City, 1949), p. 63; Forey to Randon, August 24, 1863, AMG, 1862–64.

9. Forey to Randon, September 9, 1863, AMG, 1862–64.

10. Michel Chevalier, *Le Mexique, ancien et moderne*, trans. Thomas Alpass, 2 vols. (London, 1864), I, viii–ix.

11. Miranda to Márquez, September 21, 1862, G and P, vol. IV, *Correspondencia secreta . . .* , pt. 3.

open revolt. Labastida, having returned from Europe as archbishop of Mexico as well as regent, defiantly opposed confirmation of land sales. Generally supported by other clericals he headed a powerful obstructionist movement against the French. The clergy announced that those agreeing to validate sales of church lands would not be absolved or given last rites. When the newly organized supreme court put aside all questions covering church lands, it was dismissed by the Regency, and eventually Labastida was removed from that body.[12]

A pamphlet condemning French officials as "the most inveterate enemies of religion and order" was circulated. Labastida declared "the Church has now to put up with the same attacks against its immunities and rights as those which it suffered from during Juárez's government. . . . It has never been persecuted with greater animosity."[13]

Only reluctantly did Mexicans accept civil office under the Regency. Some were pressured into taking positions but instead of displaying initiative and zeal for their duties, they generally exhibited devotion to the advancement of their own political fortunes. Their worst trait, in the judgment of Bazaine, was extravagance. Further, should the French pull out, no Mexican politician wished to be left unable to make his peace with the next regime.[14] Under those conditions slight opportunity existed for political and financial reorganization. The French fiscal agent wrote to Bazaine in exasperation, "I have patience such as I did not believe I possessed."[15]

Bazaine set out during the winter of 1863–64 to make Maximilian acceptable to the Mexicans—with the sword and a military escort. But first, in an effort to attract Liberal leaders at San Luis Potosí, where the Juárez government was doing its best to consolidate forces for defense, he sent a secret agent to treat with the Liberals.

Lerdo de Tejada, foreign minister of the itinerant Juárez cabinet, sent to Bazaine his sine qua non: complete respect for Mex-

12. Bazaine to Napoleon III, December 27, 1863, ibid., vol. XVII, *La intervención francesa en México*, pt. 3.

13. Émile de Kératry, *L'Empereur Maximilien: Son élévation et sa chute*, trans. G. H. Venables (London, 1868), p. 82.

14. Bazaine to Randon, February 23, 1864, G and P, vol. XVII, *La intervención francesa en México*, pt. 3.

15. Budin to Bazaine, February 23, 1864, ibid.

BAZAINE

As commander-in-chief of the French troops in Mexico Bazaine bungled the "regeneration" of that country toward monarchy. Later his supreme command of forces in the Franco-Prussian War ended in disgrace and the collapse of the Second Empire. Caricature by André Gill.

Illustration from Charles Fontane,
Un Maître de la Caricature: André Gill, 1840–85 (Paris, 1927).
(Library of Congress)

ico's independence and the right to choose her own government.[16] The Juaristas let it be known that they feared falling under the domination of the "Priest Party."[17]

Such a negative response to his overtures did not please Bazaine. He replied that the Liberals must realize that he was not negotiating with them; it was a question "only of adhesion, pure and simple, to the Intervention." There ought to be but one party in all Mexico, the "National Party," which all were invited to join regardless of past affiliations. Those who did not choose to enter its ranks would be marked men. Far from being a threat this was a principle arising from "a generous impulse of which the Mexican people will soon feel happy and salutary effects."[18]

This attempt at conciliation, if such it really was, came to an end by December 1863, when French troops approached San Luis Potosí. The Juárez government retreated first to Saltillo, then to Monterrey. As French troops entered town after town, resistance went underground and the number of adherents multiplied. Bazaine naïvely believed that in northern Mexico there was nothing to fear but sporadic guerrilla attacks. A Liberal army of some 3,000 in the South remained unscathed.

General Bazaine concluded in March 1864 that he had collected enough supporters of monarchy. The Marquis de Montholon, who had arrived two months before to replace Saligny, undertook to impress on the Quai d'Orsay the general's "vote-gathering success." Following a conference with Bazaine and Almonte on the subject of the nation-wide poll, Montholon reported: "I shall not hide from you, M. Le Ministre, that we who have under our eyes the people who will be called upon to vote, cannot help but consider the adherents [who] have just been added from all the important points of the country represent incontestably the real opinion of the vast majority of the nation. They were made spontaneously as a result of order and confidence created by the presence of the troops."[19] A more jaundiced view of some of the "important points of the country" came from

16. Lerdo de Tejada to Saborio, November 28, 1863, ibid.

17. Bazaine's secret agent, José Napoleon Saborio, former member of Congress, had also feared the "Priest Party" until he had been enlightened on French policy. His report to Bazaine is found in Saborio to Col. Boyer, Chief of Staff to Bazaine, December 1, 1863, ibid.

18. Boyer to Saborio, December 16, 1863, ibid.

19. Montholon to Drouyn de Lhuys, March 29, 1864, CP, Mexique, LXI.

Sir Charles Wyke who contemptuously noted they "were possibly inhabited by two Indians and a monkey."[20]

Victories over Juaristas did not end resistance to the regeneration program. Temporarily, the Liberals were drastically weakened, but Conservatives and clericals grew more and more disillusioned and restive. They were so alienated by the fall of 1863 that Corwin, watching events from the U.S. Legation, wondered how much longer they would be amenable to French direction.[21] Centered about former presidents Miramón and Santa Anna, intrigue among Conservatives was already in the making.

Called the "Paladin of Conservatism," Miramón followed the fortunes of clericalism and class, not primarily to advance personal interests, but from conviction. There were many like Miramón whose beliefs were as deep-seated and as honest as those of the Juaristas. Although Miramón was to die at the side of Maximilian, he had not originally advocated monarchy in Mexico. He had neither asked for foreign assistance nor had he associated himself with the Mexican exiles in Paris.

Santa Anna also offered his sword to the French but they had no illusions about his capacity for self-seeking and double dealing. For two years he had sought a role in the intervention which would provide an opportunity for him to return from exile. Friends in Paris, notably the promonarchist exile, Gutiérrez de Estrada, had attempted to further his interests with such lack of success that the old dictator decided to put into practice his own unique methods. He landed at Veracruz February 27, 1864, uninvited by the French but not unexpected by the Conservatives. He informed the Regency he had come to cooperate with the new throne. Reckoning he had his hands overloaded with Conservative "cooperation," Bazaine laid down strict terms. Santa Anna could stay if he lived as a private citizen with the modest title of general. He must make no political demonstration, either oral or written.[22]

Such barren fare could not nurture one who all his life had

20. Egon Caesar Corti, *Maximilian and Charlotte in Mexico*, trans. Catherine A. Phillips, 2 vols. (New York, 1928), I, 272.

21. Corwin to Seward, October 26, 1863, Dispatches, Mexico, Dept. of State, NA, XXX.

22. Bazaine to Liciaga, March 6, 1864, G and P, vol. XVIII, *La intervención francesa en México*, pt. 4.

feasted on adulation. When Santa Anna arrived at Orizaba, he
caused to be printed locally another of his periodic manifestos.
True, the document supported the empire; true, it also violated
Bazaine's terms.[23] Retribution came swifter than anything the
notorious ex-dictator had heretofore experienced: summary evic-
tion from Mexico. Upon discovering that Santa Anna had been
plotting with Archbishop Labastida and others to overthrow the
Regency, Bazaine called together those involved for explanations, after which he reported "they understand it is prudent to
keep quiet."[24]

Concurrently, European conditions were deteriorating rapidly.
Under the guidance of Bismarck, Prussian power was growing.
Possibly as a blind for Prussia's ambitions, her king was careful
to congratulate the French emperor on his victory at Puebla. The
delight of Napoleon III over the German message so disgusted
the Austrian Ambassador Metternich, whose country was the
target of Prussia, that he was moved to make a most undiplomatic
comment. Possibly, he remarked, the king of Prussia wanted to
be worthy "of the more or less fantastic plans of a Bonaparte."[25]

With Prussia soon to be an area of friction, there were the
Russo-Polish trouble, the Italian question, the Roman question,
and the Suez Canal project, to mention a few of the imperial
headaches. Napoleon III conceived what he believed to be a master stroke. In November 1863, he suggested to Great Britain that
they sponsor a new European congress to rearrange Europe. Paris
would be the locale of the congress. Napoleon III would bring
"a spirit of moderation and justice."[26] The British complimented
the emperor on his good intentions which they professed to believe but denied the need for the congress and declined to cooperate in calling it.[27] The rebuff was one of the emperor's most
profound disappointments.

All things considered, therefore, the best gamble for France
was the course she followed; namely, get the Mexican Empire on
its feet as quickly as possible so that the onus would be shifted
to the shoulders of the new ruler. From then on, success would

23. Marechal to Randon, March 21, 1864, ibid.
24. Bazaine to Randon, March 8, 1864, ibid.
25. Henry Salomon, L'Ambassade de Richard de Metternich à Paris (Paris,
1931), p. 160.
26. Napoleon III to Queen Victoria, November 4, 1863, enclosed in Russell to
Lyons, November 28, 1863, BFO 115/350.
27. Russell to Cowley, November 11 and November 25, 1863, ibid.

hinge on Maximilian's capacity for government and ability to draw allegiance from the Mexican people and on the attitude of the United States. These points were contingent on each other. If Maximilian's performance in Mexico appeared to receive popular support or if, miracle of miracles, he won control over most of Mexico, the chance of recognition by the United States would probably brighten. Granted that Washington would never like a monarchy across the Rio Grande, the State Department had repeatedly emphasized the right of the Mexican people to choose their own institutions; it was just possible that U.S. Secretary of State Seward might tangle himself in his own words and be forced to accept the new empire. If that should happen, French troops could return home and France could turn her attention to Europe. With a view to hastening this outcome, the emperor pressed Bazaine to complete the pacification of Mexico and urged Maximilian to accelerate plans for his departure.

Archduke Maximilian was of no mind to be hustled off across the Atlantic in so summary a manner. A Hapsburg could not bow to a Bonaparte. Maximilian had set two conditions for acceptance of the Mexican throne: favorable expression of that country's popular will and support by England, France, and possibly, Spain. Questionable adherents collected by Bazaine might pass as a valid substitute for a general approval of monarchy, but the British appeared resolutely disinterested.

Maximilian and Charlotte had already reconciled themselves to abandoning the second condition, but the Austrian emperor still considered it the only means of keeping the new ruler free from French domination. To satisfy his brother, Maximilian led two assaults upon the British position. Early in September 1863, the archduke's agent conferred with the prime minister and received nothing beyond the admission that England would probably recognize Maximilian as soon as he mounted the Mexican throne. Two months later a second attempt, more suitable to Maximilian's way of thinking, for influencing "the nation of shopkeepers," as he phrased it, was initiated. With propaganda similar to that which was to be leveled at U.S. business interests two years later, the archduke attempted to rally British industry and to bring the pressure of public opinion on the British cabinet. This also failed.[28]

28. England supported a proposal that Maximilian assume the Greek throne. This was approved by Maximilian's father-in-law but disdained by the archduke

Great Britain now took steps to see that Maximilian received more realistic views of Mexico than the rosy panorama spread before him. For this purpose Sir Charles Wyke, British minister to Mexico, returned to Europe in an unofficial capacity. Vienna welcomed a consultation with him. Franz Joseph's government was "terrified at the project" of a Mexican Empire and wanted more data with which to counteract the influence of France and the Mexicans.[29]

Accordingly, Wyke's mind was thoroughly probed in conversations with high Austrian officials. In these interviews the Englishman declared that the "Priest Party" was opposed by most of Mexico; he believed that only the Moderates could accomplish stability. He derided the action of the Notables and the Regency and advised that Maximilian keep himself free of this group if he wished to be regarded as a liberal. Wyke had thought monarchy possible in Spanish America, and apparently still did, if brought about through Moderates.[30] He gave the Austrian officials letters from Mexicans describing the growing antagonism toward French occupation. His conclusion was that France would have to send more troops to hold Mexico. He recommended seeking information from sources other than French.[31]

Early in September 1863, Archduchess Charlotte arrived in Brussels for a visit with "Cher Papa." Of their daily discussions she wrote each evening exhaustive accounts for her husband. The opinion of "Cher Papa" is significant because of his influence over the young couple and because of the conditions he thought they ought to make for acceptance. That Maximilian did not follow the advice of his father-in-law in itself revealed how avid he and his wife were for an imperial throne and how slight was their inclination to weigh and resist circumstances. Leopold believed a Mexican crown was possible if established under essential safeguards. He was willing to forego British aid if other conditions were met. France, he told his daughter, must guarantee a loan for the new empire. This would attract investors and give

himself. For details see Daniel Dawson, *The Mexican Adventure* (London, 1935), pp. 298–99, 320–28; Corti, *Maximilian and Charlotte in Mexico*, I, 242–44, 290.

29. Bloomfield to Russell, September 17 and September 24, 1863, Bloomfield Papers, BFO.

30. Report of Herzfeld, September 13, 1864, in Corti, *Maximilian and Charlotte in Mexico*, I, 237–38; Dawson, *Mexican Adventure*, pp. 307–9.

31. Rechberg to Maximilian, September 25, 1863, in Corti, *Maximilian and Charlotte in Mexico*, I, 239.

France a stake in the undertaking. He counseled that French troops ought to remain in Mexico for a stipulated number of years. It would not be well to make this period too long, for the new rulers must appear to be secure among their subjects. His rights as a Hapsburg archduke, particularly the right of succession to the Austrian throne, formed the greatest safeguard for Maximilian; they would free him from domination by Mexicans and emphasize their need of him rather than his of them. The Belgian king warned his daughter repeatedly against foregoing this protection.[32]

Franz Joseph's unalterable position was that support of England was indispensable to the acceptance of the Mexican crown; he never retreated from his decision that Austria could give no guarantees to the new government and must regard the whole episode as a family, not a national, question. The Austrian press was already antagonistic, the Diet more than a little irritated at the ease with which Maximilian appeared disposed to forsake his country. Already there were indications that if he accepted the Mexican throne he might be asked to renounce his right of succession.[33] When the Mexican delegation reached Miramar, no representative from Vienna was present, and all reference to the House of Hapsburg was expurgated from Maximilian's acceptance.

The archduke's meeting with the Mexican delegation, of which Gutiérrez de Estrada became the president when its members reached Paris, took place very informally on October 3, 1863, at Miramar. After a flowery prelude the veteran proponent for monarchy in Mexico extended the crown to Maximilian. In his response the archduke spoke of the action of the Notables as an "initial success" which must be sanctioned by the Mexican people. He would require, also, "such guarantees as will protect the future Empire from threats to its integrity and independence."[34] Upon the fulfillment of these conditions, he would accept the throne.

The English minister to Mexico, Wyke, appeared in Paris without official status but again acting with his government's knowledge. He gained an audience with Napoleon III on No-

32. Dawson, *Mexican Adventure*, pp. 300–307.
33. Corti, *Maximilian and Charlotte in Mexico*, I, 239–40.
34. Dawson, *Mexican Adventure*, pp. 317–19; Corti, *Maximilian and Charlotte in Mexico*, I, 216 ff.

vember 7, 1863, at which he asked permission to speak of Mexico. The French emperor amazingly said he understood the seriousness of the situation and realized he had been deceived about the true temper of the Mexican people. He still hoped, however, that monarchist feeling could be encouraged by better leadership: "I have gone to bed in a bad bed, I realize, but the affair must be liquidated." With the archduke in Mexico, conditions might take a decided turn for the better, enabling the French troops to withdraw except for a small nucleus about which a Mexican army could be organized. "This is what France wants and what I want," Napoleon III concluded.

Wyke insisted that the archduke's words to the delegation at Miramar included no expectation of the withdrawal of French troops, and he believed the archduke's power would not extend beyond the authority of French bayonets. For a moment Napoleon III reflected, then said that the archduke knew that, with the establishment of the throne, France would have completed the task she had set for herself; "one can be an ally of the new Empire without going bail for its continuance." Wyke thought the best procedure would be to dissolve the Regency and find out whether or not the nation wanted a monarchy. Napoleon III could not go along with such a course: "It would be to admit a mistake, and in France I am not allowed to make mistakes." He intended to continue the enterprise as projected and if the archduke put forward conditions which could not be carried out, the French emperor would turn his eyes toward Spain.[35]

Wyke learned that France had under consideration a second candidate, Prince de Joinville of the House of Orléans. His enthronement would check the criticism of Orleanists and might win financial and military support in Spain. Late in 1863, a close associate of Napoleon III wrote Bazaine that it would be better for French policy "to create some dictator, a Comonfort or someone else, to oppose Juárez so that as soon as possible we can bring our army back to France."[36]

By the last days of 1863, Maximilian was caught between various forces: the visionary promises of Mexican exiles; a desire of France to be relieved of her predicament in Mexico; this skepti-

35. Dawson, *Mexican Adventure*, pp. 341–42; Corti, *Maximilian and Charlotte in Mexico*, I, 286–89; Wyke to Russell, November 19, 1863, Confidential, BFO 97/297.
36. Gaulot, *La Vérité sur l'expédition du Mexique*, I, 253.

cism of the whole affair on the part of the Austrian ministers; and the argument of Franz Joseph that Maximilian hold to his condition for British support. When Wyke reported that France contemplated an alternate candidate, Maximilian was forced to decide. The die was cast on Christmas Day of 1863; next day the agent of the archduke left for Vienna and Paris.

Maximilian informed his brother that he could no longer keep the Mexicans in suspense. If Austria did not wish to defy France over Mexico she must exert pressure on the British to grant assistance or reconcile herself to dismissing that condition. He sent word to Napoleon III that he would accept the adherents to monarchy collected by Bazaine as an expression of the will of the Mexican people. There remained only the essential guarantees to be obtained from France.[37] Once these were arranged, he would strike out for the New World venture.

37. Dawson, *Mexican Adventure*, pp. 347–48.

12

"To Destroy
the Dragon of Democracy"
1864

Napoleon III in 1862 was blithely optimistic about the political redemption of the New World. He was confident of assuming
a dominant leadership from a position of strength. As events developed his position of strength became one of weakness.

Confronting the French emperor was the urgent problem of
revising the Regency's acts for the inauguration of the new empire in America. His attempts at solving other problems had left
France in a weakened position, partially brought about by the
failure of his proposals for mediation of the U.S. Civil War—by
England and France or by England, Russia, and France. Moreover, Seward's refusal to consider mediation had been stingingly
unequivocal. He had asserted that neither Congress nor any person connected with the government would entertain the idea of
adjustment "from within or without."[1]

In the summer of 1863, there took place in England and
France a series of efforts in behalf of Confederate recognition.[2]
Reports of these moves reached Seward through London with the
rumor that should England hold back again, France would act
independently. But France did not want to risk the consequences

1. Seward to Dayton, September 8, 1862, Instructions, France, Dept. of State,
NA, XVI; Mercier to Thouvenel, September 9, 1862, CP, Etats-Unis, CXXVIII.
2. Frank L. Owsley, *King Cotton Diplomacy* (Chicago, 1959), pp. 450–88.

of acting alone for a number of reasons: the disappointments in Mexico, the deterioration of the status quo in continental Europe, and victories of the Union armies. Another solution was shaping up in the mind of Napoleon III.

As early as April 1863, his Foreign Office discreetly approached United States minister to France, Dayton, giving the impression that Mexico was really a secondary issue and undoubtedly hoping to gain some expression of Washington's views. France would establish "some sort of order to the condition of affairs," and then withdraw from Mexico, vaguely remarked the French Foreign Minister Drouyn de Lhuys. "We might rest assured they were not going to charge themselves with the government of Mexico," Dayton reported to Seward. To Dayton's fear that a puppet government might be left in Mexico, Drouyn de Lhuys had replied, "No, the strings would be too long to work."[3] None of these soothing words impressed Dayton. He warned Seward that France used language to conceal thought in a masterly fashion, that the emperor's policy might change overnight, and that only United States strength promised security from his opportunism.[4]

Whether the majority of Confederates actually approved the establishment of a monarchy in Mexico is a question. Their government declared from the beginning that it viewed the French expedition with "no unfriendly eye."[5] Specific terms for a formal relationship between the Confederacy and the Mexican Empire never reached the stage of negotiations, although President Jefferson Davis and Secretary of State Judah P. Benjamin attempted to use their acceptance of Maximilian as a lever to gain recognition from France. Confederate agent John Slidell talked frequently to the Quai d'Orsay in this vein, and to Gutiérrez de Estrada. Some Southern leaders were not sympathetic to the French emperor's designs; among them was A. Dudley Mann, the Confederacy's commissioner at Brussels, who wrote Benjamin in September of 1862: "I shall be agreeably disappointed if we do not, in after years, find France a more disagreeable neighbor on our Southern frontier than the United States, at any time prior to their division, ever found Great Britain on their

3. Dayton to Seward, April 9, 1863, Dispatches, France, Dept. of State, NA, LIII.
4. Dayton to Seward, September 7, 1863, ibid.
5. Slidell to Thouvenel, July 21, 1862, *ORN*, ser. II, vol. 3, pp. 467–81.

northern border."[6] Aroused over the implications of Napoleon's manifesto of a Grand Design for America, Mann wrote Richmond, "The avowal therein made cannot fail to create general uneasiness in the minds of our citizens."[7]

Equally unwelcome to Confederate officials in France must have been the talk of expanding Mexico to include some of the territory lost to the United States. Richmond had been considerably disturbed by the inquiries of French consular officers in Texas and Virginia.[8] Each had raised with Confederate officials the identically phrased question whether it was wise for Texas to remain in the Confederacy. Placed side by side, the resemblance of these separate inquiries was more than a coincidence. Secretary Benjamin had developed an interest in history; it impelled him to urge Slidell to find out all he could about the Texas intrigue. He suspected it might be Saligny's scheme.[9] As French representative to the Republic of Texas, Saligny had always opposed Texas' annexation to the United States.

Benjamin's letter of inquiry was captured at sea and reached not Slidell but Minister Sanford to whom Seward had it sent. "The idea of making the new Empire embrace the ancient boundaries of Mexico is not an idle one," wrote Sanford, nor was the action of French consuls described in Benjamin's letter based on a myth.[10] Skeptical Confederates doubtless endorsed Mann's opinion of the Emperor Napoleon III; "He will remain anxious for us to believe that he is silently our friend. Mexico first, and then Mexico as she was previous to her dismemberment is the resolutely and faithfully cherished end at which he aims. . . ."[11]

In the fall of 1863, Maximilian's affability to Confederates had been reassuring. With one of them, Matthew Fontaine Maury,

6. Mann to Benjamin, September 1, 1862, ibid., pp. 521–23.

7. Mann to Benjamin, January 29, 1863, ibid., pp. 670–71.

8. Information about these French consular officials, B. Theron, consular agent for France and Spain in Galveston, Texas, who wrote to Governor Lubbock, and M. Tabouelle, chancellor of the French consulate, who wrote Secretary of State Benjamin, is available in Theron to Lubbock, August 10, 1862, CP, Consulaire, Etats-Unis, XIV; Lubbock to Theron, September 9, 1862, ibid.; Alfred Paul to Drouyn de Lhuys, December 12, 1862, ibid.; Theron to Count Mejan, February 4, 1863, ibid.; and Benjamin to Tabouelle, October 18, 1862, DB, AN.

9. Benjamin to Slidell, October 17, 1862, ORN, ser. II, vol. 3, pp. 556–58.

10. Sanford to Seward, August 21, 1863, private, Henry Shelton Sanford Papers, Sanford Memorial Library, Sanford, Florida, reel 99, box 58, folder 3.

11. Mann to Benjamin, May 8, 1863, ORN, ser. II, vol. 3, pp. 758–59.

the distinguished oceanographer formerly of the U.S. Navy, he had long corresponded on naval subjects. The Virginia scientist wrote from England congratulating Maximilian on receiving the call to Mexico. In discussing the common interests of Mexico and the Confederacy, Maury offered "his faith and his sword" to the Mexican Empire "since the eventualities may arise in which I can be more useful to the common cause under your banner than I am permitted to be under my own."[12]

Maury proposed commanding a Mexican navy of ironclads. He informed Maximilian that an ironclad frigate was in the course of construction in England for the Confederacy; if that government were unable to get the vessel out because of the Foreign Enlistment Act, she might be acquired by Maximilian. With a fleet, imperial Mexico could master the Pacific and detach California from the Union.[13]

Maximilian and his personal emissary were both friendly and encouraging to Confederates. To General James Williams of Tennessee, who was in London, Maximilian expressed "his earnest hope" that the Confederacy would win. Maximilian's emissary wrote General Williams that the cause of the South and Mexico "may be said to form one." Williams was urged to uphold these twin causes, especially in English circles.[14] Toward the end of November 1863, Williams visited Miramar and there received a message for Jefferson Davis. Another contact reported to Slidell that Maximilian considered Confederate victory "identical with that of the new Mexican empire;"[15] and Gutiérrez de Estrada gave Slidell assurances that he would receive an audience with the new Mexican rulers upon their 1864 visit to Paris.[16] The coveted invitation failing to materialize, Slidell sought unsuccessfully an appointment. For this change of Maximilian's attitude toward the Confederacy, Slidell believed he could thank France.

France's shift of policy had been in the making for some months. A few days after the Union victories at Gettysburg and Vicksburg in July 1863, Henri Mercier, French minister to Washington, had had a long talk with Seward. The Frenchman

12. Maury to Maximilian, October 8 and October 10, 1863, Arch. Max.
13. Maury to Maximilian, November 25, 1863, ibid.
14. De Pont to Williams, November 16, 1863, in Daniel Dawson, *The Mexican Adventure* (London, 1935), pp. 333–34.
15. Slidell to Benjamin, December 3, 1863, *ORN*, ser. II, vol. 3, pp. 968–70.
16. Slidell to Benjamin, March 16, 1864, ibid., pp. 1063–65.

admitted that recent losses were fatal to Southern hopes and he offered to suggest that his government abandon consideration of recognition. If Seward saw any connection between this sudden amiability and Mexico, he gave no hint and replied coolly that recognition of the Confederacy would be regarded as an unfriendly act.[17]

From this time on, Mercier began to believe that recognition of the Mexican Empire by the United States was not an impossibility. As he groped for a means to advance this idea, Seward slyly played mouse to Mercier's cat with the result that an effulgent beauty commenced to radiate over the relations between the French Legation and the Department of State. Mercier recounted minutely an interview in which Seward admitted that the French minister had "neglected nothing" to smooth away friction between France and the United States. Seward assured Mercier that, as in the past, he would do all he could to aid Drouyn de Lhuys to "extricate himself from a situation which I believe to be full of difficulties." Purposely, he had never protested the establishment of an empire in Mexico "for fear that such a communication might become an embarrassment to France." To calm public opinion in the United States he had refrained from making public pertinent dispatches from Dayton. Nor had he sent such communications to John Lothrop Motley, United States minister at Vienna, as they would have been an annoyance to Napoleon III in his intercourse with the Austrian cabinet. Seward admitted that Corwin had been instructed not to recognize the new Mexican regime "until further orders." On the other hand, he had not empowered Corwin to continue active relations with the Juárez government. War between Mexico and France was by no means ended.[18]

Shortly after this conference with Mercier, Seward set forth his views to Dayton for the benefit of the Quai d'Orsay. The United States, he explained, had no right or disposition to interfere in the domestic affairs of Mexico, to establish any form of government, or to intervene in the French war. Washington practiced the nonintervention it required of other nations during civil strife. Seward was sure Mexico preferred a republican form of government such as that favored by the United States.

17. Seward to Dayton, July 10, 1863, Instructions, France, Dept. of State, NA, XVII.

18. Mercier to Drouyn de Lhuys, September 14, 1863, CP, Etats-Unis, CXXX.

More than that, security for the United States depended on free institutions for other American nations; he believed these free institutions would survive European manipulations. If France persisted in a policy adverse to public opinion in the United States, collision between the two countries might follow. Constant rumors of French designs, though probably false, were deplorable and dangerous. The United States was closely watching events and was not unmindful of moves made for its own safety.[19] As the South began suffering disastrous defeats in 1863, Seward gradually changed his approach from studied neglect to firm opposition to the French machinations in Mexico.

Following the establishment of the Regency in Mexico, its undersecretary of state and foreign affairs circularized the interested powers including the United States. Events in Mexico were leading to an empire, he announced, and Mexico counted on all friendly states to cooperate. The State Department ignored this note but immediately received the Juarista, Matías Romero, who, with the higher rank of minister, had returned to Washington from the Mexican battlefield. After a formal call on Lincoln, he left cards at the legations of France, England, and Spain.[20]

As the autumn of 1863 advanced, discussions at the Quai d'Orsay assumed a graver tone. The emperor was disturbed by persistent rumors to the effect that as soon as the Union was restored, the United States would undertake an active role in Mexico. Drouyn de Lhuys believed it would not. Washington wanted peace with France, added Dayton. Drouyn de Lhuys hastened to agree that France, too, desired peace in spite of many contrary rumors; for example, that Texas and Louisiana were to be ceded to France in return for Southern recognition, or that the United States and Russia contemplated an alliance, or that an American fleet had left for Veracruz.[21]

Encouraged by a dispatch of October 1863, from Mercier, Drouyn de Lhuys spoke specifically of U.S. recognition of the new Mexican Empire.[22] His point was that the sooner this took place the sooner French troops would return to France. Dayton

19. Seward to Dayton, September 26, 1863, Instructions, France, Dept. of State, NA, XVII.

20. Romero to Lerdo de Tejada, October 29, 1863, *Corres. mexicana*, III.

21. Dayton to Seward, September 14, and September 16, 1863, Dispatches, France, Dept. of State, NA, LIII.

22. Dayton to Seward, October 9 and November 27, 1863, ibid., LIV.

explained that his country could not be expected to act quickly: relations with Juárez were unbroken and the United States "did not anticipate an early and permanent establishment of monarchy in Mexico."

United States policy during these months was hard to pin down because it was open to varied interpretations. Seward undoubtedly so intended it. In retrospect it is clear that the secretary of state had been resolutely consistent, for he never wavered from the stand so exasperating to Romero, that the Civil War in the United States must first be ended and Mexico's problems resolved thereafter; he never failed to regard Juárez openly as the rightful executive of Mexico and Romero as his envoy to the United States; he invariably maintained that it was the right of the Mexican people to determine their own institutions; he always expressed doubt that they would accept a monarchy. Yet it is possible to understand how Napoleon III could draw encouragement from Seward's views, particularly in light of the fact that France could not afford to risk the hostility of the United States. The French emperor uttered the stark truth when he declared to the British diplomat Wyke in November 1863 that war with the United States "would spell disaster to the interests of France and would have no possible object."[23]

Learning from one of his secret informers in Paris that the French foreign minister and his emperor were "overjoyed" at the new tone of Mercier's dispatches, General Sanford in reporting to Lincoln added his voice, although in a totally different key. To confidants of the emperor, those in power or those who would report to those in power, he urged that the time was ripe to repair the friendship between the United States and France. The United States could defend herself against all the rest of the world. She had more ironclads than the rest of the powers put together and Pittsburgh could turn out two hundred a year. How could France fight across the Atlantic Ocean with all the Union cruisers and privateers? The United States was destined to wield great influence in Europe "through our friends the people,"[24] was the expansive assurance of General Sanford.

Diplomats in Washington, other than Mercier, were also puz-

23. Wyke to Herzfeld, November 27, 1863, Egon Caesar Corti, *Maximilian and Charlotte in Mexico*, trans. Catherine A. Phillips, 2 vols. (New York, 1928), I, 289.

24. Sanford to Seward, December 7, 1863, private, Sanford Papers, reel 99, box 58, folder 3.

zled about what to expect from the United States. Matías Romero was certain Seward intended to keep himself unhampered by any commitments. He thought the door for recognition of Maximilian was left open by Seward's stress on the sovereign will of the Mexican people; he knew Seward did not wish to discuss Mexican eventualities and that he had warned U.S. representatives to other countries not to discuss Mexico unless instructed to do so.[25] Romero's visits to the U.S. State Department grew infrequent while he kept trying to build up support among his friends in the Senate and in the House, giving special attention to those influential in foreign affairs. Another interested minister was Count Nikolaus Giorgi of Austria. He passed word on to Vienna of Mercier's optimistic impression that Maximilian would be recognized, although he never quite believed it.[26] After conversing with Senator Sumner at a Washington dinner party, the Austrian diplomat's skepticism grew;[27] he nevertheless stopped predicting to Vienna that war between France and the United States was inevitable and imminent.

The belief that republican Mexico could expect no immediate support from the State Department was sufficiently strong to cause the Juárez government to send a new agent, Jesús Terán, across the Atlantic in January 1864. He was to convince Europe of Liberal resistance and to discourage Maximilian from accepting the offer of the Mexican Notables.

Terán went first to Madrid where he presented Prim with a letter from Juárez. The Conde de Reus accepted both the letter and the bearer. Through his efforts the Austrian minister to Spain transmitted a request from Terán to Maximilian for an interview. Subsequently, the Mexican agent was received at Miramar Palace by the archduke. There he realized immediately the hopelessness of influencing Maximilian. Thereafter he concentrated his efforts on London and Paris. He wrote letters for any publication daring to print them; he talked with anyone who would see him and provided "Les Cinq" (the five opponents of Napoleon III in the Corps Législatif) with facts about Mexico.[28]

25. Romero to Lerdo de Tejada, November 20, 1863, *Corres. mexicana*, III.
26. Giorgi to Rechberg, December 4, 1863, Etats-Unis, Auessern.
27. Giorgi to Rechberg, January 16, 1864, ibid.
28. Juárez to Prim, December 20, 1863; Prim to Juárez, February 24, 1864; Terán to Juárez, February 27, 1864, in Gabriel Saldivar, ed., *La misión confidencial de Don Jesús Terán en Europa, 1863–1866*, Archivo histórico diplomático mexicano, vol. 1 (Mexico City, 1943).

Although accredited to both Spain and Great Britain, he preferred to work as a private citizen in France until his death April 25, 1866.

When French Minister Mercier returned home from the United States in January 1864, a report was circulated that Lincoln would recognize Maximilian provided France extended no favor to the Confederates.[29] In fact, in Paris rumors that Maximilian could win Union recognition were so numerous that Dayton wrote defensively to the State Department as follows: "So far as I am concerned there is not a word of truth in them [the rumors]. I have never given nor thought of giving any such intimation as therein stated, either officially or unofficially, publicly or privately." In the same letter Dayton informed Seward that, by the advice of the emperor of France, Maximilian would abstain from recognizing the Confederacy or from entering into any diplomatic relations therewith until France should have done so. "The rumors," therefore, "of a recognition of the Confederate States by France and Mexico and an alliance between the latter Empire and the Southern Confederacy are altogether devoid of foundations."[30]

In the course of the diplomatic legerdemain no one promised anyone anything. The seeming accord between Napoleon III and Seward rested entirely on the assumed major premise of each. Seward was confident the Mexican people would not support an empire; hence the recognition issue would not arise; Napoleon III refused to admit the Mexican Empire might fail.

So necessary was this gamble to Napoleon III that a resolution against the recognition of Maximilian by the United States House of Representatives in March of 1864 provided no more than an uneasy jolt to France; Seward cushioned the blow by reminding Dayton that, while the resolution reflected public sentiment, President Lincoln still directed relations with foreign powers and he contemplated no change of policy toward Mexico.[31] Dayton added his own reassurance to the Quai d'Orsay: the intent of the resolution was little more than the policy Seward had expressed repeatedly.[32] From this time on Seward, in

29. Slidell to Benjamin, March 16, 1864, *ORN*, ser. II, vol. 3, p. 1063.

30. Dayton to Seward, March 21, 1864, Dispatches, France, Dept. of State, NA, LIV.

31. Seward to Dayton, April 7, 1864, Instructions, France, ibid., XVII.

32. Dayton to Seward, April 22, 1864, Dispatches, France, ibid., LIV.

the French view, became increasingly the wise and moderate statesman who was expected to hold in check injudicious public expression. This interpretation served the secretary of state well.

The Austrian Embassy at Paris was not entirely content with observing the Mexican situation through French eyes. Conscious that the Austrian minister in Washington questioned the conciliatory spirit of Seward, the Austrians in Paris sought further enlightenment. In a long conference in September 1864, Dayton was found surprisingly ready to talk. The United States preferred republics to monarchies, Dayton reiterated, but had no intention of conquest toward her neighbors. The potential danger to a Mexican Empire came from an independent Confederacy which would see in the new government an obstacle to its expansion. "If the people accept the new form of government which has just been established, if the Mexicans are content," said Dayton, the United States demanded "nothing more to recognize them."[33] This conference left the Austrian officials with a feeling of surprised relief.

The Confederacy's failure to win recognition was the casualty resulting from Seward's diplomacy at this point. Confederate agents might continue to urge, cajole, warn, and even threaten France, but the Southern government never won the prize sought. From Napoleon III's point of view the Confederacy had become expendable. At precisely the decisive moment Seward had trumped the Confederate ace. The rapidly rising influence of the United States and the weakening of the Confederacy were impressive evidence in 1863 that Napoleon III's virtual defiance of the Union in 1861 had disappeared. This diminished power as well as the loss of England and Spain as allies was gradually increasing French vulnerability.

Maximilian and Charlotte reached the French capital on March 5, 1864, for a final conference. The ostentatious welcome they received far exceeded their archducal status. Concerned over how he should conduct himself during the Maximilian visit, Dayton received instructions to take no cognizance of the event should Maximilian appear as Mexican emperor.[34] As events transpired, the U.S. minister might have spared himself worry; the reception in honor of Maximilian and Charlotte to which the

33. Mulinem to Rechberg, September 6, 1864, France, Auessern.
34. Seward to Dayton, February 27, 1864, Instructions, France, Dept. of State, NA, XVII.

diplomatic corps was invited took place on Sunday, and Dayton's family did not "attend balls or parties, even at the Palace,
on *Sunday nights.*"[35]

The timing of Maximilian's arrival in Paris was auspicious.
Bazaine's campaigns in Mexico were presumably meeting with
success, the number of adherents was increasing, and clouds from
the direction of the United States appeared to dissipate. The
treaty drawn up between the archduke and Napoleon III, signed
later at Miramar, was for the new Mexican empire a military
triumph and a financial catastrophe. It provided that 25,000
French soldiers should remain in Mexico until replaced by native forces to be enlisted by the Mexican emperor; the Foreign
Legion with a strength of 8,000 would remain for at least eight
years. No mention was made of a commander-in-chief nor of his
relation to France and Mexico, but whenever French and Mexican troops were used together, the French should command. A
secret article, arranging more concrete guarantees, provided that
French forces in Mexico were to be reduced only gradually, but
20,000 would remain until 1867. Finally, France promised never
to fail the new empire regardless of conditions in Europe.

Financially, the articles of this treaty resembled terms to a
fallen enemy rather than to a valued ally. Maximilian mustered
small defense against them. Extravagant and ever in debt, he had
little understanding of money; of the resources of his new country he possessed scant knowledge and even less understanding.
He agreed to reimburse France 270,000,000 francs for the expense of invasion and occupation up to July 1, 1864, and each
year thereafter 1,000 francs per soldier. All claims, so irrespon-
sibly calculated by Saligny before the allied commissioners at
Veracruz two years before, were accepted. On paper at least, the
Swiss banker Jecker finally received his satisfaction. Besides debts
and claims, Maximilian agreed to pay 6 percent interest on a
loan of over 200,000,000 francs to be raised in Europe. To show
the French people how soon money was to start rolling home-
ward from Mexico, 66,000,000 francs of the loan became the first
installment on the payment of the Mexican debt.[36] Maximilian
received 8,000,000 francs for the personal expenses of his accession to the throne.

Napoleon III's project to develop unexploited mineral wealth

35. Dayton to Seward, March 11, 1864, Dispatches, France, ibid., LIV.
36. Convention of Miramar, 1864, M et D, Mexique, X.

in Sonora and other parts of northwest Mexico was not accepted by Maximilian. The importance of this rejection lies in the insight it affords into the Austrian's own thinking on Mexico. He had just underwritten a staggering debt for his unknown realm whose chief difficulty had been financial confusion and bankruptcy. At the same time he denied what at the moment seemed the quickest means of discovering new wealth. With reference to the treaty of Miramar, Terán, then in London, asked Juárez, "What man of any dignity would have agreed that 25,000 Frenchmen should remain in Mexico, not under his orders but under a general named by the French Emperor? This treaty confirms the opinion I have already given you of the Archduke; he is what we call a cabbage head."[37]

Napoleon III also formulated a policy concerning the controversial church lands. The new rulers of Mexico expected to stop off in Rome for an audience at the Vatican en route to Veracruz. What would have been more timely than a discussion of the various controversies in which clericals played a major part? To avoid exposing this deep-seated quarrel, Napoleon III advised Maximilian against including it on the agenda of his visit to the Holy See. Oddly enough, King Leopold concurred with the French emperor; Maximilian followed the recommendation of his two mentors scrupulously.

The results of the visit to Paris, taken together, form a pattern of Maximilian's intentions. Settlement of clerical disputes was postponed until he reached Mexico. Recognition of the Confederacy was shelved to permit the wooing of Washington. Economic development of Mexico awaited the pleasure of the new ruler, yet onerous financial commitments had been assumed. From no European power was any guarantee received save that France promised to keep troops in Mexico for as long as eight years.

Of specific and practical means of discharging the responsibilities of his reign, Maximilian appeared to have little concept. Wyke, the British minister to Mexico in London at the time Maximilian and his wife paid a farewell visit to relatives there, reported that Maximilian "has no definite, settled plan and relies too much on the favorable effect he hopes will be produced by his presence among the Mexicans." The prospective Mexican

37. Terán to Juárez, May 18, 1864, Saldivar, *La misión confidencial.*

emperor's tendencies were liberal and he "disapproves of the reactionary politics of the 'Priest Party' and the Regency at present
supported by the French," continued the Englishman. Wyke's
conclusion was that Maximilian spoke "with much cleverness and
great fluency but . . . little to the purpose. . . . All his arguments
were based either on his hopes or on his good intentions."[38]

A forecast of the disappointments and sacrifices the future
would impose awaited the archduke on his return from Paris to
Austria. He was asked to sign "the Family Pact" requiring the
renunciation for himself and heirs of all rights of succession to
the Austrian throne, and all rights, specifically financial, to share
in the Hapsburg inheritance.

Maximilian regarded the pact as the most cruel blow he could
receive. He refused to accede to its terms even if it necessitated
his giving up a throne whose acceptance was all but completed.
His stand threw France, Austria, emperors, diplomats, Mexicans
all in a turmoil. The Archduchess Charlotte hastened to Vienna;
the Austrian emperor proceeded to Miramar Palace; Napoleon
III was beside himself.

The French emperor telegraphed Maximilian March 28, 1864,
"A family quarrel cannot prevent Your Imperial Highness from
undertaking your exalted mission." He wrote Leopold, "I count
on Your Majesty's influence to overcome these obstacles." As a
last resort he hustled his aide-de-camp off to Vienna and Miramar. Under the strain of uncertainty Napoleon III wrote Maximilian in phrases, some of which should have haunted him later:
"What would you think of me if, when Your Imperial Highness
had reached Mexico, I were suddenly to say that I could no longer
fulfill the conditions to which I had set my hand?"[39] In this disagreement which threatened all concerned with an international
scandal, Maximilian displayed that indecision prophetic of his
future reign.

At last the brothers reached accord; Maximilian retained his
family allowance, deposited in Austria, and he was promised
that, if he ever renounced the Mexican throne, efforts would be
made to reinstate him in a position worthy of his birth. Also a
volunteer force of 6,000 Austrians was permitted to be recruited
for the Mexican service. Maximilian neither forgot nor forgave

38. Wyke to Russell, March 15, 1864, BFO 50/383.
39. Napoleon III to Maximilian, March 28, 1864, Arch. Max.

the demand made by this family pact; torn between two choices, his Hapsburg pride met defeat in either. To cease to be an archduke galled him; to relinquish the opportunity to become an emperor was unthinkable.

The Mexican delegation created by General Forey and Minister Saligny in the Mexican capital arrived at the Miramar Palace of Maximilian on April 10, 1864. They officially offered the Mexican throne to the Austrian archduke. In his acceptance the new emperor invited "the cooperation of all Mexicans who love their motherland in the accomplishment of our beneficent though difficult task." That evening a banquet was spread but Maximilian was too ill over the controversy with Franz Joseph to attend and was represented by Charlotte. For two days he kept to his bed; on the third day he made ready his departure. He and Charlotte sailed away April 14, 1864, from the Old to the New World on the Austrian frigate, the *Novara*.

Vienna was more than a little relieved. High Austrian officials were thoroughly irritated by Maximilian's conduct, his unwillingness to face realities, and his disregard of advice. The British ambassador at Vienna, Lord Bloomfield, informed Lord Russell that the Austrian emperor and his government "had done everything possible to discourage the Mexican project."[40]

Lord Bloomfield later confided privately to Russell: "There never was a Prince departed on such an enterprise who left so few friends behind him. He is not liked in this country: nobody trusts him and his late proceedings toward the Emperor showed up his character. The blame of much is laid at the door of the Archduchess Charlotte. . . ."[41] Apparently full of his subject Lord Bloomfield sent a later message to the British Foreign Office: "I hope he [Maximilian] will find some money when he gets to Mexico but doubt it as the French are not in a habit of leaving much behind them. It is believed that he leaves debts in Europe to the amount of 6,000,000 florins. A crown and an empty treasury will be a pleasant beginning!"[42]

Maximilian's mission was not an act of ambition, wrote King Leopold of Belgium to his daughter Charlotte, "but of simple charity. . . . Once you are firmly established in Mexico it is prob-

40. Bloomfield to Russell, January 19, 1864, BFO 97/297.
41. Bloomfield to Russell, April 12, 1864, private, Bloomfield Papers, BFO.
42. Bloomfield to Russell, April 21, 1864, ibid.

able that a great part of America will place itself under your rule."[43]

From the U.S. Legation the historian John Lothrop Motley wrote, "the Archduke Maximilian . . . firmly believes . . . he is going forth . . . to establish an American empire, and that it is his divine mission to destroy the dragon of democracy. . . ."[44]

43. Leopold, Duke of Brabant, to Charlotte, November 1, 1861, quoted in Dawson, *Mexican Adventure*, p. 212.

44. Motley to Oliver Wendell Holmes, September 22, 1863, in George W. Curtis, ed., *Correspondence of John Lothrop Motley*, 2 vols. (New York, 1889), II, 138–43.

13

Monarchy Imposed on America
1864

Maximilian and Charlotte used the six weeks of their Atlantic crossing preparing for their adventure in Mexico. They studied a constitution they had sketched out the preceding year with the advice of King Leopold and Napoleon III. They drew up regulations for administrative procedures to be established in two departments, civil and military. Most meticulously, they commenced the compilation of regulations governing court etiquette; when printed, it ran to six hundred pages. Maximilian seemed determined to maintain his imperial prestige, perhaps even more determined because he considered his family had written him off.

Among those preparing for the arrival in Mexico of the Emperor Maximilian in May 1864, was the new French minister, Marquis Charles Francis Frédéric de Montholon. His father, General Charles Tristan de Montholon, had been aide-de-camp to Napoleon I at Waterloo. Assisting the French minister in the Mexican capital was the noted French journalist, Emanuel G. Masseras. Masseras, with over forty years' experience in New York, was competent to advise the new Mexican emperor on American affairs. His last assignment before arriving in Mexico was the editorship of the *Courier des Etats-Unis*, leading French language newspaper in the United States. It had been founded with funds provided by Joseph Bonaparte, former king of Spain who later lived in New Jersey.

In association with Montholon, Masseras published a brochure, *Le Programme de l'empire*, prior to the arrival of Maximilian. Its purpose was to convert a maximum number of Mexicans and describe the pattern of the new order, a pattern Montholon hoped Maximilian would follow. That such a brochure appeared without consultation with the new ruler indicated that France intended to remain in control.

Masseras wrote that time was required for the perfection of everything, a maxim Mexico had never respected. The most urgent need was a rallying point capable of raising the country in its own esteem and in the eyes of the world. Such a rallying point would be the change from a republic to an empire, provided the new empire demonstrated the truly disinterested aspect of Napoleon III's Grand Design[1] and the quality of that "far-seeing genius and energetic hand which had repaired the torn fragments of the Latin race in Europe and now wants to complete the task by raising the same race in the New World to the position it deserves."[2]

At the beginning of its independence, read the Masseras brochure, Mexico had faced a brilliant future "beside which even that of the United States might have paled."[3] In the American continent where Mexico deserved at least second place, she had now ceased to count as a power, and Napoleon III's Grand Design aimed to restore her prestige.

Masseras passed from French grandeur and Mexican decadence to the merits of an empire. Mexico had known only the name and shadow of a republic; Napoleon III had given new meaning to the imperial system by creating an "intimate alliance of the democratic and progressive principle of governmental stability."[4] The Mexican Empire would open a new era in which all civil factions would be molded into national unity. Those who had withdrawn from public life because of its precarious nature might now venture forth. Extremists would realize that they had nothing to gain by continuing a hapless struggle. But—and here was a threat—"Those who want to restore the past or upset the present will find that the moderation of the Empire does not indicate lack of firmness."[5] On the other hand, the em-

1. E. Masseras, *Le Programme de l'empire* (Mexico City, 1864), p. 9.
2. Ibid., p. 12.
3. Ibid., p. 13.
4. Ibid., p. 18.
5. Ibid., p. 23.

pire would welcome opposition. Opposition was feared only by the "timid and weak," but for the "far-seeing and strong," it was a guide. New faces would appear in government, since "a new task invites the cooperation of new men." An empire might not be republican but "it is democratic in the true sense of the term: government by the people and for the people." In conclusion, Masseras partially revealed the future by asking, "Who doubts but that the Mexican Empire is called to take the heritage of . . . prosperity so much admired by the world, and which the United States has probably lost forever."[6]

However Maximilian may have regarded the indoctrination of his subjects before he and they had seen each other, he wanted the new editor under his control. Masseras and the French Legation found his demands inadmissable.[7] The chief task of the French journalist was to establish and edit a French language newspaper, *L'Ere nouvelle*, in Mexico. It was to set there precisely the tone desired by Napoleon III.

Finally, on May 28, 1864, the Emperor Maximilian and his Empress Charlotte landed at Veracruz. As they drove through the city, they were observed by silent, undemonstrative people. Veracruzanos, who were predominately liberal, thus registered their disapproval of the empire. The new sovereigns were depressed; the empress was almost in tears. As they left the coast, en route to the capital, they noted the graves of hundreds of French soldiers who at the beginning of the invasion had succumbed to yellow fever. The imperial party proceeded inland, accompanied by Juan Nepomuceno Almonte, the reactionary Mexican who had been extremely active in planning the monarchy. As the new sovereigns passed into an area inhabited by wealthy Conservatives, the welcome became cordial.

At Puebla, an enthusiastic demonstration had been prepared. On the outskirts of Mexico City their Majesties heard mass at the Shrine of the Virgin of Guadalupe; after the service, they were met by Bazaine and Montholon. The combined cavalcade entered the capital on June 12, 1864, with a semblance of rejoicing. One note of future discord might have been observed in the prior departure of U.S. Minister Corwin.

The surface ceremonies welcoming the new sovereigns did not completely mislead Maximilian and Charlotte. "Everything in

6. Ibid., p. 30.
7. Montholon to Drouyn de Lhuys, August 28, 1864, CP, Mexique, LXII.

this country calls for reconstruction," Charlotte wrote the Empress Eugénie of France; "nothing is to be found, either physical or moral, but what nature provides." They were not alarmed, having been there only six days, the strong-willed Charlotte added; she was merely stating a fact. There would be progress "if the French Emperor stood by" them.[8] They were soon admonished by letters from Europe; one from Leopold warned his son-in-law not to rely too heavily on Europeans, and one from Napoleon III cautioned the new emperor not to be influenced by Mexicans. Thus was inaugurated the new empire imposed on America by Europeans.

In the early days of his reign, Maximilian endeavored to put into practice the advice given him. Napoleon III, Leopold, and the program of Masseras all stressed unity and the desirability of winning all factions to the throne. Furthermore, Maximilian wanted to reduce his dependence on France by drawing as much support as possible from Mexicans. If his call from the Mexican people had been genuine, no course could have been wiser but, under the circumstances, he soon discovered he was pleasing no one. Conservatives who had supported French interference in domestic affairs to restore their powers were aghast at seeing the former chairman of the Regency, Almonte, relegated to a useless, if nominally exalted, status while men like José Fernando Ramírez, a Liberal who had refused membership in the selected group of Notables, became minister of foreign affairs. Few Liberals accepted Maximilian's professions of amnesty and good will. The clericals, deeply hostile to the French, waited to see what terms might be offered the church. To most of the populace, the new emperor appeared friendly and gracious, much too unassuming for their exalted ideas of a monarch and, in spite of his halting efforts to speak Spanish, very, very Austrian. Some of those close to him soon caught on to the difficulty he usually experienced in making up his mind.

While Mexicans were sizing up their new rulers, French officials were appraising the couple for whom they had manufactured a throne. Many of them believed in 1864, as Masseras wrote later, "There was a moment when, in spite of all incredibilities, the work of the Mexican Empire was truly a work accomplished and, to make it durable, there was needed only a

8. Egon Caesar Corti, *Maximilian and Charlotte in Mexico*, trans. Catherine A. Phillips, 2 vols. (New York, 1928), II, 422.

little political sense, foresightedness, and courage on the part of the man charged with the task of consolidating it."[9] The majority of Mexicans, the French thought, were at first disposed to try Maximilian out. Many Liberals were wondering whether a fait accompli might not prove better than prolonging the struggle between Liberals and Conservatives. In the interior, the Juaristas had lost most of the important centers of population; towns were still adhering to the new banner. At that time, wrote Masseras, Mexicans thought they had a chance at stable government.[10]

Drawing on his experience as an editor in New York, Masseras believed large groups in the United States would be more sympathetic than hostile to the Mexican Empire. Mexico as a republic had been a chaotic and disorderly neighbor; but a peaceful and prosperous empire would become "a fertile field for commercial operations."[11] In fact, money was already coming out of hiding, economic operations were multiplying, and foreigners, including some from north of the Rio Grande, were thinking of investing their wealth.

Such a pleasing prospect rested on more than idle dreams. By November 1864, the French army had progressed as far to the northeast as the important city of Monterrey and the booming cotton port of Matamoros on the Rio Grande. In the southwest General Porfirio Díaz had surrendered his large army at Oaxaca and Juarista forces were disorganized and scattered. Juárez and his skeleton government, protected only by the remnants of the army that had defeated the French at Puebla, left San Luis Potosí at the end of 1863 and began retreating toward the U.S. boundary.[12] French troops controlled a part of Mexico about the size of France. Although equally large areas were unconquered, they were at a considerable distance from the capital and resistance was not on a large scale. Furthermore, hundreds of men, presumably Juaristas at heart, manned the lesser jobs of the imperial government because a job was a job. Of course, winning territory and holding it against guerrillas and other refractory elements of the population were two distinctly different operations, but the French had still to learn that lesson.

9. E. Masseras, *Un Essai d'empire au Mexique* (Paris, 1879), p. 2.

10. Ibid., pp. 9–13.

11. Ibid., p. 5.

12. For a map of the Juárez retreat showing places and dates, see Frank A. Knapp, Jr., *Life of Sebastian Lerdo de Tejada, 1823–1889: A Study of Influence and Obscurity* (Austin, 1951), pp. 80–81.

In Chihuahua, where the weakened Juárez government, protected only by guerrillas, arrived October 12, 1864, the U.S. consul considered Juárez's plight deplorable. "I did not hear in the
streets a single cry in favor of the President of the Republic," he
wrote. "The situation is very bad and would bring despair upon
any mind less faithful and hopeful than President Juárez."[13]
Washington's minister in Paris was also pessimistic. He wrote
Seward March 15, 1864, that there was little chance of republican Mexico defending itself long; he thought the United States
should not embroil herself with France "for the quixotical purpose of helping Mexico."[14]

Other observers did not subscribe to this attitude. A spokesman for the British Legation believed Mexican difficulties remained "nearly, if not quite, as entangled as ever." The proposed
regeneration of Mexico, he reported to London, had never been
popular. Many had acquiesced through sheer exhaustion but
"few, I am afraid, can actually be said to have accepted it from
conviction or of their own free will."[15] Among those agreeing
with him was William H. Corwin, who remained at the U.S.
Legation after his father, the minister, returned home. Mexicans
did not really welcome Maximilian, he explained; they were
"passively submitting to what they believed Fate had ordained
for them."[16] Their demonstrations when the imperial couple
reached the capital had no special significance, accustomed as the
people were to hailing new dictators one moment and booting
them out the next. Many prominent Liberal families had reoccu-
pied their homes in Mexico City. This meant withdrawal from
public life rather than acceptance of the empire. In general,
Liberals were far from discouraged, Corwin's son continued;
they gave Maximilian about three years of survival and were willing to tolerate him until their own strength was consolidated.[17]

By a decree of July 6, 1864, Maximilian proclaimed general
amnesty for political prisoners and exiles. Many were released
from prison or allowed to return from Europe. This action Bazaine viewed skeptically.[18] On another score the French general

13. Creel to Carter, October 18, 1864, Miscellaneous Letters, Dept. of State, NA.
14. Dayton to Seward, March 25, 1864, Dispatches, France, ibid., LIV.
15. Walsham to Russell, September 18, 1864, BFO 50/380.
16. Corwin to Seward, May 28, 1864, Dispatches, Mexico, Dept. of State, NA,
XXX.
17. Corwin to Seward, August 29 and December 28, 1864, ibid.
18. Bazaine to Randon, July 10, 1864, G and P, vol. XX, *La intervención
francesa en México*, pt. 5.

was satisfied. Miramón, who had been refused permission to join the procession to meet the new rulers, was sent abroad to study military organization in Prussia. General Márquez, another leader suspected by the French, received a commission to carry the Grand Collar of the Imperial Eagle to the sultan of Turkey. He was then to establish a convent in the Holy Land.[19]

In spite of Maximilian's efforts to draw Liberals to his government, to push aside reactionaries, to hold himself independent of France, and to make his regime truly national, his government from the very first failed to take hold. Those Liberals who accepted office gave evidence of a delaying action as Corwin's son had predicted. The French army under Bazaine continued to win victories without pacifying the country, and all the while Maximilian emerged as worse than a mediocre leader. Had he been more competent, the task of Bazaine might have been less arduous; had Bazaine met with more success, Maximilian's task would have been smoother. As it was, the French army attempted a goal beyond its capacity in the name of a foreign monarch unfitted by temperament and experience to rule. When the going grew rough, each blamed the other for the liabilities of both. The truth was that neither the French nor Maximilian had any justifiable reason for being in Mexico and this became more apparent the longer they stayed.

Six months after the beginning of Maximilian's reign, journalist Masseras believed the empire stood condemned by all except those who were afraid to face facts.[20] It was not as the French had envisioned but "a government at once autocratic and weak, rebel to all direction, and incapable of direction itself."[21] Maximilian was friendly to everyone without supporting anyone. "Promises multiplied," wrote Masseras, "without being kept, and project followed project without a chance of realization."[22]

The solution to getting along with Maximilian never ceased to be an enigma to Bazaine and Montholon. Dictating to him was impossible; yet they dared not leave him alone. The result was constant friction as Maximilian acquired an intense dislike for the two top French officials. He would seldom see Montholon, and with Bazaine he quarreled to the end. When a small contin-

19. Carlos Sánchez-Navarro y Peón, *Miramón: El caudillo conservador* (Mexico City, 1945), pp. 189–90.
20. Masseras, *Un Essai d'empire au Mexique,* p. 22.
21. Ibid., p. 56.
22. Ibid., p. 48.

gent of troops returned to France in November 1864, Maximilian openly opposed Bazaine over the decision.[23] Napoleon III had approved the withdrawal; he had hoped to pacify public opinion in France by showing that the Mexican venture was drawing to a close.

Other Frenchmen close to the Mexican Empire were critical of Maximilian. Abbé Domenech, director of the Mexican press and a reliable pipeline to the Tuileries, gave the following stiff advice when Maximilian complained of his procrastinating ministers: "Sire, you were not called to Mexico to be governed by Mexicans but to govern them. Your Majesty knows what they have made of their country during the half century they have governed. If Your Majesty continues their practices he will arrive at the same results: ruin and anarchy." Maximilian smarted under such frankness. The abbé was informed privately that, had he not been a priest, he would have been expelled.[24] Later Domenech wrote to a "personage" who would pass the letter to the French foreign minister, "Mexico is on a volcano: the Emperor and Empire used up; the insurrection triumphant."[25]

Before many weeks of his reign had passed, Maximilian must have noted the difference between actual conditions and the glowing pictures painted by France and the Mexican exiles. Large regions to the north and south were solidly in favor of the republic. Confusion in governmental processes was apparent; the financial tangle was desperate; yet Maximilian naïvely depended on Charles Corta, the French financier, for a solution. Seemingly, as a compensation for these worries, Maximilian became engrossed in building projects. Just as he had built Miramar to conform to extravagant tastes, he began making repairs on the Chapultepec Palace. Constructed on a site overlooking the Valley of Mexico, it possessed a unique and commanding view. Expenditures on the palace, in the midst of Mexico's distress, aroused severe criticism and opposition.

Another escape from pressing burdens was a series of lengthy inspection trips to distant parts of his domain. Maximilian loved to travel and the plausible excuse that he needed to know all his subjects enabled him to delay decisions crowding upon him. One

23. Charles Blanchot, *Mémoires: L'Intervention française au mexique*, 3 vols. (Paris, 1911), II, 233.
24. Emmanuel Domenech, *Histoire du Mexique*, 3 vols. (Paris, 1868), III, 168.
25. Ibid., p. 210.

journey lasted more than two months. He professed to be pleased with his reception but was disillusioned by what he observed. The worst groups he thought were judicial functionaries, army officers, and the clergy—the very classes usually regarded as pillars of the social structure. "The judges are corrupt," he charged, "the officers have no sense of honor, and the clergy are lacking in Christian charity and morality."[26]

The revision of Maximilian's first impressions of Mexico was never relayed to his kinsmen in Austria. Still strongly resentful over the treatment meted out by the Austrian government and the Hapsburgs, Maximilian continued to send home letters of enthusiasm and praise for his new kingdom. It was a paradise where people were free from all the sins of a decadent Europe, he wrote. He depicted himself as one who had come alive after years of stagnation. His extolling of New World virtues may have been in reverse proportion to the depth of his disillusionment.

It is a fallacy to assume, as many critics have, that French expeditionary officials did not realistically face up to conditions in the Mexican Empire and that Napoleon III was not adequately informed of the liabilities. Once Saligny had been removed, the dispatches crossing the Atlantic were brutally frank. Bazaine complained constantly of the Mexicans, although he praised his own troops. Montholon's reports to Paris were a continuous record of his growing alarm. Early in Maximilian's reign Montholon warned that, despite his position as minister of France to Mexico he could get very little information about what was going on.[27] Two weeks later he described "certain disturbing tendencies": the empire's debt of gratitude to Napoleon III was already difficult for Maximilian to bear, and he was surrounded by a clique of Austrians and Belgians who were mostly anti-French. Montholon observed that general restlessness was apparent in the country and that the enthusiasm with which the regal pair had been greeted was ebbing away. Mexican troops were still paid by the French, although payments by Mexico were to have begun after the arrival of the new emperor. Montholon had been told there "was no reason why . . . the [Mexican] treasury could not meet the obligation, but since the French no longer guarded the funds, they slipped away."[28]

26. Corti, *Maximilian and Charlotte in Mexico*, II, 210.
27. Montholon to Drouyn de Lhuys, June 26, 1864, CP, Mexique, LXII.
28. Montholon to Drouyn de Lhuys, July 1, 1864, ibid.

Growing more apprehensive, Montholon wrote, "Everything is in stagnation and everyone is beginning to be fearful of results." This provided an opportunity for the opposition to rally. The Moderates were holding aloof. They thought Maximilian was too French; the French considered him not French enough; to them it was inconceivable that Maximilian would rely wholly on Mexicans who were so utterly irresponsible. Others attributed the rapid degeneration of conditions to the weakness of the sovereign who they believed did not possess the requisite ability. Montholon's comment was, "Time will tell whether this is a premature judgment."[29]

Paris cautioned Montholon against surrendering too easily to discouragement. What France wanted most was a competent administration; in view of the frightful disorders of the past, not much could be expected in so short a time.[30] Napoleon III was less patient. "I fear," he wrote Bazaine in the middle of 1864, "there are many conflicts in the government and that the Emperor wishes to fly with his own wings." He urged the organization of a Mexican army "so that we can leave soon."[31]

As Bazaine paid Mexican soldiers month after month to prevent their desertion to Juárez, he pushed unsuccessfully for the necessary financial reorganization. Everywhere he encountered delay, often open hostility. Maximilian's Council of State resented French pressure; provincial officers with whom Bazaine's agents tried to cooperate had no instructions from Mexico City.[32] Montholon was also blocked when he attempted to negotiate French claims; he was accused by Maximilian of exceeding his instructions by demanding interest for delayed payments.[33] Roots of the quarrels over finances lay first in the impossible terms Maximilian had originally accepted and, second, in the understandable conflict whereby Bazaine and Montholon worked not primarily for Mexico but for France. Moreover, much of Mexico held by the French was growing restive. In November 1864, Bazaine warned, "The era of patience and indulgence is past. All those not active supporters of the Mexican Empire are declared in a state of open hostility."[34]

29. Montholon to Drouyn de Lhuys, July 28, 1864, ibid.
30. Drouyn de Lhuys to Montholon, August 22, 1864, ibid., LXIII.
31. Napoleon III to Bazaine, August 20, 1864, G and P, vol. XXII, *La intervención francesa en México*, pt. 6.
32. Bazaine to Randon, December 10, 1864, ibid., pt. 7.
33. Montholon to Bazaine, December 10, 1864, ibid.
34. Bazaine to Randon, November 9, 1864, ibid.

In one direction French guidance was generally followed; this was the new empire's relationship with her neighbors to the north, both the Union and the Confederacy. Almost as soon as he arrived, Maximilian raised the question of seeking recognition from the United States. The moment was hardly propitious inasmuch as the Republican National Convention of 1864 had condemned the Mexican Empire. Montholon prudently counseled waiting until after the presidential election the following November. He urged Maximilian to let him handle the recognition problem; he would confidentially sound out the United States and other American nations about receiving an envoy from imperial Mexico.

The previous year, the Regency had suggested that a Confederate envoy be sent to Mexico.[35] Appointed to that post was General William Preston. His mission was to outmaneuver Corwin and bring about a collision between Union forces on the Rio Grande and the French. The hope was that it would "engage France in an alliance against the United States." Preston was to expand trade with Mexico and to authorize privateers to raid the gold cargoes, totaling more than $40,000,000 annually, sailing out of California to the eastern seaboard.[36]

The assumption that the new Mexican Empire would become an auxiliary battleground for the U.S. Civil War collapsed when Napoleon III decided that the one gesture toward recognition by Washington would do Maximilian and especially himself more good than a galaxy of treaties with Richmond. News of this diplomatic turnabout, already suspected by Slidell and other Southern agents in Europe, overtook Preston at Havana en route to his assignment. Preston sent an aide from Havana to learn Maximilian's intentions toward the Confederacy.[37] Maximilian sent messages to General Preston through Montholon, urging him to defer his visit and not "put him [Maximilian] in the disagreeable necessity of eluding official intercourse with the [Confederate] government till his own troubles are removed."[38]

35. Quintero to Benjamin, November 4 and November 9, 1863, Pickett Papers, LC.

36. Benjamin to Preston, January 7, 1864, *ORN*, ser. II, vol. 3, pp. 988–90.

37. This aide, Captain R. T. Ford, spent some five months at the imperial capital during which he conferred with Almonte, Ramírez, and Montholon. In November 1864, he returned to Preston. For an account of his mission, see Ford to Benjamin, June 30, 1864, Pickett Papers, LC, and Ford to Ramírez, October 10 and November 9, 1864, Arch. Max.

38. Preston to Benjamin, November 10, 1864, Pickett Papers, LC.

The snub of Preston by Maximilian incensed Richmond. Confederate Secretary of State Benjamin and the Confederate Congress were equally irritated by the attitude of France. In the session of January 1865, several Confederate congressmen intimated the startling possibility that the U.S. Civil War, then nearing its end, might be closed by the union of Northern and Southern forces for combined action south of the Rio Grande.[39] Probably nothing more than a dig at Napoleon III was intended, but in certain quarters the proposal opened broader horizons.

More critically pressing to imperial Mexico than relations with the Union and the Confederacy was the acute controversy with the Church. A settlement satisfactory to the Holy See could have done much to strengthen Maximilian's position. Following the advice of Napoleon III, Maximilian did not discuss the problem of confiscated lands while visiting Rome en route to America. This delay discouraged French officials in Mexico who had been feuding for a year with the reactionary clergy. Abbé Domenech's conviction was that when Maximilian arrived without a concordat with the Vatican, the empire was stillborn. The variety of the abbé's twenty years' experiences and observations in Mexico and other parts of North America rendered him highly competent to judge Maximilian's controversy with the Church. The leisurely arrival of the papal nuncio[40] at Veracruz several months after Maximilian reached Mexico aggravated the already grave quarrel.

Although Maximilian had no record of church controversy behind him as did Napoleon III, he held liberal views on religious toleration and on the necessity of protecting the already secularized church lands. He had formulated a nine-point program for the Church in Mexico which contemplated a state Catholic church with toleration of other faiths and state-paid salaries for the clergy to be substituted for the nationalized church properties. To Maximilian's consternation the nuncio's proposal allowed no compromise but demanded complete restoration of all lands and clerical power. The nuncio's position reflected the denunciation by the pope in December 1864, of progress, liberalism, and modern civilization. Negotiations immediately reached a stalemate.

39. *Journal of the Congress of the Confederate States of America*, 7 vols. (Washington, D.C. 1904–5), II, 451–52.
40. Monsignor Meglia.

Maximilian was convinced that it was impossible to accede to the papal demand without causing a social upheaval. Furthermore, the church stand coincided in no degree with his own convictions. Charlotte, daughter of a Catholic king and granddaughter of a Catholic queen, had a distressing conference with the nuncio lasting over two hours. "Nothing," she wrote Eugénie, "has given me a better idea of hell than that interview, for hell, too, is no more nor less than a blind alley with no way out."[41]

Maximilian decided to act with independence on this vexatious problem. Subsequent to a consultation with his ministers he issued a decree two days after Christmas, 1864, confirming the nationalization of church property already in private hands and establishing freedom of worship for all creeds, all of which was the work of the republic under Juárez. It was then the nuncio's turn to become enraged and the people to be deeply aroused. The Liberals jubilantly declared that the principles of Juárez had triumphed. Conservatives drew farther away from the throne, and with the clergy Maximilian maintained at best an armed truce, at worst unrelenting hostility and intrigue. The nuncio returned to Rome and, throughout the remaining existence of the Maximilian empire, the church question was an unhealed wound. This and other disturbing factors gave little hope for the success of the monarchy imposed on Mexico.

41. Charlotte to Eugénie, December 27, 1864, in Corti, *Maximilian and Charlotte in Mexico*, II, 453.

14

French Humor,
Satire, and Censure
1864-1865

———————◄◆►———————

Victor Hugo, probably the most vitriolic enemy and critic of
Napoleon III, described the emperor's control of the press as "I
permit you to speak, but I require you to be silent."

Likewise, the emperor controlled the Corps Législatif so firmly
that endorsement of his policies was never in doubt. Frank if
futile opposition did, however, plague him. Criticism of imperial
policy in the Corps Législatif was led by "Les Cinq": Jules Favre,
Ernest Picard, Emile Ollivier, Adolphe Thiers, and Antoine
Berryer, all of whom were powerful orators and writers. After
the elections of 1863, their number grew from five to eleven;
after those of 1865, it was further augmented.[1]

As the years passed, more and more serious attention was paid
critics who described Napoleon III's Grand Design in America
as an indefensible drain on French resources and as a political
quagmire from which French prestige could not emerge unscathed. Loudest opposition came first from discussions about
appropriations.

For Napoleon III the decision to rescue or abandon his Grand

1. Sanford to Seward, July 28, 1865, and August 4, 1865, Henry Shelton San-
ford Papers, Sanford Memorial Library, Sanford, Fla., reel 99, box 60, folder 1;
Frank E. Lally, *French Opposition to the Mexican Policy of the Second Empire*
(Baltimore, 1931), pp. 147–50.

Design in America was imminent. With some 40,000 troops tied down in Mexico, 20,000 in Rome, and 80,000 in Algeria,[2] crises in Europe for France were growing more tense. Foremost among these dangers was the frightening expansion of Prussia and the growing restlessness of the French people.[3]

By the spring of 1865, apprehension over the Mexican situation was increasing. Despite Napoleon III's censorship, the French public was being gradually informed by critical reports of soldiers in Mexico in letters to their families. Into the reply to the emperor's *Adresse* of 1865, the opposition tried to insert a petition for peace in Mexico. With eloquence Jules Favre urged consideration of the importance of friendly relations with the United States. Said he, "It is difficult to imagine how deeply the American heart has been wounded by our expedition to Mexico." Picard questioned the rosy picture of Mexican prosperity painted by Charles Corta upon his return from Mexico. Corta had been sent there by Napoleon III to straighten out finances; he was described by Bazaine as the greatest spender in the Mexican army. Picard ridiculed the rumored peril from the United States at the close of the Civil War. The government, he declared, "keeps us under the Empire of illusions"[4] which it does not share. The plea to withdraw French troops from Mexico was ridiculed by Eugène Rouher, the minister of state. He asserted that, after the U.S. Civil War, France as an old ally and sponsor of the United States would experience "a day of joy and gladness," while in Mexico "we have accomplished a great undertaking."

From the beginning of the Second Empire to 1868, French newspapers existed by government permit; their editors and proprietors were subject to government approval, and their content to government scrutiny. "Excessive, dangerous or disagreeable" articles created an occasion for official warning; if repeated three times, these warnings were climaxed by a suspension of two months. However, censorship was usually inconsistent; it varied with the emperor's political mood. Semiofficial and official journals published articles under imperial inspiration to create desired opinions. The custom of giving and accepting compensation

2. Sanford to Seward, November 10, 1865, Sanford Papers, reel 99, box 60, folder 1. Sanford's estimate of 30,000 troops tied down in Mexico differed from Bazaine's 40,000. The latter figure is used throughout this study.
3. Sanford to Seward, July 25, 1865, ibid.
4. *Le Moniteur*, April 11, 1865.

for journalistic support was common. Despite this confusing and generally insecure situation, liberal newspapers dared to murmur against the Mexican expedition. These comments followed a variety of satire, discreet criticism, unanswered questions, and advice. Holding to the axiom that ridicule is often more damning than denunciation, the newspaper *Charivari* most consistently fed the fire of opposition. Its wit and malice were directed against the optimistic and often contradictory reports in journals bearing the intervention torch. Foremost of these torchbearers were *Le Constitutionnel, La France,* and *Le Mémorial diplomatique.* The most conspicuous target of the critics was *Le Mémorial diplomatique*; it had been commended by the emperor, and its editor, Debranz de Saldapenha, had received a citation.

In the spring of 1864, *Charivari* complimented *La France* on articles containing complete contradiction of fact. *La France* had assured the public that anarchy, revolution, violence, and disorders were a thing of the past in Mexico and that "one of the greatest undertakings of the century is accomplished." The same article volunteered the information that the new empire was "in a state of confusion and almost of war" and that the "mission of the Archduke is very difficult" because "revolutionary factions, although vanquished, are not disarmed." *Charivari* noted that these statements cancelled each other and that the reader was left to unscramble them "with that amiable light touch which, as . . . [*La France*] said the other day, is one of the piquant graces of French character."[5]

Charivari chanted "Let us colonize, let us colonize," when agitation for the so-called regeneration of Mexico was on all lips and advised those interested to seek information from *Le Constitutionnel.* The prospect was glowing: Sonora would become a second Paris; even the railroads were announcing excursions with "return in six months." Maximilian would give dowries to every daughter and protect the settlers by strong forces and artillery taken from Juárez which, from reports, must number at least 34,000 pieces. No one could say *Charivari* had not tried to help, but few colonists wanted to go; they were afraid of being killed—although this might have been a very good thing for Mexico, really, since their widows could then marry Mexicans and improve the breed.[6]

5. Clément Caraguel, "Bulletin," *Le Charivari*, April 16, 1864.
6. A. Bremond, "Patrons pour Sonora," ibid., July 2, 1865; A. Bremond, "Colonizons, Colonizons," ibid.

Much was said about Indian relations because of Maximilian's interest in the aborigines and because his father-in-law, King Leopold, had urged the use of them as an untapped bulwark of empire. *Charivari* regretted that, while the new rulers of Mexico studied Spanish in preparation for their imperial undertaking, they utterly neglected Aztec. Debranz de Saldepenha, who had gone to Mexico, was likewise handicapped by knowing Latin instead of Aztec, "a fatal lack in his literary education."[7] When the disastrous rupture between Maximilian and the papal nuncio occurred, *Charivari* consoled Paris by recalling that an agreement had just been reached with the Sonora Indians, "Life is only a series of compensations," the public was reminded, inasmuch as the Indians were a highly advanced people. Missionaries reported that the idea of the Immaculate Conception was to them "the most natural thing in the world," while one weary traveler was guided to an Indian camp by strains of "I am going to see Normandy again; it is the land where I was born."[8]

Elaborating on Napoleon III's proposal to restore proper prestige to the Latin people in the New World, the unctuous tongue of *Charivari* curled against its cheek in mock analysis: the Anglo-Saxons must yield to the Latins in America; already portents appeared. A friend from Pennsylvania wrote that Maximilian was the rage there and that Philadelphians were more and more ready to be absorbed and to adopt imperial institutions. Andrew Johnson would soon become Johnson I. Should the Mexican emperor invade the United States, he would be welcomed with open arms. There was final and absolute proof of this; had not Debranz de Saldapenha been invited to New York?[9]

Behind the fulminations of the small group of opponents in the Corps Législatif, the questioning and condoning efforts of the journals, and the ironic chuckles of *Charivari*, was a growing volume of opposition to Napoleon III. An active fomenter in this rising dissent was U.S. diplomat John Bigelow, former associate of William Cullen Bryant in the ownership of the *New York Post*. Bigelow had been in France since 1861, nominally as consul general but actually as propagandist for the Union. His ability, broad experience, and capacity to influence the press and secure the support of French liberals brought a measure of success. He had continuously denounced to Seward the aggressive

7. Clément Caraguel, "Bulletin," ibid., July 15, 1865.
8. Paul Girard, "Les Yaquis," ibid., July 1, 1865.
9. Paul Girard, "Latinisation de l'Amérique," ibid., September 24, 1865.

designs of France but when, in April 1865, he was appointed minister following the death of Dayton, the diplomacy of his position required modification of his expressed views.

Bigelow now urged improvement rather than deterioration of relations with France. "If we alienate France or even establish an unfriendly feeling here," he wrote, "it will poison all the official journalism of Europe toward us, notwithstanding the universally acknowledged folly of the Mexican enterprise."[10] Military intrigues by Grant, Sheridan, Blair, Wallace, and others did not persuade Bigelow that his compatriots were ready for another war. He assumed Americans were "too sagacious to transfer to their own shoulders the burden which is crushing France. . . . In a war not involving our national existence, like the one just closed, we should in my opinion be likely to fail. . . . Our government is based upon the will of the people who will not prosecute an expensive war for a cause which is not of vital interest to the great majority of them."[11]

Bigelow's position was based, in part, on discussions with men of influence whom he had been cultivating in Paris. For example, the Prussian ambassador told him Napoleon III probably intended withdrawing from Mexico as soon as he could do so "with decency and dignity," and that European powers were anxious for the United States not to "push him to the point of humiliation." With a weather eye out for his own country's interests, the Prussian maintained that, if the French emperor were humiliated, "he [the French emperor] would seek to preserve his prestige by troubling Europe."[12] While Bigelow did not sanction in any way a French-inspired empire in Mexico, he believed that time and emigration from the United States would solve the issue. "My theory is," he wrote Seward, "that we are to conquer Mexico but not by the sword."[13]

The U.S. minister to France then summarized his noncommittal position for Seward as follows: "My notion of my duty here . . . is substantially this: to say nothing and to do nothing which would require us . . . to compel France to leave Mex-

10. Bigelow to Seward, May 26, 1865, Dispatches, France, Dept. of State, NA, LVIII.

11. Bigelow to Seward, August 21, 1865, John Bigelow Papers, NYPL.

12. Bigelow to Seward, January 5, 1865, William Henry Seward Papers (private letters), Rush Rhees Library, University of Rochester, Rochester, N.Y., LVI.

13. Bigelow to Seward, February 14, 1865, Bigelow Papers, NYPL.

ico . . . and on the other hand to avoid saying or doing anything which would lead the Emperor to suppose we would not resort to force if ultimately necessary. . . ."[14] In approving Bigelow's revised stand on the Mexican question, Seward reiterated in detail the position of the United States. He then added that, with U.S. strife ended, the people would concern themselves with foreign affairs, chief among them, the problem of France in Mexico. Along the Rio Grande were military forces of both nations that created "a tendency, which both of them may well regret, to produce irritation and annoyance."[15] The moment for a consideration of that question was approaching.

Like his uncle, Napoleon III lent a sensitive ear to the utterances of the mass of provincial Frenchmen. He sampled the minds of his subjects through reports of local prefects, especially the *Procureurs Généraux*. These officials were legal agents of the Ministry of Justice in the twenty-eight districts of imperial courts. Their reports, required on the first day of each month and covering "an exact description of the moral and political situation," were confidential and therefore untainted by any yearning for public effect.[16]

From these sources came cumulative evidence of anxiety throughout France over the Mexican question and a genuine longing for the withdrawal of troops as soon as it could be done with honor. Delays in Forey's campaigning exasperated Frenchmen; his victories were praised largely in the hope that the expedition might be drawn nearer to a close. "The public mind wishes, expects a victory; it regrets the enterprise, would be ashamed of its abandonment, and will support its prolongation with impatience," stated one report early in 1863.[17] Similarly, the new Mexican empire was approved because it, too, seemed to bring the emperor's scheme closer to realization. When only a token return of troops was made in the fall of 1864, when the cost of the undertaking continued to rise, and when letters from sons, relatives, or friends in Mexico described confusion and uncertainty, the French people grew more restless. Many were dis-

14. Bigelow to Seward, August 21, 1865, in John Bigelow, *Retrospections of an Active Life*, 5 vols. (New York, 1909–13), III, 151–56.

15. Seward to Bigelow, September 6, 1865, Instructions, France, Dept. of State, NA, XVII.

16. Lynn M. Case, ed., *French Opinion on the United States and Mexico, 1860–1867* (New York, 1936), pt. XIV. This report was from Dijon.

17. Ibid., p. 461.

appointed that the emperor of Mexico was not French instead of an Austrian who was "accustomed to astonish the world by his ingratitude."[18] When the U.S. Civil War ended, many feared a change in U.S. policy. Mexico seemed the last place French troops ought to be held in stalemate at a time of growing Prussian militarism. Adversaries of Napoleon III capitalized on the situation for one of the most vulnerable aspects of the general outlook was the maintenance of French armies in distant lands.[19]

Skepticism over the Mexican imbroglio entered the imperial household although it is difficult to determine how candidly it was expressed. In the judgment of British ambassador Lord Cowley, Napoleon III was always a mystery to his associates. "He cannot be said to have any settled policy and his ministers are never sure whether they rightly or not interpret his feelings and intentions. Hence, they themselves are in constant hesitation and perplexity. . . ."[20] A system of government such as that of the Second Empire was weighted in favor of the emperor's will; obviously, those who sought to retain his favor must recognize that reality. Under these conditions it is impossible to determine whether Minister of Finance Fould, whose disapprobation of the Mexican expedition was made clear to Bigelow, was equally candid to the emperor.[21] Although Eugène Rouher supported the official policy toward Mexico before the Corps Législatif, he condemned it to his colleagues. The minister of war, Randon, and Count Fleury, intimates of the imperial family, testified in their memoirs that, from the start, they were dubious of the outcome of the affair in Mexico.[22]

Whatever the degree of the emperor's despair over events in Mexico, he continued in 1865 to maintain an appearance of confidence. The official press praised the stability Maximilian had instituted in Mexico. In sharper contradiction of actual conditions was the argument of the financier Corta in behalf of a second Mexican loan before the Corps Législatif on April 10, 1865. In Mexico, Corta had sensed growing apprehension. From

18. Report of A. G. Sonef, Nancy, October 24, 1863, ibid., p. 252.
19. Report of P. G. Mourier, Chambray, June 3, 1865, ibid., p. 379.
20. Cowley to Stanley, Confidential, January 29, 1867, BFO 27/1662, France.
21. Bigelow to Seward, May 26, 1865, Dispatches, France, Dept. of State, NA, LVIII.
22. Emile F. Fleury, *Souvenirs du général Fleury*, 2 vols. (Paris, 1897–98), II, 225; Jacques Randon, *Mémoires du maréchal Randon*, 2d ed., 2 vols. (Paris, 1875–77), pp. 57–62, 81–84.

the Empress Charlotte he had learned of her own discourage-
ments and fears. Yet he informed the Corps Législatif that white
Mexicans considered Maximilian the "Angel of Safety of Mexico," and Indians revered him as "their fair God." After listening
for months to complaints about the poor quality of Maximilian's
ministers, Corta characterized them as "the most capable, patriotic and devoted in all the parties, in all the classes, without
precedent."[23]

Despite the glossy window dressing fabricated by his hench-
men, Napoleon III knew the truth and could no longer hide
behind unfounded optimism. No report from Mexico was reassuring. Bazaine continued to praise the French army and deplore
the imperial Mexican administration, a feat in contradiction
which led Randon to ponder whether the military and political
sections of the general's bimonthly reports had been penned by
the same person. Praise of the French army was not wholly cred-
ible. Because of Napoleon III's unconventional habit of encouraging comments from anyone and everyone, he received
communications from officers, soldiers, and camp followers whose
tone toward Bazaine was definitely not complimentary. Bazaine
had a ready explanation; he maintained that those who complained never really understood Mexico. "In France, one always
has illusions about Mexico," he wrote, "believing that it will be
regenerated by a wave of a wand, after which the thing created
can be left to itself."[24]

More serious than the grievances of malcontents was the widen-
ing lack of sympathy between Maximilian and Bazaine. Although
no open break had occurred, the Mexican sovereign had voiced
his dissatisfaction with Bazaine to Napoleon III, and General
Félix Douay's visit home in the spring of 1865 brought criticism
of Bazaine before the Ministry of War and the Tuileries.[25] Bazaine charged that "the feeble side of the situation comes from
the direction taken by the Sovereign."[26] Maximilian blamed
Bazaine for the still unpacified state of the country despite in-
ordinately large military expenditures; he made no attempt to
hide his wish for a change in command.

23. "Discours de M. Corta," *Le Moniteur*, April 11, 1865.
24. Bazaine to Randon, July 27, 1865, AMG, 1865.
25. Egon Caesar Corti, *Maximilian and Charlotte in Mexico*, trans. Catherine A. Phillips, 2 vols. (New York, 1928), II, 485, 519 ff.
26. Bazaine to Randon, July 10, 1865, AMG, 1865.

Alphonse Dano, wisest of the French ministers Napoleon III had sent to Mexico, enlightened him on the lack of progress within the Mexican Empire. In the middle of 1865, he reported continued disaffection toward Maximilian; indeed, so serious was it that Bazaine was reluctant to arm Mexicans for fear of their going over to Juárez. The Mexican press dared to question the right of the empire to exist; some journals urged the calling of a constitutional assembly and demanded the withdrawal of French forces. Others, more prudent, reprinted extracts from the U.S. press eulogizing Juárez and condemning Maximilian. Dano asserted that three-fourths of the trouble was due to leniency. "It is time," he wrote Paris, "the Emperor [Maximilian] changed tactics if he does not want to make his task and ours impossible." He recommended that the Quai d'Orsay give Maximilian advice "so firm that he will have to follow it."[27]

A few weeks later, Dano complained that the chief weakness of Maximilian's government seemed to be procrastination. This Maximilian realized, but he was not strong enough to stop it. Laws and decrees were announced almost daily but not carried out.[28] By September 1865, the financial situation could be ignored no longer. Expenses of state had risen to 40,000,000 pesos while receipts lagged far behind at only 17,000,000. Publicly, Dano discouraged any hope of further assistance but remarked privately that "France might just as well become resigned to new sacrifices."[29]

Unbiased observers were as pessimistic as were the French. Sir Peter Campbell Scarlett arrived in Mexico City February 4, 1865, to preside over the British Legation. Cordial relations sprang up at once between the Briton and Maximilian, but enthusiasm for Mexican affairs was lacking in Scarlett's dispatches. His impression was that Maximilian often allowed himself to be misled by some narrowminded Mexican leaders, that the mercantile classes gave lukewarm support to the new dynasty and that the church party was disappointed and unruly.[30] Some six months later the British minister summed up the situation: "There is no doubt that the state of the Empire, generally depending on the protection of a very numerically inadequate

27. Dano to Drouyn de Lhuys, July 10, 1865, CP, Mexique, LXIV.
28. Dano to Drouyn de Lhuys, July 29, 1865, ibid.
29. Dano to Drouyn de Lhuys, September 28, 1865, ibid.
30. Scarlett to Russell, April 22 and April 28, 1865, BFO 50/386.

French army, ought to give real cause for apprehension in Europe and in no way justifies the optimistic opinions prevailing two months ago in London and Paris. . . ."[31] The much propagandized economic regeneration had reached a stalemate. Scarlett, under no incentive to deceive either himself or his superiors, expressed concern over it: "I need hardly speak of the want of commercial confidence in every direction and the stagnation of trade which prevails throughout Mexico, a natural result of this state of affairs."[32]

When time relentlessly forced Napoleon III to act, Bigelow inadvertently provided an opening for a turn of affairs early in October 1865. During a quiet, unofficial chat between Bigelow and Drouyn de Lhuys, the French minister admitted the desire of France to leave Mexico provided she could settle her debts and protect her prestige. Completely without authorization, Bigelow volunteered the comment that, if French troops were removed and the Mexican people supported the Maximilian empire, the United States might have to recognize it. Both diplomats speculated on possibilities during the ensuing conversation. Bigelow was firm in his stand that there could be no recognition of Maximilian without withdrawal of French troops; Drouyn de Lhuys proposed simultaneous recognition and withdrawal of troops.[33]

Following this significant interview, which Bigelow reported to Seward, Napoleon III set the wheels of his diplomatic machinery in motion by dispatching a confidential communication to Montholon, now serving as minister to Washington. After hinting on several occasions at withdrawing her troops from Mexico, France was now ready to negotiate on that subject with Washington. Montholon was told, "What we want from the United States is assurance that they will not harm the new Mexican Government." The best assurance would be in the form of recognition of the Mexican Empire; that would enable France to leave. If the United States would accept this arrangement, France would fix a date for the departure of her troops.[34]

The importance attached by the French to this negotiation is shown by a second letter to Montholon written on the same day

31. Scarlett to Russell, August 28, 1865, BFO 50/387.
32. Scarlett to Russell, July 21, 1865, ibid.
33. Bigelow to Seward, October 19, 1865, Private, John Bigelow Papers, NYPL.
34. Drouyn de Lhuys to Montholon, October 18, 1865, Confidential, CP, Etats-Unis, CXXXV.

as the first dispatch, presumably after Drouyn de Lhuys had had a second consultation with Napoleon III. The emperor wanted the dispatch to receive Montholon's earliest and undivided attention. The new instructions had been inspired, Montholon was informed, by an opening given by Bigelow a few days previously, but this information was not to be passed on to Seward.[35] Why the Quai d'Orsay chose to transfer the locale of its negotiations from Paris to Washington was not explained, but one reason immediately comes to mind. A clumsy statement attributed to Bigelow in the Corps Législatif, that the United States would not go to war over Mexico's form of government had already lessened his usefulness.[36] Direct interchange with the State Department placed the momentous bargaining on a firmer foundation.

Meanwhile, the attention of Napoleon III and Maximilian had been concentrated on such matters as a project for developing mines in Sonora in northwest Mexico, the organization of Spanish American republics against European intervention, attracting French immigrants to Mexico, combatting secret Yankee intrigues against monarchy, the settlement of Confederates below the Rio Grande, General Grant's military plot against the French, and Maximilian's failure to win recognition from Washington.

35. Drouyn de Lhuys to Montholon, second dispatch of same date, ibid.

36. Endeavoring to temper the hot winds of wrath from America, Bigelow had unwisely remarked to the French foreign minister that inasmuch as monarchy had been established in Mexico, the American people wanted it tested. He undiplomatically added that republican institutions had so far been singularly unsuccessful in Latin America. Rouher quoted Bigelow in the Corps Législatif as having given assurances that the United States would not go to war over the form of Mexico's government. Public opinion in the United States stormed its protest. For Secretary Seward's mild but straight-to-the-point rebuke see Seward to Bigelow, June 30, 1865, Instructions, France, Dept. of State, NA, XVII. Further details are found in the entry for August 13, 1865, Bigelow Papers, NYPL.

15

Back Door of the Confederacy
The Rio Grande
1861–1865

When the United States was divided, temporarily, the strife-torn Rio Grande became internationally strategic. Mexico was the only foreign nation adjoining the Confederacy; therefore, the Union blockade was inoperative on its border. With its blockade of the 3,500-mile maritime coast of the Confederacy, the Union hoped to defeat the South by cutting off the sale of its basic exchange commodity, cotton, on which the economic life of England, France, and republican Mexico was in part dependent. Consequently, the Union and the Confederacy became critically involved in those areas in Texas and in Mexico surrounding the Rio Grande. The Texas side of the Rio Grande, especially Brownsville, became the Back Door of the Confederacy. Directly across the Rio Grande from Brownsville was the Mexican custom house of Matamoros. It was the most critical gap in the U.S. blockade of the Confederacy.[1]

The population of this small town rocketed to approximately 50,000. Its fantastic growth provoked a startling statement by an observer: "Matamoros is to the rebellion west of the Mississippi what New York is to the United States—its great commercial and financial center, feeding and clothing the rebellion, arming and equipping, furnishing it materials of war and a specie basis of

1. Frank L. Owsley, *King Cotton Diplomacy* (Chicago, 1959), p. 119.

circulation that has almost displaced Confederate paper. . . ."[2]

The large number of speculators and hangers-on, drawn to Matamoros, taxed its housing and storage capacity and created boom conditions. Gambling houses, brothels, and saloons flourished and an English language newspaper, the *Matamoros Morning Call*, was established.[3] Bagdad, a shanty village at the mouth of the Rio Grande, grew to a full-fledged town. Through the Back Door of the Confederacy passed the rapidly decreasing supply of cotton to the mills of Europe; into the Back Door of the Confederacy went munitions and supplies. This two-way international trade was enthusiastically promoted by Mexicans for the critically needed export and import duties they received.

Throughout four years cotton was transported to the Rio Grande by wagon trains from East Texas and as far away as Louisiana, Arkansas, Indian Territory (Oklahoma), and Missouri.[4] From Brownsville the cotton was freighted across the river, through the Mexican port of Matamoros and then about thirty miles to the Gulf of Mexico. A treacherous bar at the mouth of the Rio Grande forced ocean-going ships to anchor several miles out in the gulf to unload and load their cargoes. In one period of nineteen months at least 449 of these freighters, mainly English, Spanish, German, Danish, and Russian, were unloaded and loaded.[5] A Confederate agent counted eighty-two vessels in March 1863.[6] The *Washington National Republican* reported on February 27, 1864, that from sixty to eighty ships were continuously loading and unloading. Their destinations were the ports of Europe and even those of New England.

Officers of blockading vessels were incensed by the purchase of Confederate cotton by Northerners; they were outraged particularly by the number of ships from New York and other Eastern ports engaged illicitly in this traffic. The wealth of Senator William Sprague, cotton manufacturer of Rhode Island and

2. Robert W. Delaney, "Matamoros, Port for Texas during the Civil War," *SHQ*, LVIII (April 1955), 473.

3. Ibid., pp. 473, 474.

4. Tom Lea, *The King Ranch*, 2 vols. (Boston, 1957), I, 184; Ludwell H. Johnson, *Red River Campaign: Politics and Cotton in the Civil War* (Baltimore, 1958), pp. 47, 64; *ORA*, ser. I, vol. XXII, pp. 952, 953; vol. XXXIV, pt. 4, pp. 638, 639; vol. LIII, pp. 971–80, 1036–39; Ronnie C. Tyler, "Cotton on the Border, 1861–1865," *SHQ*, LXXIII, no. 4 (April 1970), 456–77.

5. Notes sur Tamaulipas, M et D, Mexique, X.

6. Fitzpatrick to Benjamin, March 12, 1863, Pickett Papers, LC.

THE STRATEGIC RIO GRANDE AND THE UNION BLOCKADE

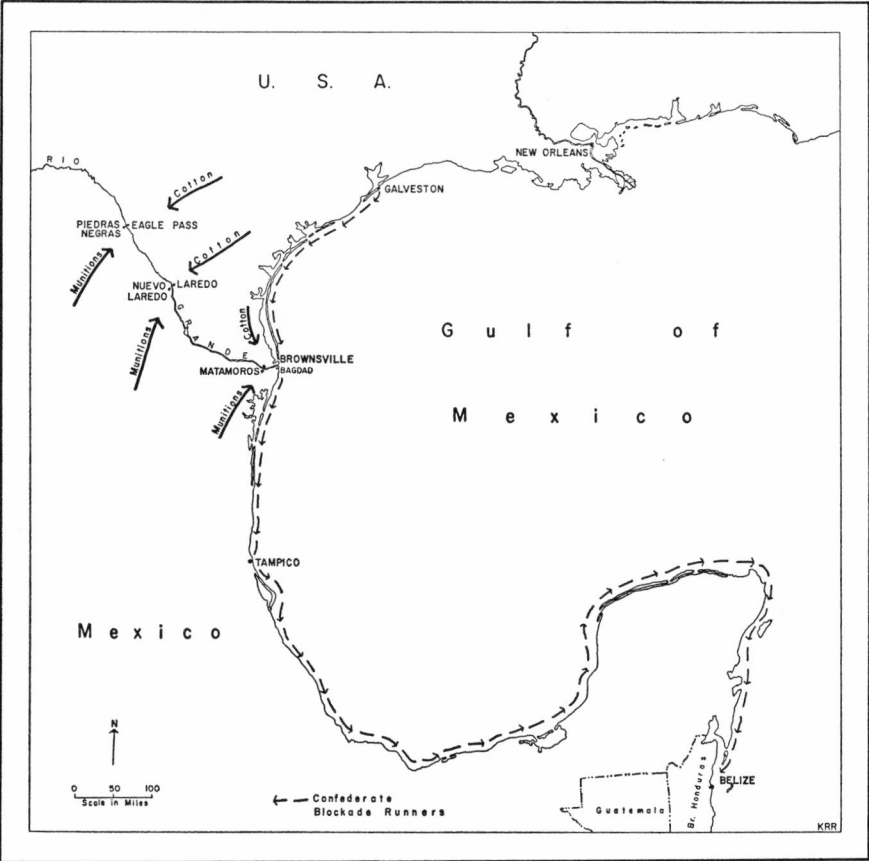

son-in-law of the future Chief Justice Salmon P. Chase, was no-
toriously increased through the Matamoros trade.[7] One ship
which profited from this cotton trade brought to a New York
firm more money than all its other ships. The admiral commanding the east gulf blockading squadron warned, "Unless this trade
can be restricted . . . the object of blockading our Southern coast
must necessarily, in a great measure, be frustrated."[8] Rio Grande
exports and imports increased so heavily that steamship lines

7. Thomas G. Belden and Marva R. Belden, *So Fell the Angels* (Boston, 1956),
pp. 56–62, 99–102, 141–49, 159–60, 227–28, 250–58.
8. Bailey to Welles, March 13, 1863, *ORN*, ser. I, vol. XVII, p. 401.

were operated from Matamoros to London and Havana, and in
1864, two steamers were added to the run to New Orleans in
which both sailing vessels and sidewheelers were engaged.[9]

Some 1,400 miles southeast of Matamoros, Belize, the capital
of British Honduras, was extensively involved in the two-way
Confederate trade. No merchants in the Caribbean were more
experienced than were those of this British port nearest Matamoros. They were highly successful in using small shallow-draft
vessels operating near the coast to avoid men-of-war and storms.
Consequently, they could choose not only Matamoros as their
destination but could proceed up the Texas coast.[10]

Access to the Confederacy by way of the Rio Grande and its
free and common use were guaranteed by a treaty. The channel
of the river meandered close to the southern bank and occasionally touched that on the north. Interruption of trade by either
the United States or Mexico without the consent of the other
was forbidden, even for the purpose of improving navigation.[11]

As the Union blockade of Southern ports grew in effectiveness
in 1862, the Back Door of the Confederacy, as the one unblock-
aded entrance to and exit from the South, assumed increased
importance.

The Union blockader *Portsmouth* was ordered to capture all
vessels anchoring in Texas waters near the Mexican boundary;
she patrolled the coast from Corpus Christi, Texas, to the mouth
of the Rio Grande. Enforcement of this order led to friction and
frustration over determining the boundary line. The captain of
the *Portsmouth* encountered another problem as winds and tides
caused vessels anchored in Mexican waters to drift to waters patrolled by the Union. This drifting provided a ready explanation
for those vessels which, discovering that unloading was easier and
safer in U.S. waters, anchored on the north side of the boundary
in the hope of escaping detection. A Union consul in Mexico
near the mouth of the Rio Grande was aroused over the failure
of the *Portsmouth* and her successors to maintain patrol at the

    9. Delaney, "Matamoros," pp. 473–87.
    10. Wayne M. Clegern, *British Honduras: Colonial Dead End, 1859–1900*
(Baton Rouge, 1967), p. 21.
    11. William M. Malloy, comp., *Treaties . . . Between the United States of
America and Other Powers, 1776–1909*, 3 vols. (Washington, D.C., 1910–23), I,
1107–21; Hunter Miller, comp., *Treaties of the United States of America*, 7 vols.
(Washington, D.C., 1896–1900), V, 207 ff.

mouth of the river; he charged that for weeks on end there was no naval surveillance whatever.[12]

Another loophole in the Union blockade was the thriving trade carried on by small Confederate blockade runners from Corpus Christi to Tampico, Mexico, where unloading of cotton to ocean-going vessels took place. The Union consul at that Mexican port reported to Washington that Tampico was more a Confederate colony than "an honorable and disinterested neighbor and whenever one of those cotton loaded vessels cast anchor off this city, all hearts are rejoiced excepting that of the writer hereof. . . . Aided . . . by the authorities they enjoy privileges of the most liberal and partial character.

"In the early part of this month this place was thronged with the agents of blockade runners who bought up all the small vessels they could find here, loaded them, and dispatched them for Texas."

The consul also informed Washington that Confederates had bought up all the percussion caps, powder, and firearms they could find in this city.[13]

The British *Phaeton* and the French *Bertholet*, men-of-war, also moved into the disputed waters off the mouth of the Rio Grande to protect cotton cargo ships operated by their nationals. The French captain discovered that Union blockaders were vague on points of international law and that books on the subject did not answer the multiplicity of questions raised. With the rapid increase of import and export duties through the Mexican custom house across the Rio Grande from Brownsville, Matamoros prospered. Inasmuch as the French occupied Veracruz and Tampico, Matamoros acquired additional importance as the only gulf port open to trade for the republicans in Mexico.

Critically involved were the outcome of the U.S. Civil War, the struggle between republican and imperialist Mexico, and the economic fortunes of thousands of individuals. In and about Matamoros lawlessness prevailed. Confederates, pro-Union refugees, and bandits raided back and forth across the Rio Grande. Filibustering forays occurred and occasionally military skirmishes

12. Pierce to Seward, March 26, 1863, Consular Reports, Matamoros, 1858–64, Dept. of State, NA.

13. Chase to Seward, September 26 and December 25, 1864, Consular Reports, Tampico, ibid., VII.

broke out. There were hazardous gambles of shrewd speculators and insidious plots of seasoned conspirators. Naval and army officers spun their webs, hatched their schemes, and pursued their prey.

One cause of border friction was the escape of Unionists from Texas. The Union consul at Matamoros wrote Seward, "My office is constantly thronged with refugees from Texas."[14] They fell into four categories: Union soldiers stationed in Texas at the time of the secession, deserters from the Texas militia, escapees from Confederate service, and foreigners. Since Texas had no notion of giving up her recalcitrant sons without a struggle, the commander at Brownsville offered to exchange Mexican for Texan refugees. Many Unionists escaping from Texas found refuge on blockading vessels at the mouth of the Rio Grande.

Occasionally military control of each bank of the Rio Grande changed. Seldom was the area free from chaotic lawlessness. In 1861 southeast Texas was held by the Confederates.

Northeast Mexico bordering the Rio Grande and along the Gulf of Mexico was controlled by pro-Confederate Mexicans. Virtual dictator of this section was Santiago Vidaurre, governor of the states of Nuevo León and Coahuila, whose power extended into Tamaulipas, the gulf state in which Matamoros was located. Vidaurre had joined the Liberals in overthrowing the dictator Santa Anna in 1855, and when the interests of his own hegemony in northeast Mexico did not conflict with those of the national government, he supported President Juárez.

A new chapter in Vidaurre's life began early in June 1861, when at the governor's palace in Monterrey he received José Quintero, Richmond's able diplomatic representative who controlled the Back Door of the Confederacy.

The thirty-two-year-old Quintero was remarkably equipped for his mission. Son of a Cuban father and an English mother, he had been sent from Havana to Harvard. After his return he dabbled in Cuban insurrections against Spain for which he was condemned to death. Escaping to New Orleans, he acquired U.S. citizenship, and became an editor of bilingual newspapers in New York and Texas. Quintero's welcome to the city of Monterrey in the state of Nuevo León was enhanced by Vidaurre's

---

14. Pierce to Seward, March 26, 1863, Consular Reports, Matamoros, 1858–64, Dept. of State, NA.

gratitude for personal services Quintero had rendered him at an earlier time in Texas.[15]

Able, experienced, and sagacious, Vidaurre foresaw great potential wealth for his northeast Mexico from the thriving trade with the Confederacy. His son-in-law, Peter Milmo, a member of the leading merchandising and banking concern, took care that the family fortunes did not suffer. Vidaurre pledged Quintero the utmost economic cooperation; further, he offered to the Confederacy a political alliance with northeast Mexico which, as the Republic of Sierra Madre, he was ambitious to head. Vidaurre would need both moral and military support from the Southern government to establish a separate Mexican republic. Jefferson Davis delayed consideration of an alliance as "imprudent and impolitic . . . at present."[16]

Vidaurre aided Quintero vigorously in channeling through Matamoros war supplies from Europe, and from northeast Mexico lead, copper, saltpeter, gunpowder, and textiles. So briskly did the caravans of supplies move across the border that within one year Quintero was able to report to Richmond that "Texas is well-supplied with ammunition."[17]

Union Minister Corwin was unable to undermine Quintero's successful operation because of the distance between his legation and the Rio Grande.[18]

Traffic on the Rio Grande was complicated by international rivalries; for instance, the Union exerted efforts to prevent supplies from reaching the Confederacy through Matamoros and favored the supply lines to Juárez. The French were determined to close Juárez's supply sources without crippling Confederate interests or, in general, dislocating commerce. Merchants who capitalized on this complicated situation sought the maximum protection for their swollen profits.

Export of cotton and import of ammunition through the Back

15. Walter Prescott Webb, ed., *Handbook of Texas*, 2 vols. (Austin, 1952), II, 424.

16. Browne to Quintero, September 3, 1861, with enclosure, James D. Richardson, comp., *A Compilation of Messages and Papers of the Confederacy Including the Diplomatic Correspondence, 1861–1865*, 2 vols. (Nashville, 1906), II, 77–81.

17. Quintero to Benjamin, August 14, 1862, ibid. See also William Diamond, "Imports of the Confederate Government from Europe and Mexico," *JSH*, VI (February–November 1940), 497–503.

18. Seward to Corwin, June 24, 1861, Instructions, Mexico, Dept. of State, NA, XVII.

Door of the Confederacy were temporarily halted. Early in November 1863, Nathaniel P. Banks, one of Seward's favorite generals, landed almost 7,000 troops from twenty-six transports at Point Isabel[19] a few miles north of the mouth of the Rio Grande and marched them seventeen miles west to Brownsville. The Union invaders hoped (1) to stop the Confederate trade across the Rio Grande, (2) to occupy Texas, and (3) to break up Confederate relations with northeast Mexico.

Union occupation of Brownsville only temporarily interrupted the export of cotton and the import of war materials. Confederate diplomat Quintero merely rerouted the two-way traffic to crossings he controlled west of Brownsville—Laredo and Eagle Pass. This readjustment of routes was expensive and time-consuming. The change was possible only because the intricacies of steamboat traffic on the Rio Grande had been mastered by several pilots who arrived there at the opening of the war between the United States and Mexico thirty-four years earlier. Guiding genius of these pilots was Captain Richard King, whose spectacular success was destined to become one of the sagas of North America. He operated primarily from his ranch 125 miles north of Brownsville. His co-workers throughout south Texas, particularly in the area of the King Ranch, were seasoned and resourceful pioneers including such Texas Rangers as Colonel John S. Ford.[20]

Strong-man Vidaurre cooperated with the Confederacy by collecting import and export duties at hastily arranged custom houses at Nuevo Laredo and Piedras Negras. That the trade through the Back Door of the Confederacy was startlingly brisk even when manipulated across the Rio Grande west of Brownsville is proved by the enormous duties collected by Vidaurre. For example, at Piedras Negras, opposite Eagle Pass, the collection was over $50,000 a month over a period of three years and some $125,000 a month at several other crossings.[21] By these circuitous routes and methods Confederate cotton nominally became Mexican and thus evaded the Union blockade. However, the sword of Damocles was descending nearer the head of Vidaurre.

President Juárez occupied Monterrey for a short time in Feb-

19. Lea, *King Ranch*, p. 205.
20. Ibid., p. 213.
21. Owsley, *King Cotton Diplomacy*, p. 128.

ruary 1863, while he took the measure of Vidaurre. Convinced that no terms could be made with the unpredictable governor, Juárez in the following April advanced on Monterrey with all the forces he could muster. Vidaurre tried unsuccessfully to rally public support. Aware of brewing discord, agents of the French appeared in Monterrey and urged Vidaurre to abandon the Liberals.[22] At length, on March 24, 1864, Vidaurre offered to retire if all action against him would be dropped. President Juárez remained inflexible; he warned that no conditions were admissible when the independence of Mexico was at stake. Juárez condemned Vidaurre as a traitor who had defied the law and communicated with the invader.[23] Defeated in the test of strength, Vidaurre fled to Texas. Later he accepted service under Maximilian, and when the empire collapsed, he was executed.

Under these erupting conditions—without the support of dictator Vidaurre and with General Banks now commanding Union troops at Brownsville—an apprehensive Quintero interviewed President Juárez. He was amazed and relieved that Juárez showed no inclination to turn over high placed Confederates to General Banks or to cut off Confederate trade. A resident of Brownsville testified years afterwards that complete neutrality was maintained at Matamoros under Juárez. Goods went through the riverport freely and agents from many places, even from New York and New England, came to make purchases. The Mexicans were indifferent to Yankees and Confederates; they partied and traded with both.[24]

The attempted interference with Confederate cotton trade by Banks and his troops lasted only eight months. Little had been accomplished by invading Texas; moreover, the danger of developing incidents with the French across the river was too acute in the judgment of Seward. In July 1864, General Banks withdrew from the Rio Grande area after stationing a small number of troops on the Gulf at Point Isabel.[25] Traffic in cotton and war supplies was immediately resumed through the main route between Brownsville and Matamoros.

22. Quintero to Benjamin, November 4, 1863, Pickett Papers, LC.
23. Santiago Roel, ed., *Correspondencia particular de Santiago Vidaurre* (Monterrey, n.d.), pp. 252, 253.
24. Testimony of Francis Latham, U.S. Congress, Senate, Joint Select Committee on Retrenchment, 41st Cong., 2d sess., Reports No. 166.
25. Paul Horgan, *Great River: The Rio Grande in North American History* (New York, 1968), II, 838.

While the Union troops were in the process of evacuation, a French army of 5,000 landed at Bagdad at the mouth of the Rio Grande in an attempt to conquer Matamoros. They were turned back by a force of 3,000 commanded by the bandit-political leader, Juan Nepomuceno Cortina, recognized temporarily by Juárez as the governor of Tamaulipas. Soon Cortina embarked elsewhere upon adventures more to his liking, such as cattle rustling.[26]

French control of northeast Mexico was finally established early in the fall of 1864, under Maximilian's able Indian General Tomás Mejía, accompanied by 2,000 troops. Maximilian had then been ruling in Mexico City since June of that year.

A Union commercial agent at Matamoros reported that trade continued unabated but that few of the traders were from the North. The town was filled with Confederates and their friends, he declared; "anyone claiming kindred with Uncle Sam is looked upon with disfavor."[27]

The phenomenal Richard King, who made a fortune out of grim conditions prevailing near the Rio Grande, was an adopted Confederate. The son of Irish immigrants, he was born in New York City in 1824. At the age of nine he was apprenticed to a jeweler. After two years of household drudgery, including rocking a cradle, he revolted. Seeking release as well as adventure, he had mixed with the roustabouts of the New York waterfront and heard how to become a stowaway. When at the age of eleven he was discovered in the hold of a ship headed south out of New York, he faced the hard-eyed, tough-handed skipper. Fortunately for this waif, the captain was favorably impressed by his personality and promise and gave him an opportunity as a cabin boy. He possessed high spirit; he was eager to venture, anxious to learn.

By the time King was eighteen, he had acquired much information and experience of the roughest nature through service on Mobile Bay steamers. One of the steamboat captains he served as cabin boy taught him to read and provided him with eight months of schooling in Connecticut.

King's next preparation for life was on a ship in the Seminole Indian War in Florida. After that his experience was broadened

26. Ibid., II, 838, 839.
27. Wood to Seward, September 26 and December 25, 1864, Consular Reports, Tampico, Dept. of State, NA, VII.

on steamboats along the Apalachicola and Chattahoochee rivers. Powerful physically and with penetrating eyes, his was a commanding and handsome presence. By 1847, King had become a remarkably experienced pilot. In that year he arrived at the mouth of the Rio Grande to join his best friend, pilot Mifflin Kenedy, and to embark upon numerous new adventures.

The King and Kenedy friendship soon developed into a partnership as they operated freight steamers under General Zachary Taylor. Where others failed, King, Kenedy, and their co-pilots became masters of the tortuous channels and viciously unpredictable currents of the Rio Grande. Meanwhile, King had begun the development of a unique livestock ranch 125 miles north of the river. In its establishment King was shrewd enough to rely on the best legal brains available. He was also fortunate in following the general advice and engineering skills of Lieutenant Colonel Robert E. Lee. In the middle 1850s Lee spent almost two leisurely years in the Rio Grande area conducting courts-martial. This long stay gave him an opportunity to make friends and among them was the developer of the King Ranch.

By 1861, when another war brought unprecedented riches to the Rio Grande, King and his partners had secured a monopoly of the steamboat trade. King's chief partner, Kenedy, was stationed at Brownsville, Back Door of the Confederacy. Another partner was at Matamoros; a third went to the Texas capital for political maneuvering; and King made his headquarters at the Santa Gertrudis Ranch. By the end of the U.S. Civil War, King and his partner, Kenedy, a devout Quaker, had so successfully met the ever-recurring crises involved in operating a business, despite war, banditry, thievery, and murder that they and several colleagues had amassed fortunes and a reputation for honesty and fair dealing startling under such conditions.

After Appomattox, King and his associates acquired pardons from the president and under entirely different Reconstruction conditions continued their success in the operation of steamers on the Rio Grande. Meanwhile King had acquired large holdings of land and developed huge herds of cattle.

In the post-Civil War period cattle drives to the Midwest were expanding, the North American continent was being spanned by a railroad, and great meat-packing plants were being built in Chicago and other population centers. The King Ranch at this time was a leader in the improvement of the quality of herds, in development of grasses, and in making adequate water by artesian wells available. Evidence that King made a fortune during the U.S. Civil War is provided by the expenditure of at least $50,000 in fencing a part of his Texas domain and his $2,000,000 loss to rustlers who drove his stock into Mexico during the last years of the French occupation of that country.[28]

No less startling was the success of Confederate diplomatic agent Quintero. General Mejía at Matamoros and French and imperial Mexican officials in the region gave them assurances they would do everything possible to aid the Confederacy. "In fact," reported Quintero, "we have never before been in such a favorable condition as we are at present in regard to our intercourse with Mexico."[29]

In four years Quintero had masterminded relations with three succeeding governments on the south bank of the Rio Grande in Mexico: (1) the caudillo Vidaurre, (2) republican President Juárez, and (3) officials of Maximilian. These Confederate successes had so magnified the resentment of General Grant and other high Union officials that their wrath against the Confederates and the French was intensified in efforts to defeat the Confederacy and to remove the French from Mexico.

28. Lea, King Ranch, I, 342–71; II, 532–75; 576–604; 647–97; 698–706.
29. Quintero to Kirby-Smith, October 21, 1864, Pickett Papers, LC.

16

The "Duke" from Mississippi
1862–1865

———————◆▶———————

Just before the close of the U.S. Civil War Napoleon III worked out a mining scheme for northwest Mexico. It was originated by Dr. William M. Gwin, who had represented the gold-rich state of California in the U.S. Senate. Gwin claimed that Mexico was potentially as rich in minerals as was California. When, early in 1864, the Marquis de Montholon succeeded Count Dubois de Saligny as French minister to Mexico, mining became his chief project.[1]

Although he had completed training at Transylvania University for the practice of medicine, Gwin decided not to become a physician. Instead he prepared himself for the practice of law. In Mississippi his success both at the bar and in politics gained him a seat in Congress. Later he moved to California, and when the U.S. Civil War broke out, Senator Gwin was jailed on suspicion of disloyalty to the Union. Released because of lack of evidence,[2] he sailed for France where he outlined a plan to Napoleon III for exploiting the minerals in northwest Mexico. Gwin's personality and striking appearance fascinated Napoleon III. He was tall and squarely built with broad shoulders; his features were rough as if hewn out of a block with an ax; his skin was ruddy and his heavy white hair was brushed back from his brows. He warned the French emperor that "if the northern boundary of Mexico

---

1. Montholon to Drouyn de Lhuys, July 28, 1864, CP, Mexique, LXII.
2. Case of Gwin, Benham, and Brent, *ORA*, ser. II, vol. 2, pp. 1009–30.

is left in its present defenseless condition" it would be overrun by soldiers of the Union army upon their discharge. His remedy was to settle Confederate refugees and other Southerners there; they would be "loyal citizens of Mexico, loyal to its Emperor and bulwarks to his throne."[3]

The always available and ever-willing Mexican exile, Gutiérrez de Estrada, hurried off a memorandum from Paris to Maximilian describing the proposed concession to France which the New York press had sarcastically dubbed Gwin's "Dukedom of Sonora." It awakened in Maximilian no response or enthusiasm for Confederates as subjects. Penciled by Maximilian on the margin of Gutiérrez de Estrada's communication is the terse comment: "They [the Southerners] have always been and always will be the sworn adversaries of Mexico whatever the form of its government." Opposite the statement that Gwin was "a real pioneer" is Maximilian's interpolation, "Yes, a pioneer for the South."[4] Maximilian's distrust of Gwin, formed so precipitately, was never dissipated.

As early as the 1840s French adventurers, speculators, and promoters had advocated the establishment of a colony in Sonora to develop mines and serve as a barrier against expansion by the United States.

By the middle of 1851, at least 20,000 Frenchmen and descendants of Frenchmen in North and South America had joined the gold rush in California.[5] Few became reconciled to that roaring frontier and were, therefore, receptive to an invitation from Mexico to find fortunes in Sonora and provide strength for Mexico's defense against United States filibusters.[6] Because of the hostility of Sonora officials and the lawless character of the French colonists, such early attempts had failed.[7] Another venture, sponsored by Gabriac, the French minister to Mexico, supported by the banking house of Jecker, Torre, and Company, was led by Count Gaston de Raousset-Boulbon.[8] He and others plainly regarded his exploit as a prelude to French seizure of Sonora; in

3. Gwin to Gutiérrez de Estrada, memorandum, October, 1863, Arch. Max.
4. Daniel Dawson, *The Mexican Adventure* (London, 1935), pp. 335–36.
5. Rufus K. Wyllys, *The French in Sonora, 1850–1854* (Berkeley, 1932), pp. 34–39.
6. Ibid., p. 47.
7. Ibid., pp. 58–65.
8. Ibid., pp. 67–75; Horacio Sobarzo, *Crónica de la aventura de Raousset-Boulbon en Sonora* (Mexico City, 1954), pp. 76–78, 83–84, 130.

fact, before his capture and execution there, Raousset-Boulbon warned that United States power was rising so rapidly that "in ten years there would not be a cannon shot in Europe without their permission."[9]

Gabriac continued his persistent campaign to keep alive French interest in unexploited Sonora. In 1860 he predicted that the nation which would develop Sonora's mineral wealth "would be mistress of the monetary course of Europe."[10] The following year Washington received a secret report that the French were investing heavily in northern Mexico.[11]

In the fall of 1863, just prior to Montholon's arrival in Mexico, Napoleon III directed Bazaine, commander-in-chief of the French expedition, to "get confidential information about the mines of Sonora and advise me if it would be possible to occupy that state."[12] Within six weeks Bazaine replied that, to occupy Sonora, four months would be required for the transportation of an army by land and sea, followed by a long struggle with the Juaristas and the savage Apache Indians but he believed the move would be advantageous to France.[13] Engineering reports forwarded to Paris were based on numerous unofficial sources rather than authentic investigation of the region.[14] By the end of the year Bazaine learned that a company was being organized in Paris to open the Sonora mines; they would be worked by colonists under the protection of a small military corps. From the profits of this enterprise both France and Mexico would receive revenue; Mexico's share would be used for the reimbursement of the cost of French invasion and occupation.

Montholon and Bazaine were instructed to win from the Regency concessions of all mining sites in Sonora not already claimed; compensation for the concessions would be deducted later from the cost of the war.[15]

9. Wyllys, *French in Sonora*, p. 167.

10. Gabriac's Memorial on the Mines of Mexico, M et D, Mexique, X.

11. Ferguson to Carleton, February 28, 1863, Miscellaneous Letters, Dept. of State, NA.

12. Napoleon III to Bazaine, September 12, 1863, G and P, vol. XVI, *La intervención francesa en México*, pt. 2.

13. Bazaine to Napoleon III, October 26, 1863, ibid.

14. Report on the Mines of Sonora, M et D, X; Memorial on Sonora by Capt. Wencelas Torbidio Claveran, G and P, vol. XVIII; Anonymous Memorial on Sonora and E. de Fleury, Notes Geographic . . . on Sonora, G and P, vol. XXII.

15. Napoleon III to Bazaine, December 16, 1863, G and P, vol. XVI, *La intervención francesa en México*, pt. 2.

PROPOSED CESSION OF NORTHERN MEXICO TO FRANCE :

"DUKEDOM" OF SONORA

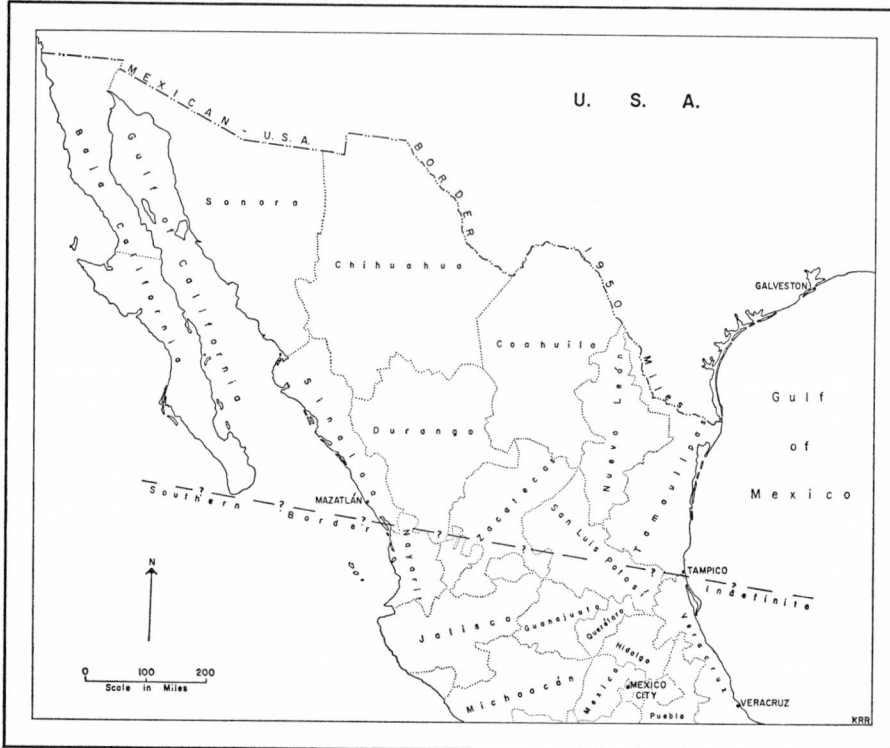

The enormous area Montholon requested the Regency to concede to France was virtually the northern half of Mexico. It extended along the United States boundary from the Gulf of Mexico 2,000 miles to the Pacific Ocean, south from the Rio Grande to Tampico, and across Mexico to Baja California. Included were the Gulf of California and parts of nine states—Sonora, Sinaloa, Chihuahua, Durango, Coahuila, Zacatecas, Nuevo León, San Luis Potosí, and Tamaulipas.

To justify the French demand for this large section, Montholon emphasized the concession was not alienation of Maximilian's imperial domain but a guarantee against invasion from the United States. Sonora and Chihuahua were the last strongholds of Juárez; if the Confederates lost the Civil War, Juárez would draw to his standard former soldiers of the United States by promising them mining sites, thereby increasing his ability to resist the empire. French troops should occupy these strategically located states at once to prevent such a catastrophe, and occupation should be consolidated by legislation giving the greatest encouragement to foreign capital by reducing taxes on mining. Under French administration the great northern expanse would be drawn closer to the empire; mines would benefit Mexico primarily, and eventually the foreign investor. This might become a second California, as no other region in the world presumably possessed such a combination of fertile soil and rich minerals! France would bring into Sonora not the riffraff and cutthroats who had settled Texas, but high-grade people from the United States who sought escape and relief from oppression of the Union. Security for life, liberty, and property which had never existed along the Mexican–United States border could be guaranteed under a government protected by France. France would also seek European immigrants.[16]

The proposal combined elements of the Spanish mining system and the public land policy of the United States. A settler who built a dwelling and tilled part of the land for two consecutive years would be permitted to purchase 120 acres at $1.25 per acre; a settler with a family would be allowed 320 acres. Gwin promised that 30,000 discontented frontiersmen, chiefly Confederates, could be drawn to northern Mexico. He had already lined up several generals for the undertaking; for example, Pierre Beauregard.[17]

Montholon, regarding himself as the architect of the so-called Gwin Dukedom, proposed that in addition to concessions turned over to a French company, northern Mexico be occupied for a period sufficiently long to exploit the mines.[18] Through this development France could repay herself "little by little." Under the guise of protecting miners, France could safeguard Mexico against expansionists from the United States, yet without title to Sonora she could not be accused of imperialistic motives.[19]

16. Note on Sonora, September 24, 1864, CP, Mexique, LXII.
17. Hallie M. McPherson, "The Plan of William McKendree Gwin for a Colony in North Mexico, 1863–1865," *Pacific Historical Review*, II (December 1933), 357–86.
18. Montholon to Drouyn de Lhuys, February 9, 1864, CP, Mexique, LXI.
19. Montholon to Drouyn de Lhuys, February 27, 1864, ibid.

Montholon forwarded to Paris on February 27, 1864, the terms of a treaty he had drawn up for the signatures of the Mexican Regency; it was a slight modification of the sample treaty he had brought from France. In his accompanying letter to Drouyn de Lhuys he stressed the importance of capitalizing on French dominance over the Regency before the empire was actually established, and condemned as absurd the assumption that Mexico could reimburse France from ordinary resources. He believed that from four sources only could Mexico raise more revenue: nationalization of church lands, immigration, mineral development, and control of transportation facilities across the Isthmus of Tehuantepec. Throughout his first year in Mexico Montholon had made progress in consultation with the Marquis de Radepont on Tehuantepec. However, Montholon's transfer to Washington as minister put an end to its further consideration.[20]

Montholon's agreement with the Regency acknowledged a debt of 210,000,000 francs to cover invasion and occupation costs prior to January 1, 1864. This amount did not include claims of French nationals or the continued maintenance of military forces in Mexico. "As guarantee of the good intentions of the present Convention as well as a testimony of gratitude to the French Emperor," the Regency would permit France to grant concessions to work the mines and maintain troops for the protection of laborers. Profits "to at least ten per cent would be applied toward the payment of the 210,000,000 franc debt and of the five per cent interest that amount carried."[21]

Two days after Montholon had sent to Paris this contemplated treaty with the Regency, Drouyn de Lhuys ordered him to stop negotiations. Repayment for French expenditures would be the subject of a conference in Paris between Napoleon and Maximilian; the prospective emperor of Mexico was too near his throne for the settlement of a paramount issue to take place without him.[22]

The terms drawn up in Paris March 12, 1864, by Napoleon III and Maximilian, which were to become the Treaty of Miramar, included no reference to Sonora. Maximilian arbitrarily refused to consider proposals for alienating any portion of the

---

20. Montholon to Minister of Foreign Affairs, October 9, 1864, *Versión francesa de México*, 5 vols. (Mexico City, 1957–67), IV, 48; Dano to Minister of Foreign Affairs, December 29, 1865, ibid., IV, 257.

21. Convention of February 27, 1864, CP, Mexique, LXI.

22. Drouyn de Lhuys to Montholon, February 29, 1864, ibid.

national domain; he also disapproved Gwin's proposition to settle Confederates on the Mexican frontier.[23]

When Montholon's proposed treaty with the Regency concerning Sonora arrived in Paris, Drouyn de Lhuys commended its author on having "perfectly penetrated in this question the views of the Government of the Emperor" and congratulated him on the results. He failed to inform Montholon of Maximilian's objection to concessions in Sonora; on the contrary, he wrote that Sonora would be the subject of discussion for additional articles of the treaty to be signed at Miramar and that he, the foreign minister, would urge their adoption.[24]

Napoleon III continued to urge Maximilian to look favorably upon Gwin's assistance in Sonora. He informed the archduke on March 28, 1864, that the finance minister, Fould, attached the "highest importance . . . to consenting to what Mr. Gwin proposes."[25]

In Mexico Montholon and Bazaine readied their plans to occupy the proposed "Dukedom" of the former Mississippi congressman. In an attempt to attract the support of the northwest area without the rigors of a military campaign, an emissary was sent to the governor of Sonora, Ignacio Pesqueira, to persuade him to give his allegiance to the empire and recognize the acts of the Regency. Governor Pesqueira spurned the offer unequivocally and declared his intention to remain loyal to the republic.[26]

Diplomacy proving abortive, Bazaine and Montholon prepared for their respective campaigns, Bazaine against Sonora, and Montholon against the new emperor. Both were confident of Napoleon III's approval. Drouyn de Lhuys had explained to Montholon that the absence of the Sonora concession in the Treaty of Miramar did not mean its renunciation by France; he advised Montholon to renew the proposal, either with Maximilian or his ministers.[27]

Senator Gwin left Paris for Mexico two weeks after Maximilian

23. Dawson, *Mexican Adventure*, pp. 358–59.

24. Drouyn de Lhuys to Montholon, March 31, 1864, CP, Mexique, LXI.

25. Napoleon III to Maximilian, March 28, 1864, in Egon Caesar Corti, *Maximilian and Charlotte in Mexico*, trans. Catherine A. Phillips, 2 vols. (New York, 1928), I, 399.

26. Arthur Zettner, French consul in Panama, was the emissary selected to win adherence from the governor of Sonora. For further details see appointment of Fourniel as agent to Sonora, April 18, 1864, Papeles del Imperio, AG, Caja 6; Zettner to Arroyo, January 20, 1864, ibid.; Pesqueira to Fourniel, July 11, 1864, ibid.; and Report of Fourniel, July 11, 1864, ibid.

27. Drouyn de Lhuys to Montholon, July 16, 1864, CP, Mexique, LXII.

sailed from Miramar, confident he was undertaking a venture comparable to the exploitation of the gold mines of California. He was received at Casa Amarilla, a villa located in the foothills overlooking Mexico City, as the honored guest of an old friend from Virginia, Colonel Andrew Talcott, then superintending the construction of the railroad between the capital and Veracruz. Bazaine acknowledged Gwin's importance by assigning him fine horses and an escort of Zouaves; their brilliant uniforms created a semioriental atmosphere not entirely reminiscent of the state of Mississippi.[28]

By the end of July 1864, Montholon was deeply discouraged. Maximilian had not granted him an opportunity to discuss the Gwin project, yet if France did not take possession soon, "this Mexican El Dorado" would be lost. Equally disturbing was Maximilian's not having received Gwin for a discussion of Napoleon III's recommendation. However, some progress was being made; Bazaine intended to move against Sonora in October and Gwin would accompany him. Montholon believed the discouraging start could be overcome and the "plan I developed in Paris . . . can be put into execution" so that the coveted prize might be salvaged for France.[29]

One month later Montholon decided to postpone discussions with Maximilian until the French army had occupied Sonora and Mexican debt had continued to grow. Maximilian had left the capital; his ministers would never agree to turn the mines over to France to be exploited by colonists brought in from the Confederacy by Gwin.[30]

By the end of September 1864, Charles Corta, the expert sent over from France to straighten out Mexican finances, was preparing to return to Paris. Corta discussed the subject of Sonora alone with Charlotte. She was unhappy over the French proposals, yet admitted that if Napoleon III "really thought it so important . . . we shall have to make the sacrifice." If the French emperor would write directly to her husband, all hesitation would cease.[31]

Upon his return to France, Corta had an audience on November 14, 1864, with Napoleon III in the presence of Charlotte's

28. Jerome B. Stillman, in the *New York World*, November 15, 1865.
29. Montholon to Drouyn de Lhuys, July 28, 1864, CP, Mexique, LXII.
30. Montholon to Drouyn de Lhuys, August 22, 1864, ibid.
31. Montholon to Drouyn de Lhuys, September 27, 1864, ibid.

father, the Belgian king, and the French finance minister.[32] Two days after the four had analyzed Corta's report on Mexico Napoleon III gave vent to his impatience. Beginning with some penetrating advice on how to found a new government, he communicated to Maximilian the combined judgment of King Leopold and himself. He realized it was impossible to "arrive at perfection all at once," but he ventured to "press you [Maximilian] to arrive at some kind of decision, anything is better than uncertainty." He referred to several "highly important points," on which Maximilian's action was "impatiently awaited." Among these, the financial organization of Mexico occupied first place, and that involved concessions in Sonora. "I know that Mr. Gwin's projects have not met with favor in Mexico," admitted Napoleon III, "and yet he is the man best able to be of service in the Sonora area." Warming up to his subject, the French emperor continued, "It is feared in Mexico that Sonora may become an American province, but, believe me, if nothing is done, it will become one by force of circumstances. . . . This will not happen if . . . [your] Government places itself at the head of the immigration, plants its flag there and organizes the country."[33]

Maximilian returned to his capital thirty days after Charlotte's conferences on Sonora with Bazaine, Corta, and Montholon. Montholon had meanwhile left for Maximilian some additional notes on the Sonora proposal.[34]

Montholon in a dispatch to Drouyn de Lhuys wrote of rumors that the Mexican emperor expected to communicate directly with Napoleon III instead of conducting further negotiations in Mexico; he hoped that since he had had "the first idea of this important guarantee of our rights and of the reimbursement of our advances, it will be my opportunity, this time, to sign the treaty which in my opinion ought to be in the future the fundamental basis of our relations with the Mexicans and of our preponderance in the New World." He was confident France would soon have the concession if, as Bazaine had intimated, French troops were in Sonora by December.[35]

Maximilian replied after a month's delay to Napoleon III's frankly urgent letter. Characteristically, he expressed coopera-

32. Corti, *Maximilian and Charlotte in Mexico,* II, 449.
33. Napoleon III to Maximilian, November 16, 1864, ibid., II, appendix, 852–55.
34. Montholon to Drouyn de Lhuys, November 10, 1864, CP, Mexique, LXII.
35. Montholon to Drouyn de Lhuys, November 28, 1864, ibid.

tion, but was eloquent in his postponement of action. The establishment of a regular government, he wrote, "under the simultaneous protection of the French and Mexican flags" in Sonora "was one of his aims": he hoped it would enable him "in a not too distant future to enhance the resources of this interesting portion" of his empire. With what might well have been irony, he added, "I shall then be charmed to see Mr. Gwin attract there the many American colonists who appear to be merely awaiting a sign from him to come and group themselves around him to seek their fortune."[36] This was the surrender Charlotte had agreed must be made, if France insisted. But her husband failed to answer the one question on which all plans hinged—when would it take place?

Meanwhile, according to Montholon's information, the three hundred Californians who had gone to Sonora early in 1864 were followed by others intent on trade and settlement. Estimates showed that U.S. citizens owned capital in Sonora totaling $1,000,000 invested chiefly in silver and copper mines and cotton plantations.[37] Steamship service from San Francisco south to La Paz on the peninsula of Baja California and then up the Gulf of California to Guaymas in Sonora had considerably increased. A French journalist made the exaggerated estimate that some 3,000 emigrants from the United States had entered Sonora and Sinaloa in 1862 and 1863 and that the majority were Confederates.[38] In the summer of 1864, Seward was informed that many secessionists were in Baja California and Sonora and that a plot to wrest the southern portion of the state of California was to be financed by French mercantile houses.[39]

Two agents of Gwin, provided with a letter from Montholon to the French consul in San Francisco, left Mexico in December 1864. Upon their arrival in California they talked so freely of the assured success of the Sonora enterprise that these reports spread throughout much of the United States. Hundreds of prospective immigrants in California, Oregon, and Nevada prepared to seek

36. Maximilian to Napoleon III, December 27, 1864, Corti, *Maximilian and Charlotte in Mexico*, II, appendix, 860–62.

37. Alden to Seward, September 30, 1864, Consular Reports, Guaymas, Dept. of State, NA, I.

38. *L'Estafette*, March 29, 1864.

39. Savage to Seward, July 8, 1864, Consular Reports, Havana, Dept. of State, NA, XLVII.

easy fortunes in Mexico. They were prevented from leaving by orders from General Irving McDowell.[40] Aroused over this incident the California governor, Frederick F. Low, repeated to Seward the warning he had sent six months before. He feared that Baja California, in which the mouth of the Colorado River was located, would fall under the control of the French emperor or his viceroy, Gwin. Pacific coast residents were alarmed over the safety of their commerce. The governor declared the most serious danger lay in the possibility that the scheme of Napoleon III for Sonora would succeed; this would place all the Pacific states in jeopardy because of their proximity to French dominated regions.[41]

But the Sonora bubble had already been pricked in Paris. On November 29, 1864, Drouyn de Lhuys reviewed for Montholon the decision reached by "the Emperor and his Council of State" regarding the proposed new article to the Treaty of Miramar. He emphasized the part played by the Council of State in making the decision; this was doubtless either a subtle indication that the ministers had successfully kept the emperor's feet on the ground, or that Napoleon III wished to placate Montholon's feelings with the subterfuge that his ministers were really to blame. Drouyn de Lhuys went on to say that, much as the emperor and the Council of State appreciated Montholon's zeal for the interests of France, they disapproved his proposal to occupy northern Mexico. The suggested concession was excessive in amount, and control over so large a part of Mexico would change the apparent motive of the Grand Design. Many handicaps stood in the way, including civil disorder, lawsuits over controversial land titles, and the long process of granting concessions to companies. Furthermore, the necessity of providing security for these companies would mean the permanent occupation of Mexico by France. These hazards would open the door to "too many malevolent critics"; consequently, the Council of State had found it "wiser and more opportune to give up a project which in many respects merited our attention." France was grateful for Charlotte's good will but remembered that Maximilian did not yield without hesitation. Therefore, the French government had decided to abandon its request for the concession of northern Mexico. Hope

40. *New York Herald*, November 15, 1865.
41. Low to Seward, February 4, 1865, Miscellaneous Letters, Dept. of State, NA.

was expressed that the Mexican government would do everything possible to pay the French debt by some other means.[42]

The cancellation of the Gwin project can be attributed mainly to the French emperor's unpredictability, to Montholon's over-ambitious expansion of the scope of the concession, but perhaps most of all to the stark realism of Alphonse Dano who was soon to succeed Montholon as minister to Mexico. One of the ablest of French diplomats and the only capable minister appointed by Napoleon III to Mexico, Alphonse Dano was already conversant with Mexican conditions. As chargé d'affaires there in the early 1850s he had been instrumental in resolving the tragic confusion resulting from the Raousset-Boulbon fiasco. Drouyn de Lhuys's dispatch canceling the Sonora proposal followed the line of reasoning which Dano was to embody in a memorandum, "On the Mines of Sonora." In it Dano referred to data submitted to him about which he had already expressed his judgment. Evidently, he had held earlier conferences with French officials during which he reviewed the complete file on Sonora.

In the Dano memorandum was the statement that many adventurers had sought fortunes in Sonora but had become discouraged and left. Failure had been due neither to faint heart nor lack of zeal. The region was inaccessible and forbidding; water was scarce and agriculture difficult. There was potential mineral wealth, but the expense of mining operations in a remote area which necessitated protecting workers would be prohibitive. The Sonora mines were not as amazingly rich as earlier reports hinted; if they had been, nothing could have prevented settlers from the United States from taking them over; Californians would have moved south en masse when their veins of gold began to shrink. It would be more difficult to attract Europeans to Sonora than Americans; North Americans, irresistibly susceptible to the gold fever, were never assimilated by other peoples, were undisciplined, and lived revolver in hand. To maintain in Sonora troops essential for keeping order would antagonize the United States, complicate Maximilian's position, and make Mexico subject to all the schemes of exploitation which had proved so disastrous.[43]

When, early in January 1865, Montholon received the incred-

42. Drouyn de Lhuys to Montholon, November 29, 1864, CP, Mexique, LXII.
43. On the Mines of Sonora, February 20, 1865, memorandum by Dano, M et D, Mexique, X.

ible news that the Sonora proposal had been abandoned, he was aghast. Gwin left for Paris at once to revive his own fortunes and to protect this golden opportunity. Montholon also sympathized with the Southerners. He urged Gwin to discuss with Napoleon III their future; he suggested a haven might be arranged for the Confederates in Algeria.[44]

Possibly to Gwin's surprise and certainly to his relief, he discovered the French emperor still was interested in Sonora. Having received Maximilian's grudging assent, Napoleon III appeared to reason that, although his Council of State had rejected it, the colonization of Sonora might still become a profitable enterprise of imperial Mexico. Extraordinarily cautious about French participation in the venture, he urged Gwin to return to Mexico. Gwin agreed, fully expecting the French support he assumed was implied in the emperor's conversation.[45] Actually, Napoleon III had no such intention; he sent Bazaine a letter which, ironically, Gwin carried, advising the general that it was up to Maximilian "to decide what he can get from his [Gwin's] efforts and intelligence." Bazaine was cautioned to be prudent about giving support and not to "embark on a new expedition which can be expensive and dangerous."[46]

From this time on, Gwin was the victim of events. Before his return to Mexico following his audience with Napoleon III, the U.S. Civil War had ended. When Gwin pushed his plan of settling Confederate refugees in Sonora, he found Maximilian, released at last from French pressure, indifferent and even hostile. "I fear him [Gwin] most of all because of his extreme finesse and the great ability which I see in him," was Maximilian's secret comment. Reminded that Napoleon III thought well of Gwin, the Mexican emperor retorted that he had fascinated Napoleon III but "he did not fascinate me."[47]

The return of Gwin revived Mexican fears that Sonora might yet be turned over to France. To combat such rumors, Maximilian issued a specific denial in *El Diario del Imperio*. Read the court announcement: "Dr. Gwin has been figuring in all

---

44. Montholon to Drouyn de Lhuys, January 8, 1865, CP, Mexique, LXIII.

45. Gwin to Napoleon III, March 25, 1865, reproduced in Evan J. Coleman, "Senator Gwin's Plan for the Colonization of Sonora," *Overland Monthly*, XVII (May 1891), 497–519, and (June 1891), 593–607.

46. Napoleon III to Bazaine, March 3, 1865, G and P, vol. XXVII, *La intervención francesa en México*, pt. 8.

47. Dano to Drouyn de Lhuys, June 11, 1865, CP, Mexique, LXIII.

these accounts as governor, as viceroy and with the title of Duke, and as having derived his powers from the Emperors of Mexico and France. We are authorized to say that these statements are absolutely false. . . . Dr. Gwin has not obtained from His Majesty any commission or title. . . . Neither connection nor relationship binds him to the Government. We understand, moreover, that his person is not recognized by the personnel of the Court. . . . Also, we are authorized to say that the magnanimous and intelligent monarch who rules the destinies of France has made an official notification to us . . . that he has not participated in any combination formed in relation to Sonora, our government being free to work out any arrangement for the national interest."[48]

On the day following this announcement, Gwin left Mexico City for San Antonio. The Quai d'Orsay was warned that Gwin's state of mind was inflammable and because of his grievances he might do harm.[49] Under regulations of the U.S. Army all persons connected with the Confederacy were to be detained if they attempted to cross the border to or from Mexico. Accordingly, Gwin was arrested and packed off to General Sheridan at New Orleans. For a second time the former Mississippi congressman who had fascinated the French emperor and who aspired to be the Duke of Sonora peered out through the window of a Yankee prison.[50]

48. *El Diario del Imperio*, June 26, 1865.
49. Dano to Drouyn de Lhuys, August 11, 1865, CP, Mexique, LXIV.
50. Case of William M. Gwin, *ORA*, ser. II, vol. 8, p. 755. For a full treatment of Gwin see Hallie M. McPherson, "William McKendree Gwin, Expansionist" (Ph.D. diss., University of California, 1931).

Uncle Sam Finds Two Fine Mushrooms Nearly Fit to Pull

MAXIMILIAN AND THE DUKE OF SONORA

The "Duke of Sonora" was a Confederate refugee, Dr. William M. Gwin, who had been a congressman from Mississippi and a U.S. senator from California. He schemed with Napoleon III to acquire and exploit a strip of Mexico contiguous to the U.S. border from the Pacific to the Gulf of Mexico. This area allegedly was richer in gold and silver than California and would produce some $50,000,000 a year.

Frank Leslie's Illustrated Newspaper, 11 March 1865
(Library of Congress)

17

"Crowns against Liberty Caps"
1864–1866

By 1864, Napoleon III's Grand Design for America was only partly initiated. This, the "deepest thought of the Second Empire" of France, had undergone some serious modifications. For example, Spain had not followed the lead of France but, with England, had withdrawn her troops from Veracruz and the Tripartite Treaty had been broken. A strongly reinforced French army in its advance toward the capital of Mexico had been disastrously defeated at Puebla. After a delay of one year and with the aid of even more veterans, Puebla had finally been taken. Then the republican government headed by President Juárez had fled from the Mexican capital and the French had entered. Under French dictation a regency had been set up by representatives of the Conservatives and the Church, two elements Juárez had defeated in the War of the Reform. Maximilian, elected emperor, had begun his reign, and with military protection General Bazaine had begun the regeneration of Mexico by virtually forcing various areas to approve establishment of the monarchy.

At this time, the United States was prevented by its Civil War from enforcing the Monroe Doctrine. However, Secretary of State Seward had repeatedly warned France that the Americas opposed monarchy. Although Spanish America was not sufficiently strong to aid militarily in the defense of Mexico, many statesmen and diplomats from American republics surmised, as did President Ramón Castilla of Peru, that behind the tripartite expedition of England, France, and Spain to Veracruz was a malevolent motive. It was, Castilla asserted, a "war of the crowns against the Liberty Caps."[1] Confirmation of such suspicions lay in a dispatch by Edmond de Lesseps, a French diplomat in Peru. Before the landing of the monarchical invaders at Veracruz, de Lesseps predicted that monarchies would be established in the Western Hemisphere. "The symptoms of Mexican illness you are about to cure," he informed the French Foreign Office, "begin to appear here." He gave assurances that, although the prevailing disgust over republicanism was "not openly visible," nevertheless, it was "deep and complete."[2]

One of the foundations of Napoleon III's Grand Design in America, wrote Michel Chevalier in 1863, was "to save from irreparable ruin not only Mexico but also the whole branch of Latin civilization." He added that "Without France, without her intelligence, her elevated sentiments and her military power . . . Latin nations would be reduced to make out a very humble figure in the world, and would long since have been completely eclipsed."[3] In other words, France was the soul and the arm of Latin civilization. The French accepted heroically the responsibility of their heritage and set about lifting the Latin nations of America from the degradation of republicanism.

Austrian though he was, Maximilian had no difficulty in being indoctrinated with this idea. He saw himself as the symbol of political rejuvenation in the New World. He dreamed of expanding his Mexican empire over Central America after which he and his cousin, the emperor of Brazil, might jointly divide Spanish South America.[4] He had even tried, unsuccessfully, to promote a marriage between his brother, the Archduke Ludwig Victor, and the daughter and heir of Pedro II of Brazil, who was then shopping for a husband. Thus, two Hapsburg empires in the New World might vie with merely one in Europe. Ludwig Victor, with more perspicacity than he himself probably realized, declined to exchange Vienna for Rio de Janeiro.[5]

1. Robinson to Seward, February 25, 1862, Dispatches, Peru, Dept. of State, NA, XVIII.

2. De Lesseps to Thouvenel, November 29, 1861, Papiers de Thouvenel, DB, AN, XIII, 31.

3. Michel Chevalier, *Le Mexique, ancien et moderne*, trans. Thomas Alpass, 2 vols. (London, 1864), II, 182–85, 201.

4. Daniel Dawson, *The Mexican Adventure* (London, 1935), p. 381.

5. Egon Caesar Corti, *Maximilian and Charlotte in Mexico*, trans. Catherine A. Phillips, 2 vols. (New York, 1928), II, 280–81.

SPANISH AMERICAN   REPUBLICS   NAPOLEON Ⅲ
PROPOSED   TO   CHANGE   INTO   MONARCHIES

Most of the Spanish American republics had long resented attempts at European intervention in their hemisphere and in
their national affairs. This opposition fostered a unifying sentiment for republicanism and a modest concept of inter-American
continental defense. By linking support of republicanism and
territorial integrity with denunciation of slavery and disavowal
of expansion, President Lincoln focused Latin fears on the Confederacy and on France.

A basis for suspicion of European aggression already existed.
Prior to the invasion and occupation of Mexico, the concern of

republicans over the threat of thrones in America had been aroused by a series of Spanish intrigues. The boldest of these plots occurred as early as 1848, when recruits were drilled in Spain for an expedition to Ecuador.[6] Two years later a lesser plot was organized to set up a monarchy in Bolivia.[7] In 1861, Spain's reincorporation of the Dominican Republic into her imperial domain appeared to initiate the long-suspected monarchical aggression. However, the change of government there was due, primarily, to Pedro Santana's determination to place the eastern two-thirds of Hispaniola under the protection of a stronger power as a defense against the threatened conquest by Haiti.[8]

In 1862, Peru suggested a congress for a continental alliance backed by the United States and expressed her willingness to send a military force of some 5,000 men to aid in the defense of Mexico.[9]

This proposal for a continental alliance, also supported by Chile, ran into difficulties when U.S. Secretary of State Seward declined to acknowledge that Mexico's sovereignty was in danger of being violated. Peru persisted in her efforts to interest the United States by proposing that American republics adopt a joint policy of nonrecognition of the Confederacy. Federico L. Barreda, Peruvian consul in New York and later minister at Washington, in consultation with agents of Chile, Colombia, Mexico, Peru, and some Central American countries, drew up a pact guaranteeing the independence, territorial integrity, and autonomy of political divisions in the New World and denying recognition to revolutionary governments until they had been accepted by a free vote. Seward again refused to join the movement for fear of involving the Union in a second war.[10]

When in 1863, Manuel Nicolás Corpancho assumed his duties as minister from Peru to Mexico, he secured the adherence of President Juárez to the Continental Treaty. Chile, Ecuador, and

---

6. Ralph W. Haskins, "Juan José Flores and the Proposed Expedition against Ecuador, 1846–1847," *HAHR*, XXVII (August 1947), 467–95.

7. Humberto Vasquez-Machicado, "La monarquía en Bolivia," *Revista de historia de América*, Numero 32 (December 1951), 21–82.

8. Charles C. Hauck, "Attitude of Foreign Governments toward Spanish Reoccupation of the Dominican Republic," *HAHR*, XXVII (May 1947), 247–68.

9. Romero to de la Fuente, January 7 and 9, 1862, *Corres. mexicana*, II.

10. Robert W. Frazer, "Latin American Projects to Aid Mexico during the French Intervention," *HAHR*, XXVIII (August 1948), 381–84.

Peru had already signed it to guarantee their independence and the integrity of their boundaries. Corpancho hoped to direct the force of this treaty against France, but not all American republics shared his faith in the document. Argentina rejected it on the ground that the Americas as an independent political entity did not exist. Moreover, she did not believe that any combination of enemies would be powerful enough to change republican institutions.[11]

Between 1861 and 1863 there was an improvement in the attitude of republican Spanish America toward the United States. One reason for the change was Lincoln's selection of able and zealous diplomats and consular officials. Another influence was the use of pro-Union press materials to counteract the anti-Union news releases from Europe, on which the neighbor nations had been almost entirely dependent.[12]

Lincoln's Latin American policy was so widely accepted that it aligned as inseparable the welfare, even the existence, of all American republics. In time, Juárez and Lincoln were pictured as white knights fighting identical battles for the freedom of the Americas. Consequently, with a restored North American Union, the independence of the New World and republicanism were joined in partnership.

The only sour note was Seward's noncommittal and evasive response to entreaties for all-American action. Romero, inspiration and central figure of plans for collective security based on aid from the United States, wrote as late as March of 1865, just before the collapse of the Confederacy, that Seward informed the Latin diplomats that his country could not complicate her position with European powers. Asked if the United States would modify its policy after its internal war ended, Seward replied he could not answer inasmuch as modification of policy might lead to war with France. When a first step was taken, he warned, a nation should always be ready for the second.[13]

The proximity of the five Central American republics to Mexico placed them in an acutely vulnerable position. On Mexico's southern border, Guatemala had been ruled for more than a

11. Ibid.

12. Nathan L. Ferris, "The Relations of the United States with South America during the American Civil War," *HAHR*, XXI (February 1941), 51–78.

13. Romero to Lerdo de Tejada, March 8, 1865, *Corres. mexicana*, V.

quarter of a century prior to 1861, by Rafael Carrera, an uneducated but extraordinarily shrewd dictator of Spanish, Indian, and Negro descent. Looked upon by the Indians as a messenger from God, he enjoyed the quasi-monarchical title of President for Life with the ardent support of Conservatives and clericals. He had been decorated by the pope in recognition of the great power he had accorded the Church in negotiating the first concordat of any Latin American republic; he had also been decorated by Santa Anna for the attributes despots have in common.

When in 1863, Spain belatedly recognized the independence of Guatemala, Carrera sent as his representative to Madrid, Felipe Neri del Barrio, whom Juárez had expelled from Mexico. According to Romero, Neri del Barrio was instructed to aid the establishment of a monarchy in Mexico and to assure the European interventionists that, if the monarchy succeeded, Guatemala would become a part of the Mexican Empire. Romero's assertion was denied by Antonio José de Irisarri, noted writer and politician who represented Carrera in the United States from his Brooklyn residence.[14]

Filling the post of minister to Guatemala was Elisha O. Crosby, a product of the gold rush in California. Crosby encountered strong pro-French influences around the president of Guatemala. However, he succeeded in preventing the use of Guatemalan ports by Confederate cruisers seeking supplies, especially the port of Livingston on the Rio Dulce, part of the Bay of Honduras. Crosby had become a friend of Carrera on a previous visit to Central America. He suspected in March 1862 that secret negotiations were going on, or about to be initiated, between Carrera and the three powers intervening in Mexico. He believed that the Central American republics would be annexed to Mexico with Carrera the viceroy of them all, and that the old orders of nobility, still respected and keenly sought after by the Guatemalan aristocrats, would be restored.

Crosby later reversed this opinion. The vice president, representing the aristocracy in Carrera's government, had just died; he had been responsible for the monarchical scheme, Crosby reported, and since no other leader was likely to acquire his influ-

14. Romero to de la Fuente, March 29, 1862, ibid., II; Irisarri to minister of foreign relations, August 22, 1863, Legajo B 99–6–3, Tomo 4430, Archivo General del Gobierno, Guatemala.

ence, the movement for monarchy would probably subside.[15]
The Union minister believed his own influence with Carrera
was gradually increasing; he overlooked no opportunity to win
the president away from monarchical machinations.[16] The following December the foreign minister told Crosby that recognition of any regime in Mexico would be withheld until the
"leading nations of the world, and especially the United States
had set the example."[17]

Six months later, Crosby assured Washington that Carrera
would oppose any connection of monarchy with Mexico because,
as viceroy under Maximilian, the Guatemalan would wield less
power than as president for life. Some advisers of Carrera, as well
as certain members of Congress, favored a monarchy but were
not powerful enough to carry out their aspirations.

Rival of the United States minister was the French consul
general, Dominique Edouard Tallien de Cabarrús; he was as
eager to woo Guatemala to the crowns as was Crosby to gain
advantage for the Liberty Caps. The French diplomat had sent
an encouraging message to Paris in June 1863: "Guatemala continues to be quite favorable to us," he wrote, "and her policy
toward Mexico is invariably loyal to France."[18] In September
1864, the French representative claimed he had induced Carrera
to support a French protest over insults to Maximilian and Bazaine published in El Salvador. Carrera was quoted as declaring
that Guatemala was ready to give moral and material support
to force other Central American republics to respect France.[19]

In the fall of 1864, Maximilian sent his aide, Count Ollivier
Resseguier, on a secret mission to Guatemala to explore the possibility of drawing Central America into the Mexican Empire.[20]
The energetic French minister, Cabarrús, advised the aide it
would be necessary, first of all, for Mexico to conclude a frontier convention to soften the distrust of Guatemalans over their
boundary dispute with Mexico. After this gesture of good will,
but not before, Maximilian's agents could plot out with the
French further enticement of Guatemala. The Frenchman be-

---

15. Crosby to Seward, July 6, 1862, Dispatches, Guatemala, Dept. of State, NA,
IV.
16. Crosby to Seward, July 21, 1862, ibid.
17. Crosby to Seward, December 8, 1863, ibid.
18. Cabarrús to Drouyn de Lhuys, June 17, 1863, CP, Amérique Centrale, XIX.
19. Cabarrús to Drouyn de Lhuys, September 16, 1864, ibid., XX.
20. Corti, *Maximilian and Charlotte in Mexico*, II, 443–45.

lieved Carrera might be able to unite and annex all Central America to the Mexican Empire.[21]

Cabarrús's activities after the recall of Crosby in 1864, and the death of Carrera in April 1865, were watched by the U.S. minister to Honduras and El Salvador, the competent James L. Partridge of Maryland. He wrote that Guatemalan aristocrats were eager to be affiliated with Maximilian for protection against the Indians, and that the official newspaper was almost entirely filled with articles in favor of building Mexico into a strong Latin power of the Roman faith to serve as a barrier against the rapacity of "Northern heretics." Other publications regularly carried articles slanted to prepare the public for a change in the form of government. Authors of these articles asserted that a change had become imperative because of the failure of republicanism. In all of this the subtle influence of Cabarrús was "plainly visible."[22]

In El Salvador and Costa Rica the press carried articles hostile to France, the French emperor, and the French government.[23] A publication in El Salvador claimed that country had made the first strong protest against the "unjustifiable invasion," and that the protection offered Spanish Americans by Napoleon III was "masked servitude."[24]

The clashing ideologies and interests of El Salvador and Guatemala led to war in 1863. Gerardo Barrios, liberal president of El Salvador, wrote, "The moment I suspected the war was going to begin . . . I informed the Government at Washington . . . of the tendencies of Guatemala to unite herself with Mexico in the wrong concept of an empire in Spanish America. It was my firm conviction that neither the Government nor the people of the United States would tolerate monarchical institutions in our continent or even the intervention of European nations in the political problems of America."[25] When the forces of El Salvador were defeated by Carrera, Barrios fled to the United States.

Maximilian suffered a severe rebuff from Honduras. That

21. Cabarrús to Drouyn de Lhuys, December 2, 1864, CP, Amérique Centrale, XX.

22. Partridge to Seward, March 29, 1865, Dispatches, El Salvador, Dept. of State, NA, I.

23. Cabarrús to Drouyn de Lhuys, June 17, 1865, CP, Amérique Centrale, XIX.

24. Cabarrús to Drouyn de Lhuys, April 26, 1863, ibid., XVII.

25. Barrios to Seward, January 13, 1864, Central American legations, Dept. of State, NA, IV.

country's president, José María Medina, received an offer from Maximilian's foreign minister of a title of nobility with other honors and emoluments in exchange for recognition of the Mexican Empire and his influence in annexing the whole of Central America. The Honduran was to be made governor or viceroy of the five states. Rejecting the proposition indignantly, Medina informed Maximilian that no consideration whatever could induce him to become a traitor to his country or be false to republican principles.[26]

Nicaragua attempted to organize in Central America a concerted resistance to French penetration. Costa Rica, backed by Peru and Colombia, attempted to arrange a continental congress for defense.[27]

Colombia realized her peril if France demanded passage across the Isthmus of Panama for transporting her troops to the Pacific coast of Mexico. Even so, her liberal press violently abused Napoleon III and his representatives; the British chargé d'affaires fared but little better.[28] When in the summer of 1864 Maximilian inquired, through the French Legation, if he might send a minister to Colombia, the recently established liberal president, Manuel Murillo, refused.[29] The following year the Colombian Congress endorsed the republican government of Mexico and praised Juárez. Also from Colombia came an offer from General Tomás de Mosquera to raise an army of 15,000 men and march across Central America to aid republican Mexico.[30]

Bordering Colombia on the east, Venezuela, also strategically located with regard to Mexico on the Caribbean Sea, was active in the advocacy of continental union. Realizing that only after the defeat of the South would Washington consider resisting European encroachments in the New World, her representative

26. Rousseau to Seward, November 16, 1866, Dispatches, Honduras, ibid., II.

27. Frazer, "Latin American Projects," pp. 385–86.

28. Burton to Seward, September 12, 1862, Dispatches, New Granada, Dept. of State, NA, XVII. For consular reports from Mexico on intervention developments, see Official Records, Colombia, in the bibliography.

29. Goury du Roslan to Drouyn de Lhuys, August 17, 1864, CP, Nouvelle Grenade, XXIX.

30. Diario oficial, 1865, Ministry of Foreign Affairs, Bogotá, February 2, 1865; for General Mosquera's offer see General Mosquera to Romero, February 28, 1865, Archivo histórico de Matías Romero, Banco de Mexico, D.F. (microfilm copy, University of California, Berkeley, fol. 00587), cited by R. R. Miller, "Matías Romero: Mexican Minister to the United States During the Juárez-Maximilian Era," HAHR, XLV (May 1965), 234.

in Washington offered, in the fall of 1863, to send Venezuelan cavalry to the Army of the Potomac or to Grant's operations in the West. Why not place 1,000 Venezuelan officers in command of Negro regiments, he asked. Out of the versatility of racial mixtures available, any shade of color desired could be sent, from lieutenants to generals.[31]

South of Colombia Gabriel García Moreno had led in 1859, a successful revolt against the government of Ecuador. He appears to have appealed to the Spanish and French legations to set up a protectorate. Later, he concentrated his efforts on France because of the unpopularity of Spain. His alleged purpose in seeking foreign aid was fear of aggression from Peru on the south, Colombia on the north, and the "rapidly advancing destructive torrent of the Anglo-Saxon race."[32] Once president in 1860, Gabriel García Moreno continued his approach to France according to de Lesseps, French chargé d'affaires at Lima. "After you have established in Ecuador a government just like that of France, in the name and under the influence of Napoleon III," de Lesseps wrote Paris in November 1861, "Peru and Bolivia, seduced by the example of their regenerated neighbor through the powerful inspiration of France, will ask you, even beg you, to admit them to that beneficent status." He cautioned against hasty action but was confident that in time "monarchy will replace the republican form of government with which these countries have had a very bad experience."[33] Gabriel García Moreno, implacable enemy of "godless liberals," hailed Maximilian as Mexico's deliverer from the "excesses of a rapacious, immoral, and turbulent demagoguery."[34]

Ecuador's location between Peru and Colombia, both strong advocates of republicanism, conditioned her actions and reactions. The Ecuadorian foreign minister told Friedrich Hassaurek, United States minister, that in the event of serious threats of conquest by Peru or Colombia, Ecuador would seek protection from any available quarter.[35] Hassaurek was forced to contend

31. Blas Bruzual to Seward, October 19, 1863, Funcionarios Diplomáticos, Caracas, 1863–67.
32. Hassaurek to Seward, August 28, 1861, Dispatches, Ecuador, Dept. of State, NA, V.
33. De Lesseps to Thouvenel, November 29, 1861, Papiers de Thouvenel, DB, AN, XIII.
34. Hubert C. Herring, *History of Latin America* . . . (New York, 1955), p. 505.
35. Hassaurek to Seward, September 20, 1861, Dispatches, Ecuador, Dept. of State, NA, V.

with highly complicated problems, social and political. Ecuador was probably the most reactionary of Spanish American republics. Its president, Gabriel García Moreno, had become during a trip to Europe an arch conservative after observing the revolutions of 1848, and he reached the conclusion that Catholicism would be the salvation of Ecuador. Hassaurek had fled from his native Austria after the uprisings there in which he took part. Joining the large German-American colony of Cincinnati, he immediately attained in journalism a radical, anticlerical reputation. Endowed with prodigious energy, he studied at night and soon became a lawyer, less radical and more prosperous. He had been drawn to the Republican party because of abolition and its popularity among German-Americans, whose vote was mighty, and he was instrumental in establishing the Republican party in the Cincinnati area. Because of his popularity and ability as a campaigner, he helped nominate and elect Lincoln.[36] That Hassaurek was able to carry out Lincoln's Latin American policy in Ecuador under these circumstances was a tribute to his diplomacy. Hassaurek feared that monarchical sentiment was daily gaining strength; the head of the army was a monarchist, the minister of finance was extremely pro-French, and "if France were willing to accept . . . a proposed annexation, a most powerful effort could be made to support the scheme."[37] Early in 1862, Hassaurek informed Washington that the Ecuadorian government through its official organ, El Nacional, had denied ever having made a proposal to France, although the French Yellow Book of 1862 stated that France had declined the Ecuadorian invitation.[38] The sincerity of France's official pronouncements was questioned by Hassaurek.[39] Hassaurek improved friendly relations with Ecuador, and was initiator and member of a mixed commission to handle troublesome U.S. claims.

Promonarchists in Peru were not aided by a regenerated neighbor state as de Lesseps, the French minister, had optimistically prophesied. Rather, they faced in Ramón Castilla, a president who had fought for independence from Spain under San Martín and Bolívar and wanted no truck with monarchy in any guise.

36. Friedrich Hassaurek, Four Years Among the Ecuadorians, ed. C. Harvey Gardiner (Carbondale, Ill., 1967), pp. vii, xiv–xvi, xviii.

37. Hassaurek to Seward, December 19, 1861, Dispatches, Ecuador, Dept. of State, NA, V.

38. Hassaurek to Seward, January 6, 1862, ibid.

39. Hassaurek to Seward, April 17, 1863, ibid.

"The Republics of the New World . . . will be free, independent and sovereign," he declared, "because it is their will, it agrees with their democratic instincts and sound convictions, and because in America monarchy is impossible."[40] President Castilla was pleased with the new Union minister, Christopher Robinson, former attorney general of Rhode Island, who had represented that state in Congress. A strong abolitionist, for that reason he was especially acceptable to President Castilla, who had freed the Negro slaves and put an end to the cruel exactions from the Indians. Robinson needed all the help he could get. Peru's relations with the United States had been suspended in 1860 by President James Buchanan over claims controversies. So effectively did Robinson promote the new Lincoln policy of mutual respect and friendship that, by the middle of 1862, he was able to inform Washington that Peruvian officials believed the restoration of unity in the United States would "interpose an insuperable barrier to the scourge of European despotism."[41] On July 4, 1863, a benefit was held in Callao for Mexican hospitals. Its announcement carried pictures of Washington and Juárez. During a brief pause in the performance, a shout was heard throughout the theater, "Death to Frenchmen!"[42]

An even more popular supporter of the Lincoln Latin American policy was the sagacious Hoosier friend of Lincoln, Thomas H. Nelson, minister to Chile. Courtly in bearing, and ingratiating in personality, he settled claims readily and soon convinced Chileans that the Union was the defender of free Spanish America.[43] On July 4, 1863, Nelson was honored by a national celebration for his heroism in saving lives in a church fire in which some 2,000 worshipers were burned to death.

Nelson notified Seward that the Chilean minister to London had warned the British Foreign Office that, if England, France, and Spain intervened in Mexico, they would incur serious losses in commerce and general animosity throughout Spanish America.[44]

40. Frazer, "Latin American Projects," p. 387.
41. Robinson to Seward, June 10, 1862, Dispatches, Peru, Dept. of State, NA, XVIII.
42. De Lesseps to Drouyn de Lhuys, July 13, 1863, CP, Peru, XXXII.
43. For a summary of the Chilean attitude, see Angel Núñez Ortega, *Memorias sobre las relaciones diplomáticas de México con los estados libres y soberanos de la América del Sur* (Mexico City, 1878), pp. 79–81.
44. Frazer, "Latin American Projects," pp. 384–85.

Nelson forwarded an excerpt from the newspaper, *El Ferro-Carril*. It read: "Even should the Mexican monarchy establish itself . . . who believes it possible that it will count one day of existence after the reconstruction of the Union? How will it be possible to maintain a monarchy . . . at the side of a republic powerful by her liberty and powerful in the moral aid which the whole of South America would lend her against [Imperial] Mexico."[45]

Continuing disorders in Bolivia and Uruguay led to rumors that France, supported by Italy, considered establishing a monarchy in the Plata region. When the Union minister, Charles A. Washburn, a publisher from California, discussed this rumor with Francisco Solano López, dictator of Paraguay, he received the impression that López had already asked Napoleon III to approve his becoming the king of Paraguay but that no response was received from the emperor of the French.[46]

Washburn claimed that López, from his youth, had dreamed of changing Paraguay into an empire, possibly encouraged by the example of Pedro II of Brazil. However, when the Paraguayan despot's hope of marrying one of the Brazilian princesses was blasted by their taking European husbands, Washburn believed López precipitated in 1865 the most disastrous war in South American history in the hope of establishing an empire consisting of Paraguay, Argentina, Brazil, and Uruguay.[47]

Argentina, under the powerful and widespread influence of its president, Bartolome Mitre, ceased to be an inviting field for European intervention. In 1863, Mitre expressed the hope that the day was at hand when the United States would be able to enforce the Monroe Doctrine; he declared Chile represented the sentiment of the continent when she called upon Washington to protect Mexico from France.[48] The influence Mitre exerted later by founding *La Nación*, one of the world's great newspapers, continues.

Two extraordinarily able diplomats and ardent patriots represented the United States during President Mitre's administra-

45. Nelson to Seward, May 1, 1862, enclosing an issue of *El Ferro-Carril* of April 10, 1862, Dispatches, Chile, Dept. of State, NA, XVIII.
46. Ferris, "Relations of the United States with South America," pp. 68–69.
47. Charles A. Washburn, *History of Paraguay*, 2 vols. (Boston, 1861) I, 522, 525, 571.
48. Webb to Seward, January 17, 1863, Dispatches, Brazil, Dept. of State, NA, XXVIII.

tion. The first of these was Robert C. Kirk, formerly lieutenant governor of Ohio, who brought about the remarkable adjustment of claims due citizens of his country, aggregating more than $4,000,000. Kirk was succeeded as minister to Argentina by the amazing Alexander S. Asboth, Hungarian refugee. Having fought under Lajos Kossuth in Hungary in 1848, Asboth accompanied Kossuth to the United States and became a U.S. citizen. In 1861 Major General John C. Frémont stationed at St. Louis appointed Asboth his chief of staff with rank of brigadier general. Asboth's record in the Union army was heroic. Wounded at the battle of Pea Ridge, Asboth was in action the next day at the head of his division. Later he was in command at Columbus, Kentucky, and Fort Pickens, Florida. At Marianna in Florida he received wounds that eventually proved fatal. His final promotion was to major general. In 1866 General Asboth was honored for his long fight on behalf of political freedom in Europe and in North America. But his congenial association with President Mitre in South America was cut short by his death in 1868.

Argentina's neighbor, Brazil, was the only Latin American state to receive a minister from imperial Mexico. This recognition was due, in part, according to the historian Manuel de Oliveira Lima, to a desire to maintain friendly relations with France where a Brazilian battleship was being constructed.[49] Obviously, Maximilian had expected happy relations with the only other American empire. His longest cruise with the Austrian navy had been to the former Portuguese colony.

The Mexican Minister Pedro Escandon arrived in Rio de Janeiro in the middle of January 1865; for an entire month he waited impatiently before an audience with Emperor Pedro II was granted. In addressing the emperor, Escandon enlarged upon the bonds and interests shared by Brazil and Mexico. Pedro II expressed appreciation with definite restraint. Upon reading in the press severe criticism of his speech to the emperor, Escandon grew seriously disturbed. He was surprised to note that the leading political parties opposed the change of government in Mexico and that the newspapers accompanied "their commentaries with reflections which do not reveal much respect for the Emperor of the French."

Escandon did his utmost to build prestige for his Hapsburg

49. Ferris, "Relations of the United States with South America," p. 73.

master in this unfriendly atmosphere. He inaugurated a series of lavish entertainments. When no favorable results were forthcoming, he returned to the softer life in Paris, to consort there in luxury with other Mexican émigrés. "As Minister," he complained, "I have received not a manifestation, nor invitation, nor a glass of water from the Monarch or his government." Slightly more than one year later, the chargé d'affaires whom Escandon had left in the Brazilian capital likewise exhausted his endurance and closed the legation. From the very beginning, he reported, the Brazilian press had been antagonistic. As an illustration, he quoted a newspaper, "From New England to Patagonia . . . Maximilian can count on the sympathy of no people. . . ."[50]

Escandon attributed the Mexican failure in Brazil to the influence of the U.S. minister, James Watson Webb. A more discerning diplomat would have interpreted the situation otherwise. Webb's eight years in Brazil have been described as "a horror story in Latin American relations." A former publisher and editor of the newspaper which later became the powerful *New York World*, Webb was neither popular nor influential at the court of Pedro II, but trade with the United States was increasingly important to Brazil.

Lincoln's minister to Brazil visited his belligerence upon all who disagreed with him. He conducted private warfare against Confederate privateers and the Union navy when its officers did not hearken to his dictation, but he reserved his most caustic diatribes for the British minister. Occasionally, the Brazilian foreign minister was firm with Webb to the point of brusqueness; he could hardly have experienced less than intense irritation over Webb's two-year quarrel as to whether Brazil should regard Confederates as rebels or belligerents. That battle Webb never won.[51] Possibly, Webb's rambunctious behavior served one purpose. It kept aggressively before Brazil the widespread American antagonism against French interference in the New World.

A number of factors limited the war of the "Crowns against the Liberty Caps" in Spanish America to words rather than muskets. The undeviating refusal of Lincoln and Seward to allow

50. Richard B. McCornack, "Maximilian's Relations with Brazil," *HAHR*, XXXII (February 1952), 176–78; see also Núñez Ortega, *Memorias*, pp. 39–40, 46.
51. Lawrence F. Hill, *Diplomatic Relations between the United States and Brazil* (Durham, N.C., 1932), pp. 146–76; see also James L. Crouthamel, *James Watson Webb: A Biography* (Middletown, Conn.: Wesleyan University Press, 1969).

the Union to become vulnerable to European retaliation by assuming the lead in continental action deterred Latins from sending troops and other material aid. It is questionable whether Spanish America could have been of military assistance to republican Mexico. The elimination of Castilla from the presidency of Peru removed from that country leadership for international unity. Certainly the conservative stand of Guatemala dissipated what could have formed the semblance of defense on the southern border of Mexico. Disorders in the majority of republics, serious in Colombia, Venezuela, Ecuador, Bolivia, and Uruguay, produced uncertainty and consumed domestic energy.

From 1862 to 1866, Peru and Chile, and to a lesser extent other Spanish American republics, were concerned primarily with their own defense against the last futile attempt of Spain to regain her colonies. Using the provocation France had employed in Mexico, the collection of claims, Spain sent a naval expedition to the Pacific and attacked both Peru and Chile. A continental congress for defense held in Lima in the fall of 1864 was attended by delegates from Argentina, Bolivia, Chile, Colombia, Ecuador, Guatemala, Peru, and Venezuela. But nothing of a practical nature resulted.[52]

However, faith in a growing unity of purpose in the face of European aggression persevered. Attempts were made to establish media for the expression of New World cooperation and freedom. Among such efforts was the publication in New York in 1864 and 1866 of two newspapers, the *Continental* and the *Voice of America*. As late as January 8, 1866, a large and important public meeting was held at Cooper Union in New York to promote hemispheric security, to aid the defense of Mexico against France, and to strengthen the resistance of Chile and Peru against Spain. Among speakers were the poet, William Cullen Bryant, then editor of the *New York Evening Post,* and the Union general, William S. Rosecrans. Letters were read from highly placed political leaders advocating the enforcement of the Monroe Doctrine.

Summing up the issue for the Western Hemisphere the former Mexican minister of foreign affairs, Francisco Zarco, told a New York meeting in 1865: "The Mexican question involves the fate of the continent. In it is to be decided the antagonism which

52. *Exposición de secretario del interior sobre relaciones exteriores al congreso de los estados unidos de Colombia, Memorias, 1865* (Bogotá, 1865), pp. 22–25.

exists between despotism and liberty, between monarchy and republicanism; therefore, it is a continental question, an American question which no people in the New World can contemplate with indifference without being false to their destiny."[53]

These classic declarations from Spanish America, nurtured by Lincoln's ministers—Corwin in Mexico, Robinson in Peru, and Nelson in Chile, as well as other crusaders from the United States—generated powerful forces of hemispheric unity in the battle of the "Crowns against the Liberty Caps." The most resourceful and dedicated leader was Matías Romero, Mexican minister in Washington. Day by day, week by week, year by year, he marshaled the diplomatic battalions destined to triumph over the Emperor Maximilian's efforts to slay the dragon of democracy.

53. *Proceedings of a Meeting of Citizens of New York to Express Sympathy and Respect for the Mexican Republican Exiles* [Cooper Institute, July 19, 1865] (New York, 1865).

18

"To Overcome Degradation
and Demoralization"
1863–1865

It was Napoleon III's dream to raise Mexico to the level of a modern state by upgrading its population through large-scale immigration. This was to provide Mexico with needed leadership, stability, and prosperity through the development of natural resources. Propagandists for this panacea were military officers, civil servants, journalists, and special agents all in the service of France. They argued that at least 600,000 new settlers must be drawn to Mexico in four years, or 150,000 each year. Only by this means could the strife-torn country be pacified, the standard of living raised, the economy stimulated, and new wealth produced.[1] The idea of strengthening the Americas by European immigration was drawn obviously by Napoleon III from the studies and writings of Michel Chevalier and enlarged upon from the experience of the United States with immigration. For example, a total of two and one-half million immigrants arrived in the United States in the decade that preceded the invasion of Mexico by French troops. In his interpretation of Napoleon III's "regeneration" of Mexico, *Le Mexique, ancien et moderne*, Chevalier explained that immigrants to be attracted there were to be selected in contrast to the mass of ignorant, unskilled poor who had migrated to the United States.

1. Emmanuel Domenech, *Le Mexique tel qu'il est* (Paris, 1867), pp. 250 ff.

[199]

Seeking to entice new settlers to Mexico was not a novel idea to her citizens. It had been advocated in the reform period of the 1850s[2] and later received official recognition and endorsement from the government of Juárez.[3] Again, as in the confiscation of church lands, the policy of the Mexican Liberals was carried out by France. Conservatives, following faithfully their Spanish heritage, generally regarded newcomers dubiously, fearing their influence in changing the status quo.

The Mexican press reflected the widespread debate on immigration during and after the Regency.[4] Arguments centered not only on the desirability of immigration but also on the characteristics prospective Mexicans should possess, countries from which they should come, naturalization policies, freedom of worship, inducements to be offered in transportation and subsidies, the survey and allotment of lands, the process of assimilation, and administration of the entire undertaking.

Foremost advocate of immigration was the French language newspaper, *L'Estafette*. Its editor had lived some twenty years in Mexico and, in 1863, received a subsidy from the Regency.[5] To associate immigration with the new empire, *L'Estafette* declared on October 5, 1863, that Maximilian would be the first of these forerunners of progress.

Immigration as a defense against the United States was also advocated by *L'Estafette*. At the close of the U.S. Civil War, bands of soldiers, unfit for peacetime occupations and avid for spoils, would threaten the lands below the Rio Grande.[6] Mexicans were warned that they should not be deceived into counting on that war to exhaust their "natural antagonist." Before its close they must place a protecting barrier of Europeans on the northern frontier.[7]

2. A. de Lachapiele to Vidaurre, July 30, 1856, Correspondencia de Vidaurre, Archivo General del Gobierno del Estado de Nuevo León.

3. Juárez decree of March 13, 1861, concerning immigration, *L'Estafette*, March 19, 1861.

4. Alfred J. Hanna and Kathryn Abbey Hanna, "The Immigration Movement of the Intervention and Empire as Seen through the Mexican Press," *HAHR*, XXVII (May 1947), 220–46; Henry Lepidus, *History of Mexican Journalism* (Columbia, Mo., 1928), 47–50.

5. Eugène Lefèvre, *Documents officiels recueillis dans la secrétairerie privée de Maximilien*, 2 vols. (Brussels, 1869), I, 336; Lepidus, *History of Mexican Journalism*, pp. 47–48. *L'Estafette* had been the leading French language newspaper of Mexico until the establishment of *L'Ere nouvelle*. French officials felt the editor of *L'Estafette*, Charles Barrès, was not an ardent supporter of the Mexican Empire.

6. *L'Estafette*, July 4, 1865.

7. Ibid., May 4, 1864.

By the beginning of Maximilian's reign in June 1864, opposition to immigration was in full bloom. *El Cronista* of Mexico City, *El Ferro-Carril* of Orizaba, and *El Eco de comercio* of Veracruz represented the opposing Conservative thought. "Let us consolidate peace, reestablish order, and guarantee public confidence," declared *El Cronista*. "Once this is done there will be no need of seeking immigration."[8]

L'Estafette classified proponents of this obstructionist attitude into four groups: (1) those content with only the restoration of peace; (2) those who, rather than allow their country to be developed by foreigners, were willing to let it fall into political insignificance; (3) those who recognized the need of new blood but recoiled from disclosing to strangers the secrets of their disgraceful political and social life; and (4) those timid, sick souls, who, afraid of law and justice, feared they would be dispossessed of their habits, customs, privileges, and authority over the ignorant Indians and mestizos. This last group consisted of "speculators in abuses" who had "fattened on bad politics."[9]

Hostility toward foreigners was traceable to colonial days, maintained the Liberal newspaper, *La Sombra*, of Mexico City; it remarked that "if the conquistadores had permitted immigration, Mexico today would not resent the introduction of vast numbers of foreigners" or tremble lest it become the "victim of ambition and avarice of the immigrants who can exploit advantageously the ignorance and stupidity left over from the conquest."[10]

Some Mexicans who accepted the principle of immigration were apprehensive of its effect. One pamphleteer agreed that the population was too sparse for the development of natural resources, which could not be appreciably increased without more manpower, but feared that a large influx of foreigners would submerge "our race, ways, and customs."[11] *L'Estafette* retorted that Mexico must choose between immigration and annihilation, that it would be wiser to welcome foreigners than to risk their being imposed, better to accept them under established policies than to be invaded by dispossessed peoples.[12]

El Ferro-Carril of Orizaba accused *L'Estafette* of being will-

8. *El Cronista*, January 25, 1864.
9. *L'Estafette*, July 12, 1864.
10. Ibid., October 27, 1865.
11. José Jesús Cuevas, "La Colonisation," *L'Estafette*, January 18, 1865. Cuevas printed these views also in a pamphlet under the same title in Mexico City, 1866.
12. Ibid., February 8, 1865.

ing to "abolish the great Mexican family to establish Mexican nationality." This was denied; the French newspaper claimed that all groups stood to gain by immigration; landowners, by an increase in land values; artisans, by more work; and Indian laborers, by generally improved conditions.[13] *El Ferro-Carril* admitted the necessity of immigration but not to the extent of subjecting Mexicans to the degradation of haste. It contended that, until public order could be restored and the government stabilized, immigration would be impossible, even dangerous. Moreover, "If we cannot live in good order, being few in number, how shall we succeed with a great increase in population?" This sophistry almost suffocated *L'Estafette*, which replied, "To propose postponing the coming of immigration until the complete solution of the Mexican problem by Mexicans alone is to put it off indefinitely. . . . If, four years from now the Intervention has not retired leaving behind 600,000 colonists rooted in the soil, the final catastrophe will begin."[14] *L'Ere nouvelle* dryly commented, *"Ferro-Carril* wants the train to run without the locomotive."[15]

Violent controversy arose over freedom of worship as a means of attracting Protestant immigrants. Forey had proposed in June 1863, freedom of worship as "the great principle of modern society."[16] *El Cronista* asserted, "The Catholic religion is the only one in the world; all other religions are the personification of evil, or the germ of evil, or the achievement of evil, which weigh on humanity. . . . Religious toleration is, in its essence, indifference to faith, and indifference is the triumph of immorality in social dissolution." *L'Estafette* reprinted this statement as the most "bloody satire against toleration" ever to come under its observation and demanded, sarcastically, "Is it then because she is so intolerant that the Mexican nation is one of the most enlightened of the world and that she marches in the vanguard of civilization?"[17]

A strong opponent of toleration was *El Pájaro verde*, leader of Conservative newspapers in Mexico City. It insisted that freedom of worship and immigration had little in common, that "in

---

13. *L'Estafette*, May 26, 1865.
14. Ibid., June 6, 1865.
15. *L'Ere nouvelle*, June 9, 1865.
16. Emmanuel Domenech, *Histoire du Mexique*, 3 vols. (Paris, 1868), III, 110–13.
17. *L'Estafette*, January 13, 1865.

all the projects for colonization the conditions applied for refer to personal security and opportunity to prosper without any mention of churches or denominations."[18]

La Orquesta, a Liberal humorous semiweekly in Mexico City, declared that the clerical origin of *El Pájaro verde* was well known, and that "its horror of all that is related to liberty and progress is notorious."[19] *La Sombra* supported freedom of worship and declared "religious tolerance and immigration have come to be today the two stars shining in a perennially dark horizon."[20]

Debates on types of immigrants caused scores of individuals, some of them experienced in the migration of peoples, to air their views. A former prospector for gold in Australia advocated the exploitation of mines. His conviction was "the future of Mexico is there and only there." Moreover, the exploitation of mineral wealth in isolated areas would not disturb the landowners; 2,000 mines could produce sufficient wealth to bring prosperity to the entire nation. He believed 400,000 miners could be brought to Mexico within six months; to strengthen his argument he cited the development of Australia.[21]

"What suits Australia would be a calamity for Mexico," rejoined a critic of this scheme. There would not be enough food for so large a number of nonagricultural workers. He considered miners undesirable colonists; their sole object was to amass money and then go elsewhere; the farmer was the ideal immigrant.[22]

A Polish baron wrote that if offered adequate aid thousands of farmers would emigrate from his country; 20,000 young people from various parts of Europe could be counted on, and, including Slovac farmers, a total of 100,000 could be brought over.[23] *L'Ere nouvelle* expressed reservations about Polish stability; they might hurry home to fight the Russians as they had done after migrating to France.[24]

Charles Thiele, former editor of a French language newspaper in California, recommended French nationals already in North America; they wanted to enter Mexico, they would make excel-

18. *El Pájaro verde,* April 21, 1865.
19. *La Orquesta,* June 8, 1865.
20. *La Sombra,* October 27, 1865.
21. L. Simon in *L'Estafette,* April 6, 1865.
22. Dr. Max Lilienthal in *L'Estafette,* April 9, 1865.
23. Baron de Gost in *L'Estafette,* May 12 and May 17, 1865.
24. Ibid., May 19, 1865.

lent citizens, and they were readily available; 800,000 in Canada, 20,000 in California, and 200,000 in other sections of the United States.[25] Of them, he said the French in California were the most desirable; for fifteen years they had been ill-treated by Californians.

Two other groups in the United States were reported as available: German immigrants in the more densely populated centers who wanted to move, and some 20,000 farmers in the West who were discouraged by conditions and were ready to start for Mexico with their families, tools, and that rare commodity, money.[26]

Nearest Mexico were the Confederates. As early as 1863, *L'Estafette* had explored this source and found it good. After the fall of Vicksburg and Gettysburg this newspaper prophesied that refugees would seek new homes and urged that they be received in Mexico. Like the Poles they were a conquered people experiencing bitter hardships and humiliations; unlike the Poles, they were near at hand.[27] A Southerner from New Orleans, with other Confederates who had already found homes in Mexico, promised that if Mexico would adopt a policy favoring his compatriots her coasts would soon be "populated with thousands of planters from Louisiana, Alabama and Texas, whose energies and intelligence will open for their adopted country incalculable riches and whose implacable resentments will constitute her best defense on the seacoast and along the northern frontier."[28]

Thiele counseled caution. To count on the hatred of the South for the North was to misunderstand entirely the causes of the Civil War in the United States, he argued. The South had seceded because relations with the North had become too burdensome; the North had resisted the rupture because she had much to gain from the South. "No question of human principle of nationality divided them," Thiele was convinced, "and when they are reunited both will turn to Mexico, which for twenty years they have regarded as their property when the moment came to take it." He advised against repelling them completely; he believed that they should be carefully supervised to prevent their getting out of hand.[29]

25. *L'Ere nouvelle,* May 19, 1865.
26. *L'Estafette,* February 1, 1865.
27. Ibid., August 8, 1863.
28. Ibid., October 5, 1863.
29. *L'Ere nouvelle,* May 19, 1865.

El Pájaro verde appeared to approve a communication it quoted from Guadalajara supporting the proposal for attracting Confederates, but maintained that the frontier should be strongly guarded. In that event, "such forceful immigration would be of immense value to us; but if not protected, it would result sooner or later . . . in the ruin of Mexico."[30]

The one subject on which there was unanimity was opposition to Orientals. Asiatics in general and Chinese in particular had been suggested by a foreign officer in the Mexican service. *L'Estafette* was bitingly explicit; Orientals had been tried for twelve years in the Spanish Antilles and "after a thousand experiences have given only deplorable results"; the Chinese were "incapable of hard tasks, infatuated with superstitions, obstinately attached to their way of life, tricky beyond the imagination of honest men, incompatible, coldly cruel, inclined to gambling, shame, suicide, and theft—a depraved race, scorned by mankind."[31]

As the press continued a lively examination of immigration, news of Maximilian's New World adventure spread throughout Europe accompanied by glowing descriptions of Mexico's riches and opportunities, all within the grasp of the pioneer. Hundreds of adventurers and underprivileged in many lands wrote for information as they dreamed of discovering their pot of gold at the end of the ancient Aztecan rainbow. The Mexican consul at Bordeaux reported on November 29, 1865, that all Europe was interested in Mexican colonization.[32]

In anticipation of receiving new settlers, Maximilian, early in January 1865, urged proprietors of uncultivated lands to make them available on modest terms.[33] An average rate of one peso per acre with payments over a period of five years was recommended. Some *hacendados*, assuming their holdings would increase in value, notified the government that they had acreage for sale.[34] The press commended their action and cooperated by listing their lands. A government representative, Emilio Longue-

30. Ibid., February 14, 1865.

31. *L'Estafette*, November 16, 1864.

32. The cajas of the Papeles del Imperio contain a large number of petitions, memorials, etc., from individuals in Western Europe for land concessions, authorization for colonization projects, etc. A letter of the Bordeaux Consul is in Caja 7. See also E. Masseras, *Le Programme de l'empire* (Mexico City, 1864), pp. 19 ff.

33. *El Diario del Imperio*, January 12, 1865.

34. *El Pájaro verde*, March 10, 1865.

maire, was stationed at Veracruz to consult with immigrants upon their arrival.[35] Later, a hostel was established.[36] Of the extent and location of public lands ready for settlement, the government had only meager information. Maximilian's officials insisted that two-thirds of the proprietors claimed ownership of more land than could be proved by deeds.[37] By a series of decrees the emperor ordered a clarification of titles and a survey of the public domain.[38] Many landowners, conscious of the vague extent of their enormous estates, petitioned the emperor to stop what they charged was a policy undermining the most stable element of the nation; they implied he was biting the hand of his chief support.[39]

As immigrants began arriving, innumerable questions arose. Under a new law, purchasers of land became, ipso facto, citizens. This was opposed by various groups, particularly foreigners interested in promoting colonization projects.[40] So severely was the law criticized by L'Ere nouvelle that the newspaper was given a censorship warning.[41] Controversy ended when Maximilian interpreted the provision to mean that foreign landowners were subject only to Mexican statutes.[42]

The most critical problem of the average immigrant was how to get settled before the small amount of money he had brought with him was exhausted. This situation provoked such questions as, should immigrants who could not finance themselves be discouraged? Should colonization companies be licensed? Should the government grant an outright subsidy? Eventually, the Mexican Empire employed all three practices.

By July 1865, four charters for colonization companies had been granted: one to a German, one to a Frenchman, and two to United States entrepreneurs. A subsidy of 10,000 pesos had also been approved for immigrant aid, an action strongly denounced by L'Ere nouvelle. Its position was that Mexico needed to attract capital, not individuals who were a financial liability; furthermore, the new empire did not have adequate funds for such

35. El Diario del Imperio, February 17, 1865.
36. L'Ere nouvelle, May 2, 1865.
37. Domenech, Histoire du Mexique, III, 261.
38. El Diario del Imperio, February 27, March 10, March 22, 1865.
39. Petition of April 1, 1865, Caja 5, Papeles del Imperio, AG.
40. L'Estafette, April 9, 1865.
41. L'Ere nouvelle, April 9, April 13, April 18, 1865.
42. Ibid., May 23, 1865.

expenditures. Mexican newspapers generally disapproved this policy on the ground that it showed favoritism to foreigners.[43]

Reviewing the immigration program at the conclusion of the first year of Maximilian's reign, L'Estafette found disagreement everywhere; one critic complained that the ministers of Maximilian's cabinet appeared "not to propose but to oppose everything useful to Mexico."[44] L'Estafette's conclusion was dismal: "A year ago everyone had 'regeneration' on his lips; now, no one has it in his heart." The various criticisms were that Anglo-Saxons were heretics, Poles were unreliable, Germans were not pure Catholics, drank beer and smoked pipes, the French were too radical, and Southerners were rebels. These were the "practical scruples" which had followed Mexico's "great protest of good will."[45] A remedy had to be discovered for overcoming the "apathy of the whites, the degradation of the Indians, and the demoralization of the mestizos." Those who should have shouldered responsibility had done nothing.[46]

Maximilian was discouraged. "Never had anything been more confused, less directed and in contradiction of all logic," he wrote. "These good people have learned nothing, have seen nothing, and think they know better than the rest of us."[47]

Notwithstanding this pessimism, progress had been made. The minister of public works had issued several circulars for the use of immigrants and on March 28, 1865, a commission of colonization had been created. It consisted of twelve members, four Mexicans and eight foreigners; it was to serve as a clearing house for immigration enterprises.[48] In each governmental department of Mexico an auxiliary commission was to be organized to work with the department prefect. Departmental juntas had five members, two Mexicans and three foreigners. Thus, a majority of non-Mexicans controlled immigration machinery.

Mexicans had a picture of the much publicized regeneration of their country by the summer of 1865. An Austrian emperor, a French army of occupation, and foreign investors, colonists, and

43. Hanna and Hanna, "Immigration Movement," pp. 236–37.
44. Domenech, Histoire du Mexique, III, 210 ff.
45. L'Estafette, June 22, 1865.
46. Ibid., August 23, 1865.
47. Maximilian to Domenech, July 23, 1865, in Domenech, Histoire du Mexique, II, 323.
48. Decree of March 28, 1865, Caja 22, Papeles del Imperio, AG; El Diario del Imperio, April 21, 1865, gives the organization of the junta.

concessionaires were to refashion the nation in their composite alien image. Landowners were to be divested of holdings to which they could not prove title, to make room for new settlers irrespective of the fact that landowners, as a class, had been foremost in support of the establishment of the new empire. *L'Ere nouvelle* voiced the French position in an editoral May 17, 1865: "It is useless to discuss it [immigration]; the matter is already settled; regeneration can only be accomplished by this means. . . . It remains only to decide what element is destined to people Mexico, and if one nation is to be favored more than another, which will be this nation."

Inevitably, a people whose Spanish heritage had inoculated them with suspicion of foreigners, resented the attitude expressed by *L'Ere nouvelle*. A few *hacendados* appeared to accept the French inspired vision. For the most part, however, procrastination and ineffectual acquiescence formed a variety of defenses; the *mañana* technique, which over the centuries had approached virtuosity in crises, was brought into play with deadening effectiveness.

19

Infamous Yankee Intrigues
1865–1867

Far to the north of Mexico City in Chihuahua, the imperturbable President Juárez had issued his 1865 New Year's proclamation. "After three years of bloody struggle," he announced, "we are as resolved as we were the first day to continue defending our independence and our liberty." These were the dark days of the Mexican republic, when deep-seated faith and obstinate determination were its main assets. To Americans the Juárez proclamation was an appeal to fighters for democracy; while to jingoists the prospect of chasing the French out of Mexico offered an incentive for closing the U.S. Civil War; to the Yankee expansionists, the defense of Mexico provided a glorious excuse to carry the Stars and Stripes to the Isthmus of Panama.

As critical losses of the Confederacy foreshadowed the end of hostilities, a series of Yankee intrigues developed in Washington; some were abortive, some dangerous, all hostile to France and formidably predatory. Conspicuous in these intrigues were the military who saw no reason why the largest army the United States ever possessed should not be used for triumph over foreign interlopers once the Union was restored. Recalling the leadership which Southerners and Westerners had exerted prior to the 1860s in expansion and filibustering, Yankee expansionists dreamed of eliminating the hatred between North and South by uniting the armies of both sections in a border foray. Confederates had no reason to favor France; for four years she had deceived them with vain hopes.

Foremost of these northern plots to assume more than nebulous form was that of the elderly journalist-politician, Francis Preston Blair, father of Union General Francis P. Blair, Jr., and Montgomery Blair, a member of Lincoln's cabinet. His stratagem was to stop the U.S. Civil War by inducing Jefferson Davis to lead Confederate forces, later to be augmented by Union officers and soldiers, into Mexico to drive out the French, destroy the Maximilian empire, and restore Juárez to power. He believed also that at least a portion of Mexican territory might, in the course of this otherwise noble gesture, fall under the sovereignty of the United States. This evil aspect of his plot was not to be revealed to Mexican eyes.

At the Mexican Legation in Washington, Romero, a close friend of the Postmaster General Blair, was brought into the virtuous part of the scheme and reported it to Juárez on January 10, 1865. Vitally interested and in the main approving, Romero sensed the danger to the independence of his country.[1] Nevertheless, Mexico's immediate need of aid was so desperate that later risk of possible territorial loss was secondary.

Five days after Romero reported to Juárez, Postmaster General Blair sent Romero a secret message in which he confided his belief that the Confederates would be willing to settle with the Lincoln government by undertaking an expedition to Mexico; he assured Romero Mexicans need not fear Southerners as aggressors, pointing out that they sympathized with the Mexican republic and would probably oppose the annexation of territory by the United States; he urged Romero to involve Confederate troops in a move against Maximilian.[2]

Juárez responded speedily to Blair's proposition. Romero was empowered to appoint the commander-in-chief of the proposed expedition who would become general of a division in the Mexican army and, with Romero's approval, appoint other officers. Enlistments were to last only for the war against the French invaders; and, although citizens of the United States would retain their citizenship, they must consider themselves as Mexicans during this service. Officers might remain in the Mexican army, but

---

1. Romero to Lerdo de Tejada, January 10, 1865, *Corres. mexicana*, V.

2. Montgomery Blair to Romero, January 15, 1865; Romero to Lerdo de Tejada, February 4, 1865, ibid.

soldiers, if they stayed, were to become colonists on land provided by the Juárez Law of August 1, 1865. The commander-in-chief was to receive 100,000 pesos in money or land; the next ranking generals would be paid 30,000 and 20,000 pesos respectively. The corps was to bring its own arms, equipment, and funds for six months' maintenance. Eventually, reimbursement was to be made from the sale of public lands, from the national income, and from the confiscation of property belonging to Mexican imperialists.

Juárez required Romero to secure, if possible, from the U.S. government a specific guarantee that Mexican independence and territorial integrity would not be violated; at least he must insist on a moral commitment. If the United States preferred to send a division of its own army, the Mexican government would draw up a treaty governing its operation. Provisions regarding subordination of U.S. troops to Mexican command might be waived, but not more than one-third of the men should be Southerners.[3]

During the exchange of reports and instructions between Romero and Juárez, the elder Blair received permission from Lincoln to pass through the army lines; at Richmond on January 12, 1865, he interviewed the president of the Confederacy. By that time, the Davis government had almost despaired of securing recognition from Europe. Drawing from Davis the information that the waning Confederacy had no commitment with European powers, Blair proceeded to paint Napoleon III as the arch-enemy of the United States, the Confederacy, and of Spanish America.

Blair told Davis that the moment Napoleon III "perceived our frenzied people engaged in perpetuating a national suicide, he invaded Mexico to take up a position on the southern flank of this Republic, to avail himself of its distractions as well as those of Mexico, to give effect to the daring scheme of the Bonapartist dynasty," namely, "to make for the Latin race in all our regions on the Gulf a seat of power under the auspices of France."

Blair appealed to Davis as the logical leader to shatter "this formidable scheme of conquest" and "baffle the designs of Napoleon to subject our Southern people to the 'Latin Race.' " Success would put the Confederate president alongside Washington and Jackson as "a defender of the liberty of our country."

3. Lerdo de Tejada to Romero, March 29, 1865, ibid.

Blair spun out his tempting web by promising Davis reinforcements. If the combined Juárez and Confederate armies
needed more manpower to vanquish the French, officers and
soldiers of the North would undoubtedly "be found ready to
embark on an enterprise vital to the interests of our whole Republic. . . ." He pledged that his younger son would resign his
generalship in the Union army, expatriate himself, and "join
all the forces he could draw to the standard borne on a crusade
of the expulsion of the European despotism now threatening our
confines. . . ."

Davis was assured he might carve out a new career for himself
as dictator of Mexico. Here Blair's line of persuasion degenerated from the heights of patriotic fervor over the Monroe Doctrine to the depths of a filibustering adventure, as the far-seeing
Juárez had suspected. If in delivering Mexico from the clutches
of a foreign power, persisted Blair, Davis "should model its States
in form and principle to adapt them to our Union and add a new
Southern constellation to its benignant sky," he would, "while
rounding off our possessions on the continent at the Isthmus . . .
[also] complete the work of Jefferson, who first set one foot of
our colossal government on the Pacific. . . ."

In conclusion Blair said, "There is my problem, Mr. Davis;
do you think it possible to be solved?"

"I think so," Blair quoted Davis in response.

"You see that I make the good point . . . that the war is
no longer made for slavery but against monarchy," encouraged
Blair.

As Blair recorded the interview, Davis was somewhat cautious
about means of reconciliation between the North and South.
Time and events must determine this course, Blair admitted, but
"no circumstances would have a greater effect than to see the
arms of our countrymen from the North and the South united in
a war upon a Foreign Power assailing principles of government
common to both sections and threatening their destruction."[4]

Blair made a second trip to Richmond for another talk with
Davis, in spite of the cold water with which Lincoln doused his
hopes by declaring he favored nothing not preceded by the immediate reunion of the North and South. However, persuaded by
General Grant, Lincoln agreed to meet with Confederate leaders

4. Memorandum of F. P. Blair, January 1865, Lincoln Papers, LC, CLXXXV.

at Hampton Roads. On board the *River Queen* a four-hour conference took place on February 3, 1865. Alexander H. Stephens, vice president of the Confederacy and head of the Confederate mission to Hampton Roads, suggested an armistice during which Confederate troops would be sent secretly to Mexico. Lincoln's adamant refusal to discuss peace on any terms other than the surrender of the Confederacy ended the conference and with it Blair's intrigue. He had proposed a conspiracy of conquest and annexation, to be carried out under the guise of friendly aid to an harassed neighbor.[5] The motives of the Confederacy were also suspect. Evidence reached the U.S. Department of State that caused Secretary of State Seward to surmise a connection between the Hampton Roads conference and a last effort to break down the French emperor's policy of neutrality.[6] At any rate, France learned immediately of the event.

What Blair failed to accomplish in the Confederacy as a whole, General Lew Wallace undertook on the Texas border with the blessing of Grant. Brought up on the Indiana frontier where his father was governor, Wallace helped organize volunteers with whom he had marched off to fight against Mexico in 1847. Back home after the Mexican War, he practiced law, served four years in the Indiana Senate, and in the Civil War rose to the rank of major general of volunteers. His life was as full of action as were his fantastically successful novels, *Ben Hur* and *The Fair God.* Generally speaking, Wallace's activities in and about Mexico partook of the character of fiction. He claimed to have talked to Lincoln as early as 1865 about aiding Mexico.

"I suppose it is right we should help the oppressed," was Lincoln's alleged response to Wallace. "But do you know, young man, what you are asking? This is the argument of the thief—all right if you don't get caught. Go to Seward. . . ."[7]

In common with many others, Wallace did not regard the State Department, and especially the secretary of state, as sympathetic

5. For the Blair intrigue see John G. Nicolay and John Hay, "Abraham Lincoln: A History," *Century Magazine,* XXXVIII (May 1889), 838–56; see also E. M. Coulter, *Confederate States of America, 1861–1865* (Baton Rouge, 1950), pp. 551–52.

6. Seward to Adams, March 1, 1865, Instructions, Great Britain, Dept. of State, NA, XX.

7. Quoted in Irving McKee, *"Ben Hur" Wallace* (Berkeley, 1947), p. 92. Wallace wrote Porfirio Díaz, August 15, 1889, that Lincoln "admonished me not to mention the business to Mr. Seward." See *Lew Wallace: An Autobiography,* 2 vols. (New York, 1906), II, 843.

to unconventional secrets. Instead, he attached himself to the more credulous Grant. From a former schoolmate and refugee from Texas, Wallace told Grant, he had learned that Confederates west of the Mississippi were thoroughly disheartened and ready to unite with the Unionists to aid Juárez.

"The adoption of the Juárez flag on the bank of the Rio Grande as the basis of compromise would stagger the Rebellion. . . ." Wallace promised.[8] Grant authorized Wallace "to inspect the condition of military affairs" near the mouth of the Rio Grande.[9]

Accompanied by a staff of three, Wallace hurried to New Orleans, collected $4,520 of Secret Service funds and continued on his journey toward Mexico. Unwilling to risk being captured, he sent an emissary to General James E. Slaughter, Confederate commander at Brownsville on the Rio Grande. Under the pretext of discussing extradition of Union men from Mexico, the emissary gained an interview with Slaughter in which he brought the conversation around to a meeting with Wallace at Point Isabel on the Gulf of Mexico not far from Brownsville.

When Wallace greeted the Confederate officers March 11, 1865, he made good his promise to provide "a supply of refreshments" paid for by the U.S. treasury.[10] For forty-eight hours, discussions continued, now and then interrupted by potent refreshment and rest. Wallace enjoyed the role of host; he wrote his wife, ". . . if our good people could have seen General Slaughter and myself lie down to sleep together . . . I fear my character for loyalty would suffer. . . ."[11]

Wallace sent a report to Grant that both Slaughter and Colonel John S. Ford "entered heartily into the Mexican project. It is understood between us that the pacification of Texas is the preliminary step to a crossing of the Rio Grande. . . . General Slaughter was of the opinion that the best way for officers in this situation to get honorably back into the Union was to cross the river, conquer two or three states from the French and ultimately annex them, with all their inhabitants, to the United States."[12]

The record of the Point Isabel conversations, prepared by Ford

8. January 14, 1865, Wallace, *Lew Wallace*, II, 814.
9. Ibid., II, 814–15.
10. Wallace to Grant, January 14, February 22, and March 14, 1865, ibid., II, 813–16, 823.
11. Wallace to Mrs. Wallace, ibid., March 14, 1865, II, 821.
12. Wallace to Grant, March 14, 1865, ibid., II, 821–22.

for Slaughter's superior, Major General John G. Walker, differed sharply from the version Wallace sent Grant. Ford wrote that he and the other Confederates doubted Wallace's statement that he had no authorization from the Washington government because of his assertion that Grant would confirm anything he, Wallace, thought it wise to arrange. They were suspicious of his claim that "the political men have nothing to do with such a subject," that the Union and Confederate armies should execute terms of peace.

There seemed to be nothing on which Wallace hesitated to speak with finality. He informed the Confederates, according to Ford, that the Union had decided to enforce the Monroe Doctrine, would continue refusing recognition to the Maximilian empire, and would eventually assume a protectorate over Mexico. When he asserted that Lincoln was preparing to send three hundred warships to the Mediterranean to make a demonstration of force, Ford inquired if this would not precipitate war with France and England. Without hesitation, Wallace answered yes.

Startling also was the simplicity with which Wallace dismissed the question of slavery. "I will tell you confidentially," he was quoted by Ford as saying, "that we consider the Emancipation Proclamation a great mistake. The most intelligent men of the North, outside the Abolitionist radicals, regard it as a nullity, and consequently, it is thus they will treat it. As for the Constitutional Amendment [to abolish slavery], it seems probable that it will not be ratified by a sufficient number of states for many years to come, if ever."

Although Texas and other Southern states had the right to withdraw from the Confederacy, Slaughter told Wallace, "we are united with our brothers on the other side of the Mississippi by bonds stronger than those of the Constitution. It is the vow which we have taken to stand together in danger. Honor keeps us from abandoning them voluntarily."

Refuting this argument, Wallace maintained that civil government should be submissive to military authority; he said a military despotism existed in Washington. "Everything Grant recommends," he claimed, "Lincoln will do. I suppose that it is the same with the government at Richmond and General Lee."[13]

Aspiring to win fame by bringing back into the Union the Trans-Mississippi states of Texas, Arkansas, and Louisiana, the

13. Ford to Lieut. L. G. Aldrich, March 13, 1865, AMG, 1865.

adolescent-minded Wallace seems never to have questioned the favorable outcome of his fanciful dream. In summarizing for Grant the results of the Point Isabel conference he explained that Ford, whom he regarded as the "most influential Confederate," politically, in Texas, would take his proposition to Walker at Houston after which he would confer with both Walker and General Edmund Kirby-Smith, Commander of the Trans-Mississippi Department.[14]

When Wallace reached Galveston March 29, 1865, for the anticipated rendezvous, a communication from Walker grimly put the situation back in focus.[15] "Stripped of all disguise," Walker wrote Wallace, "your proposition is nothing less than that we lay down our arms, surrender at discretion, take an oath of allegiance to the United States government and, in return, to accept such terms of amnesty, pardon, or foreign exile as our conquerors shall graciously accord us."[16] Walker informed Slaughter that this would be "the blackest treason to the Confederacy. . . . The fact that an officer of . . . [Wallace's] rank in the enemy army is found at so remote a corner of the Confederacy has in itself something sinister and suspicious."[17]

Walker was "of the last ditch variety," Wallace complained to Slaughter and Ford, "his indignation was both childish and discourteous." The sudden end "of the conference held so agreeably" at Point Isabel was deplorable. Since Walker was not a Texan, Slaughter and Ford might take matters into their own hands, all for the good of their state,[18] argued Wallace.

Confederate indignation did not end with Walker's denunciation of Wallace and his intrigue. Copies of the entire correspondence were sent across the Rio Grande to the Mexican imperialist, General Tomás Mejía, who warned the commander at Tampico to be prepared for an invasion. "It will not be long," in Mejía's opinion, "before there will be great events on this frontier."[19] Mejía also forwarded the Wallace correspondence to Bazaine who hurried it across the Atlantic for inspection by the French government. At face value the documents outlined a policy of the United States which included enforcement of the

14. Wallace to Grant, March 14, 1865, *ORA*, ser. I, vol. 48, pt. 1, pp. 1276–79.
15. Wallace to Grant, April 18, 1865, ibid., pt. 2, p. 457.
16. Walker to Wallace, March 27, 1865, ibid., pt. 1, pp. 1275–76.
17. Walker to Slaughter, March 27, 1865, ibid., p. 1448.
18. Wallace to Slaughter and Ford, April 6, 1865, ibid., pt. 2, pp. 462–63.
19. Mejía to Francisco Cassanova, April 11, 1865, AMG, 1865.

Monroe Doctrine, ejection of French forces from Mexico, and the reestablishment of the republic under Juárez or the creation of a protectorate over Mexico.

Both the Blair and the Wallace plots were discussed in *L'Ere nouvelle*, a French language newspaper of Mexico City, early in May 1865. What these two conspirators had proposed was related with surprising accuracy, followed by comment on the gravity of the situation and the apparent increase of danger from the North following Lincoln's assassination. Grant was credited with responsibility for intrigues to dazzle the South into an attempt to annex Mexico. *L'Ere nouvelle* believed the leniency of terms given Lee by Grant had a connection with these schemes. It warned that the peril of invasion would have been less serious if internal conditions in Mexico were less vulnerable; that "peace is not assured; the guerrillas are everywhere at large and defiance is spreading throughout the Empire, paralyzing its efforts."[20]

Shortly after Wallace's conference with the Confederates, Grant lost his enthusiasm for Wallace. When, a few months later, Romero suggested that Wallace be associated with plans for aiding Mexico, Grant was unresponsive. The irrepressible Wallace was concocting his most ambitious Mexican adventure with the equally imaginative and impractical General José M. J. Carvajal.

Ever contemptuous of the messianic Lew Wallace since his division had been lost at Shiloh, General Sheridan from the Rio Grande reported to Grant in the summer of 1865 that Wallace, with "some other sharks," had arrived but doubted "if they can do much good."[21] The Maximilian-sponsored Confederate newspaper in Mexico City, the *Mexican Times*, heaped the severest ridicule on the Indiana conspirator. "This remarkable worthy," it reported, "has been definitely located at last, and now turns out to be a first class filibuster in Matamoros. . . . Wallace is a wheezy, ramshackle ex-officer of the Volunteer Federal army, barely saved from disgrace at Shiloh. . . . He comes to Mexico with six Parrott guns and 1,000 kindred adventurers."[22]

In sharp contrast to the futile maneuvers of Wallace and Carvajal was the surprisingly efficient accomplishment by Herman Sturm, whom Carvajal at Wallace's suggestion had commissioned a Mexican general. Financially secure and with European

20. "Intrigues in Texas," May 5 and May 6, 1865, *L'Ere nouvelle*.
21. Richard O'Connor, *Sheridan the Inevitable* (Indianapolis, 1953), p. 282.
22. *Mexican Times*, October 1, 1866.

experience, Sturm had served with distinction during the U.S. Civil War as chief of ordnance at Indianapolis. He assumed the responsibility of providing munitions and supplies and, to safeguard secrecy, of taking general charge of immigrants prior to their departure for Mexico. He also undertook to find means for their transportation.

By the summer of 1866 Sturm had ready for shipment supplies for 7,000 men and, almost as important, the ways and means of transportation. First of the Sturm argosies was the steamer, *General Sheridan*; the second, the *Everman*, which sailed from New York, July 26, with arms, ammunition, a group of Mexican officers, Lew Wallace, and Colonel George E. Church of the *New York Herald*.

The *Everman* docked at Brazos de Santiago after fifteen days out of New York and there was met by a lighter sent by Carvajal on which the cargo and passengers were transported to Matamoros. After Carvajal had begun storing the cargo in government warehouses, his enemies suddenly staged a revolt. They attempted to assassinate Carvajal, but he escaped to Texas; they imprisoned the passengers, including Wallace, and proceeded to take possession of the cargo. Order was finally restored and Wallace and the others were released. The salvaged cargo was stored in Brownsville.[23]

The persevering Wallace accompanied by Church set out from Matamoros by wagon for Monterrey to locate a responsible agent of the Juárez government who would accept and give a receipt for the *Everman*'s cargo. He spent one month in Monterrey in futile efforts to secure from the governor the necessary documents and then, as blithely as if on a holiday jaunt, he and Church started the toilsome twenty-day journey to Chihuahua, more than eight hundred miles westward. "Such an opportunity to 'do' northern Mexico," wrote Wallace, "seldom comes."

Juárez and his reduced government were hospitality personified when the U.S. travelers reached Chihuahua late in September 1866; they were given a prominent spot on the program of an eight-hour official dinner. Wallace opened negotiations with Juárez, whose cabinet he considered superior to that at Washington. Enchanted by northern Mexico, he and Church succumbed to the age-old U.S. habit of seeking concessions. They offered to

23. McKee, *"Ben Hur" Wallace*, pp. 104–5.

defend the states of Coahuila, Nuevo León, Chihuahua, and northern Durango against the Indians and to bring in five hundred colonists annually for a concession of 2,700 square leagues of arable land in northern Chihuahua (including mines located there), provided they were given coinage monopoly and exemption from taxes. There followed happy days of dreams, pleasure, and plans, but no contracts were executed, and no business was ever transacted about the *Everman* cargo except the penning by the secretary of foreign affairs of two letters of thanks. In December 1866, the Juárez government and army moved southward. Wallace was left alone late the next month at Zacatecas, he claimed, "without escort, to find my way, as best I could, through the desert and over the infested highway to Saltillo."[24] The engineer-journalist Church remained with Juárez.

The implications of the Yankee intrigues, personified by Blair and Wallace, were significant because they sustained French and, indeed, European fears of what might happen once the Union was restored. Even though General Henry Shelton Sanford's claim that the United States was now the most powerful nation might not be accepted, there was no doubt that the size of its trained forces, the number of its ships, and the quality of its arms presented an impressive and foreboding picture. Few informed Europeans believed this arsenal would be quietly disbanded and some million Union soldiers resume their civilian status. Sanford, the echo chamber of European opinion, emphasized this apprehension to Seward in dispatch after dispatch. "All see we are a most formidable power,"[25] he wrote. By March stocks were falling on the Paris Bourse and prospective Mexican investments were paralyzed. "I think you could make a good bargain with the Emperor if you would only help him out of his Mexican scrape,"[26] was Sanford's prophetic advice. Baron Rothschild confided to Sanford that he had refused to handle a new Mexican loan even though the commission was $17,000,000.[27]

Greatest cause for concern was the restoration of a common boundary between Mexico and the United States along the Rio Grande. Such proximity bred military incidents. No one in

24. Ibid., 106–11.

25. Sanford to Seward, February 24, 1865, Sanford Papers, Sanford Memorial Library, Sanford, Florida, reel 99, box 60, folder 1.

26. Sanford to Seward, March 5, 1865, ibid.

27. Sanford to Seward, August 1, 1865, ibid.; see also William Henry Seward Papers, Rush Rhees Library, University of Rochester, Rochester, N.Y.

France, wrote Sanford, believed that twenty to thirty thousand French in Mexico impressed the United States which could put 500,000 troops there. France knew her intervention in Mexico had been a serious mistake, one Frenchman told him, and intended to withdraw, but if public opinion in the United States insulted the French flag, "I know my country well enough to vow to you that the whole of France will take up the cause and never give in."[28]

At this critical juncture of relations between France and the United States, Seward's physical condition entered into the course of events. On April 5, 1865, a carriage accident fractured Seward's jaw and broke an arm. Nine days later at almost the same hour that Booth was shooting Lincoln, a deranged ex-Confederate soldier broke into Seward's room and stabbed repeatedly the bedridden secretary of state, slashing open his right cheek. Had it not been for the iron brace protecting Seward's jaw, he would have been killed.

His powerful reserve strength enabled him to make such a recovery that within five weeks he was going to the State Department and shortly thereafter attended cabinet meetings.[29] It was fortunate that Seward recuperated so miraculously. Within a few months he was to render his country a service unsurpassed by any of his predecessors.

28. Sanford to Seward, August 31, 1865, Sanford Papers, reel 99, box 60, folder 1; Seward Papers, vol. 52.
29. Glyndon G. Van Deusen, *William Henry Seward* (New York, 1967), p. 415.

20

Commodore Maury's "New Virginia" 1865–1866

———————◄◆►———————

The arrival in Mexico of Commodore Matthew Fontaine Maury created new optimism for the immigration program. As a high officer in the U.S. Navy, he had made such fundamental contributions to the science of oceanography as to give him a worldwide reputation. He was described by Douglas Southall Freeman as "a keen-eyed man with a great dome of a head and pleasant composure of countenance." Because he was one of the best-known Confederates, his relatives and friends had warned him that if, after the war, he returned to his native land, he would be imprisoned. After completing a mission for the Confederacy in England, he therefore headed for Mexico where he offered his services to Maximilian. His enthusiastic idea of establishing a "New Virginia" in Mexico so impressed Maximilian that the Virginian was appointed head of the entire colonization program.

Maury's scientific contribution to the United States and all maritime nations occurred prior to the U.S. Civil War. He compiled works dealing with winds and currents of the Atlantic and Pacific oceans. In the days before steam revolutionized ocean transportation, the utility of this work was such that ten to fifteen days' sailing time could be saved in the passage from New York to Rio de Janeiro. Even more important during the California gold rush was the saving of approximately forty-seven days by the use of his charts in the run from New York to San Francisco.

CONFEDERATE COLONIES IN MEXICO

Honors, medals, purses, and honorary degrees were bestowed upon Maury, including the LL.D. from Cambridge University.

His reflections on drawing colonists from the United States to Mexico revealed his earlier dream to see the seemingly endless Amazon Valley become a flourishing center of world trade. An important result, he hoped, would be the transference there of slaves from the United States.

After the loss of Vicksburg in 1863, Southern states west of the Mississippi were isolated from the Richmond government and left to shift for themselves. And, as the Confederacy sank toward collapse, the eyes of potential émigrés turned toward Maximilian's empire. As early as May 1, 1862, when New Orleans fell, some Louisianians expatriated themselves and went to eastern Mexico. In the West, Union control of California alienated Confederate sympathizers, some of whom fled to western Mexico.

One of the earliest Confederate recruiters in California was Alonzo Ridley,[1] a New Englander who had served as an Indian agent in the West.[2] He and some of his recruits accompanied Brigadier General Albert Sidney Johnston from California to Virginia.[3] After Ridley had served in the Confederate army, he joined other Confederates in Mexico.[4] He was appointed immigration agent by Maximilian, with his office at Mazatlán on the Pacific coast. He sent circulars to California hoping to attract settlers.[5] Remaining in Mexico until the 1870s, he finally returned to Arizona.[6]

Edmund Kirby-Smith, commander of the Trans-Mississippi Department, in February 1865 undertook to find out what the future held for the Confederates. He commissioned Robert Rose, a lawyer of Galveston, to inform the emperor that if an "unexampled catastrophe" befell the Confederacy, he intended to seek asylum at the imperial court and could bring with him intelligent and daring soldiers to aid in consolidating the Mexican Empire.[7]

Two months later, when General Lee surrendered, Kirby-Smith sent another message to Maximilian expressing the desire of Confederates to enter into an agreement with the Mexican Empire "for mutual protection" from their common enemy. The emperor was assured that 9,000 Missourians and not less than

---

1. San Bernardino (California) Weekly Patriot, July 27, 1861.
2. Los Angeles News, April 3, 1866.
3. ORA, ser. I, vols. 4, 19.
4. Interview with Martin Calderwood, Phoenix (Arizona) Republican, March 26, 1909.
5. Constance Wynn Altshuler, Latest from Arizona! (Tucson, 1969), p. 276.
6. Ibid., p. 277.
7. Kirby-Smith to Rose, February 1, 1865 (two letters), ORA, ser. I, vol. 48, pt. 1, pp. 1358–59.

10,000 Confederates from other states "would gladly rally around any flag that promises to lead them to battle against their former foe."[8]

The debacle of the Confederate government and the surrender of its army created general apprehension over the fate of its high officialdom even before the assassination of Lincoln touched off in the North a virtual crusade for retribution. Radicals in the U.S. Congress stood ready to capitalize on the emotional turmoil resulting from this tragedy. In addition to economic bankruptcy and social revolution under which the Southern people were already staggering, there was now the fear of imprisonment and confiscation of property. Thousands of Southerners prepared to take refuge in foreign lands; Mexico was the most accessible.

Alarming rumors spread in the North that armed, organized bodies of Confederates were entering Mexico and that many were en route to Sonora to join ex-Senator Gwin in setting up a French protectorate. In June 1865, Grant was notified that soldiers and civilians were transporting war equipment, horses, and mules into Mexico.[9] Early in July a body of armed troops variously estimated from several hundred to 1,000 crossed the Rio Grande, sold their arms to Juárez officials at Piedras Negras and proceeded to Monterrey. Some enlisted in the Juárez army, others started toward the Pacific en route to California or sought homes in countries to the south or in Europe, but the majority followed Major General Joseph O. Shelby and his Iron Cavalry Brigade of Missouri to Mexico City and offered their services to the Emperor Maximilian.[10]

The mounting tide of Southerners seeking refuge below the Rio Grande posed many problems for both Maximilian and the French. On the one hand, such immigrants provided a faltering empire with new citizens—intelligent, skilled, and able to contribute in many ways to their adopted land. If trouble broke out between the United States and France, Confederate refugees would support the French. On the other hand, nothing would infuriate Northerners more than to watch the men whom they

8. Kirby-Smith to Rose, May 2, 1865, ibid., vol. 48, pt. 2, pp. 1292–93; Emile de Kératry, La Créance Jecker: Les indemnités françaises et les emprunts mexicains (Paris, 1868), pp. 71–76.
9. Sheridan to Grant, June 28, 1865, Miscellaneous Letters, Dept. of State, NA.
10. John Newman Edwards, Shelby and His Men; or The War in the West (Cincinnati, 1867), pp. 535–50; see also Edwin A. Davis, Fallen Guidon (Santa Fe, N.M., 1962).

had spent four years defeating range themselves for a new struggle in support of a pseudo-American monarchy Washington had refused to recognize. If anything could demolish all hope of reaching an accord between the United States and the Mexican Empire, it would be a warm welcome by Maximilian and Charlotte to Confederate refugees.

In early June 1865, circumstances forced Maximilian to adopt a policy which was reported "very confidentially" to Paris by Alphonse Dano, who had succeeded Montholon as French minister. Dano wrote that Maximilian would not allow Southerners to settle near the northern boundary as ex-Senator Gwin had urged and as many of the recent arrivals had requested. "They will be faithful for a while," was Maximilian's judgment, "but I must think of the future. What will happen when a compact Anglo-Saxon group is established on the frontier? They will become rich, and will they follow our rule or want to be independent?" he queried, no doubt with Texas in mind. He likewise opposed locating Southerners on the Isthmus of Tehuantepec but would allow them to settle throughout the central part of the country, though not in large numbers in any one locality.[11] Eventually, in at least one-half the states of Mexico, Confederate settlements of colonists were established.

Maximilian hoped the exodus of Confederates would provide a basis for negotiation and discussion of a common problem with the United States, and that imperial Mexico might thereby find herself in a favorable relationship with her northern neighbor. Probably with this in mind, the emperor required all Confederate soldiers to turn in their arms at the border and sent one of his ministers to establish friendly relations with Union officers in Texas.[12]

The desire of Confederate veterans to serve in the imperial army created another problem. According to Confederate Major General John B. Magruder, Maximilian declined their offers; he knew their inclusion would offend Washington and his judgment was "that no government . . . can exist permanently in Mexico which fails to win the good-will of the . . . United States." However, Magruder quoted the Mexican emperor as saying, "I will

11. Dano to Drouyn de Lhuys, June 11, 1865, Very Confidential, CP, Mexique, LXIII.

12. Dano to Drouyn de Lhuys, June 29, 1865, ibid.; Imperial Minister of Fomento was Luis Robles.

avail myself with great pleasure of the services of such of you as may remain here . . . to introduce into this country your admirable public land system and . . . [your] system of immigration."[13] General Bazaine devised a more practical solution. He quietly placed a limited number of Southerners in the Foreign Legion and in the counter-guerrillas.[14]

The Quai d'Orsay gave guarded approval to such procedures, interspersed with cautious advice. Mexico should make it clear that she did not really desire Confederate immigration: rather, she merely fulfilled a duty to humanity by affording desolate men a refuge after they had been disarmed and sent to the interior.[15] Yet it would be unwise to allow them to go unsupervised. They might join Juárez, become guerrillas, or even raid the United States to exact vengeance. As for enlistments in the Foreign Legion, care should be taken not to concentrate a sizeable group in any one division, to prevent the impression that enemies of the Union were reorganizing on foreign soil. Bazaine was repeatedly urged to exercise the utmost prudence.[16] From this avowed policy of French humanitarianism and neutrality, Maximilian, as usual, deviated.

Among the Confederates who were accepted for military service under Maximilian was Judge Alexander W. Terrell of Virginia, who had attained the rank of brigadier general in the Confederate army. After his repatriation, Terrell was appointed U.S. minister to Turkey by President Grover Cleveland, first post-war democrat in the White House.

A considerable number of high-ranking Confederates were associated with Maury's immigration organization. Director of land distribution was Major General John B. Magruder, physically magnificent and known as "Prince John." Others surveyed and made available lands for immigrants, organized colonies, and administered settlements.

First and best known of Confederate settlements in Mexico was Carlota, named in honor of the Mexican empress. It was on

13. John B. Magruder, "Our Mexican Problem," *New York Times*, April 2, 1916, reproduced from a statement written fifty years before; Campbell to Seward, November 21, 1866, Dispatches, Mexico, Dept. of State, NA, XXX.

14. Dano to Drouyn de Lhuys, August 10, 1865, CP, Mexique, LXIV; Alexander W. Terrell, *From Texas to Mexico and the Court of Maximilian in 1865* (Dallas, 1933).

15. Drouyn de Lhuys to Dano, July 15, 1865, CP, Mexique, LXIV.

16. Drouyn de Lhuys to Dano, August 21 and August 30, 1865, ibid.

the railroad to Mexico City, seventy miles west of Veracruz. Its chief promoters were Brigadier General Sterling Price, governor of Missouri, perhaps the leading secession figure west of the Mississippi, and Governor Isham G. Harris of Tennessee, who fled to Mexico with a price on his head and who helped Commodore Maury draw up immigration regulations. After repatriation Harris represented Tennessee in the U.S. Senate. Others settled in Cordova and Orizaba in the general vicinity of Carlota.

Perhaps the most spectacular high Confederate official in Mexico was Major General "Jo" Shelby. Refusing to surrender, he and his Iron Cavalry Brigade of Missouri escaped to Mexico. En route they were joined by others of like convictions.

Shelby was given a valuable *hacienda* near Carlota where he planted coffee and established a freighting line from the Cordova area, where the Veracruz–Mexico City Railroad construction had then reached. Shelby used ten-mule wagon trains. This business venture was prosperous when not interrupted by guerrilla attacks. Later he was active in the Confederate colony of Tuxpan.

After the collapse of the Maximilian empire, General Shelby returned to Missouri and later was appointed U.S. marshal in Kansas City by President Grover Cleveland.

Perhaps the Confederate refugee in Mexico most hated by the North was the Virginian, Lieutenant General Jubal A. Early, West Pointer by training but "prosecuting attorney by impulse and choice," he of the Shenandoah apple toddy memories. In 1864, when Early was marching his troops down the Shenandoah Valley to attack Washington, he ordered the Union city of Chambersburg, Pennsylvania, to pay him a ransom of $100,000 in gold to escape destruction. When this ransom was not paid, Early ordered the burning of Chambersburg. After the war he fled to Mexico. The Confederate who carried out Early's order to destroy Chambersburg, Brigadier General John McCausland of Missouri, endeavoring to escape vindictive action, finally found refuge in Mexico. Because of his experience as a military engineer he was appointed one of the principal surveyors of lands for immigrants.

Among other Californians seeking a new life in western Mexico was Confederate Brigadier General David S. Terry. A native of Kentucky, Terry had gone to Galveston as a boy to study law with an uncle. At the age of thirteen he enlisted as a Texas militiaman when Texas was fighting for its independence.

After completing his study of law and fighting with the Texas Rangers in the U.S. war against Mexico, Terry moved to California, built a prosperous practice and became, at the age of thirty-four, chief justice of the California Supreme Court.

Terry left his law practice to serve the Confederacy, and when the Confederate army surrendered, Terry joined those who sought refuge in Mexico. He established a cotton-growing community of Confederates near Guadalajara in the state of Jalisco, not far from the Pacific coast. Early in that venture, however, Terry decided that Mexico was doomed to anarchy and bloodshed. Therefore, in 1867, before his first crop was picked, he returned to California and practiced law successfully there for the next two decades.

Terry was courageous and quick to anger. He lived and died by the then current code of honor among gentlemen. In his youth he was adept in the use of the bowie knife. Later, in California, he challenged U.S. Senator David C. Broderick to a duel to redress an insult, and killed the senator. Adherence to this code, in fact, led to his own death; Terry impulsively slapped a judge who questioned the legality of his wife's former marriage, and was shot to death by the judge's bodyguard.

Inland from Mazatlán Brigadier General William P. Hardeman surveyed lands in the state of Durango, where the Palacio colony was established. Here Confederate Major George W. Clark of Arkansas was in charge of the settlement of Southerners. His newspaper, the *Two Republics*, was begun after the fall of the empire. He gathered much information about Confederate refugees and was able to maintain his publication until the 1870s.

A major contribution by Confederate engineers in Mexico was that part of the railroad designed to connect Veracruz with Mexico City. Of these engineers several were well-trained and widely experienced graduates of West Point.

This group included Chief Engineer Andrew Talcott of Connecticut whose U.S. Army duties included building fortifications and canals, improving rivers, and determining boundary lines in eight states. His civil experience was even more extensive, including as it did considerable railroad building. Talcott married in Virginia one of the Randolphs and was an associate and very close friend of Robert E. Lee.

Another Northerner appointed by Maximilian to help build the Veracruz–Mexico City Railroad was Brigadier General Danville Leadbetter of Maine, also a West Pointer and former Chief Engineer for the state of Alabama.

Thomas C. Reynolds, a South Carolinian, was the superintendent of the Mexican Railway Company. He had attended the University of Virginia and Heidelberg University in Germany and entered politics in Missouri where he was lieutenant governor. His turbulent life there and in Mexico included numerous personal controversies with leading Confederates. To his credit it should be noted that when he left Mexico, he was on friendly terms with President Juárez and General Porfirio Díaz.

Manning M. Kimmel of Missouri, a graduate of West Point, was unique in that as an officer in the Union army he fought the Confederacy in defending Washington. He then resigned from the U.S. Army in which his cousin, Anthony Kimmel, was a major general, to join the Confederacy, and in time became Confederate brigadier general.

In Mexico Kimmel was assigned to an engineering post on the railroad. His full rights of citizenship were restored through a friend, who was private military secretary to President Andrew Johnson. His son, Rear Admiral Husband E. Kimmel, was commander-in-chief of the U.S. fleet when the Japanese attacked Pearl Harbor[17] December 7, 1941, and sank the U.S.S. *Arizona* with the loss of 1,104 lives.

The search for assassins of Abraham Lincoln extended to the group of Confederates in Mexico. Among those charged with this and related crimes was the famous Virginian, Beverley Tucker, for whom a $25,000 reward was offered. Tucker had been engaged by the Escandons, a great family of Mexico, to manage their huge *haciendas*, famous for their fine bulls, in the state of San Luis Potosí. Tucker suffered a long period of humiliation before the charge was dropped for want of evidence.

Maury's vision was to attract to Mexico as many planters as could be induced to accept expatriation. Maximilian, having fallen under the spell of Commodore Maury, authorized him to proceed with his plan to reproduce in Mexico the agreeable way

17. Letter from Rear Admiral Husband E. Kimmel to A. J. Hanna, July 11, 1938, and four letters from Major M. M. Kimmel to others (all in possession of the author).

of life he had treasured in Virginia.[18] His "New Virginia" would provide an escape from an intolerable situation and would be a powerful spur to the growth and security of the new empire. For the information of Napoleon III, Maury also described the enterprise in a letter to his old friend, Admiral Chabanne.

"The wreck of the Southern Confederacy is rich in the materials of Empire," Maury explained to Chabanne. "It is in the power of the Emperor Maximilian to transfer these people with their emancipated Negroes to Mexico and to convert them instantly into the most loyal, true and devoted subjects: and through their instrumentality to establish firmly and at once his empire. It is for this that I am here. . . .

"If the Empire were sprinkled with settlements consisting of not more than a dozen or so of these Southern families," continued the Virginian, "they would leaven the agricultural industry of the whole country. Every settlement would be an agricultural school of the first class, teaching by example . . . [and the émigrés] would at once surround the throne with the elements of an elegant aristocracy such as few sovereigns have ever found themselves able to create. . . ."[19]

Under Maury's guidance, the Junta of Colonization worked out new plans.[20] A series of decrees by Maximilian opened Mexico to immigrants of all nations, and outlined regulations.

Included in these announcements were provisions for former slaves. Employers were responsible for feeding, clothing, and sheltering the laborer and his children on a contract basis. The laborer was to be paid a wage, one-fourth of which was to be deposited in banks created for that purpose. Aside from these safeguards, the Negro laborer and his children (until they became of age) were bonded to employers for periods of not less than five or more than ten years; they could not change employers without consent; if they ran away, they could be returned legally.[21]

---

18. Alfred J. Hanna, "The Role of Matthew Fontaine Maury in the Mexican Empire," *Virginia Magazine of History and Biography*, LV (April 1947), 105–25.

19. Maury to Chabanne, June 1 and June 10, 1865, Pièces Diverses, unbound folder, 1865, Affaires Diverses, Etats-Unis, AN; Maury to Chabanne, June 9, 1865, and "Project of a Design to Encourage Immigration to Mexico of Planters from Virginia with their Former Slaves," June 13, 1865, Matthew Fontaine Maury Papers, LC, XXII.

20. Campbell-Scarlett to Russell, September 1, 1865, BFO 50/387.

21. *El Diario del Imperio*, September 5 and 9, October 7, 1865.

Jubilant over immigration prospects, the French language newspaper, *L'Estafette*, proclaimed this program "the greatest act of the Empire."[22] Although opposed to subsidized immigration and having previously sounded a warning against admitting Negroes,[23] *L'Ere nouvelle*, the other French language newspaper, approved, on the whole, the practical steps taken, but warned that "the phalanx of resistance [to immigration] is closing its ranks and presenting a more solid front than ever." It predicted more passive antagonism than open opposition by Conservatives.[24]

Confederate immigration agents were appointed in Virginia, the Carolinas, Missouri, California, Louisiana, and Alabama. Among supporting publications was a sixteen-page pamphlet in English, describing Mexico as an Elysium for the dispossessed. A more effective propaganda organ to attract Confederates was an English language newspaper, the *Mexican Times*. Supported by a subsidy, it appeared as a weekly in mid-September 1865.

Editor of the *Mexican Times* was Brigadier General Henry W. Allen whose military career had ended with the shattering of his right leg. Elected governor of Louisiana, he was later singled out by Douglas Southall Freeman, Lee's noted biographer, as the only "great administrator produced by the Confederacy."[25] Penniless, Allen borrowed $500, set out for Mexico, and fortified his courage by quoting from Aristotle that "banishment is desirable, because a banished man has the choice of places in which to dwell."[26] In his appeal to prospective immigrants, editor Allen summarily disposed of the Monroe Doctrine as a "bloated humbug" and reminded his readers that the largest portion of the Western Hemisphere was held by three monarchies other than Mexico; namely, England, Russia, and Brazil.[27]

General Grant attempted to counteract the Confederate migration to Mexico. He instructed General Sheridan, who was in charge of Union forces along the Rio Grande, not to allow Con-

22. *L'Estafette*, September 10, 1865.

23. *L'Ere nouvelle*, June 18, 1865.

24. Ibid., September 12, 1865.

25. For a biography of Allen, see Vincent H. Cassidy and Amos E. Simpson, *Henry Watkins Allen of Louisiana* (Baton Rouge, 1964).

26. Sarah A. Dorsey, *Recollections of Henry Watkins Allen, Brigadier-General Confederate States Army, Ex-Governor of Louisiana* (New York, 1866), pp. 307–10; Alfred J. Hanna, "A Confederate Newspaper in Mexico," *JSH*, XII (February 1946), 67–83.

27. *Mexican Times*, November 18, 1865, and February 17, 1866.

federates to pass over the boundary line into Mexico. Sheridan placed troops to guard the main crossings of the Rio Grande and to inspect vessels leaving New Orleans and nearby ports.[28] A refugee who arrived at San Luis Potosí one month after this regulation went into effect, declared that more than five hundred families with their wagons and property had been turned back from the Mexican border.[29]

Another serious handicap confronting Southerners was the warning that they could not reenter the South without permission from President Andrew Johnson and that persons "implicated in the rebellion" who applied for passports would be dealt with according to the merits of each case.[30] Many prospective colonists were restrained by the fear that, if the golden fruit of Mexico turned sour, they might not be allowed to return home.

The exodus of Confederates heated a cauldron of seething wrath in the North after Mexican diplomat Matías Romero distributed Maximilian's decrees relating to Confederate refugees. The U.S. minister in Paris was instructed to discuss the subject with the French government. Reacting to widespread indignation, the U.S. House of Representatives asked President Johnson for a report on the "re-establishment of slavery or peonage in the Republic of Mexico," and the Senate requested information about what Senator Gwin and Commodore Maury were doing "to induce into the so-called Mexican Empire . . . dissatisfied citizens. . . ."[31]

The Quai d'Orsay was more disturbed by the growing tension in Washington than its outward calm indicated. Attempts were made in Paris to brush aside the issue when the U.S. minister called to make inquiry, but a subsequent note sent to Mexico was far from phlegmatic. In effect, it said that Maximilian's policy was producing the reverse of the unobtrusive assimilation of Southern colonists which had seemed to be a providential source of strength for the empire.

28. Philip H. Sheridan, *Personal Memoirs*, 2 vols. (New York, 1888), II, 218–19.
29. Bazaine to Randon, May 9, 1866, AMG, 1866–67.
30. Seward to Maury, September 5, 1865, Miscellaneous Letters, Dept. of State, NA, LXX. For announcement of August 25, 1865, see James D. Richardson, comp. *A Compilation of the Messages and Papers of the President, 1789–1897*, 10 vols. (Washington, D.C., 1896–1900), VIII, 3347.
31. Resolution of December 11, 1865, U.S., Congress, *House Ex. Doc.*, 39th Cong., 1st sess., No. 13, and Senate Resolution of December 19, 1865, U.S., Congress, Senate, *Congressional Globe*, 39th Cong., 1st sess., 17. For retort to criticism of the Northern press, see *L'Estafette*, November 11, 1865.

L'Ere nouvelle spoke frankly of the rising danger from the United States and the lack of wisdom in featuring Maury. "The illustrious scholar left in the United States singularly lively animosities," warned this newspaper. "One sees in him one of the most irreconcilable personifications of the antagonism between the North and the South. . . . It is no wonder that the favors of which the eminent exile was the object in Mexico were regarded as an act of positive unfriendliness toward the North" as was the "back-handed attempt to revive slavery on Mexican soil for the benefit of Confederates."[32] Denouncing numerous enticements put out by Maury's Immigration Office, *L'Ere nouvelle* asked, "What must . . . [immigrants] think, what must they say among themselves, men who come on the faith of such declarations and find neither lands, nor agents, nor guides and are forced to go home? . . . It is unfortunate that so many promises have been spread abroad in the name of the Emperor."[33] Another journalist accused Maury of an entire lack of interest in other groups because of his overdevotion to his own compatriots.[34]

When Dano, armed with the latest dispatch from Paris, took Maximilian to task for his immigration inconsistencies, the Mexican emperor was easily won over. He knew it had been a mistake to favor Southerners so openly, but—and here he borrowed the technique of the first Adam—Charlotte had advised it. Actually Dano explained to Paris, Charlotte's deep sympathy for Confederate refugees had resulted in the appointments of Maury, Magruder, and other high immigration officials in Maximilian's absence. The offending indenture system was a kind of slavery, Maximilian admitted; but he would revise the decree. He would not dismiss Confederates he had appointed to high offices and thus admit his mistake; instead, he would render their positions so illusory that they would ask to resign.[35]

Maximilian's decision to double-cross Southerners was one of the few he seems actually to have carried out. That determination was rendered easy by a bankrupt treasury, a disintegrating government, and opposition to immigration by the Mexicans themselves.

The Southern press was either lukewarm or opposed to ex-

32. *L'Ere nouvelle*, January 19, 1866.
33. Ibid., March 28, 1866.
34. *El Cronista*, March 31, 1866.
35. Dano to Drouyn de Lhuys, January 28, 1866, CP, Mexique, LXV.

patriation. Some editors expressed the growing sentiment that Southerners should not abandon their homeland in her humiliation and distress, but work through her Gethsemane into a new era of prosperity and social health. The *Richmond Times* predicted that "[Confederates] in Mexico will soon return to their homes in view of the clemency of the government of the United States, and if the Emperor Maximilian has counted on them for colonization projects, he has been deceived."[36] In declining Maury's invitation to migrate, General Lee wrote, "I prefer to struggle for its [the South's] restoration, and share its fate rather than give up all as lost."[37]

Maury himself did not escape further criticism. Another newspaper charged that the "attempt made last year under Mr. Maury to promote colonization on a large scale proved . . . abortive, mainly because it was controlled by incompetence and conducted in utter defiance of common sense and with not much regard for truth and common honesty. Its failure seemed for a time to have completely discredited and put an end to all attempts to introduce American settlers in Mexico."[38]

Maury became disillusioned. He reported confidentially to Maximilian that Mexican officials would not cooperate; they failed to provide lands for prospective settlers and procrastinated in rendering urgently needed service. Imperial ministers were paralyzing the emperor's good will and ruining the empire by untrustworthiness and greed. He accused the clergy of ignorance, spite, and treason, as well as immorality; he declared that public security and communication were seldom maintained and that the Mexican army had degenerated.[39]

In February 1866, Maury left for England, ostensibly to visit his family. Two months later, the illusory technique Maximilian had promised Dano became evident; he informed Maury that for "motives of economy" he had abolished the Imperial Commission on Colonization and expressed appreciation for the efforts Maury had "so successfully made in the Empire to augment its population. . . ."[40]

36. *La Sociedad*, November 14, 1865, quoting the *Richmond Times*.

37. Lee to Maury, September 8, 1865, Maury Papers, LC, XXIII.

38. *Mexican Times*, December 11, 1866, after it became independent.

39. Maury to Maximilian, October 15 and November 19, 1865, and January 8, 1866, in Egon Caesar Corti, *Maximilian and Charlotte in Mexico*, trans. Catherine A. Phillips, 2 vols. (New York, 1928), II, 538–40, 561.

40. Maximilian to Maury, April 19, 1866, Maury Papers, LC, XXIII.

Although prospective settlers came to Mexico from Africa, Austria, Belgium, China, the Dutch East Indies, Egypt, France, the German States, Italy, Ireland, Poland, Portugal, Spain, and Switzerland, Southerners formed the largest number of immigrants. Yet the final total fell far short of the optimistic figure of 600,000 set by Napoleon III in his plan for the regeneration of Mexico.[41]

41. *La Sociedad*, July 19, 26 and 28, 1865; B. R. Carmen to Seward, October 22, 1864, Consular Reports, Mazatlán, Dept. of State, NA, 1864–69.

21

Mr. Secretary Seward
and the Brass Hats
1865–1866

———————————

War between France and the United States had been somewhat casually threatened as early as 1864. In his campaign for
the vice presidency, Andrew Johnson declared: "The time is not
far distant when the Rebellion will be put down and then we will
attend to this Mexican affair and say to Louis Napoleon, 'You
can get up no monarchy on this continent.' An expedition into
Mexico would be a sort of recreation to the brave soldiers of the
Union, and the French concern would quickly be wiped out."[1]

Across the Rio Grande French soldiers occupied northeastern
Mexico. At any moment the danger that some rash incident there
might invoke national pride was averted by the patience and
skill of Secretary of State William H. Seward. Following his recovery from the assassination attempt he appeared to gain new
vigor in meeting the challenge of the French in Mexico. His
policy was to capitalize on the ineffectiveness of Maximilian and
on Napoleon III's desire to abandon overseas entanglements.
Seward was convinced the Mexican republic could be restored
and the French eliminated without military intervention of the
Union. Seward's enemies—and he had many—denounced his policy as vacillating and weak. Many of these enemies were so-called

1. Lloyd P. Stryker, *Andrew Johnson* (New York, 1929), p. 132.

SEWARD

Secretary of State William H. Seward was described by Charles XV, king of Sweden and Norway, as "the most wise and sagacious statesman of modern times." In his extensive state papers Seward forcefully and appealingly condemned the interference in the New World by Napoleon III and other European monarchs, thereby giving to the democratic ideals and aspirations of the Americas worldwide respect and distinction.

Anonymous, 1863; Illustration from *Vanity Fair*
(The Bettmann Archive, Inc.)

fire eaters in Congress who from time to time passed resolutions that provoked embarrassment in Paris.

Most powerful opponent of Seward's policy was General Grant. The General took advantage of his ready access to Lincoln's successor to expound his views on Mexico and to develop yet another scheme from Washington for interference in Mexico. He contended that an honorable and permanent peace must be secured while "we still have in service a force sufficient to insure it." He maintained that the Mexican invasion and occupation would never have taken place had the U.S. Civil War not led European powers to expect the United States to be dismembered and republican institutions thus weakened. Grant reminded President Johnson that from the time the Maximilian empire had been established, the Rio Grande region had been pro-Confederate.

French hold on the northern states of Mexico was weak in the spring of 1865. In reporting that French troops were few and lines of communication feebly guarded, a United States secret agent wrote, "Perhaps Maximilian or his tutor, General Bazaine, really believe that the task is already accomplished and that now nothing is required but the titles of nobility and the gold embroidered coats which have been promised in profusion to traitors and rascals who have endeavored to sell the inheritance of freedom . . . for a mess of pottage."[2]

As the U.S. Civil War ended, Grant sent Sheridan and under him more than 50,000 veteran troops, to carry out very secret projects against the French along the Rio Grande. The first of Grant's plans to provoke the French in that region was the display by Sheridan of hostility on the Texas boundary line and the passing of supplies over the river to the Juarista forces. Arms and munitions were left quietly near the river bank and as quietly disappeared.

Early in the fall of 1865, Sheridan staged a second demonstration along the border. After reviewing the cavalry at San Antonio, Texas, with much ostentation, he proceeded southward to Eagle Pass and through a staff officer opened communication with Juárez, "taking care," he explained, "not to do this in the dark." Rumors spread like wildfire that Sheridan's invasion of northern Mexico was in readiness and awaited only the arrival

2. Reuben Creel to James H. Carleton, April 12, 1865, Adjutant General's Office, War Dept., Miscellaneous Branch, NA.

of additional troops already on the march. By this time Bazaine had prudently moved French troops back from the border to Monterrey. Since imperialist forces in Matamoros and vicinity were thus materially weakened, the Juaristas under General Mariano Escobedo, improved their position and increased their strength with supplies from Texas. Of the considerable war materials Sheridan made available to the republican forces, at least 30,000 muskets were drawn from the Baton Rouge arsenal.[3]

When news of the Sheridan posturing reached Washington, the French minister protested vigorously to Seward that the truculence at Brownsville and other points was not compatible with the policy of moderation Washington had announced.[4] Immediately, strict neutrality was enjoined on Sheridan's troops by Washington, a move that Sheridan could not understand, aware as he was of Grant's negotiations with President Juárez through Romero.

As early as August 1864, Juárez had offered land bounties to foreigners who would aid in the defense of the Mexican republic. A year later after the close of the U.S. Civil War, Mexican recruiting offices were opened in Washington, New York, and other cities. Inquiries from demobilized men poured into the Mexican legation in such profusion that Romero worked out a form letter for his replies.[5] Submitting it to the U.S. Department of State, Romero was informed that armed immigration could not be permitted under the neutrality laws.[6] However, with the backing of Grant Romero continued to encourage immigration. In discussing with Grant the likelihood of war between France and the United States, the Mexican minister prophesied that Americans could control Mexico in six or eight months.

Success of the proposed armed immigration to fight with Juárez against the French depended on the enlistment of an influential general. After Grant refused to consider the command, Romero and Francis Preston Blair, Sr., decided on General William Tecumseh Sherman, whom Blair approached; Sherman declined. After further shopping about Grant suggested General John M. Schofield, then stationed at Raleigh, North Carolina. It was re-

3. Philip H. Sheridan, *Personal Memoirs*, 2 vols. (New York, 1888), II, 223–26. See also Richard O'Connor, *Sheridan the Inevitable* (Indianapolis, 1953), pp. 278–81.
4. Montholon to Seward, October 19, 1865, Notes, France, NA, XVII.
5. Romero to Lerdo de Tejada, May 9, 1865, *Corres. mexicana*, V.
6. Romero to Lerdo de Tejada, May 11, 1865, ibid.

ported that Schofield was interested and would make a trip to Washington for conferences.[7]

Through Grant's intercession, Romero was permitted to consult with President Johnson without going through the State Department. The Mexican minister assured the president that Mexico was asking for nothing except the release of a general to lead immigrants to Mexico, the right to purchase arms freely, and permission to float a private loan. President Johnson asked if Seward had been consulted. Romero admitted that he had not done so but explained that Seward had been ill and furthermore, he wanted to keep the proposal in the "hands of Mexico's friends."[8]

President Johnson requested Grant to present the project in writing for cabinet consideration. His statement, submitted to the cabinet June 16, 1865, recommended the release of "one of our general officers for the purpose of going to Mexico to give direction to such immigration as may go to that country" and also permission for the Juaristas to purchase arms. This uninstructed officer would be permitted to take service under the Republic of Mexico.[9] Grant argued that the United States would not have to declare war on France; she could merely allow Mexico to buy whatever munitions were needed and to enlist about 10,000 men. This procedure would be similar to the neutrality practiced by England and France in the U.S. Civil War. Upon hearing the proposal for the first time, Seward gave it his emphatic disapproval. He declared it would unite France and imperial Mexico. Other cabinet members received the Grant proposal with reservations. Secretary of War Edwin M. Stanton was of the opinion that the intentions of Schofield should be known before he was granted his leave to go to Mexico.

Late in June 1865, Schofield arrived in Washington. He first called at the Mexican Legation but would not talk business before he had seen Grant. The next day a meeting was held in Grant's office. Schofield said he was interested, provided terms could be arranged and permission received from the War Department. He expected to see the president in company with Grant, but President Johnson was ill. Schofield then left for a

7. As Schofield was unknown to Mexican officials, Ignacio Mariscal, secretary of the legation, interviewed him. Mariscal's report of Schofield's interest is contained in a communication of June, 1865.

8. Romero to Lerdo de Tejada, May 11, 1865, *Corres. mexicana*, V.

9. Grant to Johnson, July 15, 1865, *ORA*, ser. I, vol. 48, pt. 2, pp. 1080–81.

month's visit with his family, his head full of plans. If all went well, military operations might get under way by August. Romero was confident that under impressive military leadership the enterprise would possess an irresistible appeal. The arguments Grant, Schofield, and Romero expected to use with President Johnson included domestic as well as international aspects. Not only could the Monroe Doctrine be sustained, but the Republican party also steered away from a possible split over the question of Negro suffrage. Romero thought the president, even though he stood in awe of Seward, would favor the views of Grant.[10]

Acceding to the president's request, Romero at last faced Seward. Recognizing the desire of the United States to preserve neutrality, he explained that he had thought out a plan whereby, without violating that policy, the sympathetic support of the United States could be channeled to Mexico. He assured Seward that nothing of an irregular nature was contemplated. The Juárez government desired to make a loan, buy arms, and accept the services of a few army officers placed on furlough for that purpose. He explained that Mexico's above-board dealing was demonstrated by his consulting the State Department before proceeding; he hoped no objections would be raised.

Seward told Romero the Washington government must reduce expenses and could not pay officers not actually serving. Romero replied that Mexico wanted only two or three officers; while in Mexico they would not receive pay from the United States. Seward failed to see how invaders from the United States would be more welcome than those wearing French uniforms. He thought it would be better if Mexico could save herself. However, he agreed to study the proposition and for that purpose asked that it be sent to him in writing. Romero hesitated to do this for fear Seward would discover the steps already taken and undermine the proposed conference with President Johnson.[11]

En route back to Washington late in July, Schofield stopped at West Point to consult Grant about Mexico. Together they proposed an inspection tour of the Texas border, thus enabling Schofield to reach the Rio Grande without arousing suspicion; the War Department would grant him a year's leave of absence

---

10. Romero to Lerdo de Tejada, June 18, 1865, Corres. mexicana, V.
11. Romero to Lerdo de Tejada, July 22, 1865, ibid.

with permission to leave the country.[12] Grant ordered Sheridan to hold supplies, captured or otherwise, pending Schofield's arrival, and to discharge soldiers desiring to go to Mexico and allow them to retain their arms. War with France should be avoided, in deference to Johnson's desire, but if it came, France must be made to seem the aggressor. Schofield discussed the plan with the president on July 27, 1865. Johnson appeared to endorse it, but declined to disclose his decision immediately.

In all this harmony Schofield's demands for remuneration sounded a discordant note. As a reward for his services, he wanted 100,000 pesos paid in advance as adequate provision for his family. Should the Mexican venture misfire, he foresaw that his reputation might be ruined. Romero offered a 10,000 peso advance which was not at all acceptable. He explained that the Mexican government intended to make payment in public lands; furthermore, if full rewards were advanced to him, other officers would make similar demands entirely beyond Mexico's capacity to pay; she expected to finance the expedition from a loan yet to be raised.

A second rift followed. Schofield proposed that he command Mexicans as well as immigrants, and that his army total at least 40,000. Romero firmly opposed any prearrangement of command. The general would have to take whatever position the Mexican government gave him. When the French and Mexican imperialists fought together, the French always commanded and Mexicans resented this. A similar arrangement Juárez would never permit. As to the size of the army, Romero could agree to only 20,000 troops.

Despite these unresolved basic differences, arrangements for a small army of immigrants progressed. Schofield proposed two generals of division and to these posts he expected to appoint General Francis Preston Blair, Jr., and the former Confederate general, Joseph E. Johnston. Armed immigrants would enlist for three years and assemble at convenient locations in Mexico. They would have the rights of Mexican citizenship and the pay of Mexican soldiers. Officers only would receive bonus money.[13]

Against this fantastic enterprise which had the tacit, if not the open approval of the high brass, Seward proceeded adroitly. To stop Romero's running in the side door of the White House

---

12. Grant to Stanton, July 25, 1865, Letterbook, 1865, War Dept., NA.
13. Romero to Lerdo de Tejada, July 30, 1865, *Corres. mexicana*, V.

and, no doubt, to educate a president unversed in diplomatic protocol, the secretary of state issued a circular to all legations in Washington. "Instances of irregularity having recently occurred," read the circular, "it is deemed desirable, with a view to prevent misunderstandings, to announce that the United States Government will expect from members of the diplomatic body an observance of the same rules and courtesies which are required from diplomatic officers of the United States in foreign countries. Official business will be transacted through the head of this Department. The President will, however, receive on occasions of ceremony, only such diplomatic representatives as pursuant to their grade, may be accredited to him."[14]

Both Johnson and Romero having thus been set firmly in their respective official places, Seward next invited Schofield to Cape May, New Jersey, where the Seward family was spending the summer. Since the two had never met, Secretary of War Stanton provided a letter of introduction; in it he stated that Schofield was about to proceed on a tour of inspection along the Rio Grande and had received a year's leave of absence.[15]

Thereafter, the secretary of state maneuvered the situation with consummate skill. Not for a moment did he minimize the dangers of the Grant-Romero-Schofield cabal. Schofield must not be allowed to lead an army of immigrants across the border; on the other hand, Grant, who was being hailed as the savior of the Union, must not be flouted publicly.[16] How better could the needed time be gained than by removing Schofield from the United States and as far as possible from Mexico?

When Schofield arrived at the Seward summer home, the bait was spread astutely before him. The secretary of state readily consented to his inspection of the Texas border; that undertaking would easily consume several weeks. But before Schofield embarked on the military expedition to Mexico, Seward urged him to undertake a special mission to Paris. As Schofield recorded the interview in his memoirs, Seward said to him, "I want you to get your legs under Napoleon's mahogany, and tell him he must get out of Mexico." The general was attracted by the enticing offer, partly because a role in deciding the fortunes of his

14. Circular to the Diplomatic Corps, July 26, 1865, Notes, Mexico, NA, VII.
15. Stanton to Seward, July 28, 1865, William Henry Seward Papers, Rush Rhees Library, University of Rochester, Rochester, N.Y., LI.
16. John Bigelow Papers and Journal, NYPL, March 27, 1869.

country appealed to his pride and patriotism, partly because his financial arrangements with Romero were far from satisfactory.[17] For Schofield a trip to Paris with the blessings of the State Department offered security and prestige with which a highly irregular undertaking in Mexico could never compete. However, before accepting, the general told Seward he must consult Grant and Romero.

Romero, less naïve than Schofield, realized immediately what was afoot. "Unfortunately," wailed the Mexican minister, "General Schofield does not know the true spirit of Seward and is captivated with the idea of going to France on a special mission." Making the best of his disappointment, he insisted on one change only: there must be no waste of several weeks in making an inspection tour along the Rio Grande. Romero urged Schofield to go directly to Paris and, during his absence, preparations for the Mexican expedition could be completed.[18] It thus came about that ten days later Schofield found himself safely within the jurisdiction of the State Department.[19] About the same time Stanton ordered Sheridan on the Rio Grande to discharge all the white soldiers he could spare. This disturbed Schofield but Seward assured him it meant nothing.

For several weeks Schofield waited daily for instructions to leave for Paris. Finally, when his suspicions regarding the mission were aroused, he pressed Seward to set a date for his departure. Seward explained he must wait for an answer to his latest note to Paris, each delay strengthening the position of the secretary of state. Grant returned to Washington in September from a trip through the country, in the course of which he found the North thoroughly in sympathy with Juárez and resentful of Napoleon III and Maximilian.[20] Grant assured Schofield that Sheridan would not discharge any of his men until their services could be channeled into the Mexican expedition. Impatient over continued delays, Grant and Schofield called on President Johnson late in October 1865, only to discover he was implicitly following Seward's advice. Grant complained to Romero that nothing could be done in Mexico so long as Seward was secretary

17. John M. Schofield, *Forty-Six Years in the Army* (New York, 1897), pp. 383–85.
18. Romero to Lerdo de Tejada, August 4, 1865, *Corres. mexicana*, V.
19. Echert to Seward, August 14, 1865, Miscellaneous Letters, 1865, Dept. of State, NA.
20. Grant to Johnson, September 1, 1865, *ORA*, ser. I, vol. 48, pt. 2, p. 1221.

of state,[21] and an effort was started to dislodge him. But Johnson flatly refused to request the resignation. Seward was regarded as the most prominent civilian in public service, and the attack on his life when Lincoln was assassinated had increased his hold on the public.[22] Grant next interviewed Seward who mollified him somewhat by cryptically elaborating on his own procedure and guaranteeing it could not fail to remove the French army from Mexico. The general was convinced that Seward was thoroughly pro-Juárez and that his purpose was to avoid a general war.[23]

Within a few days Schofield received the long-awaited instructions; on November 15, 1865, he sailed for Liverpool. Preceding him was a dispatch to the legation in London introducing the general as a visitor to Europe. The minister there, Charles Francis Adams, was asked to make Schofield's stay in London pleasant and to advance the object of his mission.[24] Seward's instructions to the minister in Paris, Bigelow, were likewise casual and totally lacking in clarity. After announcing Schofield's impending arrival, Seward wrote, "I recommend him to your confidence and authorize you to communicate with him, whenever occasion shall require, to pass between yourself and any of our representatives whom you may wish to consult informally upon the general situation."[25]

The complete omission of any suggestion that Schofield might get his legs under Napoleon III's mahogany left Bigelow in the dark concerning the nature of the mission. Visiting generals had not been infrequent in Paris since Lee's surrender, and their reception by the legation had been expensive. Seward never saw fit to explain his dispatch to Bigelow. When Napoleon III inquired of Bigelow if Schofield had come to Paris on a mission, the minister innocently answered no.[26] News of Schofield's arrival had already started rumors that he had brought demands from Washington. Bigelow corrected "what was correctable in this impression" by reading Seward's dispatch.[27] To Sanford he

21. Romero to Lerdo de Tejada, October 27, 1865, *Corres. mexicana*, V.
22. Romero to Lerdo de Tejada, October 31, 1865, ibid.
23. Romero to Lerdo de Tejada, November 14, 1865, ibid.
24. Seward to Adams, October 31, 1865, Instructions, Great Britain, Dept. of State, NA, XIX.
25. Seward to Bigelow, November 4, 1865, Instructions, France, Dept. of State, NA, XVII.
26. Bigelow to Seward, December 26, 1865, Dispatches, France, Dept. of State, NA, LIX.
27. Bigelow to Seward, December 8, 1865, Seward Papers.

confided, "He [Schofield] is accredited to me but to no other person that I am aware of." However, the president would doubtless approve having the general "meet the Emperor somehow" and tell what the U.S. military think of his adventure in Mexico.[28]

Bigelow briefed his visitor on the realities of the Franco-Mexican situation of which the general appeared to be entirely ignorant. To his credit the pupil learned rapidly and profited by the instruction. For the present, he wrote the secretary of state, he would make no effort to see the French emperor or his foreign minister.[29] The Mexican situation was improving and "it seems advisable . . . to leave the French government free to work out its solution in its own way."[30] He would confine himself to watching the emperor.

While in Europe Schofield met many persons of high rank, spoke at a Thanksgiving Day dinner in Paris, received with Bigelow at the U.S. Legation's New Year's reception, and in January 1866, some five weeks after his arrival, met Napoleon III and Empress Eugénie at a soirée. Bigelow appeared to inform Schofield on events as they transpired, but in his continuous conferences at the Quai d'Orsay, Schofield did not participate. Late in February 1866, Schofield asked permission to travel for one month and then return home. Seward approved, probably with tongue in cheek and relief in heart. After some five months pleasantly spent in Europe, Schofield in June 1866, reported back to Washington.

Schofield undertook to justify to Grant the reversal of his views on the French in Mexico. Many Frenchmen realized, he explained, that the Maximilian empire was not "consolidating," but by ignoring this evidence Napoleon III found an excuse to withdraw his troops. The situation was absurd, the general admitted, but he thought it "well to let . . . [the French emperor] make the most of his audacity in the creation of convenient facts. . . . Would it not be wise for us to abstain for a few months from all interference, direct and indirect, and thus give Maximilian time to carry out their farce?"[31]

In this manner the plot of the brass hats lapsed into limbo

28. Bigelow to Sanford, December 5, 1865, Henry Shelton Sanford Papers, Sanford Memorial Library, Sanford, Fla., reel 72, box 115, folder 13.

29. Schofield to Seward, December 8, 1865, Dispatches, France, Dept. of State, NA, LIX.

30. Schofield to Seward, December 21, 1865, ibid.

31. Schofield, Forty-Six Years in the Army, pp. 390-91.

until the presidential campaign of 1868, when, to the irritation of Johnson and Seward, campaign literature gave Grant full credit for the collapse of the Maximilian empire. Bigelow, then back in private life, was asked to "prepare a true statement of the case." Unlike President Johnson, he was not interested in campaign controversy and urged that errors of statement could better be corrected after the campaign was over.[32] Bigelow was still not clear as to the relations between Grant and Schofield. After Seward's retirement Bigelow learned from him for the first time the strategy of restraining Grant. Bigelow wrote in his diary that Seward "sent Schofield to Paris merely to avoid such a proceeding"—that is, Mexican meddling by Grant—since the secretary of state was confident the French emperor would quit Mexico as rapidly as he could.[33]

At last satisfied about a situation which had never ceased to puzzle him, Bigelow forgot Schofield. In 1896, General Schofield broke into print with an article about his mission to France and, one year later, wrote his memoirs, *Forty-Six Years in the Army*. Bigelow was then asked to corroborate Schofield's interpretation of his mission to France; this, of course, he could not do. In his diary he wrote, "Schofield had no commission of any kind but was merely commended to my courtesies as a person enjoying the confidence of the Government at Washington." Seward's sole purpose in sending him was to "squelch the wild scheme" of Grant "who was all powerful in Washington." But Schofield, "no longer . . . head of the army . . . begins to feel neglected and has taken to chewing the end of sweet and bitter memoirs in the hope of prolonging his reign through the echoes of the Press."[34]

32. Bigelow Papers, September 21–23, 1868.
33. Ibid., March 27, 1869.
34. Ibid., December 9, 1896.

22

Maneuvers
for White House Recognition
1864–1866

Against the backdrop of Confederate migration, border tension, military opposition, and general public irritation over the existence of a Mexican empire, diplomatic discussions between the United States and France went on during 1865. The first goal of France was to win recognition for Maximilian.

Henri Mercier, prior to his retirement from the French Legation at Washington in the spring of 1865, had encouraged Napoleon III to hope for ultimate recognition of the Mexican Empire once it was actually established. Chargé d'affaires M. L. Geofroy, whom Mercier left at Washington, did not share this optimism.

Geofroy found hostility to France in both the Congress and the press although from Secretary Seward he invariably received professions of peaceful intention. So long as Seward remained in power, thought Geofroy, there would be no war between France and the United States. However, he cautioned Paris, Seward "will not always be Secretary of State." Suspecting that even Seward was playing for time and might change his policy at the end of the U.S. Civil War, Geofroy tried to peek into the secretary's hand. "You cannot deny that the general sentiment is for war after the Rebellion is over," the Frenchman argued. Seward responded candidly, "That is my personal opinion if guarantees which we have never stopped demanding for Mexico are not given." When Geofroy reminded the secretary of state of the notorious chaos of preceding republican regimes in Mexico, Seward sadly agreed. But he added that an empire in Mexico had no better prospect of establishing order.[1]

Geofroy was agreeably surprised at the restraint of the U.S. press when Maximilian began his reign in Mexico. There seemed to be a naïve astonishment at the deliberate violation of the Monroe Doctrine by the French.[2] Two months later Geofroy mentioned the Maximilian empire to Seward. The noncommittal response was that the United States was satisfied with its Mexican policy, and if an agent of Maximilian came to Washington, he would be given treatment identical to that of representatives of other unrecognized governments. Geofroy and Seward agreed that "nothing they had said had been official," a caution which encouraged the French diplomat to report that Seward seemed not unwilling to see Maximilian succeed but "will only open the door in the future."[3]

When the French Legation in Mexico City, prodded by Maximilian, sounded out the feasibility of announcing officially to Washington his ascension to the throne, Geofroy discouraged it. He warned that 1864 was the year of elections and that to win, a presidential candidate must uphold the Monroe Doctrine; hence no commitment would be made.[4] After Lincoln was reelected the suggestion was revived that Maximilian send a minister to Washington in the hope that the president would not dare rebuff him. Geofroy wrote: "Today Mexico and the United States are in the position of two powers who will not speak; after one has refused to speak it is easier to quarrel."[5] He was appalled that Mexican imperialists expected early recognition. He had never given any such impression; moreover, the approaching end of the U.S. Civil War caused popular feeling against the French to rise higher.[6]

Geofroy neither categorically stated that the United States would not recognize the Mexican Empire, nor did he minimize the wide gap in points of view between France and the United

1. Geofroy to Drouyn de Lhuys, May 30, 1864, CP, Etats-Unis, CXXXI.
2. Geofroy to Drouyn de Lhuys, June 20, 1864, ibid.
3. Geofroy to Drouyn de Lhuys, August 1, 1864, ibid., Confidential, CXXXII.
4. Geofroy to Montholon, July 21, 1864, ibid., CXXXI.
5. Geofroy to Drouyn de Lhuys, January 15, 1865, ibid., CXXXIII.
6. Geofroy to Drouyn de Lhuys, January 30, 1865, ibid.

States. That France was kept in this twilight zone of hope and suspense month after month was part of the genius of Seward. An interview with Geofroy early in 1865 revealed the Seward technique. The Frenchman referred once more to the possibility of war between France and the United States over Mexico and to the heat of sentiment in the United States; Seward answered that his people were too practical to go to war. And then he added, "If you want to know my personal opinion, I think your Emperor wishes to withdraw from Mexico; we do not wish to enter; consequently our interests are identical. If the point of honor does not become involved, you will see we shall never have to fight." When Geofroy volunteered the comment that recognition of the Maximilian empire might improve conditions, the secretary waved him aside. "We in America have the habit of never taking up two questions at once," said Seward. "Now we are thinking only of re-establishing the Union, and keeping neutral with our neighbors. The Administration is sufficiently strong for that, and it will prevent all physical aggression against Mexico. Let us not go beyond that, and let time work it out."

From this conversation Geofroy assumed Seward thought solely of the moment. "Since the opening of the war," insisted the Frenchman, Seward had "tried patriotically to follow the only course which could keep the rebellion from succeeding by holding us off and keeping us asleep; and he does it more effectively because he is genuinely conciliatory." While in the presence of Seward, Geofroy believed the secretary's intentions; afterwards he asked himself, "What of tomorrow?"[7]

Late in March 1865, Geofroy informed Paris that everyone in the United States, even prudent, peaceful people, expected Washington to protect Mexico from foreign usurpation and, once blood was spilled across the Rio Grande, war with France was inevitable. When the *New York Times*, regarded as the mouthpiece of the State Department, conceded this point of view, Geofroy once more sought out Seward but gained small comfort from the interview. The secretary of state brought forth a clipping reporting that a New York regiment had taken a vow to aid republican Mexico. Penciled on the margin, in Seward's handwriting, was "My impression is that fighting regiments never take idle vows." Somewhat puzzled, the French diplomat re-

7. Geofroy to Drouyn de Lhuys, February 27, 1865, ibid.

marked that French regiments were reprimanded for political actions. That, responded Seward, was the regrettable difference between French and American regiments.[8] A few days later, a secret agent gave Geofroy a report on the conference in Richmond between Blair and Davis.[9] The situation was rapidly growing complex.

After the Confederacy had fallen and Lincoln had been assassinated, Geofroy recoiled from President Andrew Johnson's lack of restraint. "What will become of the Republic," he queried, "in the hands of such a tempestuous man?"[10]

To cope with the rapidly changing conditions and to protect an already unsatisfactory state of affairs, Drouyn de Lhuys in the French Foreign Office spelled out the policy of Napoleon III. Not only was the U.S. minister in Paris enlightened by the French foreign minister's statement and Geofroy instructed for future conversations, but also the prospective French minister to Washington, the Marquis de Montholon, received the exact text of the address he should give as the incoming envoy.[11]

In his interview with Bigelow, Drouyn de Lhuys dwelt nostalgically on the stream of good will which had flowed so long from France to America. France could not be responsible for rumors of favoritism toward the South, rumors the French emperor had done nothing to start. France liked to dwell on the dramatic and triumphant role she had played in the founding of the first republic in the New World and in the extensive commercial relations which had grown yearly between the two peoples. Napoleon III had viewed the conflict between North and South with genuine regret; he had offered mediation in good faith and, above all, had tried not to prejudice the issue but leave it to "strength of arms and the will of God." Stuffing into the closets the skeletons of pro-Confederate activities in France where it was hoped they would remain, the Quai d'Orsay insisted that France was on the same footing with the United States as she was prior to the U.S. Civil War. Napoleon III conceded that some feeling inimical to France existed in the United States but he trusted the good sense of its people and was confident they would recover from the passions of war and "do justice to our inten-

8. Geofroy to Drouyn de Lhuys, March 30, 1865, ibid.
9. Geofroy to Drouyn de Lhuys, April 6, 1865, ibid.
10. Geofroy to Drouyn de Lhuys, April 17, 1865, ibid.
11. Drouyn de Lhuys to Montholon, March 23, 1865, ibid.

tions." Frenchmen rejected the prospect of war with the United States over Mexico; rather, they expected the United States to "reciprocate in friendship and neutrality." No acquisition of territory was contemplated in Mexico by France; only the reconstruction of life and property on a more favorable basis than the preceding republican regimes had provided.[12]

In May 1865, the Quai d'Orsay issued a circular to French envoys in London, Mexico, Vienna, Brussels, and Washington. The gist of it was that the United States, while preferring a republic on its frontier, recognized the right of all peoples to choose their own form of government and would never oppose what had been freely accomplished. American disapproval over the Mexican situation sprang from the notion that France intended to propagandize and advance the monarchical system in the New World. But France had no plan of monarchical restoration antagonistic to the United States. She went to Mexico to secure recognition for just claims from a government unable to control the country. When that government fell at the approach of the French flag, a new one was assisted into being. The new government was attempting to bring greater peace and prosperity than Mexico had ever before experienced. Closer relations, from which political agreements might well emerge, ought to be promoted between the United States and the Mexican Empire.[13]

These devious effusions from the Quai d'Orsay, continuously reported in General Sanford's communications, might have amused Secretary Seward had he not still been fighting for his life after the attempt on it by assassins. Possibly, however, Seward would have resented the French zeal to enrobe itself in garments of purity. Although he might not have known the full story of French chicanery in Mexico, his breadth of information and his political insight must have revealed Napoleon III's duplicity quite as much as the falsity of the Quai d'Orsay's statements.

When recruiting stations were opened in the United States for armed immigrant volunteers to join the Juárez forces,[14] the French Legation protested and U.S. officials promised to investigate violations of an 1818 statute forbidding foreign enlistments.

12. Drouyn de Lhuys to Geofroy, March 23, 1865, ibid.
13. Drouyn de Lhuys to French legations and embassies in London, Mexico, Vienna, Brussels, and Washington, May 2, 1865, ibid.
14. These recruiting stations were set up by González Ortega with some help from Romero.

France professed confidence in the Johnson administration, although the new president was expected to be less circumspect than Lincoln. Regarding the people of the United States, the French felt less assurance. Of them Geofroy wrote, "Americans are sensible and calculating but en masse they are the most unreasonable and chimerical people on earth."[15]

In the midst of this tangle of events, the Marquis de Montholon arrived in Washington to discharge the responsibilities of minister. He had come from Mexico where he held a similar position. Son of the famous General Montholon who had been the companion of the first Napoleon at St. Helena, he was highly qualified for filling this key post of French minister to the United States. One year after he had become, while still in his twenties, an attaché in the French Legation in Washington, Montholon married a citizen of the United States, the daughter of Brigadier General Charles Gratiot. Gratiot had been appointed to West Point by President Jefferson, being one of the four French youths of Missouri Territory selected for this distinction with the object of conciliating the French population after the cession of Louisiana to the United States. Gratiot had distinguished himself in the War of 1812 and as an engineer had been stationed in both Charleston and Fortress Monroe.[16] Therefore, his daughter, Montholon's wife, had spent much time in two southern states, South Carolina and Virginia, in addition to New York. Additional experience in the United States was acquired by the Montholons in 1842 when he became consul in Richmond and in 1853 when he was appointed consul general in New York. This broad acquaintance with people of the United States in various sections of that country gave Montholon perhaps undue confidence in his ability to induce Washington to accept monarchy in Mexico despite odds which would have submerged a less optimistic envoy.

Montholon's prefabricated address to President Johnson, as he presented his credentials as minister, included felicitations on the restoration of the Union and assurances of the abiding interest of France in the welfare of the United States. Diplomatic amenities accomplished, the new minister confidently settled to his task. He pressured William Hunter, who presided over the

15. Geofroy to Drouyn de Lhuys, May 2, 1865, CP, Etats-Unis, CXXXIII.

16. *Encyclopedia of the History of St. Louis*, ed. William Hyde and Howard L. Conrad, 2 vols. (New York, 1899), II, 928–29.

State Department pending Seward's recovery, to put an end to the recruiting of volunteers for republican Mexico and recommended legal action against promoters of enlistments. Hunter temporized on the question of prosecution but gave assurances that the United States would never allow an expedition to be fitted out. After a trip to New York, Montholon believed the enlistment efforts were faltering in the East although still popular in the South and West. Mexican recruiting agents were without funds, and volunteers were already disappointed by their prospects. The whole undertaking would in time fade out.[17] The minister warned his superior to let the matter rest without pressing for a statement of policy; Drouyn de Lhuys wisely concurred.[18]

When resentment against France flared up over the arms carried across the border by Confederate refugees, Montholon quickly sought redress. He reported to Paris he did not want France to "lose ground which we are gaining every day in our relations with this country about Mexico."[19] Munitions and stores were at once returned to Unionists in Texas. Important as it was to France to speak frankly about Confederates in Mexico and detailed as were the instructions from Paris in explanation of the French position on the problem,[20] Montholon restrained himself to a simple declaration that the Mexican Empire welcomed all immigrants, regardless of origin. There was too much hostility toward Southern refugees to permit calm discussion.[21]

Montholon spent the summer of 1865 organizing his strategy and lining up his contacts. He endeavored to win over senators and representatives and military leaders such as General Rosecrans, as well as James Gordon Bennett of the *New York Herald*, and other powerful editors. He realized that the success of his mission depended on the extent to which the Mexican Empire could find favor with extremists in Congress and, in turn, on the influence of these extremists with the new president. He also knew that quick and decisive victories over republican forces in Mexico were essential. Confident that Juárez would be driven out of the country, Montholon prophesied that on the day im-

17. Montholon to Drouyn de Lhuys, May 29, 1865, CP, Etats-Unis, CXXXIII.
18. Montholon to Drouyn de Lhuys, June 20, 1865, ibid., CXXXIV.
19. Montholon to Drouyn de Lhuys, June 13, 1865, ibid.
20. Drouyn de Lhuys to Montholon, July 20, 1865, ibid.
21. Montholon to Drouyn de Lhuys, August 8, 1865, ibid., CXXXV.

perialist and French forces achieved that triumph, "we shall find the United States very well inclined to let us re-establish order in Mexico."[22]

The French diplomat was far too astute to force the issue of recognizing the Mexican Empire; his approach to the State Department was one of friendly persuasion and he never pressed for anything definite but urged cooperation in Mexican affairs. His plea was, "Help us in this disinterested task of giving you a neighbor who will always be useful to you and never useless. Join your protection to ours and the United States and France will have an understanding which some day will be very advantageous. . . . To push away . . . would be to keep us forever in Mexico to accomplish our tasks without you and in spite of you."[23] The State Department agreed, he felt sure, but the moment had not come for reason to prevail over public passion. No control of public opinion was possible in this democratic land, but domestic matters would soon become absorbing and soldiers restored to their homes would not want to fight again. "I repeat," Montholon wrote Paris in June 1865, "that everything is well and if nothing comes up suddenly to compromise the situation which is created, the question will be presented under favorable circumstances and nothing will longer oppose the recognition of the Empire by the Cabinet at Washington."[24]

That Montholon put wings on his hopes during the early summer of 1865 there can be no doubt. Dispatch after dispatch bears out this evidence notwithstanding occurrences which admittedly caused him concern. Furthermore, he was not enthusiastic over Maximilian as a ruler and appears to have lost confidence in the stability of the Mexican Empire. As Napoleon III's minister in Washington his strenuous attempts to secure Maximilian's recognition were motivated solely by loyalty to his own country; it was what France wanted and needed. Maximilian's agents criticized Montholon for not working more aggressively, condemned the caution with which he played his hand, and misinterpreted his reluctance to press the State Department for a definite commitment. Montholon thought he knew the people of the United States better than his critics did; obviously this was true. Convinced that Seward wanted no rupture with France, he waited

22. Montholon to Drouyn de Lhuys, June 27, 1865, ibid.
23. Ibid.
24. Montholon to Drouyn de Lhuys, June 13, 1865, ibid., CXXXIV.

for the subsiding of passions aroused by the U.S. Civil War and by the murder of Lincoln. In short, he was endeavoring to follow the intricate pattern of political life in the United States which the editor of *L'Ere nouvelle* had explained.

Political leaders in the United States had to remain alert to public opinion and feign temporary opposition to the very policy they considered wise, Masseras wrote in *L'Ere nouvelle*. "This is the kind of action peculiar to public men in the United States, which is hard to understand without long practice but which must be understood to avoid being misled by their acts. European governments know this; and proof of it is that their relations with the Washington Cabinet are different from other international affairs." Seward had tried to forestall congressional action by being as firm as possible, short of war. He knew Congress liked "to play with fire only if it is far away."[25]

However reconciled the French became to this play and counterplay, the less-informed Maximilian was unimpressed. Wanting to start his regime by negotiations with the United States, he was frustrated by a year of inaction. The moment for agreement was at hand, he thought; to be restrained at French behest was another aspect of the Paris domination he increasingly resented. Consequently he took the offensive when Confederate refugees began crossing the Rio Grande. Probably he agreed with Masseras that Confederate migration might strengthen his hand with Washington. "Mexico has precisely the same weapons against the United States that the latter has against her," Masseras had written in *L'Ere nouvelle*. "If the Americans can increase the difficulties of the Empire, the Empire in turn would have little trouble in reviving the [U.S.] Civil War. The thousands of refugees from the South who have preferred exile to submission would welcome the occasion to return to their country with means to raise the Confederate flag. . . . This is the side of the situation which Mexico has not seen before now. However, it gives the Imperial government a force by means of which it can trade power for power. Perhaps it is not improper to let it be understood that it is already in mind."[26]

Before Maximilian ascended the throne, several commercial agents of the Mexican Regency had appeared in the United

25. "Affaires de Jour," *L'Ere nouvelle*, February 1, 1865.
26. Ibid., July 29, 1865.

States. After the emperor's arrival in Mexico, one of them was directed by Maximilian's foreign minister to seek an interview with Seward. His later overtures to the State Department were tersely rebuffed.[27] A second agent of Maximilian tried to pry a crack in the door of the State Department by extending condolences over Lincoln's assassination; he then expected to fling it wide open by discussing the Confederate refugees, a question of importance to the Union. This agent was no more successful with the State Department than the first. He retired to New York where he concentrated his efforts on a campaign to stir up sentiment favorable to Maximilian and attract capital to the Mexican Empire.

But Maximilian's efforts to promote recognition and attract capital were not limited to Mexicans. He also selected two Austrians; his friend and aide, Count Resseguier, who had represented him in Guatemala, and Chevalier Charles Frederick Loosey, Austrian consul general in New York from 1850 to 1870, whose "keen intelligence and . . . ability" Maximilian said he recognized. The Austrian minister in Washington viewed Loosey as "a consummate swindler."[28]

Maximilian wrote a long exposition of Mexican needs for Loosey and sent it to New York by Resseguier. Now that the U.S. Civil War was over, the statement read that it was imperative, "not only to prepare ourselves for the developments which are about to take place in the United States but to exploit them as far as possible for our own advantage. . . ." Government in the United States, contended Maximilian, depended almost entirely on public opinion and public opinion could be molded only by interesting big capital which almost completely controlled the masses. In view of the "predominantly materialistic tendency of the people of the United States, a complete change in the opinion of the masses could be brought about by proving to them that their interests were identified with those of the Mexican Empire." To retain its support of the electorate, the Washington government appeared to be waiting for this turnabout in public opinion before opening friendly intercourse between the two countries.

27. Memorandum to Corwin, March 12, 1865, Dispatches, Mexico, Dept. of State, NA, XXX.

28. Egon Caesar Corti, *Maximilian and Charlotte in Mexico*, trans. Catherine A. Phillips, 2 vols. (New York, 1928), II, 601.

To further the enlightenment of the masses, Loosey was commissioned to establish and direct a well-organized press agency for which Maximilian appropriated $30,000. With his accustomed lack of restraint about financial matters, the Mexican emperor assured Loosey there was more where that came from. Accompanying the $30,000 was a power of attorney enabling Loosey to form three companies in the name of Maximilian. These companies would provide a rail communication between Mexico City and the Pacific, a transit across the Isthmus of Tehuantepec, and a direct steamship line between New Orleans and Veracruz. Dangling before the supposedly greedy eyes of New York merchants were plans to buy all manner of supplies, to be financed by alluring loans to Mexico.[29]

The diet to be fed New York capitalists was to be a mixture of bait and bully. Only the recognition of imperial Mexico would produce the recall of French troops, a recall desired as warmly by the Mexican Empire as by the United States. Loosey was instructed to mention "confidentially" that the Mexican emperor was engaged in working out a convention with France for the withdrawal of French troops, a bit of information which would have surprised the French. Blocking the consummation of this desired end was the stubborn insistence of Washington that Juárez was president of a Mexican republic which Maximilian insisted no longer existed.

Instructions to Loosey enumerated the fictitious virtues of the Mexican Empire, that it rested on the expression of popular will and that Mexicans were highly gratified over its establishment. Furthermore, the Mexican sovereigns could not be "more attached to the American people, whose activity and energy they do not cease to praise. . . ." A "most sincere affection" for people of the United States had been felt by Maximilian "from his younger years." He and Charlotte were devoted to the noble pronouncement of President Monroe which was "as much in the intentions of Mexico as of the United States." The first speech of Maximilian to Mexicans, made two years before, contained "a marked support of the Monroe Doctrine."

If a combination of love of the United States, adherence to the Monroe Doctrine, efforts to achieve French military withdrawal,

29. Maximilian to Loosey, August 23, 1865, Charles Frederick de Loosey Collection, New-York Historical Society Library, New York, N.Y.

and tempting commercial ventures did not titillate the U.S. palate, a mild threat was added. If Washington delayed recognition and the U.S. Civil War was rekindled in the Southern states, "Mexico would find herself in a critical position, not knowing to which side she should incline. In the absence of all recognition she would not be bound to the North by any international obligation."[30]

The zealous work of Loosey produced two corporations. The first was organized to offer inducements for development of mining, agricultural, and industrial lands. The scope of the second corporation was broad; in addition to colonization, it would transport mail, freight, and passengers, and engage in banking and exchange. Within six months it would provide a transport line from Mexico City to the Gulf or the Pacific.[31] Ten trustees, all from the United States, were to preside over its destinies; two of them were General Henry S. Sanford and Clarence A. Seward, nephew of the secretary of state.[32]

In an attempt to play both the imperial and the republican sides of the street, the impression was conveyed that both Maximilian and Juárez approved the corporation. When this claim reached the Mexican Legation at Washington, Romero acted swiftly to prove it false. The Juarist minister upbraided the company for deluding the public; he complained to Seward,[33] who was already embarrassed by his nephew's association; he scotched the reports of Juárez's approval by the simple device of writing his superiors in Mexico and making public their answers. Juárez had never heard of the "gentleman or his projects" and could not "approve of what has never come to my knowledge."[34] To make assurance doubly sure, Romero announced that the Republic of Mexico had already declared invalid all concessions of the Hapsburg usurper.

But the tenacious Romero was not through; he sent the State Department full information about the company and the policy

30. Instructions to Loosey, n.d., ibid.

31. "Faits Divers," *L'Ere nouvelle*, June 20, 1865; "Colonisation et Transport," *L'Estafette*, June 21, 1865.

32. Prospectus of Imperial Mexican Express Company, enclosure with Courcillon to Romero, October 24, 1865, Notes, Mexico, Dept. of State, NA, XIV.

33. Romero to Seward, October 27, 1865, ibid.

34. Juárez to Romero, December 22, 1865; Juárez to Navarro, December 1, 1865, ibid.

of Juárez. Through Grant, Seward was heckled about the commitment of his nephew.[35] The situation was sufficiently serious to cause Seward to instruct the U.S. district attorney in New York to watch the company closely and to remove from his ambitious nephew all hope of official blessing or protection.[36] The House of Representatives requested the president to turn over correspondence relating to the company. Romero was elated over the ensuing publicity. He assembled and made available additional information and succeeded in having the pertinent documents reprinted in the *New York Herald.*[37]

At least three other agents were involved in Maximilian's attempt to secure recognition from the United States. But all their efforts came to naught as the implacable Secretary Seward refused to budge from his steadfast position.

After these propaganda failures by Maximilian's agents, relations between them and the French Legation in Washington cooled. The agents claimed French Minister Montholon was aloof and indifferent to their interests and charged him with frustrating their enterprises. If true, it was because there was considerable question about their methods and their integrity. He had no time for petty intrigues, entrusted as he was with a grave responsibility by his government. One agent complained that Montholon's ideas "were exclusively French" and that all "his hopes and anxieties were with reference to the position of France in the Maximilian question. . . ."[38] He was entirely correct. Only when the interests of France and imperial Mexico ran parallel was Montholon pro-Maximilian. When the ends of the two governments separated, Montholon devoted himself unswervingly to the interests of France.

35. Grant to Seward, November 1, 1865, U.S., Congress, *House Ex. Doc.*, 39th Cong., 1st sess., No. 73, pt. 2, 252–53.

36. Seward to Dickenson, November 1, 1865, ibid., 255; Seward to Clarence Seward, November 1, 1865, ibid.

37. Romero to Lerdo de Tejada, February 12, 1866, *Corres. mexicana*, VIII; *New York Herald*, February 3, 1866.

38. Estvan to Castillo, February 23, 1866, Arch. Max. Estvan wrote *War Pictures from the South* (New York, 1863).

23

Imposed Monarchy "Disallowed"
1865–1866

———◄◆►———

Two events of October 1865 alarmed French diplomats in Paris. One was a decree by Maximilian imposing the death penalty on armed republicans when captured; the other was the appointment of a U.S. minister to republican Mexico, a post vacant since Corwin withdrew at the approach of Maximilian seventeen months before.

This ruthless decree condemning to death Mexicans who fought against the monarchy was inspired by France. French troops had twice driven the Juárez government out of its temporary capital in Chihuahua. Each time the severely reduced republican army and government had perched precariously on the Mexican banks of the Rio Grande across from the present Texas city of El Paso. Why imperialist forces did not make a supreme effort to capture Juárez or, at least, force him across the Rio Grande was probably due, first, to the perils involved in border campaigning so near Texas and, second, to the exorbitant expense and danger of sustaining a supply line through some nine hundred miles of hostile territory west of Matamoros.

The French asserted that one of Maximilian's most persistent mistakes lay in his leniency toward those bearing arms against him. The French theorized that if Juárez could not be run out of Mexico the alternative was to blot out his ardent supporters. Finally, Maximilian was persuaded to issue an edict by which all armed supporters of the republican government were to be

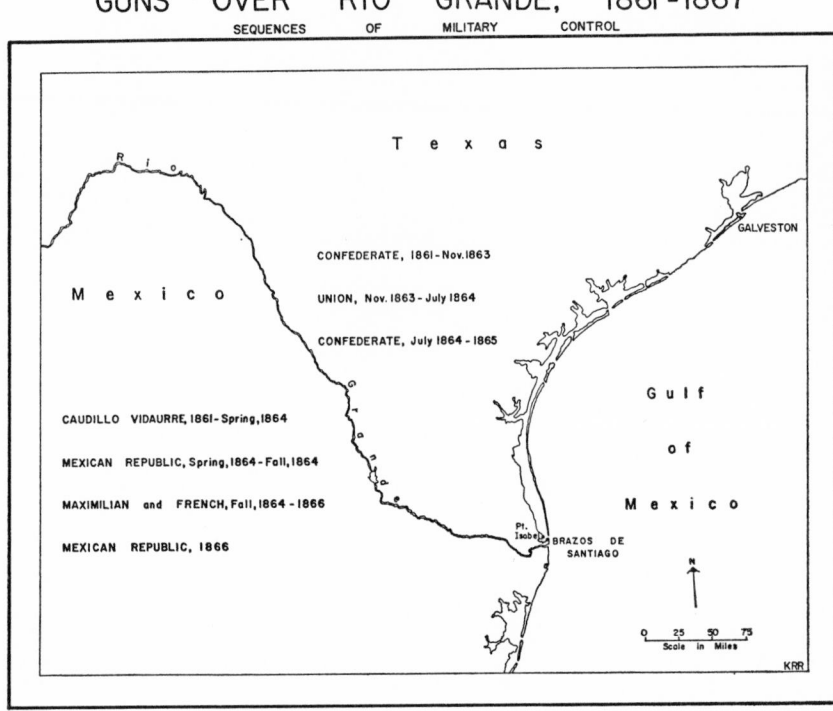

GUNS   OVER   RIO   GRANDE,   1861-1867

SEQUENCES   OF   MILITARY   CONTROL

T e x a s

R i o

GALVESTON

CONFEDERATE, 1861-Nov.1863

M e x i c o   UNION, Nov.1863-July 1864

CONFEDERATE, July 1864-1865

Gulf

CAUDILLO VIDAURRE, 1861-Spring,1864

of

MEXICAN REPUBLIC, Spring,1864-Fall,1864

MAXIMILIAN and FRENCH, Fall,1864-1866   M e x i c o

Pt.
Isabel
MEXICAN REPUBLIC, 1866   BRAZOS DE
SANTIAGO

N

0   25   50   75
Scale in Miles

KRR

branded brigands and, when caught, handed over to the summary treatment of courts-martial; in other words, to death. Bazaine strengthened the decree by instructing officers to take no prisoners. He wrote Paris, "His Majesty finally decided, on my advice, to give proof of the firmness which had had such good effect when used by the Conservatives."[1] The measure had been long overdue, added French Minister Dano.[2] The United States was outraged by such merciless treatment of prisoners. The Juaristas never forgave Maximilian; the memory of men pitilessly shot for no offense other than the will to be free was to be a factor in the emperor's own execution. The French, as well as Maximilian, later defended the Decree of October 3 by claiming that

1. Bazaine to Randon, October 9, 1865, AMG, 1865.
2. Dano to Drouyn de Lhuys, October 9, 1865, CP, Mexique, LXV.

they had believed Juárez had been driven into Texas; but dispatches to Paris at the time and other evidence do not support this.[3]

Secretary Seward asked U.S. Minister Bigelow to call the decree to the attention of France.[4] He protested more strongly when, some weeks later, news of the first executions reached Washington. Seward insisted that France "can never countenance proceedings which are so repugnant to the sentiments of modern civilization and the instincts of humanity."[5]

Drouyn de Lhuys squirmed under this barb from across the Atlantic. At first he disclaimed responsibility for Maximilian's action and asked why the United States did not deal directly with the Mexican emperor.[6] A second thought moved him to mollify Union wrath. Suppose Confederates had turned themselves into guerrillas operating at large throughout the United States; would they, he asked, have been accorded belligerent rights? How could Maximilian give belligerent rights to similar groups in Mexico? The United States would not proffer such rights to a well-organized Confederacy. Where was the Juárez capital? Who were the officials of his government? Montholon was instructed to plant such questions in the mind of Seward.[7]

It was amid this tension that Seward replied to the French proposal to withdraw from Mexico in exchange for recognition of the Mexican Empire. He instructed Bigelow to inform the French that the president would neither recognize nor pledge to recognize hereafter any political regime in Mexico in opposition to the Juárez government. "The United States have hitherto practiced the utmost frankness on that subject," Seward continued. "They still regard the effort to establish permanently a foreign and imperial government in Mexico as disallowable and impracticable." So far, France had made no move indicating a

3. Evidence that Juárez never left Mexico is in I. S. Bartlett, "President Juárez at Old El Paso," *Bulletin of the Pan American Union*, XLI (November 5, 1915), 641–58.

4. Seward to Bigelow, November 3, 1865, Instructions, France, Dept. of State, NA, XVII.

5. Seward to Bigelow, November 28, 1865, ibid.

6. Bigelow to Seward, November 30, 1865, Dispatches, France, Dept. of State, NA, LIX.

7. Drouyn de Lhuys to Montholon, November 29, 1865, CP, Etats-Unis, CXXXV.

plan to eliminate the cause of discord. This was regrettable because the United States wished to preserve French friendship.[8] Ten days after this dispatch went to Paris, a new minister from the United States was appointed to the Republic of Mexico.[9] It was an action timed to affect the international situation as well as the domestic scene. The minister-elect was John A. Logan, who, as a congressman from Illinois, had acquired a national reputation for spread-eagle oratory and contentious spirit. An outspoken partisan of war with France and a twice-wounded volunteer, Logan was promoted to major general after Vicksburg. The secretary of legation-elect was Colonel Orville Hickman Browning, a powerful political adviser to President Andrew Johnson.

Logan's appointment appeared to be a part of the cat and mouse game being played at Washington and Paris. Congress at its previous session had provided an appropriation for sending a representative to "Republican Mexico." Obviously it would be wise for President Johnson to fill the position before a critical Congress reconvened. General Schofield was on the eve of departure for France, happily under the illusion he was undertaking a mission of profound import. Grant was resentful that Seward had diverted Schofield from the proposed armed expedition to Mexico and not wholly convinced that Seward knew his business. President Johnson had previously intimated to Grant that the post of U.S. minister to Mexico would be filled. Apparently, Logan's appointment, whether or not it was accepted, had much to do with an attempt to mollify Grant.[10]

The appointment pleased Romero in view of Logan's strong advocacy of the Juárez government. Logan and the jingoists, especially those in the army and in Congress, agreed that until Maximilian fell, the Southern rebellion could not be crushed. In the course of a harangue to a Brooklyn audience, Logan had inelegantly advised the State Department to say to Maximilian, "Little Gentleman, get up and dust."[11]

Logan's reluctance to "get up and dust" off to Mexico, after he was given an opportunity to help solve the crisis, might well

8. Seward to Bigelow, November 6, 1865, Instructions, France, Dept. of State, NA, XVII.

9. Seward to Logan, November 16, 1865, Instructions, Mexico, Dept. of State, NA, XVII.

10. Romero to Lerdo de Tejada, October 27, 1865, Corres. mexicana, V.

11. Freedman's Journal and Catholic Register, November 25, 1865.

have been due to the peripatetic nature of the Juárez government. Logan's friends correctly predicted that he would never accept the post. However, the assignment, in suspense for some weeks, produced the effect the president and Seward evidently desired. Possibly Grant contributed to this end; he warned Logan that if he intended to refuse the proffered favor, he *must* see Seward first.[12]

The day Logan's appointment was announced, Seward invited the French minister to dinner. Reassuring words were spoken; the president would have been negligent not to have filled an office for which Congress had voted funds, explained Seward. He urged Montholon to report this to Napoleon III. The bewildered diplomat, groping for his bearings, answered that he could only view the appointment as a provocation and as the first hostile act of the United States. Surely, Montholon suggested, the danger far outweighed the advantages. "I hope you are wrong," answered Seward, and dinner was served.

Montholon was not so easily calmed. Why, *why* had the appointment been made? he reiterated. Was it the work of President Johnson, Grant, the radicals in Congress, or of all three? Had Seward abandoned conciliation? Montholon was aghast at Bigelow's ever having mentioned the recognition of Maximilian as the price of withdrawal of French troops from Mexico. Flames of resentment against Maximilian, he reported to Paris, soared higher than ever in the United States. Added to condemnation of Maximilian's death penalty decree was their resentment over favors shown Confederates, especially the selection of Commodore Matthew Fontaine Maury, a former high official of the U.S. Navy, as one of Maximilian's counselors of state. No less amazed than Montholon over Logan's appointment were members of the diplomatic corps in Washington. They tried to console Montholon by declaring that, if the French really intended leaving Mexico, there might be no trouble.[13]

Sir Frederick Bruce, British minister to the United States, took a practical view of the Logan appointment. It was, he believed, a move for domestic political consumption and would sacrifice good feeling abroad. But the U.S. government frequently oper-

---

12. Grant to Logan, November 23, 1865, Headquarters, Dept. of the Army, NA, Letterbook B, 1865.

13. Montholon to Drouyn de Lhuys, November 30, 1865, Confidential, CP, Etats-Unis, CXXXV.

ated in that manner. However it might hesitate before actual hostilities, the United States never recoiled before sacrificing understanding if some portion of public opinion might be propitiated. Foreign powers needed to bear this in mind when dealing with the United States and "not be easily moved by demonstrations which are due to its form of government rather than to the deliberate and unfettered action of the Executive,"[14] concluded the British diplomat, virtually echoing the warnings of editor Masseras.

Montholon's important instructions of October 18 on the withdrawal-recognition proposition which, by order of Napoleon III, had been marked for immediate action, were still in his pocket at the end of November. Up to that time he had been afraid to present the proposal to Seward; however, when he learned that Bigelow had discussed it in Paris and had so notified Washington, he asked Seward to read the dispatch unofficially. He hoped the possibility of negotiations taking place might restrain the language of Johnson's annual message to Congress, though he saw little prospect of success for the ends France sought.[15]

On December 4, 1865, Congress listened to Johnson's summary of the State of the Union. He dealt primarily with domestic issues regarded as of "transcendent importance." A passage that gave Montholon encouragement was the announcement that the army was being reduced to a 50,000 peacetime basis; 800,000 volunteers had already laid aside their uniforms and the military budget had been cut some 80 percent. This did not look like war.

On the subject of international affairs, the president touched on country after country, arriving at France at last. Without naming either Maximilian or Mexico, Johnson alluded to monarchy and convulsions in its behalf. The United States had always refused to act as a propagandist for republicanism although it was the only suitable form of government for the Union. On the whole, the president's message summarized, Europe and the Americas had dwelt in harmony through the years in which European dynasties had flourished or faded as the people decreed. "This consistent moderation may justly demand a corresponding

14. Bruce to Clarendon, November 20, 1865, BFO 5/1021.
15. Montholon to Drouyn de Lhuys, November 28, 1865, Special CP, Etats-Unis, CXXXV.

moderation. We should regard it as a great calamity to ourselves, to the cause of good government, and to the peace of the world, should any European power challenge the American people, as it were, to the defense of republicanism against foreign interference." The United States neither foresaw nor wished to contemplate occasions which might present themselves on this score; the nation had no wish to depart from its traditional course. Then, almost as an afterthought, came these words, "The correspondence between the United States and France in reference to questions which have been subjects of discussion between the two governments will at the proper time be laid before Congress."[16] The message was a victory for Secretary Seward over the military wire-pulling which had advocated immediate U.S. interference in Mexico.

Below the Rio Grande and along the river Seine there was relief over the prospect of no immediate armed intervention from the United States. General Bazaine concluded that Logan's appointment might not be a dagger at his throat after all. The Quai d'Orsay took heart. Montholon formally presented the dispatch of October 18. Then Romero decided to break a five months' boycott of the State Department as Seward daily became more solidly entrenched with President Andrew Johnson. Moving out of the camp that had opposed Seward, Romero enumerated for the secretary of state fortunate developments in Mexico. Seward said he had always considered it best that the Mexicans save themselves.[17]

Two days after the president's message was read to Congress, Seward's reply to Montholon's dispatch of October 18 was a repetition of the opinion already forwarded to Bigelow. As the secretary of state observed the problem, France wanted to withdraw from Mexico but found it difficult unless the United States agreed to be "friendly or tolerant" toward Maximilian. "I regret to be obliged to state that the condition the Emperor suggests is one which seems quite unpracticable," wrote Seward. Napoleon III did not sense the basic discontent of the Western Hemisphere toward the "foreign monarchical government" set up in Mexico. Above all, a people must be able to choose its institutions with-

16. James D. Richardson, comp. *A Compilation of the Messages and Papers of the Presidents, 1789–1897*, 10 vols. (Washington, D.C., 1896–1900), VIII, 3562, 3566 ff.

17. Romero to Lerdo de Tejada, December 28, 1865, *Corres. mexicana*, V.

out foreign interference. It would be equally unfortunate, slyly added Seward, if the United States tried to force out monarchies in Europe in favor of republics. In conclusion, he hoped France would see her way clear to abandon her "aggressive attitude in Mexico."[18]

This reference to European monarchies was deliberate. General Sanford had repeatedly reported to Seward on the deepening unrest in Europe and the increasing probability of revolutions. In the summer of 1865 he wrote, "The political atmosphere is full of electricity and a storm is approaching."[19] At a shooting festival in Bremen, some German soldiers who had returned from service in the Union armies made speeches to the effect that they expected to aid in making the thirty sovereigns of Europe "smell republican powder." Sanford added, "Europe is mined for revolution and our triumph makes it certain."[20]

Still optimistic, Montholon commented favorably on Seward's reply as he packed it off to the Quai d'Orsay and requested instructions for the next approach. As soon as he learned what was in the emperor's mind, he thought progress could be made; Seward was apparently willing to negotiate on the basis of non-intervention or neutrality. He even believed the recognition of Maximilian as the de facto ruler of Mexico might climax an agreement.[21]

At Christmas time, the French Legation learned that Congress had asked the State Department for documents pertinent to French and U.S. conversations over Mexico. As a review of congressional proceedings would reveal, such a demand was not new. Since the French invasion of Mexico began, the State Department had been delivering packages of documents, both large and small, for the edification of committees of Congress. Nevertheless, the timing of the December request upset French nerves. Very probably, earlier congressional resolutions requesting Seward to submit records to Congress had not been noticed by the French, or if they had, were not considered alarming. But as the year 1865 ended, both the disintegration of Maximilian's empire and

18. Seward to Montholon, December 6, 1865, Notes, France, Dept. of State, NA, XVII.
19. Sanford to Seward, July 25, 1865, William Henry Seward Papers, Rush Rhees Library, University of Rochester, Rochester, N.Y., LI.
20. Sanford to Seward, July 4, 1865, ibid.
21. Montholon to Drouyn de Lhuys, December 11, 1865, CP, Etats-Unis, CXXXV.

the menace of U.S. hostility were somber realities. Having con-cluded she must extricate herself from Mexico, France began maneuvering for the least embarrassing terms possible.

Chairman of the House Foreign Affairs Committee was Gen-eral Nathaniel P. Banks of Massachusetts, who had just resumed his seat in Congress after military service including several months on the Rio Grande. Sumner, chairman of the compara-ble committee in the Senate, was regarded at the French Lega-tion as friendly to France. Banks urged the senator to hold back action by the Committee of Foreign Relations as long as pos-sible or, at least, until after the emperor's *Adresse* to the Corps Législatif the following month.[22] Sumner acceded; the senator also informed Romero that resolutions against the French occu-pation of Mexico would be introduced only if Napoleon III did not make a statement concerning the withdrawal of French troops. Even President Johnson put off Romero's pleading for permission to float a Mexican loan on the ground that it would be politic to hear what the emperor had to say.[23]

Seward contributed his own delaying tactics. Two months were allowed to pass before he responded to the request of Con-gress, and even then the correspondence with France that he sent was judiciously selected. Mindful of the pressure that congres-sional curiosity over these documents might exert, Seward la-mented to Bigelow that relations with France were in jeopardy.

Bigelow needed no such reminder. He had been studying ways and means of reducing the mounting tension. He worked out a resolution which "some person of no special political significance might introduce to Congress"; in it was a request that France take steps to restore political independence to Mexico since she had "taken an unworthy advantage of the domestic troubles of the United States" to overthrow the Mexican republic, had en-dorsed fraudulent debts against Mexico, and had maintained a ruler imposed by foreign troops. Bigelow argued vehemently for this resolution: it would enlighten Europe as well as America on the policy of the United States, and it contained no allegations which could not be demonstrated and no pretensions statesmen of any nation dared contest.[24]

22. Montholon to Drouyn de Lhuys, December 26, 1865, ibid.

23. Romero to Lerdo de Tejada, January 11, 1866, and January 20, 1866, *Corres. mexicana*, VI.

24. Bigelow to Seward, December 14, and December 21, 1865, Strictly Con-fidential, John Bigelow Papers and Journal, NYPL.

Bigelow rushed a second suggestion across the Atlantic after he learned from Drouyn de Lhuys that the emperor intended to speak of Mexico before the Corps Législatif, and the French thought that what he intended to say would be satisfactory to the United States. To promote friendship between the two nations, Drouyn de Lhuys asked Bigelow if it would not be wise for the two heads of state to exchange notes. Bigelow agreed and suggested that Johnson be prevailed upon to move first by requesting Napoleon III to express his intent in Mexico. Bigelow believed that, if President Johnson followed this course, he would neither lose dignity nor incur injurious results. His letter might be sent by a special emissary without offering the press a preview. Generosity toward France would produce its own reward, he contended, because "every nation has to bleed in some way for every gratuitous wound that it gives to the pride of another."[25] Napoleon III wanted to leave Mexico, provided nothing happened to detain him for honor's sake.[26]

But Seward hewed to his original line. No such resolution was proposed in Congress; no letter from Johnson to Napoleon III was composed. The secretary of state knew only too well how easy it would be for the president to take matters into his own hands. Having survived the intrigues of the generals, he had no desire to borrow their tactics.

At the beginning of 1866, Paris sought to clothe defeat in garments of victory. In its reply of January 9, 1866, to Seward's communication of December 6, 1865, over which the emperor had carefully cogitated, the Quai d'Orsay described the nobility of France's Mexican position. Napoleon III was convinced that "the divergence of view between the two Cabinets is the result of an erroneous appreciation of our intentions." Never had France been hostile to New World institutions or to the American Union for whose birth she had shed her own blood. Proof of the disinterested motives of France was not wanting; the United States had been asked to join the tripartite expedition to Mexico and Napoleon III had been strictly neutral throughout the U.S. Civil War. Would such policies have been followed by France had her designs been nefarious?

Furthermore, wrote Drouyn de Lhuys, who must have thanked

25. Bigelow to Seward, December 21, 1865, Strictly Confidential, ibid.
26. Bigelow to Seward, December 26, 1865, Dispatches, France, Dept. of State, NA, LIX.

the fates for the secrecy in which diplomacy was then enveloped, Napoleon III had never carried monarchy to Mexico in the fold of his flag. He had merely judged it timely to attempt to rescue an exhausted people from disorders permitted by Juárez. The calling of Maximilian had been submitted to Mexican suffrage. All Napoleon III desired was that Mexico be "born into a new life." Surely the United States must understand that claims should be satisfied; indeed, U.S. force had been employed on far less provocation.

Following this attempted justification of the past, the note flowed gracefully into the future. France wished to withdraw from Mexico as rapidly as "safety for our nationals and dignity for ourselves" would permit. Both countries wished to respect the national will of Mexico, and Seward had professed no desire to propagandize for republican institutions. Let France solve the problem of her claims with Maximilian and all would be well. Of course, the new empire, as all new governments, faced problems. "A few military chiefs" still kept alive opposition but the Maximilian government would prevail; it was quite independent of France in spite of Bazaine and the French army overseas. France served as a friend of Mexico; "What nation does not need friends?" The purpose of this argument which distorted or omitted facts resting on evidence that had been accumulating for over four tense years, constituted an attempt to prevent the United States from intervening in Mexico.[27]

Before Seward answered this sophistry, Napoleon III addressed the Corps Législatif on January 22, 1866. He announced that France, having accomplished a noble task for civilization, was preparing to bring her troops back from the New World. The Mexican Empire approached the moment when it could stand alone.

This Bonaparte duplicity deceived no one. Few believed that Maximilian was consolidating his government; it was simply a rationalization for withdrawal. Opposition in the Corps Législatif was especially candid in commenting on the emperor's *Adresse*. "History will have a hard page for this expedition," declared one member; it will tell how foolish it was and reveal the diplomatic duplicity that it caused. How are we to get out of the scrape?"[28] The emperor's ministers were not prepared to answer that ques-

27. Drouyn de Lhuys to Montholon, January 9, 1866, CP, Etats-Unis, CXXXVI.
28. *Le Moniteur*, January 28, 1866.

tion. Communications had already been sent to Maximilian, it was explained; debate should await his answer.[29]

Exactly how and when Napoleon III decided to withdraw troops from Mexico was reported to Seward by the flamboyant James Watson Webb. En route home from his post as minister to Brazil in the fall of 1865, Webb stopped in France to see Napoleon III, with whom he had become acquainted in New York when the emperor was there in 1836 as a refugee.

On November 10, 1865, by Webb's account, a dramatic conversation followed Webb's breakfast with Napoleon III. Webb quoted the emperor as having remarked that he "got into the Mexican affair very unintentionally" and wanted to withdraw, but difficulties had interposed. He wished the United States would recognize Maximilian. Webb told him that this was impossible and, furthermore, Americans would probably go into Mexico by the thousands to become soldiers of the republic. Napoleon III hoped nothing would happen to compromise French honor. It would be folly, agreed Webb, for the United States and France to clash: the result would be to give England the trade of the world. There had been no specific limit set to the Mexican occupation, mused Napoleon III. Webb proposed that the French army leave in three sections, consuming in all, eighteen months; in this case the United States might accept the Mexican Empire as de facto and leave the rest to time. "An inspiration!" Webb quoted Napoleon III as exclaiming. Before Webb sailed from France he claimed he received telegrams confirming his conversation with Napoleon III from both the emperor and the foreign minister.[30]

Immediately upon his return to the United States Webb called on Seward and informed him that, beginning November 1866, French forces would be evacuated at six-month intervals. That same evening Seward allegedly told Webb that the president was pleased with his report and authorized Webb to communicate his satisfaction to Napoleon III. When the diplomatic correspondence sent to Congress was published, Webb was exceedingly angry that Seward did not credit him with negotiations for withdrawal of the French. Webb then wrote in his best jour-

29. Ibid., March 3, 1866.

30. Memorandum, November 29, 1865, in Diplomatic and Business Correspondence, July–December 1865, Webb Family Papers, Sterling Library, Yale University, New Haven, Conn.

nalistic style an account of the breakfast conference with Napoleon III, acknowledging himself as the originator of the method of French evacuation and requesting Napoleon III to insert it in *Le Moniteur*.[31] Webb's article was never printed; obviously the emperor could not acknowledge a foreigner as the source of imperial policy. Since Napoleon III's reputed words to Webb over the breakfast table bound no one, Seward could not adopt them as a basis for action.

31. Webb to Napoleon III, April 27, 1866, Dossier de J. Watson Webb, Papiers de Tuileries, AN.

24

General Sherman's Mexican Odyssey 1866

———————◄◆►———————

General Henry S. Sanford described the French emperor's Mexican dilemma in homely phrases, "He is like a man with his fingers between two cogwheels in motion."[1] The historian Ollivier characterized the dilemma more philosophically: "Placed between catastrophe if he persisted, and humiliation, if he retreated . . . [Napoleon III] resigned himself to humiliation. . . ."[2]

One week before Napoleon III announced French troops would be withdrawn from Mexico the Quai d'Orsay informed Dano of the emperor's decision and explained that the situation must not continue. The expedition had been undertaken to collect French credits and the claims of nationals. Aid had been proffered a people struggling to restore order, and support had been granted a prince willing to undertake the process of regeneration. But, as the Convention of Miramar had stipulated, that assistance had limits. The Mexican Empire could no longer meet its obligations. France could not support it with renewed advances. "We have been deceived in our expectations," Dano was informed by Paris, "by the ineffectiveness of those with

1. Sanford to Seward, May 24, 1865, William Henry Seward Papers, Rush Rhees Library, University of Rochester, Rochester, N.Y., LI.

2. Emile Ollivier, *L'Empire libéral: Etudes, récits, souvenirs,* 17 vols. (Paris, 1895–1915), VII, 546.

whom we had a contract and we cannot sacrifice further."[3]

Napoleon III broke the news of his abandoning Mexican regeneration to Maximilian in a letter of January 15, 1866; the cause was financial. No additional appropriation could be asked of the Corps Législatif, and Maximilian had already stated he could not pay anything himself. Although temporary weakness might result from the departure of the French, the Mexican throne would be strengthened ultimately by removing all pretext for intervention by the United States. Arrangements for withdrawal of troops should be made in such manner as to leave public order undisturbed.[4] Thus, Maximilian and the French Legation were notified of French withdrawal prior to its announcement to the French nation.

Pride dictated Maximilian's reply to the ally who had abandoned him. He wrote Napoleon III he did not wish to imperil either the position of the French throne or the Bonaparte dynasty; consequently, he suggested that French troops be removed at once. He would take his chances in the new country like a true Hapsburg.[5] Having thus delivered himself of a statement regarded as worthy of his forebears, Maximilian began to waver before uncompromising reality.

By the time Dano was finally granted an audience, Maximilian had become almost hysterical over his predicament. On the one hand, he insisted that French forces prepare to withdraw en masse; on the other, he demanded a new treaty to replace the Convention of Miramar. First, the emperor promised to pay all his commitments, knowing full well that it was impossible; then, he declared he might repudiate all obligations to France, on the theory that Napoleon III had abandoned him, and appeal for support to the Mexican people. Dano, touched by the pathetic condition of the Mexican sovereigns, wrote Drouyn de Lhuys, "Their position . . . is sad and painful beyond anything they expected. They are desperate and frightened. . . ."[6]

Throughout the spring of 1866 when hope and despair alternated in Mexico, France held steadfastly to her decision to withdraw. Dano was to undertake the negotiation of a treaty

3. Drouyn de Lhuys to Dano, January 14, 1866, CP, Mexique, LXVI.

4. Napoleon III to Maximilian, January 15, 1866, in Egon Caesar Corti, *Maximilian and Charlotte in Mexico*, trans. Catherine A. Phillips, 2 vols. (New York, 1928), II, 580.

5. Maximilian to Napoleon III, February 18, 1866, Arch. Max.

6. Dano to Drouyn de Lhuys, February 28, 1866, CP, Mexique, LXVI.

empowering France to administer the customs of Veracruz, Tampico, and other ports and to apply the receipts toward the repayment of the staggeringly heavy expeditionary debts. "Those matters having been taken care of and French interests thus safeguarded," wrote Drouyn de Lhuys to Dano, presumably without a trace of irony, "the Emperor will continue to show, in no less effective manner, his sympathy for the person of the Mexican monarch and the gracious task to which he had committed himself."[7]

While Paris clung to the illusion that the Mexican Empire would survive French evacuation, Dano tried to impress upon the Quai d'Orsay a sense of its certain disintegration. No matter how sincere Seward's predilection for neutrality, Dano claimed U.S. generals on the Texas border had never heard of the word; any day an incident might precipitate war between France and the United States. If war did not break out and even if the United States recognized the Mexican Empire, Maximilian's government could not survive the departure of the French.[8] Dano began to urge that Maximilian leave with the troops.[9]

In the spring of 1866, reports from Dano, and from many unofficial sources[10] continued to depict the Mexican Empire as tottering. Napoleon III's patience ebbed and his temper grew short. His orders to Bazaine were contradictory; only to Dano was he entirely consistent. This minister's conduct was repeatedly endorsed; instructions to negotiate a customs convention were stated again and again and, finally, Dano received the first indication that Napoleon III at last questioned continuance of the Mexican Empire. Should Maximilian renounce the throne and refuse to solve the crisis, a message in code instructed Dano, May 30, 1866, to have Bazaine call an assembly to organize a provisional government, name a president, adjust French relations with the new government, and leave.[11]

Possibly Maximilian would have mustered enough moral courage to abdicate had Charlotte not intervened. Throwing the weight of her decidedly stronger personality behind her arguments for riding out the storm, she finally announced that to

7. Drouyn de Lhuys to Dano, February 10, 1866, ibid.
8. Dano to Drouyn de Lhuys, January 9, 1866, ibid.
9. Dano to Drouyn de Lhuys, February 28, 1866, ibid.
10. A collection of such letters which were given Napoleon III is in the Papiers de Tuileries, AN.
11. Drouyn de Lhuys to Dano, May 30, 1866, in code, CP, Mexique, LXVII.

save their throne, she herself would cross the ocean to win back the support of Napoleon III. As Maximilian wavered, Charlotte wrote a lengthy memorandum appealing to the honor of his lineage and moralizing on the disasters that had befallen various princes whose resolution had prematurely buckled.[12] A mind more perceptive would have realized that Charlotte's arguments ignored the rising strength of republican guerrillas and mounting deficits.

In August 1866 Charlotte arrived at Paris and made her dramatic appeal to Napoleon III for funds. The stormy interviews between the two sovereigns created by political opportunism have been told and retold. Napoleon III's final word was that France would stay in Mexico until February 1867, provided Maximilian abdicated and returned with the French army. Almost prostrate with despair, disillusionment, and indignation, Charlotte next visited the pope. While at the Vatican Charlotte's overburdened mind gave way and the mental illness continued until her death in Belgium sixty-one years later in 1927.

Later in that dismal year of 1866 Maximilian made another surrender, one probably more humiliating than his enforced fealty to the French: it was the renunciation of his liberal ideas. Finally submitting to Gutiérrez de Estrada and other arch-reactionary Mexicans, Maximilian named one of them, Theodosio Lares, as minister-president. Lares had served in Miramón's cabinet and as president of the Assembly of Notables. Maximilian admitted to Dano that it was most degrading to substitute reactionary principles but he had no alternative. He told the French minister that, if France abandoned him, he would, if necessity demanded, defend his realm from mountain fastnesses: his Indian general, Mejía, had taught him how an army could operate without money. Only Maximilian regarded these vague assertions seriously.[13]

Finally, Seward received the long-awaited French dispatch of April 6, 1866. It declared that there was no occasion to continue debating the pros and cons of differing theories of actions long since passed. The United States did not support any intervention and France accepted that position as sufficient basis to begin withdrawal of her troops. The first contingent would leave in November 1866, the second in March 1867, and the third the

12. Corti, *Maximilian and Charlotte in Mexico*, II, 636 ff.
13. Dano to Drouyn de Lhuys, August 28, 1866, CP, Mexique, LXVII.

following November.[14] A second note soon followed after the Quai d'Orsay learned of mounting tension in Washington; it gave assurances that the emperor's intention was to permit no delays in the evacuation.[15]

If Paris believed these assurances had resolved the issues with Washington, she was soon undeceived. Aroused over reports from Bigelow at Paris and Motley at Vienna that plans were being made to send more troops to Mexico, Seward urged an earlier date for the removal of French troops. He also instructed Bigelow to sound out French intentions and told Motley to protest vigorously to Vienna the raising of Austrian volunteers.

The first addition to the French who fought in Mexico was made in 1863. It was an Egyptian force of 500 troops, including 50 Sudanese Negroes, shanghaied from Alexandria. Larger contingents arrived later from Belgium and Austria. The Belgians, known as the Empress Charlotte Guard, totaled 2,000 volunteers, and the number of auxiliaries from Austria was estimated at 6,000.

Before Seward's dispatch to Vienna reached its destination, the New York press carried a review of the instructions to Motley. This violation of diplomatic protocol disturbed Montholon. He concluded that this strong reaffirmation of the Monroe Doctrine, although not mentioned by name, must stem from domestic political pressure on President Johnson and Secretary Seward. He reported to Paris regretfully that Seward's timing was shrewdly effective as Europe was too tense and preoccupied with other problems to take umbrage.[16]

Heretofore, in exchanges of correspondence, Vienna and Washington had ignored the Mexican question. Late in 1863, Motley had been instructed not to discuss Maximilian.[17] The Austrian minister to the United States was informed by his superior that Austria considered the Mexican crown to be the private business of the former Austrian archduke.[18] The prospect of Austrian replacements broke this reserve. As early as March 1866, Motley had been instructed to express, firmly but discreetly, the displeasure of the United States if Austria should

14. Drouyn de Lhuys to Montholon, April 6, 1866, CP, Etats-Unis, CXXXVI.
15. Drouyn de Lhuys to Montholon, April 25, 1866, ibid.
16. Montholon to Drouyn de Lhuys, May 1, 1866, CP, Etats-Unis, CXXXVI.
17. Seward to Motley, October 9, 1863, Instructions, Austria, Dept. of State, NA, I.
18. Instructions to Wydenbrook, February 11, 1865, Etats-Unis, Auessern.

become the protector of Maximilian.[19] Two weeks later, Seward was more emphatic. Austria must realize that actions supporting Maximilian would cause her to be at war with the Republic of Mexico and under such circumstances the United States could not promise neutrality.[20] Seward's third dispatch to Motley was virtually an ultimatum. Austria was asked for assurances that the enlistment of volunteers for Mexico would be stopped; if she refused, Motley was to withdraw from Vienna.[21]

The plight of the Austrian capital faced by a hostile Prussia was critical. Her record of neutrality during the entire period of Maximilian's entanglement in Mexico had been consistent. On the other hand, Maximilian was the emperor's brother and Austrians who had gone to Mexico when the archduke accepted the crown had already fought on Mexican soil. To permit their reinforcement seemed innocuous enough until the United States made it a *casus belli*. An advance guard of 1,000 volunteers out of a possible total of 4,000 had been assembled on May 15, 1866, for embarkation.

Prior to the receipt of Seward's drastic demand, Motley had warned the Austrian foreign minister that Austria and the United States stood on the threshold of grave danger. The time at last had approached when the Mexican people might express their will without intimidation. Washington hoped Vienna would continue nonintervention by holding up the enlistment of volunteers.[22]

On May 21, 1866, Motley received the required assurances. The government of Franz Joseph had repeatedly expressed neutrality toward Mexico, but Austria's efforts had not, apparently, convinced the United States. Therefore, the departure of the volunteers had been stopped although Austria did not subscribe to all of Washington's views. The Austrian note ended with a hope for continued U.S. neutrality south of the Rio Grande.[23] This action of Seward was probably his most emphatic use of the Monroe Doctrine by inference, though not by name.

Motley believed the critical Prussian situation plus U.S. pro-

19. Seward to Motley, March 19, 1866, Instructions, Austria, Dept. of State, NA, I.

20. Seward to Motley, April 6, 1866, ibid.

21. Seward to Motley, April 30, 1866, ibid.

22. Motley to Foreign Minister Mensdorff, May 6, 1866, Dispatches, Austria, Dept. of State, NA, VII.

23. Mensdorff to Motley, May 21, 1866, ibid.

test accounted for Austria's abandonment of Maximilian. A third line of reasoning, and possibly as potent as the other two, probably influenced the Austrians. Should United States filibusters be unleashed over the border as a result of Austrian replacements, it would expose Maximilian to a danger out of all proportion to the aid he would receive from volunteers.[24]

Bigelow fared less satisfactorily. The temper of Drouyn de Lhuys was somewhat short when Bigelow finally saw him. He remarked that France had proclaimed her "intention to retire from Mexico because it suited her convenience and interests to retire, and for no other reason": the French government made its declaration in good faith and intended to keep it, but the method of evacuation depended on considerations "of which France is the only competent judge." Bigelow mildly inquired whether any U.S. official had questioned the good faith of France. Drouyn de Lhuys, still prickly, said no, but that the U.S. press had. "The press," Bigelow retorted, was a "law unto itself and we had better not accept it as a law unto us." He had been instructed, he continued, to ask why troops were being sent *to* Mexico when France was pulling out. Somewhat mollified, the French foreign minister explained that replacements for the Foreign Legion had left, but no new troops; the Austrian volunteers were no concern of France.[25]

Similar truculence crept into Paris dispatches to Montholon. It was not easy to transport thousands of troops from Mexico to France; numerous precautions had to be taken. Drouyn de Lhuys did not like the inferences which were creeping into U.S. dispatches that France had yielded to pressure. France had acted entirely on her own initiative, and her evacuation of troops did not alter her recognition of Maximilian as the legal ruler. However, it was admitted frankly, delays in financial arrangements handicapped evacuation.[26]

No proud words could hide for long the imminence of disaster in Mexico or the acknowledgment that, in the liquidation as in the initiation of the Grand Design, no major undertaking in the Americas had met Napoleon III's expectation. And, as in other crises binding the French to Mexico, Napoleon III had made another of his many modifications. Montholon was di-

24. Mensdorff to Metternich, May 9, 1866, France, Auessern.
25. Bigelow to Seward, June 4, 1866, Dispatches, France, Dept. of State, NA, LX.
26. Drouyn de Lhuys to Montholon, June 7, 1866, CP, Etats-Unis, CXXXVII.

rected on July 24, 1866, to determine cautiously if Washington would assume responsibility for preventing anarchy in Mexico after French withdrawal and Maximilian's abdication. If Washington responded, Montholon was to inform Drouyn de Lhuys "what practical means of approach was most proper."[27]

Others had speculated on the aftermath of French withdrawal. Months before, Romero had predicted to General Grant that France would want the United States to negotiate an armistice while the French were withdrawing.[28] Montholon had talked to Seward and found him firm in his conviction that the Mexican Empire would fall. He was strongly opposed to U.S. interference. Upon receiving instructions to sound out the United States on undertaking responsibility in Mexico, Montholon buttonholed Seward's son, Frederick. Young Seward agreed that Mexico should have an orderly government but was unequivocal in his rejection of any proposal that the United States support Maximilian, even to prevent chaos. "The presence of our flag is a secondary question," Montholon regretfully wrote Drouyn de Lhuys. To the United States "the form of government is everything."[29]

With the return of northeast Mexico to the republicans, and after the departure of Charlotte for Europe, the United States in general believed the end of the Mexican Empire was rapidly approaching. In his position Montholon could not concede such a situation. What would the United States do, he asked Seward, "if France departed, leaving the Empire upright behind her?" The secretary of state dryly responded, "That is a hypothesis not likely to happen." Seward would not admit the existence of the Mexican Empire in the future any more than he had in the past.[30]

The U.S. minister in Paris guardedly watched through the summer of 1866 the diplomatic moves and countermoves. Acting on Seward's prodding, he asked at regular intervals the now almost mechanical question, has French policy governing troop withdrawal been modified? The answer was invariably in the negative.

27. Drouyn de Lhuys to Montholon, July 24, 1866, ibid.

28. Romero to Lerdo de Tejada, April 23, 1866, *Corres. mexicana*, VII.

29. Montholon to Drouyn de Lhuys, August 22, 1866, Confidential, CP, Etats-Unis, CXXXVII.

30. Montholon to Lavalette, October 1, 1866, ibid.

"My dear Jules," wrote a French soldier identified only as the author of a letter captured in the spring of 1866 by republican guerrillas, "We are running like crazy people after an enemy that cannot be caught."[31] This elusive guerrilla fighting increased throughout the summer and into the fall of 1866 as General Bazaine began moving his troops toward the capital for departure from Mexico. As the French withdrew, each village, town, or city was occupied by Juaristas, often within twenty-four hours.

Also, in the spring of 1866, Doña Margarita, wife of President Juárez, was in Washington; she had made the long trip to nurse Romero's mother. President Johnson gave a reception for her, the first since Lincoln's death, and Seward complimented her with a dinner at which he predicted eloquently that the French would be out of Mexico by the end of 1866. A ball in her honor given by General Grant was attended by President Johnson who broke precedent to express U.S. friendship for republican Mexico.[32]

Juárez prepared to march southward from the upper reaches of Chihuahua. He had gained control over the northern states, including the important city of Monterrey. In the south republicans held the Isthmus of Tehuantepec and parts of Yucatán. Not even locations near the capital were safe from the Juaristas.

Maximilian stormed against this shrinkage of his empire. Unyielding, Bazaine followed the orders of Napoleon III to prepare for embarkation. Maximilian vacillated between depression and futile optimism. Angered by Austria's yielding to Seward's demands, the Mexican emperor feebly tried to retaliate by informing Vienna that his empire had withdrawn from the convention entered into before Maximilian left Europe.[33]

An astonishing compromise of Maximilian's liberal principles was the appointment of Father Agustín Fischer as secretary of his cabinet. A German Protestant, Fischer migrated to Texas and later to California, became a Jesuit, and at one time served the Bishop of Durango as secretary. He appears to have led a disorderly life and his ethical standards were questionable. How Fischer gained over the Mexican emperor the power to exert

31. Malgraive to "My Dear Jules," March 13, 1866, enclosed in Romero to Seward, July 10, 1866, Notes, Mexico, Dept. of State, NA, XVII.

32. Ralph Roeder, *Juárez and His Mexico* (New York, 1947), II, 633–34.

33. Corti, *Maximilian and Charlotte in Mexico*, II, 648.

an insidious influence must be laid to Maximilian's infallible inability to judge character.

In this turmoil Bazaine found himself helplessly in the center. The fatal defect of his command lay neither in his own ambitions, though they were limitless and sometimes devious, nor in the character of the Mexican emperor, but in the Grand Design itself. Nothing less than a miracle could have brought together a ruler with a commander-in-chief who owed allegiance to another sovereign.

Bazaine complained that Maximilian openly tried to discredit the French army as it began to withdraw. Perhaps, hinted Bazaine, this criticism was but a pretext for explaining the poor returns of revenue and the delay of unification which "will remain the same as long as the Emperor wishes to be more Mexican than the Mexicans, more Juarista than Juárez, because no party has confidence in his political capacity or in his character, which is that of a dreamy German."[34]

In September 1866, Bazaine sent to the minister of war an even more scathing denunciation. The continued existence of the Mexican Empire was not a question of years but of "days and hours." The temper of Mexicans was not monarchist; temporarily inactive Liberals would at French withdrawal rise "as one man against the Emperor who has no prestige." Bazaine blamed Maximilian and Charlotte for the disillusionment and despair. Mexicans had forgiven much the first year on the score of ignorance and inexperience, but Maximilian's continued weakness invited defiance, even scorn. The emperor told "more lies than the biggest Mexican liar," while Charlotte was "proud, disagreeable, vain, and believes herself a superior statesman."[35] While these strictures were being written, the first contingent of troops was embarking. Before the vessels left Veracruz, two telegrams arrived from Napoleon III. One suspended evacuation until all troops could leave at one time; the other announced the departure from Paris of General François Castelnau as a special emissary of Napoleon III with supreme authority.[36]

As Castelnau was crossing the ocean in the leisurely fashion of the 1860s, the affairs of Maximilian reached still another crisis.

34. Bazaine to Randon, March 9, 1866, AMG, 1866.
35. Bazaine to Randon, September 27, 1866, ibid.
36. Dano to Drouyn de Lhuys, September 28, 1866, CP, Mexique, LXIX.

It developed by degrees. First came Napoleon III's letter of August 29, 1866, a last blunt attempt to convince the Mexican ruler that French help had terminated. Not a franc more, not a single additional soldier could be expected. If Maximilian believed he could maintain himself, French troops would leave the following year. Should Maximilian decide to abdicate, Napoleon III advised him to issue a proclamation setting forth his reasons. This would be followed by the calling of a general assembly to elect a government before the French left.[37]

This letter reached Mexico October 1 by the same post which brought letters from the distracted Charlotte—scarcely coherent narratives whose sole lucid expression was the admission of failure.[38] Two courses of action thus tore at Maximilian, both disagreeable: one was to place his crown before a national assembly for adjudication with a corollary of abdication; the other was to try, with Conservative support, to maintain his empire. European members of his court urged the former; his council and Father Fischer strongly advocated the continuance of the empire, mindful that a Juarista firing squad might otherwise be their lot.

Sensing the powerful opposition of the Conservatives to abdication, Maximilian's advisers made efforts to protect him, on the pretext of illness, from such persuasions. Behind the scenes there was the utmost confusion; the Conservative ministry resigned and then reconsidered. The emperor drew up, but never issued, a proclamation announcing his withdrawal and appointing a regency of Lares and Bazaine until a congress could be called.[39]

French troops were to be concentrated for mass embarkation in March 1867, thus anticipating the original date set for final evacuation.

Napoleon III informed Dano that Castelnau was to find answers to two questions. Could Maximilian maintain himself after the French departed? Could the empire survive if the troops remained the allotted time, namely, one year? If the answer was no, "as I believe," Maximilian must be induced to "give up the power already slipping away from him." Bazaine would then proclaim to Mexicans that France never wanted to impose an unpopular government on the country and that a national as-

37. Ollivier, *L'Empire libéral*, IX, 79.
38. Corti, *Maximilian and Charlotte in Mexico*, II, 685.
39. Ibid., II, 737.

sembly, to be convened at once, would decide the nature of the new government. Men hostile to French interests, such as Santa Anna and, above all, Juárez, were to be excluded from the next regime. If a responsible government came into existence, Bazaine was authorized to support it, but should confusion and disorder result, the French were ordered to leave immediately. Napoleon III wanted Castelnau "to bring the government of France out of the state of uncertainty in which it has been for three years." He wearily added, "The more it is said that the government of Maximilian can maintain itself, the more the contrary shows up."[40]

Having decided on the procedures by which a new Mexican government would be established, Castelnau and his colleagues turned their attention to the liquidation of the old. No argument whatever had been needed to convince Castelnau that the Mexican Empire was doomed. In the capital he communicated with Maximilian's ministers and, indirectly, with the Austrian. Abdication again was urged. Maximilian's ministers were shaken but unconvinced.[41] If the emperor intended to abdicate, it should be done from the capital and after a new government had been set up. The French expected Maximilian to leave Mexico at once.

Calling a national assembly to decide the form of government was strongly rooted in Maximilian's mind. He had no intention, he insisted, of surrendering his authority to any party or faction but only to the nation whence he had received it, a lofty sentiment but scarcely consistent with hard facts.

Maximilian, the cause of all the international commotion, spent hours in the woods near Orizaba under the spell of his fatal malady, indecision.

On November 18, 1866, he called a conference of ministers and others to meet with him at Orizaba to reconsider the whole question of abdication.

As Maximilian's vacillation moved him inevitably toward destruction, a mysterious mission left New York. Its members were General William Tecumseh Sherman and a new minister to Mexico, Lewis D. Campbell of Ohio. An editor and hack politician, Campbell had served five terms in Congress and in 1864

40. Drouyn de Lhuys to Dano, December 8, 1866; Note of Napoleon III, September 1866, Notes Lettres et Rapports sur la Mission de Général Castelnau, M et D, Mexique, X.

41. Castelnau to Napoleon III, November 9, 1866, AMG, 1866.

SHERMAN'S   SECRET   MISSION   TO   MEXICO

had boomed Johnson against Lincoln for the Presidency.[42]

Sailing south aboard the sidewheeler *Susquehanna*, Campbell and Sherman first stopped in Havana to confer with M. D. L. Lane and Marcus Otterbourg, who were returning to their United States consular posts at Veracruz and Mexico City, respectively. Campbell and Sherman held another conference while in Havana with the former confederate general, John B. Magruder. He delivered a message entrusted to him by Bazaine for President Johnson. "The moral influence of the United States has destroyed the Empire," Bazaine was quoted as asserting, "and thus the obligation rests upon the United States to keep Mexico from anarchy and protect the thousands of foreigners residing

42. Campbell to Johnson, December 20, 1865, Andrew Johnson Papers, LC, LII. For information about Campbell's relations with Senator Sumner see Campbell to Johnson, May 1, 1866, Andrew Johnson Papers, LC, XCIV.

there. Ten or fifteen thousand American troops properly distributed through northern Mexico and a similar number of French soldiers, all working together, would do the trick."[43]

Campbell and Sherman decided to remain at Havana until Lane and Otterbourg reached their destinations and reported on conditions.[44] When Otterbourg reached Mexico City, he was told by Bazaine that the U.S. mission would be welcomed.[45]

The possible visit of the U.S. mission to Mexico City depended on Maximilian's abdication and departure. When the *Susquehanna* steamed into the harbor of Veracruz November 28, Maximilian, still undecided, was at Orizaba; consequently, the mission from Washington remained on board. An emissary from the French authorities assured the mission that French troops were being assembled for embarkation as rapidly as possible and, if the French had their way, Maximilian would then be en route to Europe.[46]

The *Susquehanna* lingered off Veracruz four days. Maximilian, according to the British chargé d'affaires, sent his own agent to invite Campbell and Sherman to Orizaba.[47] The agent arrived at Veracruz after the *Susquehanna* had left. What desperate final plea was in the emperor's mind remains unknown; the day after the sidewheeler steamed away to Tampico, Maximilian finally announced his intention of remaining in Mexico. After a brief stop at Tampico, Campbell and Sherman continued their odyssey to Brazos de Santiago in Texas and thence to Brownsville. Before starting on the mission, General Sherman had requested that President Juárez be notified of the mission's departure and that U.S. troops along the Mexican border be readied for his call in case temporary occupation of forts was requested.[48] At Brownsville the mission met General Sheridan on an inspection tour of the border, and General Mariano Escobedo, commander of republican forces. Sherman learned about Juárez's plan of

43. Campbell to Seward, November 21, 1866, Dispatches, Mexico, Dept. of State, NA, XXX.

44. Campbell to Seward, November 23, 1866, ibid.

45. Dano to Moustier, November 28, 1866, CP, Mexique, LXVIII.

46. Lane to Seward, December 3, 1866, Consular Reports, Veracruz, Dept. of State, NA, 1861–66.

47. R. J. C. Middleton to Stanley, December 10, 1866, Confidential, in cipher, BFO 50/397.

48. Sherman to Grant, November 3, 1866, William T. Sherman Papers, LC, XX.

campaign toward Mexico City and the number and equipment of his forces.[49] Juárez was still in Chihuahua, although he contemplated moving his headquarters to Monterrey. Neither Sherman nor Campbell considered going to distant Chihuahua; each was beginning to believe that he had wandered about long enough in pursuit of the republican government. The travel-weary Sherman wrote in rugged Shermanic prose that he suspected that Juárez was "away up in Chihuahua for no possible purpose other than to be where the Devil himself cannot get at him. I have not the remotest idea of riding on mule back 1,000 miles to find . . . [the] chief executive. . . ."[50]

After thirty-six days the commissioners separated. Sherman continued on the *Susquehanna* to New Orleans while Campbell lingered timidly and fruitlessly at Brownsville for about one week or until he learned that Juárez would be still further delayed in reaching Monterrey. Then Campbell too left for New Orleans.

Campbell was described grotesquely by Gideon Welles, U.S. secretary of the navy: "The Minister with his thumb in his mouth stood off, went up the coast where Sherman left him and the whole turns out a *faux pas*, a miserable, bungling piece of business."[51]

Seward had instructed Campbell not to hamper or embarrass the departure of French forces, and no arrangement was to be made with either the French or with Maximilian. The United States wished to see Mexico freed from foreign interference and restored to self-government without dictation from anyone. However, if President Juárez needed Campbell's good offices to further the reestablishment of national authority, he might confer with Juárez, or "with any other parties or agents should such an exceptional conference become necessary, but not otherwise." It was possible that "some disposition might be made of the land and naval forces of the United States."

Sherman had been appointed to accompany Campbell as a military adviser with "discretionary authority as to the location

49. Sherman to Grant, December 16, 1866, Headquarters of the Army, War Dept. Records, NA, Letters Received.

50. Sherman to "Dear Brother," December 7, 1866, Sherman Papers, XX.

51. Gideon Welles, *Diary*, 3 vols. (Boston, 1911), II, 649; see also Henry D. Flint, *Mexico under Maximilian* (Philadelphia, 1867), pp. 145–46.

of [United States] forces . . . in the vicinity of Mexico."[52] The general reluctantly accepted the appointment after his close friend General Grant had refused it three times. As Sherman explained to his brother, President Johnson wished to ease Grant out of Washington in the hope of making Sherman secretary of war and commander of the army. He confided, "I have to make this trip to escape a worse duty and to save another person from a complication that should be avoided."[53]

Sherman's reluctance was not surprising. It was an uncertain mission which had to be played by ear, by both him and Campbell.

Had Secretary Seward intended to place a minister in a crucial area to advance the interests of the United States, someone more capable and experienced than Campbell should have been sent. Had Seward intended to demonstrate that Juárez was the only Mexican with whom the United States would treat, the tour of the *Susquehanna* was an expensive exhibition. Had Seward felt constrained to soothe U.S. public opinion before Congress convened in December 1866, the sending of a diplomat and the second most famous Union general to Juárez was a purchase of time, as had been Schofield's journey to France. In both cases it mattered little that the missions accomplished nothing. Some months later, Seward told Romero his preference was that Campbell should reach Juárez after the republican government had been reestablished in the capital.[54] Campbell admirably served this preference. He never reached Juárez at all.

To all appearances Juárez neither sought nor avoided a meeting with the U.S. envoy accredited to him but continued about his business, apparently unruffled by the U.S. mission's disinclination to travel. Thus, near the end of a five-year ordeal, republican Mexico appeared willing to wind up the long struggle through her own efforts.

52. Seward to Campbell, October 25, 1866, Instructions, Mexico, Dept. of State, NA, XVII.

53. Sherman to "Dear Brother," November 11, 1866, Sherman Papers, XX; see also "Notes of Col. W. C. Moore, Private Secretary to President Johnson, 1866–1868," *AHR*, XIX (October 1913–July 1914), 99–132.

54. Romero to Lerdo de Tejada, April 19, 1867, *Corres. mexicana*, IX. See also Martin H. Hall, "The Campbell-Sherman Diplomatic Mission to Mexico," *Bulletin of the Historical and Philosophical Society of Ohio*, XIII (October 1955), 254–70.

25

Maximilian's Fatal Indecision
1866–1867

Four days before Sherman and Campbell arrived off Veracruz, Maximilian on November 24, 1866, called together his Council of Conservative Ministers in Mexico City. Their deliberations were reported by the British Minister Scarlett and the French Minister Dano, although neither attended the sessions.

Scarlett informed London that the council voted nineteen to two to support Maximilian if he continued on the throne and to raise $2,000,000 for military defense. Scarlett thought Maximilian might be able to salvage the crown and "in the face of a threatened partition of Mexican territory by the United States . . . [Mexicans would] drop their party differences and rally round the throne."[1] In Dano's account there was no demand for continuance of the empire; even Lares, president of the council, urged only that the emperor not abdicate before the French left. In that event, the Conservatives would be able to prepare their own defense with arms and munitions left by the French. Some ministers insisted that Maximilian remain as emperor until he could get a guarantee from Washington and Paris for Mexican autonomy and for the protection of imperialists.[2]

On November 28, 1866, Maximilian announced he would postpone abdication pending the calling of a congress. Should he be asked to stay, he listed conditions for acceptance. With the

1. Scarlett to Stanley, November 28, 1866, Confidential, BFO 50/397.
2. Dano to Moustier, November 20, 1866, CP, Mexique, LXVIII.

[290]

exception of freedom from French control, these stipulations represented objectives he had promoted with total failure ever since he arrived in Mexico.[3]

The following day, November 29, *El Diario del Imperio*, the official organ of the empire, announced the emperor and his council of ministers were considering the crisis; namely, the continuation of civil war and the threat of Franco-American intervention to abolish the empire and change Mexican institutions. The newly established conservative newspaper, *La Patria*, became belligerent: "We have finished with the epoch of magnanimity and pardons. A period now begins in which the sword will decide."

The French Legation promptly set the record straight; it seemed ironical, Dano replied, that such a statement should come from a council which would have had no place to meet had it not been for French bayonets. The French were not responsible for any crisis since they knew little of Maximilian's plans; they renounced henceforth all responsibility for the empire. They would have no relations with a government seeking to prolong civil war; as soon as possible their troops would be removed. According to Dano, this declaration caused a sensation. However, Maximilian was to have the last word. On December 9, the French Legation received a circular prepared by Maximilian's Foreign Office for the Diplomatic Corps. "For political reasons," it read, Napoleon III was removing his troops prior to the date set by treaty. Negotiations were in progress for Franco-American intervention to suppress the empire. The Mexican Empire intended to maintain itself.[4]

The circular aroused French ire because of its veiled attack on Napoleon III and its claim of Bazaine's complicity. For weeks Castelnau had suspected that the *maréchal* had been playing a double game. The U.S. consul Otterbourg had informed Seward that Bazaine had interviewed various Mexican groups; when Castelnau also acquired this information, he refused to permit Bazaine to attend the November 24 meeting of the Council of Ministers because he did not know what the *maréchal* would do or say.[5] Castelnau collected evidence on Bazaine's conduct, sent

3. Egon Caesar Corti, *Maximilian and Charlotte in Mexico*, trans. Catherine A. Phillips, 2 vols. (New York, 1928), II, 751.

4. Dano to Moustier, December 10, 1866, CP, Mexique, LXVIII.

5. Castelnau to Napoleon III, November 28, 1866, in Luis Sonolet, "L'Agonie

copies to Paris, and faced Bazaine. The evidence consisted of alleged conversations in which Bazaine had purportedly toyed with means of delaying the French evacuation. Bazaine denied the charges, declaring that he had been misrepresented and misunderstood. Castelnau ordered him to make no statements which were not sanctioned by Dano and himself.[6] When news of this friction among French authorities reached Paris, the Austrian Legation there, already worried over the outcome in Mexico, questioned the Quai d'Orsay. "Was it true," the legation spokesman asked, "that Bazaine was actually preventing the abdication of Maximilian?" "Not at all," firmly responded the French foreign minister, "we have too much interest that the Emperor Maximilian will leave Mexico, with or without an act of abdication, for the version you heard to have the least truth."[7]

Convinced that "bloody anarchy" was just around the corner unless Maximilian could be brought to immediate abdication, Castelnau and Dano set out toward Orizaba on December 20 to confer with the emperor. Meanwhile, Maximilian had started toward Mexico City. At Puebla, Castelnau saw Maximilian for the first time, and found him seemingly reasonable, even gracious. He told Castelnau he realized he could not keep the crown but he wanted to renounce it honorably for himself and usefully for the country. He was calling a national congress and seeking an armistice to give Mexicans an opportunity to express their will. Castelnau argued that such a plan, however praiseworthy, was one year too late to be successful.

On December 22, Castelnau, accompanied by Dano, again saw Maximilian and renewed the argument. Abdication would be a great and noble action, "worthy of his character," the Frenchman pleaded. A soldier, replied Maximilian, did not leave his post until relieved of duty. He was determined to call a congress and would even accept the mediation of the United States to force Juárez to an agreement. Furthermore, Napoleon III had advocated the calling of a congress. There was no question of the outcome; Juárez would be sustained since the country was not monarchy-minded. He, Maximilian, would accept the decision,

---

de l'empire du Mexique," *La Revue de Paris*, XXXIV (August 1 and August 15, 1927), pt. 1, p. 624.

6. Castelnau to Napoleon III, December 28, 1866, ibid., pt. 2, pp. 875–82.

7. Mulinem to de Beust, December 21, 1866, Confidential, France, Auessern.

congratulate his successor and, "with a light heart and head high," set out for Europe.

To the discomfiture of Castelnau and Dano the emperor produced a telegram from Bazaine, sent the day before, encouraging him to keep the crown. Everyone knew Bazaine had been dealing with both sides, said Maximilian, and then with a sly smile remarked, "You do not seem accustomed to the methods of the Maréchal."[8]

Before this bland, confident, utterly unrealistic visionary who saw conditions only as he wished them to be, Castelnau and Dano were powerless. They returned to Mexico City frustrated, exhausted, and furious; their fury was directed at Bazaine. Castelnau considered removing him from his command and consulted officers in his confidence about it. Regardless of their opinion of Bazaine, they strongly advised against it; such drastic action would be a rebuff to all French *maréchals*; besides, it would prolong evacuation. During this critical period, Castelnau saw Otterbourg frequently and explained to him the situation in detail as insurance against the risk of rumors reaching Washington to the effect that the French were delaying evacuation.[9]

The third French attempt to bring about abdication occurred after Maximilian's return to the capital, January 5, 1867. Public reaction to the emperor's reappearance was not encouraging. Even those who had voted against abdication appeared frightened by the situation. On January 6, Bazaine saw Maximilian. "If I can believe the Maréchal," wrote Castelnau to Napoleon III, "he [Bazaine] had advocated Maximilian's abdication and promised to call a Council of Notables following the precedent of 1863." Pending their decision, the republican leader most capable of maintaining order would be placed in command; the French would withdraw, taking with them Miramón and Márquez, by force if necessary. Maximilian told Bazaine he knew he had been betrayed by those who urged him to remain. No longer did he believe a national congress could be called but he must wait to be sure. The Diplomatic Corps and many foreign residents added their advice to that of the French. Many suggested

---

8. Castelnau to Napoleon III, December 28, 1866, in Sonolet, "L'Agonie de l'empire du Mexique," pt. 2, pp. 875–82; Dano to Moustier, December 23, 1866, CP, Mexique, LXVIII.

9. Otterbourg to Chew, December 17 and December 29, 1866, Consular Reports, Mexico City, Dept. of State, NA, XI.

Letting Him Slide

Napoleon (to Maximilian of Mexico): "I am really very sorry, but I must let go, or you might pull me over!"

NAPOLEON III AND MAXIMILIAN

U.S. minister to Austria John Lothrop Motley asserted that Maximilian accepted the Mexican crown to "destroy the dragon of democracy in the Americas." Controversy has long raged over the final days of Maximilian in Mexico. Official records prove that Napoleon III did everything in his power to induce Maximilian to embark for Europe with the French troops, and Austria even sent a ship for his return. After immature vacillation Maximilian remained in Mexico, and on June 19, 1867, he was executed at Querétaro.

Harper's Weekly, 20 October 1866
(Library of Congress)

the Juarista general, Porfirio Díaz, as the republican most appropriate to receive the surrender of Mexico City.[10]

On January 14, Maximilian called a meeting of thirty-five men of influence, including officials and clergy, to consider whether or not the empire could pacify the country. A fantastic picture was painted by the reactionary clique; they unrealistically estimated the emperor's military resources at 26,000 men and his revenue at the ridiculous sum of $11,000,000. Bazaine, who had been invited to the meeting, spoke strongly against continuation of the empire. He insisted that the majority of the people favored a republic and, although he had had an estimated 40,000 French and 20,000 Mexicans under his command, he had not found them strong enough to transform republicans into monarchists. He was convinced that the emperor should depart for his honor as well as for his safety.[11] When the vote was taken, twenty-four favored continuance of the empire, six opposed it, and five abstained. Among abstainers were the clergy; they declined to express themselves on subjects they considered beyond their competence. This restraint about political affairs after their previous record was startling. The favorable vote induced Maximilian to persist in his efforts to maintain the throne.[12]

Meanwhile, both Maximilian and Bazaine tried to negotiate with the nearest republican general, Porfirio Díaz. On February 14, 1867, Díaz announced that an agent of Maximilian offered him the surrender of Puebla and Mexico City after which Maximilian would leave the country. "Was it for this," queried Díaz, "that I spent part of 1865 in jail?" With some difficulty he convinced the agent that his only relations with Maximilian would be those of war.[13]

Probably Bazaine's overture to Díaz was conditioned by dispatches received from his agent, Vicomte Ludovic M. François de Noue, who spent December 1866, and January 1867, in Washington and New York. De Noue consulted the French Minister Montholon in Washington and the French consuls in New York, New Orleans, and elsewhere about U.S. attitudes. The tenor of

10. Castelnau to Napoleon III, January 9, 1867, in Sonolet, "L'Agonie de l'empire du Mexique," pt. 2, pp. 887 ff.

11. Address of Bazaine at meeting of January 14, 1867, A. de Vouvielle, "Enquête sur l'expédition de Mexique," *La Liberté*, August 28, 1867.

12. Middleton to Stanley, January 28, 1867, BFO 50/405.

13. Statement of Porfirio Díaz, February 14, 1867, CP, Mexique, LXIX, Maximilian's agent was M. E. Burnouf.

his frequent communications to Bazaine was that in the United States "there was no hope whatever of any guarantee of French interests." In his opinion, (1) the United States had but one candidate for the presidency of Mexico, Benito Juárez; (2) Seward was cool toward Maximilian's notion of calling a national assembly, disinclined to foster a truce between the imperialists and the republicans; and (3) the best that could be hoped for from Washington was strict neutrality. One point de Noue stressed repeatedly was that the French must depart even if it meant leaving Maximilian behind.[14]

Bazaine could hardly be expected to seek negotiations with Juárez even had it been geographically possible. The logical approach was General Díaz, in central Mexico. Equally logical was Díaz's refusal of Bazaine's offer on the assumption that the French wished to sow discord in Juarista ranks. But such an assumption was not necessarily correct. By this time Bazaine was operating on a *sauve qui peut* basis; only too apparent was the advantage to his sovereign, himself, and the prominent family of his Mexican wife of reaching some understanding with the enemy.

On January 10, 1867, Napoleon III cabled Castelnau not to force Maximilian to abdicate but to bring the troops out of Mexico by March as scheduled.[15] Thereafter, preparations went forward speedily. The last contingent marched from the capital early in February 1867, with Bazaine at its head. Accompanying them were fugitive Mexicans from the interior and many prominent persons from Mexico City who, leaving for Europe, took advantage of the safe conduct to the coast offered by withdrawing troops. Bazaine made a last appeal to Maximilian and, when he arrived at Puebla, sent word that a safe conduct to the coast could still be provided.[16] Thus ended, after five years of cruel bloodshed and wide destruction, Napoleon III's futile attempt to regenerate Mexico as the beginning of his Grand Design for the Americas.

Dano remained in Mexico City; he had been instructed by Na-

14. Vicomte Ludovic M. François de Noue Papers, Geneva. See especially de Noue to Bazaine, December 9, 1866, December 12 and 24, 1866, and January 4, 15, and 20, 1867.
15. Napoleon III to Castelnau, January 10, 1867, CP, Mexique, LXIX.
16. Far more tragic was Bazaine's last action in France, when as commander-in-chief of the French in the Franco-Prussian War, he surrendered his army of 140,000. For this action he was court-martialed and sentenced to death but escaped to Spain.

poleon III to stay until Maximilian abdicated or Juárez occupied the capital.[17]

Count Jules Berthemy, the minister who had succeeded Montholon at Washington, immediately conferred with Seward about the preservation of order in Mexico and the protection of French nationals after the troops left. Seward was noncommittal. The United States must be prudent, said he, but he was willing to relay messages to Romero.[18] At Berthemy's suggestion Seward spoke to the Mexican Legation. Romero suspected the French of trying to strengthen Maximilian. However, he was willing to talk with Berthemy even though results more tangible than a meeting of the minds would have to be reached in Mexico.[19] Accordingly, Seward passed on to Berthemy the suggestion that Juárez and Bazaine arrange an armistice. Berthemy replied rather huffily that France needed no armistice; she was well able to protect her troops as long as they remained in Mexico.

In January and February 1867, the French Legation in Washington tried one means after another to entice the U.S. State Department toward taking a positive stand to prevent anarchy in Mexico after French withdrawal. Berthemy conferred with Senator Sumner, chairman of the Foreign Relations Committee, about a resolution favoring American action. Sumner was still interested in Mexico, friendly to France, but disinclined to tamper with the status quo. The American attitude was not precisely antagonistic, Berthemy believed; rather, the United States apparently intended to keep for herself complete freedom of action; back of everything else was something akin to a feeling of triumph which enhanced her own prestige and deepened French distress. It became difficult to get the State Department to say anything about Mexico. Napoleon III resigned himself to failure and to impending humiliation. Berthemy had been asked to attempt the impossible; after troops left Mexico, normal interests between the United States and France might be given consideration.[20]

For the stubborn, indecisive Maximilian, left to the mercy of his alleged friends and the hatred of his enemies, the denouement of his career in America was approaching. Throughout

17. Moustier to Dano, March 6, 1867, CP, Mexique, LXIX.
18. Berthemy to Moustier, January 10, 1867, CP, Etats-Unis, CXXXVIII.
19. Romero to Lerdo de Tejada, January 9, 1867, *Corres. mexicana*, IX.
20. Moustier to Berthemy, February 15, 1867, CP, Etats-Unis, CXXXVIII.

Maximilian's three-year reign, opposition to the Mexican monarchy was increasing steadily, not only throughout the United States, but in Spanish America. Although men from the United States were known to have served Juárez as mercenaries, there is no exact record of the number or reliable information about them. Estimates range from a Legion of Honor numbering 25,[21] organized in California, to the exaggerated figure of 3,000,[22] including those recruited by General Lew Wallace on the eastern seaboard of the United States.

The Legion of Honor was financed by "Sam" Brannan. A leader in the Mormon church, he had transported almost three hundred members of that faith from New York around the tip of South America to the Golden Gate when that region still was a part of Mexico. Brannan prospered and was California's first capitalist. He became a supporter of the Juarista cause through his friendship in California with a recruiter for Juárez, General Sánchez Ochoa, one-time governor of a central Mexican state, Zacatecas. Later Ochoa was in command of Juarista forces at Mazatlán.[23]

The legion left California in the spring of 1866 and traveled overland by horse and wagon to El Paso, Texas, then to Chihuahua where President Juárez accepted them into the Mexican service.[24]

First commander of the legion was Colonel George M. Green, who, a member of the Mexican army since 1858, had been Ochoa's chief of staff. Accompanying Ochoa to California in 1865, he recruited the initial men for the legion. His brother, Francis L. Green, also a member of the legion, fought in the battles of Zacatecas, Querétaro, and the siege of Mexico City.[25] Another member of the legion was Captain Harvey Lake, a veteran of the U.S. Army.[26]

Mazatlán, largest Pacific seaport of Mexico, located near the entrance to the Gulf of California, was the most important Pacific port through which Californians entered or left Mexico.

An American merchant and mining engineer, Frederick G.

21. Robert B. Brown, "Guns Over the Border" (Ph.D. diss., University of Michigan, 1951), p. 74.
22. Ibid., p. 86.
23. Ibid., p. 39.
24. Ibid., pp. 74, 75.
25. Ibid., p. 78.
26. Ibid., p. 74.

Fitch, turned from his Sinaloa mine at Copala to direct the fortification of Mazatlán in May and June of 1863. His newly erected works protected that city from attacks by the French frigate *Cordellière*. Fitch managed to bring in 100,000 percussion caps aboard the schooner *Juanita*, running the French blockade and landing at the mouth of the Chametla River, where he turned the caps over to the Juaristas.[27]

Another spectacular American from California was Francis F. Dana. He had been living in Mazatlán and volunteered May 1, 1865, to help Juárez. On March 16, 1866, with nine men under his command, he boarded and captured the Maximilian steamship *John L. Stephens* off Cape St. Lucas. Dana took her into La Paz, Baja California, and discharged her cargo, turning the booty over to the Juaristas.[28]

In San Francisco General Placido Vega, former governor of Sinaloa, the state in which Mazatlán was located, endeavored to recruit U.S. citizens for the Juárez army and to purchase urgently needed guns and munitions.[29]

During February and March 1867, radical changes occurred in various parts of Mexico. In the northern states the military forces of Juárez were rapidly enlarged by guerrillas from the central and southern areas, and the French were marching to Veracruz in preparation for their return trip to France.

The French had been gone from the capital only one week when Maximilian's ministers, forsaking the empty hope of continuing the monarchy, urged upon him the opening of negotiations with President Juárez in a city held by the empire.[30] Accordingly, the emperor and General Márquez, at the head of imperial troops, rode out of the capital on the morning of February 13, 1867, and headed for Querétaro, having been preceded by generals Miramón and Mejía. Maximilian's departure was so unexpected that few in the capital knew of it.

Querétaro, some 160 miles northeast of Mexico City, was founded by Montezuma I in the fifteenth century. Its picturesque setting embraced a lush valley surrounded by low hills. This topography was to prove virtually a trap for the imperialists.

Time and again, Maximilian tried unsuccessfully to confer

27. Ibid., p. 51.
28. Ibid., p. 52.
29. Ibid., p. 21.
30. Corti, *Maximilian and Charlotte in Mexico*, II, 773.

with Juárez. When the emperor's overtures were contemptuously ignored, he lost time and military advantage waiting, waiting forlornly for reinforcements or some break in an increasingly tense situation. The republicans, increasing their forces daily, began the siege of Querétaro. This time there was no military support from the French. After sixty-seven days the siege ended suddenly during the early hours of May 15 when the emperor was captured through the treachery of Colonel Miguel López, a former favorite.[31] Slightly less than a month later, Maximilian was charged with traitorously taking up arms against the republic, tried by court-martial, and convicted. Pleas for mercy from European governments and from the United States were lodged.

The case of the Republic of Mexico against Maximilian, as prepared by Foreign Minister Lerdo de Tejada, rested on the premise that an act of clemency would be dangerous to the nation. Maximilian had known exactly what he was doing, it was argued, when he agreed to build an empire, aided by a foreign army, on the subversion of a constitutional government. To allow him to return to Europe would create a center of intrigue against the republic where all disgruntled elements, such as the exiles in Paris had been in 1861, could congregate and which European sovereigns might support if their demands for claims on Mexico were not satisfied. Mexico could not exist in such turmoil as she had endured since her independence.[32]

Maximilian was executed before a firing squad on June 19, 1867, on a hill overlooking the city of Querétaro. As the news of his death leaked out to the world, the Juarista minister to Washington, Matías Romero, scanned the American political horizon anxiously. The New York press condemned the execution as virtual assassination. In Washington, French Minister Berthemy summed up U.S. sentiment when he reported to Napoleon III that the people of the United States were embarrassed by the outrage to humanity but satisfied with the humiliation inflicted on Europe and European princes.[33]

31. Prince Felix zu Salm Salm, *Diary in Mexico*, 2 vols. (London, 1868), I, 189 ff; II, 180–256. The author, a Prussian, had fought in the Union army during the U.S. Civil War. He then joined Maximilian's forces and appears to have become one of Maximilian's closest friends.

32. Memorandum sobre el proceso de Archiduque Fernando Maximiliano de Austria, prepared by Mariano Riva Palacio and Rafael Martines de la Torre; Records of Maximilian's Trial, enclosed in Romero to Seward, July 7, 1867, Notes, Mexico, Dept. of State, NA, XX.

33. Berthemy to Moustier, May 31, 1867, CP, Etats-Unis, CXXXIX.

Thus in the summer of 1867 the struggle of the New World against interference from the Old was finally ended. This significant turning point in the political life of the Americas was the subject of an inter-American observance in 1869, at the Mexican capital when former U.S. Secretary of State William H. Seward declared that in the struggle "the United States became for the first time, in sincerity and earnestness, the friend and ally of every other Republican state in America and all the Republican states became, from that hour, the friends and allies of the United States."[34]

This visit of Seward to Latin America established an important tradition that in time was to bring the United States closer to its republican neighbors by the exchange of visits of the highest officials.

The Lincoln-Seward policy toward Latin America was based on a determination of the American nations to give each other the utmost cooperation in time of attack from abroad and respect for the different heritage, culture, and customs of each. Even though the foundations Lincoln and Seward laid for uniting the American republics have subsequently been neglected and even abused, some of the basic principles have endured. They did not rely on superficial slogans such as "Alliance for Progress." They were devoted wholeheartedly to the unity of the Americas.

After Seward closed his eight-year service as secretary of state and before he visited Mexico, he spent a short time in Alaska. One of his last acts in office had been to direct the complicated political maneuvers by which Alaska was added to the national domain of the United States. The acquisition of this vast area removed another crowned head from the Americas—that of the Russian tsar. Moreover, it added strategic value to the northwestern boundary of the United States. Although Seward's foresight in purchasing Alaska was not to be recognized for years to come, eventually that act would enhance his world-wide reputation.

Although severely handicapped by progressive paralysis, Seward undauntedly embarked upon an extremely difficult tour of the world.[35] In doing so he set still another important precedent for high ranking political figures of the United States. Leaving

34. Frederick W. Seward, *Reminiscences of a War-Time Statesman and Diplomat, 1830–1915* (New York, 1916), p. 414.

35. Glyndon G. Van Deusen, *William Henry Seward* (New York, 1967), pp. 557–61.

his Auburn home in the summer of 1870, he stopped in Chicago, then a city of only 300,000, where he saw the new president, Ulysses S. Grant. At Salt Lake City he attended services at the tabernacle where Brigham Young introduced him to nine of his fifteen wives. From Ogden, Utah, to San Francisco he rode in the luxurious private car of the directors of the Union Pacific.

He sailed leisurely across the Pacific to Japan where he was extended the high honor of a face-to-face audience with the Mikado. Leaving the Orient he traveled to the Middle East and Europe. At Paris, which still bore the marks of the Franco-Prussian conflict, Seward revived memories of France in Mexico with Drouyn de Lhuys, still the foreign minister.

Revived, too, was the recollection that the drumming of Seward's fingers on his desk in Washington had increasingly reverberated through the salons of the Tuileries and had inexorably indicated to Napoleon III that time, which has no allies, had run out for his Grand Design for the Americas. At the time Seward was in Paris Napoleon III and Eugénie were living quietly in England.

Among Seward's contemporaries who understood the achievement of this remarkable American was the great champion of "pan-Scandinavianism," Charles XV, king of Sweden and Norway. He declared that Seward was "the most wise and sagacious statesman of modern times."[36]

36. Ibid., p. 495.

26

"The Deepest Thought
of the
Second Empire"

The attempted regeneration of Mexico by Napoleon III, 1861–67, was the forerunner of his Waterloo. What was to have been Napoleon III's "deepest thought of the Second Empire" ended as did the adventure of Napoleon Bonaparte, in disaster.

Napoleon III was determined to substitute monarchies for republics below the Rio Grande and to make of them a powerful barrier to expansion of the United States. He had envisioned populating these monarchies with European immigrants qualified to form nations in the image of the Second Empire. He succeeded in subverting, briefly and temporarily, the republican form of government of Mexico and in substituting three years of insecure monarchy (1864–67) under Maximilian. The attempt of Napoleon III and Maximilian to set up monarchies in other parts of Spanish America was not extended beyond Mexico. This scheme was not supported by Brazil, the only other Latin monarchy in the New World. Moreover, it was severely condemned by the then stronger Spanish American republics, such as Argentina, Chile, and Peru.

At the time of Maximilian's execution, Jules Berthemy, French minister to Washington, was convinced that: "What happened in Mexico is first of all a defiance of Monarchical Europe from Republican America."[1]

1. Berthemy to Moustier, July 5, 1867, CP, Etats-Unis, CXXXIX.

In the summer of 1867, after the issue of monarchies versus republics in the New World was settled, Alphonse Dano, the only able, well informed, and clear thinking minister Napoleon III sent to Mexico, wrote a lengthy commentary to the Quai d'Orsay on Napoleon III's Grand Design. Since the day Maximilian was shot, began Dano, interpreters everywhere have tried to shed light on the tragedy. "Never has such foolishness been written," he added, saying the blame had been placed everywhere except where it belonged. "Why not have the courage to look for the obstacle where it can really be found? That obstacle was created all at once by the taking of Richmond, the surrender of Lee and the reconstruction of the Great American Union. . . . From the moment . . . [the French decided they] did not want war with the United States—and there were 100 reasons for not wanting it—the Mexican question entered a crucial phase."[2]

Minister Dano maintained that second to the opposition of the United States, the most serious obstacle to the success of Napoleon III's Grand Design was Maximilian. "The Austrian reasoned well," wrote Dano, "and acted entirely to the contrary."[3] Maximilian welcomed an opportunity to work out a new destiny not handicapped by the decadence of the Old World. However, he was unable even to symbolize the vitality of this professed altruism. Had he possessed the humble virtue of common sense, he might have accepted reality, however unpalatable, and saved his life. Maximilian apparently never understood the absurdity of attempting to live in Mexico according to the protocol proper to Hapsburgs; neither did he understand the vitriolic hate with which the Juaristas regarded him and his adventure. When Maximilian was about to be executed at Querétaro, President Juárez replied to pleas for his life: "If all the kings and queens of Europe were in your place, I could not spare that life. It is not I who take it but the people and the law, and if I should not do its will the people would take it and mine also."[4]

Many theories and rationalizations have been suggested as responsible for Napoleon III's final decisions and actions under

2. Dano to Moustier, September 1, 1867, CP, Mexique, LXIX.
3. Dano to Moustier, ibid.
4. Agnes Salm Salm, *Ten Years of My Life*, 2 vols. (London, 1875), vol. 2, *Leaves from the Diary of Princess Salm Salm*, p. 82. She was an American who tried valiantly to save Maximilian's life. See also *My Diary in Mexico* by her husband, Prince Felix zu Salm Salm, 2 vols. (London, 1868). Prince Salm Salm was closely associated with Maximilian in the pre-execution period.

which in 1870 the Second Empire collapsed. There was a drastic difference between the emperor who instigated the American adventure and the Napoleon III at the time his empire collapsed. The English scholar Frederick Arthur Simpson argued that the French emperor's unpredictable, inconsistent, and contradictory decisions and actions could be traced, at least in part, to the suffering experienced during his imprisonment. Simpson wrote: "Another and not less unfortunate consequence must be noted. Naturally meditative—almost ruminative—in his process of thought, Louis Napoleon emerged from . . . [prison] a confirmed visionary. If in his later life we find at times a certain aloofness from the actual, an indefinable remoteness from the realities of political life, we may confidently assign as cause . . . [this isolation]. . . . A habit of mind to which he was naturally prone was there fostered and encouraged. For it was good for him then that he should be able to subject the sordid present to a glorious future, to blot out his prison walls by visions of his kingly palace. But it was not good that when the great future had become the actual present, when the hermitage had really been exchanged for the palace then its master's mind should still be groping forwards into a yet further futurity."[5]

Another interpreter of Napoleon III's motivation, the Austrian ambassador, Prince Richard Metternich, told Lord Cowley it was impossible to conceive all the artifices Napoleon III instigated, or how perseveringly he carried them out. His Majesty seemed irresistibly drawn toward such involvement. Whenever a difficulty arose, it was immediately met by some fresh maneuver. In short, wrote Metternich, he is *"un prestidigitateur de premier ordre."*[6]

Metternich here seems to support the assumption that the "deepest thought of the Second Empire," the Grand Design, was ever nebulous and was probably not clearly thought out by Napoleon III and, therefore, certainly not understood by others. The French emperor's hope to create out of the Confederacy a permanent adversary of the United States, as well as an econom-

5. F. A. Simpson, *The Rise of Louis Napoleon, 1808–1848* (London, 1909), pp. 233, 234.
6. Lord Cowley, British ambassador to France, reported this conversation with Metternich to Lord Russell, Private, May 6, 1862, Public Records Office, F.O. 519/229, cited by Carl Bock, *Prelude to Tragedy: The Negotiation and Breakdown of the Tripartite Convention of London, October 31, 1861* (Philadelphia, 1966), p. 450.

ically useful ally of France, obviously was unfulfilled. So was the French emperor's dream of achieving superiority for the Latins in America over Anglo-Americans in world trade and culture. Napoleon III did succeed in giving the French capital a seemingly enduring magnificence, but Paris did not become the arbiter of the world as he had hoped.

The failure of the Grand Design left the Empress Eugénie with a heavy heart because it was her false conviction that she had persuaded her husband to interfere in the Americas. One of her strong motivations, derived from her inherited love of reactionary Spain and her loyalty to the Roman church, was to counteract the spread of Protestantism in the New World by the United States.

The Empress Eugénie's émigré co-workers such as Gutiérrez de Estrada, Juan Nepomuceno Almonte and José Manuel Hidalgo, who were entirely dependent on the French army, lost all with the downfall of the neofeudal political tradition of Mexico.

After the triumph of 1867 of the American republics all Europe was restive, as General Sanford repeatedly reported to Seward. Napoleon III's peace of mind was frequently unsettled by unexpected developments and by his poor health. The cold rebuff of England to the French emperor's proposal for another European Congress was evidence that the power of his leadership had declined. Enmity between Prussia and Austria and the swift rise of Prussia under Bismarck menaced France and challenged her prestige. One year before the execution of Maximilian, Prussia's slashing defeat of the Austrians at Sadowa foreshadowed the final tragedy Napoleon III was to suffer in 1870 from the Prussian army. Had he not been tied down in Mexico, he could have been more active and possibly more effective in Europe; of this Prussia was keenly aware.

Napoleon III's Grand Design failed of its own weaknesses, but it was not without gains for Mexico. Had the proposal for paying European claims from a U.S. loan succeeded, even to the point of frustrating monarchical schemes, Mexico would have been left with her lands mortgaged to the United States and her customs offices managed by alien commissioners. Republican victory over Maximilian freed Mexico from monarchy; from exorbitant and frequently dishonest demands of foreign nationals who looked to their respective governments to enforce their claims; and from the efforts of exiles who for years had schemed and plotted in foreign lands for the restoration of their power, their class privileges, and vested interests. Patriots of the Mexican republic, poorly equipped and always short of money and resources, scattered at the point of imperial bayonets and reappeared to fight on uncompromisingly. They served not just their national cause, they served the New World as well, to make the "Liberty Caps prevail over the crowns."

"We have obtained our victory," declared the exultant Mexican statesman, Matías Romero, "by our own efforts without the aid of any foreign nation—in spite of the moral influence of all Europe and the material force of France and the continental powers. We have opposed this gigantic combination with nothing more than the suffering and patriotism of our people and the firm sympathy of the United States."[7]

7. Romero to Barney, May 31, 1867, *Corres. mexicana,* IX.

BIBLIOGRAPHY

———◆———

1. OFFICIAL RECORDS

Austria

Haus- Hof- und Staatsarchiv, Vienna.
Microfilm reproductions of documents from the Archiv Kaiser Maximilians von Mexiko; cartons 51 and 57, correspondence of Matthew Fontaine Maury, General James Williams, and William M. Gwin.
Photostatic reproductions, in the Library of Congress, of documents from the Archiv Kaiser Maximilians von Mexiko; cartons 137, 140, 141, 144, and 146, correspondence between Maximilian and Napoleon III and correspondence relating to the activities of Thomas E. Massey, Bela Estvan, Mariano Degollado, José Miguel Arroyo, and Louis Borg.
Photostatic reproductions, in the Library of Congress, from the Politisches Archiv des k. k. Ministerium des Auessern, instructions to and dispatches from diplomatic representatives in Belgium, England, France, Spain, and the United States.
For additional records belonging to Maximilian, see Official Records, Mexico.

Colombia

Ministry of Foreign Affairs, Bogotá.
Diario oficial, 1865.
Instructions to and dispatches from diplomatic and consular representatives in Mexico and the United States, 1863–65.

Memorias, No. 8610: message of President Manuel Murillo to Congress, February 1, 1865.
Noticias de Colombia, vol. III.

Confederate States of America

Library of Congress, Washington, D.C.
    Department of State records in Pickett Papers.
National Archives, Washington, D.C.
    United States War Department records; Texas Cotton Bureau records.
Journal of the Congress of the Confederate States of America, 1861– 1865. 7 vols. Washington, D.C., 1904–5.
Richardson, James D., comp. *A Compilation of Messages and Papers of the Confederacy Including the Diplomatic Correspondence, 1861–1865.* 2 vols. Nashville, 1906.
    For additional records of the Confederate States of America, see Official Records, United States.

France

Archives du Ministère de la Guerre, Château de Vincennes, Paris.
    Political reports of Forey and Bazaine to the minister of war; also letters from and to Napoleon III.
Archives du Ministère des Affaires Etrangères, Quai d'Orsay, Paris.
    Correspondance Politique: Instructions to and dispatches from diplomatic representatives in Austria, 1861–64; Central America, 1861–63; Colombia, 1861–63; England, 1860–65; Mexico, 1852– 67; Republic of Texas, 1839–43; Spain, 1860–62; United States, 1861–67.
    Correspondance Politique des Consuls: Instructions to and dispatches from consular representatives, 1861–67, as follows: Mexico (Matamoros, Mazatlán, Tampico, Veracruz); Peru (Lima); Spain (Havana, Cuba); United States (Baltimore, Boston, Charleston, Galveston, Los Angeles, New Orleans, New York, Philadelphia, Richmond, San Francisco, St. Louis).
    Mémoires et Documents: A wide variety of memorials and papers prepared by or submitted to the minister of foreign affairs, relating to the Mexican situation.
Archives Nationales, Paris.
    Archives du Ministère de la Marine et des Colonies: Reports of commanders to the Navy minister and to the minister of foreign affairs on conditions at the mouth of the Rio Grande and along the Pacific coast.
    Papiers des Tuileries: Letters to Napoleon III.

Dossiers Biographiques: Biographical information was provided by the Bureau du Secrétariat Général, Grande Chancellerie de la Légion d'honneur; Papiers de Thouvenel: private correspondence to Thouvenel as foreign minister from French diplomatic representatives abroad; unclassified: papers relating to the Confederacy. Records of the Ministry of Finance and of the Tuileries (except those cited) were destroyed by fire. In 1867 Alphonse Dano destroyed the records of the French Legation in Mexico City relating to the Mexican Empire.

Great Britain

Library of Congress, Washington, D.C.
Photostatic reproductions, Foreign Office papers:
Instructions to and dispatches from the British minister to the United States with extensive enclosures from British diplomatic representatives in Austria, France, Mexico, and Spain.
Public Records Office, London.
British Foreign Office Papers:
Dispatches from diplomatic representatives in Mexico: Sir John Walsham, Sir Peter Campbell Scarlett, and R. J. C. Middleton, October 1863 to December 1867, bearing on relations with the United States, the Confederacy, France, the Mexican Empire, and specifically on Scarlett's relations with Maximilian, F. O. 50, vols. 376–408.
Dispatches from Lord Cowley, ambassador to France, July 1866 to August 1867, F. O. 27, vols. 1620–25 and 1659–65.
Bloomfield Papers: Private letters from Lord Bloomfield, ambassador to Austria, to Earl Russell and to succeeding foreign secretaries, 1862–64.
British and Foreign State Papers. London, 1841–   .
Instructions to and dispatches from diplomatic representatives in Austria, France, Mexico, Spain, and the United States: vol. 52, 1861–62; vol. 53, 1862–63; vol. 54, 1863–64; vol. 55, 1864–65; and vol. 56, 1865–66.

Mexico

Archivo General de la Nación, Mexico City.
Papeles del Imperio: These documents, papers, and correspondence of the Mexican Empire remained in Mexico. They were described by Herbert E. Bolton, *Guide to Materials for the History of the United States in the Principal Archives of Mexico* (1913), as consisting of sixty cartons and were then located in the Archivo

General de Relaciones Exteriores. When in 1944 the authors of this study began research in Mexico, the sixty cartons could not be located. Search was resumed in 1946; finally, as a result of persistent inquiry and search, the cartons were located in the storage rooms of the Archivo General de la Nación. As the contents were examined by the authors of this study the cartons were designated and numbered by them at the request of Dr. Edmundo O'Gorman of the archival staff. The materials cover, in part, the work of the Mexican Empire from October 1866 until its collapse. Included also are some unimportant documents prior to October 1866, and considerable valuable data on the proposed immigration program.

Archivo General de la Secretaria de Hacienda, Mexico City.
Miscellaneous materials.

Archivo General de la Secretaria de Relaciones Exteriores, Mexico City.
Correspondence between the secretary of foreign affairs and the minister to the United States.

Archivo General del Gobierno del Estado de Nuevo León, Monterrey.
Correspondence of Santiago Vidaurre with various military and civil leaders, principally in Texas, 1856–64.

Biblioteca Nacional, Mexico City.
Miscellaneous materials.

Museo Nacional, Mexico City.
Miscellaneous materials.

Estrada, Genaro, ed. *Don Juan Prim y su labor diplomática en México*. Archivo histórico diplomático mexicano, 25. Mexico City, 1928.
Prim's two addresses before the Spanish Cortes as well as his correspondence with the republican government of Mexico and with the intervening powers.

————, ed. *Las Relaciones entre México y Perú: La misión de Corpancho*. Archivo histórico diplomático mexicano, 4. Mexico City, 1923.
Corpancho was the minister from Peru to republican Mexico.

García, Genaro, and Pareyra, Carlos, eds. *Colección de documentos inéditos ó muy raros para la historia de México*. 36 vols. Mexico City, 1903–11. Vol. XIII, *Correspondencia secreta de los principales intervencionistas mexicanos*; Vols. XIV–XXXVI, *La intervención francesa en Mexico*.

Peña y Reyes, Antonio de la, ed. *Notas de Don Juan Antonio de la Fuente, ministro de México cerca de Napoleon III*. Archivo histórico diplomático mexicano, 10. Mexico City, 1924.

Roel, Santiago, ed. *Correspondencia particular de Vidaurre*. Monterrey, n.d.

Romero, Matías, ed. *Correspondencia de la legación mexicana en Washington durante la intervención extranjera, 1860–1868: Colección de documentos para formar la historia de la intervención.* 10 vols. Mexico City, 1870–92.

Consisting of almost 30,000 documents (reproduced from the official archives), these volumes include highly important records bearing on the French Intervention, Mexican relations with the United States as well as with other countries, the Civil War in the United States, Romero's correspondence with Seward and other officials and leaders of the United States, newspaper clippings, extracts from speeches, and similar materials.

Saldivar, Gabriel, ed. *La misión confidencial de Don Jesús Terán en Europa, 1863–1866.* Archivo histórico diplomático mexicano, 1. Mexico City, 1943.

Versión francesa de México, 1808–1867. 5 vols. Mexico City, 1957–67.

This series is invaluable because it gives information about the history of Mexico not otherwise readily accessible. The precursor volume includes materials of the period 1808–39. The prologue, text, and notes are by Ernesto de la Torre Villar. Contents of the other four volumes were translated by Lilia Díaz. Volume 1 covers the years 1853–58; volume 2, 1858–62; volume 3, 1862–64; and volume 4, 1864–67.

See also Official Records, Austria. Reproductions of a selection of these documents are in the archival depositories of Mexico.

Spain

Diario de les sesiones de Cortes, congreso de los deputados. Madrid, 1861–62.

Documents presented to the Department of the Interior, first appendix to no. 133, 1861–62; second appendix to no. 5, 1861–62.

United States

National Archives, Washington, D.C.
Department of the Army: Sherman mission to Mexico.
Department of the Navy: Captain's Letters, January–March, 1860, concerning the capture by U.S. naval forces of the *General Miramón* and the *Marquis de la Havana*; log, U.S.S. *Susquehanna*, November 10–December 20, 1866, Campbell–Sherman mission.
Department of State: Consular reports and letters from Mexico (Chihuahua, Matamoros, Mazatlán, Mexico City, Monterrey, Tampico, Veracruz) and from Spain (Havana, Cuba); instruc-

tions to and dispatches from diplomatic representatives in Austria, Brazil, Chile, Colombia, Costa Rica, Ecuador, El Salvador, England, France, Guatemala, Honduras, Mexico, Nicaragua, Peru, and Spain; Miscellaneous Letters; Notes.

General Records Division, Foreign Affairs Section: Dockets of U.S. citizens to U.S. and Mexican Joint Claims Commission of 1868 for satisfaction in damages from Republic of Mexico (for serving against Maximilian).

Malloy, William M., comp. *Treaties, Conventions, International Acts, Protocols, and Agreements Between the United States of America and Other Powers, 1776–1909.* 3 vols. Washington, D.C., 1910–23.

Miller, Hunter, comp. *Treaties and Other International Acts of the United States of America.* 7 vols. Washington, D.C., 1931–42.

Official Records of the Union and Confederate Navies in the War of the Rebellion. 31 vols. Washington, D.C., 1894–1927.

Richardson, James D., comp. *A Compilation of the Messages and Papers of the Presidents, 1789–1897.* 10 vols. Washington, D.C., 1896–1900.

War of the Rebellion: A Compilation of the Official Records of the Union and Confederate Armies. 130 vols. Washington, D.C., 1880–1901.

Venezuela

Ministry of Foreign Affairs, Caracas.

Instructions to and dispatches from Blas Bruzual, 1863–65, including correspondence with Seward.

2. MANUSCRIPTS

Bibliothèque Nationale, Paris.

Léonce Angrand Collection: Letters to Madame Hortense Cornu, almost a foster sister of Napoleon III, from Angrand, former consul general of France in Mexico, and notes on Mexico, 1862.

De la Londe Collection, Paris.

The diary (1862–63) of Comte de la Londe is now in possession of Loïc de la Londe, great grandson of Comte de la Londe and great-nephew of the Marquis de Radepont. The diary is supplemented by various memoranda. Comte de la Londe was a banker at Veracruz and an official of the French Legation in Mexico from 1856 to 1863 in which year he was made an officer of the Légion d'honneur for services rendered there. The owner of this collection gave the authors valuable information about Radepont's experiences in the United States and his connections with the French expedition to Mexico.

De Noue Collection, Geneva.

Papers of Vicomte Ludovic M. François de Noue, a French officer who joined the French expedition to Mexico and served as political adjutant to Marshal Bazaine. De Noue was sent to Washington for consultations about an arrangement between France and the United States for a "caretaker" government to be established in Mexico after the exodus of the French army.

Alphonse Dano, French minister to Mexico, objected to de Noue's undertaking this mission because de Noue's wife, the former Eliza Harney, daughter of U.S. Brigadier General William Selby Harney and granddaughter of John Mullanphy of St. Louis, who had served under Napoleon I, was a Southerner, and because the de Noue home in Mexico City had been the center of Confederate social activities in that country. Nothing came of the French proposal to the United States that a "caretaker" government be set up in Mexico to maintain law and order after the exodus of the French army. Selected letters from de Noue to Bazaine were made available in 1962 by Count Jehan de Noue of Geneva, Switzerland, direct descendant of the Vicomte Ludovic M. François de Noue.

Houghton Library, Harvard University, Cambridge, Mass.

Marquis de Radepont Papers: Aimé Louis Léon de Bosc, Marquis de Radepont, was the architect of the so-called French Intervention in Mexico. These papers include correspondence with Duc d'Aumale, Walewski, Napoleon III, Clarendon, Saligny, Judah P. Benjamin, Clermont-Tonnerre, and documents, 1857–64, relating to the expansion of the United States, the proposed development of Mexico as a buffer state against her northern neighbor, and plans for establishment of transportation facilities over the Isthmus of Tehuantepec. They supplement the official correspondence of Radepont with the French Foreign Office.

The significance of Radepont's connection with the French expedition to Mexico was discovered by the authors in the records of the French Foreign Office in Paris. They received supplementary information from Abel Doysie who made an inventory of some Radepont papers which were sold in 1930 to Jesse Isidor Straus, U.S. ambassador to France. In 1936 Straus gave the supplementary Radepont papers to his alma mater, Harvard University. So far as the authors have been able to determine, this collection has not previously been used.

Library of Congress, Washington, D.C.

Grant, U. S. (Papers, 1865–67).
Johnson, Andrew (Papers, 1865–67).
Lincoln, Abraham (Papers, 1861–65).
Mason, James M. (Papers, 1861–65).
Maury, Matthew Fontaine (Papers, 1864–67).
Pickett Papers (Archives of the Confederate State Department).
Plumb, Edward L. (Papers, 1864, 1866, 1867).
Schofield, John M. (Papers, 1865–67).
Sheridan, Philip H. (Papers, 1865–67).
Sherman, William T. (Papers, 1866–67).

New-York Historical Society Library, New York City.

Beekman Collection: Letters from Romero to James W. Beekman, 1864–68, relating to conditions in Mexico.

Charles Frederick de Loosey Collection: Letters to his agents in the U.S., memoranda, and related papers, 1865–67, from Maximilian, relating to the establishment of a propaganda agency to "influence public opinion in favor of Mexico"; newspaper clippings, 1863–67. With the Loosey Collection are the correspondence and related papers of Luis de Arroyo, confidential agent of Maximilian, with Mexican officials, 1865–66.

New York Public Library, New York City.

John Bigelow Papers and Journal, 1865–66, 1868–69, 1896.

Rush Rhees Library, University of Rochester, Rochester, N.Y.

William Henry Seward Papers: Private letters, 1863–67. Of chief value for this study was the Seward-Sanford correspondence. Most of these letters were examined at the Seward residence in Auburn, N.Y., through the courtesy of William Henry Seward III before the collection was given to the University of Rochester.

Sanford Memorial Library, Sanford, Florida.

Henry Shelton Sanford Papers (1823–91): The library and papers of Henry Shelton Sanford were preserved for many years by one of his daughters, Carola Sanford Dow, at The Homestead in Derby, Connecticut, the home of the Sanford family. In her last will and testament Mrs. Dow appointed Dr. Alfred J. Hanna, vice president of Rollins College, and Hon. Leo T. Molloy of Derby, Connecticut, literary executors of the library and papers, and left these valuable materials to the Henry Shelton Sanford Memorial Library and Museum, Sanford, Florida. Under the leadership and direction of a deeply interested kinsman, Gifford Cochran, the grandchildren of General Sanford, Sarah Jane Sanford Pansa, Gertrude Sanford Weeks, and Stephen Sanford, financed the processing of the papers.

The Civil War section of these papers consists of 2,000 items and relates to Sanford's activities as U.S. minister to Belgium, 1861–70, in charge of secret service in much of Europe. The collection became available only in 1960. Sanford was an astute observer of European events. He was an excellent linguist, had spent many years in Europe and had broad contacts with influential Europeans. Brussels was a strategically located listening post, close both to London and Paris. Sanford's correspondence with Seward, official and especially private, was an indispensable source. The authors of this study were among the first historians to use these valuable materials hitherto unavailable.

Sterling Library, Yale University, New Haven, Conn.

Webb Family Papers: Correspondence of James Watson Webb with Napoleon III, 1861–66.

3. Contemporary Accounts

Basch, Samuel. *Recuerdos de México: Memorias del médico ordinario del emperador Maximiliano, 1866 à 1867.* Translated by D. Manuel Peredo. Mexico City, 1870.
    In this translation from the original German by Maximilian's physician, published in Leipzig, 1868, is an essay by Hilarion Frias y Soto noting Basch's errors and inaccuracies.
Blanchot, Charles. *Mémoires: L'Intervention française au mexique.* 3 vols. Paris, 1911.
    A colonel on Bazaine's staff, the author was closely associated with former U.S. Senator Gwin.
Blasio, José Luis. *Maximilian: Emperor of Mexico.* Translated by Robert Hammond Murray. New Haven, 1934.
    The author, Maximilian's private secretary, accompanied Charlotte to Europe.
Bonaparte, Louis Napoleon. *L'Extinction du paupérisme.* Paris, 1844.
    Written in prison, this work by the future Emperor Napoleon III was, according to David I. Kulstein, "Louis Napoleon's most direct and most striking effort to convince workers that Bonapartism

called for basic social reforms." It was included in *Oeuvres de Napoleon III*, 5 vols. (Paris, 1856–69). It was translated from the third Paris edition by James H. Causten, Jr., in 1853.

Chevalier, Michel. *Le Mexique, ancien et moderne.* Paris, 1863.

Mexico, Ancient and Modern is an English translation by Thomas Alpass, 2 vols. (London, 1864). See elsewhere in this study numerous references to Chevalier and the significance of his writings.

————. *Lettres sur l'Amérique du Nord.* Paris, 1836.

The first of these letters, appearing in the *Journal des débats*, preceded Tocqueville, *Démocratie en Amérique* (1835) as an interpretation of the United States. In 1836 the original Chevalier letters were combined with his additional interpretations of the United States to form the first edition of his book, *Lettres sur l'Amérique du Nord.* Relatively unknown, the Chevalier observations are superior in some respects to those of Tocqueville. Chevalier and Tocqueville occasionally reached similar conclusions. Some critics claim that the more descriptive and concrete work of Chevalier is more profound than that of the more philosophic Tocqueville.

Chevalier's *Lettres sur l'Amérique du Nord* was published in the United States in translation in 1839 by T. G. Bradford under the title, *Society, Manners and Politics in the United States: Being a Series of Letters on North America.* In 1961 John William Ward translated and edited another edition of Chevalier's work. For an important evaluation of the career of Chevalier, see Arthur Louis Dunham, *Anglo-French Treaty of Commerce in 1860 and the Progress of the Industrial Revolution in France* (Ann Arbor, 1930), pp. 28–63, 351–67.

Détroyat, Léonce. *L'Intervention française au Mexique.* Paris, 1868.

Maximilian became attached to the author of this book, a captain in the French navy. The emperor, once an admiral himself, dreamed of establishing a navy for Mexico. The French treasury made substantial advances to guard the coasts against smugglers. Détroyat was appointed secretary of this nonexistent navy which, according to Sara Yorke Stevenson (see her book, *Maximilian in Mexico*, p. 137), never became operative—it did not even possess a canoe.

Domenech, Abbé Emmanuel Henri Dieudonne. *Histoire du Mexique.* 3 vols. Paris, 1868.

The third volume, recording the history of the French in Mexico, reproduces valuable documents and Maximilian letters. Domenech was a journalist and a missionary in the United States and Mexico. As press director in Maximilian's cabinet, he played a minor role in the Grand Design. His other six books are devoted to experiences in travel in the United States and Mexico.

Dommartin, Hippolyte du Pasquier de. *Les Etats-Unis et le Mexique: L'Intérêt européen dans L'Amérique du Nord.* Paris, 1852.
Illustrated in color.

Gaulot, Paul. *La Vérité sur l'expédition du Mexique.* 3 vols. Paris, 1889–90.
Based in part on some of the correspondence between Napoleon III and Bazaine which had been acquired from Bazaine by Ernest Louet, finance officer with the French army in Mexico.

Hans, Alberto. *Querétaro: Memorias de un oficial del emperador Maximiliano.* Translated by Lorenzo Elizago from the original French. Mexico City, 1869.

Hassaurek, Friedrich. *Four Years Among the Ecuadorians.* Edited by C. Harvey Gardiner, Carbondale, Ill., 1967.
Reprint of Hassaurek's *Four Years Among the Spanish-Americans,* published in London in 1868.

Héricault, Charles Joseph d'. *Maximilien et le Mexique: Histoire des derniers mois de l'empire mexicain.* Paris, 1869.
The author supported the French interference in Mexico, had scant respect for Mexicans, and was critical of the United States.

Hidalgo, José Manuel. *Apuntes para escribir la historia de los proyectos de monarquía en México desde el reinado de Carlos III hasta la instalación del emperador Maximiliano.* Mexico City, 1869.
Defensive in nature and unreliable, the author was Maximilian's minister to France; he was active in events leading up to the establishment of the Mexican Empire.

————.*Un hombre de mundo escribe sus impresiones: Cartas.* Edited by Sofía Verea de Bernal. Mexico City, 1960.
Although a contemporary account, it was not published until the date indicated.

Iglesias, José María. *Revistas históricas sobre la intervención francesa en México.* Mexico City, 1868–69.
The author, minister of finance, accompanied Juárez as the government moved into northern Mexico.

Jecker, Jean B. "La Créance Jecker," *Revue contemporaine,* LXI (January 15, 1868), 128–49.
Response to charges published by Kératry.

Kératry, Emile de. *La Créance Jecker: Les indemnités françaises et les emprunts mexicains.* Paris, 1868.

————. *La Contre-guerilla française au Mexique (Souvenirs des terres chaudes).* Paris, 1869.

————. *L'Empereur Maximilien: Son élévation et sa chute.* Amsterdam, 1867.
Published shortly after Maximilian's execution, this is a carefully documented treatment by an officer of the French army in Mexico.

He described relations between Maximilian and Bazaine by reproducing much of their correspondence; included, also, are documents from Napoleon III, Seward, Eloin, and others. Count Kératry was prejudiced in favor of his commander, Bazaine, severely condemned Napoleon III for his "contempt for plighted faith," was critical of the United States for her "arrogant threats" and antimonarchical stand, and dismissed Maximilian as inadequate due to his "strange contradictions," his "indecision," and his "fickleness of temper as well as his ignorance of the Mexican character." After serving with the French army in Mexico, Kératry returned to Paris and wrote frequently for the chief reviews, particularly the *Revue Moderne*. Translated into English by G. H. Venables and published in London, 1868.

Kollonitz, Countess Paula. *The Court of Mexico*. 3rd ed. Translated by J. E. Ollivant. London, 1868.

Lady in waiting to the Empress Charlotte, the author accompanied Maximilian and Charlotte to Mexico in 1864. This book consists of her impressions of that journey and includes her observations in Mexico. It is almost entirely superficial, devoid of facts and poorly written.

Lefèvre, Eugène. *Documents officiels recueillis dans la secrétairerie privée de Maximilien: Histoire de l'intervention française au Mexique*. 2 vols. Brussels, 1869.

_____. *Le Mexique et l'intervention européenne*. Mexico City, 1862.

The author, a French journalist, was hostile to the Mexican Empire, a political opponent of Napoleon III, and a supporter of the republican government in Mexico. He edited the *American Review* in London during the French occupation and later edited the *Mexico City Tribune*. According to Count Corti, the Juárez cabinet purchased one thousand copies of this book.

Masseras, E. *Un Essai d'empire au Mexique*. Paris, 1879.

Montluc, Léon de, ed. *Correspondance de Juárez et Montluc*. Paris, 1885.

Based on the Armand Montluc Papers in Hôtel de Ville, Paris.

Niox, Gustave Léon. *Expédition du Mexique, 1861–1867: Récit politique et militaire*. 2 vols. Paris, 1875–77.

The author, a captain on the French general staff in Mexico, included many important documents in his account.

Pola, Angel, ed. *Los Traidores pintados por sí mismos*. Mexico City, 1900.

Collection by Eloin, these criticisms of leading Mexicans who were associated with Maximilian portray a black picture.

Randon, Jacques Louis César Alexandre. *Mémoires du Maréchal Randon*. 2d ed. 2 vols. Paris, 1875–77.

After Forey captured Puebla, the author, minister of war, and other council members appear to have convinced Napoleon III that the French troops should be withdrawn from Mexico.

Riva Palacio, Mariano, and Martínez de la Torre, Rafael. *Memorandum sobre el proceso del archiduque.* Mexico City, 1867.

Rivero Cambas, Manuel. *Historia de la intervención, Europa, y Norte América en Mexico y del imperio de Maximiliano.* 3 vols. Mexico City, 1888.

Rivière, Henri. *La Marine française au Mexique.* Paris, 1881.

Upon the recommendations of Captain Vichot, director of the Naval Museum in Paris, this book was examined and in it was found information about ships and conditions not otherwise available.

Romero, Matías. *Mexico and the United States: A Study of Subjects Affecting Their Political, Commercial and Social Relations, Made with a View to Their Promotion.* New York, 1898. Vol. 1.

For an enlightening description and evaluation of the writings by Romero, see the *American Historical Review*, IV, no. 3 (April 1899), 580–82. The author of these comments, the eminent George Parker Winship, for twenty years librarian of the John Carter Brown Library and later at Harvard University, wrote:

D. Matías Romero was appointed Secretary to the Mexican Legation at Washington in 1859, and for nearly twenty-five of the years between that date and his death in December last [1898], he resided in the United States as the diplomatic representative of Mexico. Throughout this period he devoted himself with earnest intelligence and with unremitting diligence to the task of developing by every legitimate means more intimate relations between the neighboring republics. Possessed of solid qualities rather than brilliant talents, his work attracted comparatively little attention even from those whom it affected most directly, but his long term of almost uniformly pleasant and successful service gave him a position of distinct influence in official circles at Washington and with the representatives of commercial interests in the large cities. He was frequently called upon by influential organizations, by learned societies and by magazine editors to explain the problems which complicate relations with our South American neighbors and to throw light upon the puzzling questions whose solution demands an understanding of the social and political characteristics of the Mexican people. His responses to these various demands have contained a very large amount of information upon many sides of Mexican life and history. Written by one of the best informed Mexicans of his generation for the people of the United States, whose wants and ideas he had come to understand very thoroughly, these papers have for some time been regarded by those best acquainted with Mexico as among the most reliable of the sources of information available to English readers.

Almost the last important service rendered by Señor Romero to the two republics which he served so faithfully was the revision of the more important of these occasional essays and addresses for publication in permanent form. The statistical and geographical notes, originally prepared for the American Geographical Society, were carefully corrected and wherever feasible completed by the most recent data obtainable from the officials in Mexico, the whole being arranged so as to give an extended descriptive account of the actual condition of Mexico in its various physical aspects. The articles on the silver question, on the problems of wages and labor, on tariff relations and on the Pan-American movement were expanded by the ideas and the supplementary facts which had been brought to his attention since their first publication. Where the expression of his opinion had given rise to controversies, Señor Romero carefully explained the grounds upon which objection was made to his statements, inserting also his replies and such confirmatory data as he could secure. Putting all these things together, Señor Romero was able to provide his publishers with material for a bulky volume which contains the most trustworthy available compendium of all sorts of information relating to modern Mexico.

The more strictly historical portion of this volume is based upon two articles which appeared originally in the *North American Review* in 1895 and 1897, and which in their revised form are entitled, "Genesis of Mexican Independence" and "Philosophy of Mexican Revolutions." Both papers have been considerably enlarged and to some extent rewritten; minor errors have been corrected, objections to theories or to statements of fact answered, and one or two important recent works on the most exciting period of Spanish American history drawn upon for additional data. All this fills a hundred large pages which contain a lucid account of the course of the vital events by which Mexico and her sister republics to the south won their independence from Spain, and of the subsequent events which showed the Mexican people the disadvantages of political controversies conducted by force of arms. Señor Romero's idea, however, in writing these papers was largely philosophical. His essays were intended to explain to the people of the United States that their southern neighbors are able to take care of themselves, and that they are not afflicted with an incurable desire for revolutionary turmoil and physical political disturbance. It is, therefore, from this point of view that any criticism of his arguments ought to be directed. Agreement with his main thesis is easy, to the extent that it is beyond question a great deal nearer the truth than is the current conception of the Spanish American peoples derived from Mr. R. H. [Richard Harding] Davis and other newspaper reporters or casual visitors. As for the facts stated by Señor Romero, detailed criticism is of little value in the existing condition of knowledge respecting the history of Spanish America during the first half of the nineteenth century. The events of these years have been narrated by many writers, and the prosperous governments of the southern republics have recognized their obligations to their liberators by publishing voluminous series of documents connected with every phase of the struggle for independence. There can be no doubt that the facts of this period will some day be made intelligible. It is quite as true that no satisfying exposition of the significance of these events has yet been given. The Spanish American appreciates to a remarkable extent the curious but indubitable fact that the important thing for the world to know is never what actually happened in the historical past, but is rather the thing which is said to have happened. Inasmuch as something must have happened, it becomes necessary, from this point of view, not to find out what that thing was, but for historical writers to agree upon what it may fairly be supposed to have been. Being essentially logical by birth and breeding, the Spanish American historians are able to assume the truth of the accepted narrative of the course of events during the revolutionary period. It is quite beside the question to ask whether such were really the facts and the motives which governed the succession of events and the development of character among the leaders in the struggle. Such it is agreed that they were, and as such they must be accepted until a more searching and less logical study of the character of individuals and the nature of events has been made. There are, indeed, difficulties in the existing situation, as Señor Romero might have thought had he noticed the cases—comparatively rare in his revised work—where he has occasion to make diametrically opposed statements of fact within a few paragraphs of each other. But each statement is derived from authoritative printed works, and each admirably illustrates the point which ought to be brought out in its particular connection.

Señor Romero has given English readers a very useful summary of the accepted facts of a most interesting period of Mexican history, and he has expounded certain important conclusions which, whether they follow from the facts or not, unquestionably are based upon an intimate and accurate knowledge of the Spanish American character, frankly recognizing its weaknesses and its misunderstood strength.

For a biographical sketch of Mrs. Romero (Lucretia Allen of Philadelphia) see the *Washington Star*, July 30, 1898, p. 7.

Schönovsky von Schönwiese, Adelbert Andreas. *Aus den Gefechten des österreichischen Freicorps in Mejico.* Vienna, 1873.

This publication is disappointing in that it is concerned primarily with that part of Mexican history preceding the Maximilian empire, instead of describing the military activities of the Volunteers who came from Austria to support their former archduke.

Sheridan, Philip H. *Personal Memoirs.* 2 vols. New York, 1888.

Stevenson, Sara Yorke. *Maximilian in Mexico.* New York, 1899.

Sara Yorke Stevenson (1847–1921), archaeologist, historian, and writer, was born in Paris. Her parents were originally from Louisiana. Although her unique record was not published until 1899, it is an eyewitness account of conditions in Paris from 1860 to 1862 and in Mexico from 1862 to 1867. The author recalls and describes both French and Mexican participants.

After her return in 1867 from Mexico she spent the remainder of her life in Philadelphia, engaged in intellectual pursuits. She was elected a member of the American Philosophical Society, was a Chevalier of the Legion of Honor, and was the first woman to receive an honorary degree from the University of Pennsylvania, with whose programs she was closely associated. Mrs. Stevenson's description of the Mexican adventure of Napoleon III was, according to the *American Historical Review*, VI, no. 1 (October 1900), 178, "in very many respects one of the most intelligible of the numerous accounts of what took place during that curious episode in the American drama. Writing from the standpoint of personal observation, Mrs. Stevenson has succeeded with quite unusual skill in maintaining the balance between what she saw and heard for herself, and what she, like others who study the affair, must have learned from the books in which those who participated officially have published their recollections of what they did. Knowing these participants, as table companions, partners at court balls, and as powerful protectors in times of serious danger, she understood how to use their books, and the result is a clear, reasonable narrative of what happened, with some shrewd suggestions as to why. . . . The footlessness of the whole affair, the entire absence of justifying motive or of any sort of profit in the outcome to those who were responsible for the intervention, all that makes this episode the despair of those who would see some philosophy in history, were never more clearly shown than on Mrs. Stevenson's pages. . . ."

Thouvenel, Louis, ed. *Le Secret de l'empereur*. 2 vols. Paris, 1889.
     Confidential correspondence of the foreign minister with the Duc de Gramont, Count Flahaut, and Mercier, compiled by his son.

Timmerhans, Léon François Lambert Emile. *Voyage et opérations du corps belge au Mexique*. Liège, 1866.

Uliczün, Julius. *Geschichte des österreichisch-belgischen Freikorps in Mexico*. Wien, 1868.

Wallace, Lewis. *Lew Wallace: An Autobiography*. 2 vols. New York, 1906.

Washburn, Charles A. *History of Paraguay*. 2 vols. Boston, 1861.

4. Contemporary Pamphlets

Arbelli, H. P. *Les Renards, les dindons et le Mexique*. Bordeaux, 1863.
     The author charged that a secret understanding between Russia and the United States to divide the world—giving Europe to Russia and the Western Hemisphere to the United States—provoked the Crimean War.

Barreyrie, F. de la. *Révélations sur l'intervention française au Mexique de 1866 à 1867*. Paris, 1868.
     The author, editor of *Journal d'Orizaba*, maintained that nine-

tenths of Mexicans thought in 1864 that the French flag promised the restoration of order and free exploitation of natural wealth; also he made charges similar to those of Kératry that civil officials of the Mexican Empire frequently gave orders directly opposed to those of Bazaine.

Belleyme, Adolphe de. *La France et le Mexique.* Paris, 1863.
    The author, a member of the Corps Législatif, opposed the expedition to Mexico.

B[onaparte], N[apoleon] L[ouis]. *Canal of Nicaragua.* London, 1846.
    Prepared and written by the future Napoleon III while he was in prison at the fortress of Ham and completed in London.

Brant, Lucien. *Le Mexique d'hier et le Mexique de demain.* Paris, 1865.

Chesténet, E. *De Notre système financier.* Paris, 1864.

Chevalier, Michel. *La France, le Mexique et les Etats-Confédérés.* Paris, 1863.
    Unsigned but attributed to Chevalier. See explanation under English translation in next entry.

————. *France, Mexico and the Confederate States.* Translated by William Henry Hurlbert. New York, 1863.
    Although this English translation was published as having been written by Chevalier, the translator Hurlbert wrote in the preface that he did not accept that explanation.

————. *L'Isthme de Panama.* Paris, 1844.

Church, George E. *Mexico, Its Revolutions.* New York, 1866.
    The author, a noted engineer, accompanied Juárez in 1866 as a correspondent of the *New York Herald.* See Lewis Hanke, "A Note on the Life and Publications of Colonel George Earl Church," *Books at Brown,* XX (1965), 131–63.

La Chute de l'empire du Mexique par un Mexicain. n.d.
    This anonymous Mexican defended the pope, the Mexican clergy, and the Mexican Conservatives.

Cluseret, Gustave Paul. *Mexico and the Solidarity of Nations.* New York, 1866.

Corta, Charles. *Discours de M. Corta.* Paris, 1865.
    Report on conditions in Mexico delivered before the Corps Législatif.

Cuevas, J. J. *La Colonización.* Mexico City, 1866.
    The author feared immigrants would submerge "our race, ways and customs."

Domenech, J. Passame. *L'Empire mexicain: La Paix et les intérêts du monde Mexique.* Mexico City, 1866.

Kingsley, Vine Wright. *French Intervention in America; or, A Review of "La France, le Mexique, et les Etats-Confédérés."* New York, 1863.

    The author strongly condemned Napoleon III for attempting to establish a monarchy in Mexico.

Malespine, A. *Solution de la question mexicaine.* Paris, 1864.

Masseras, E. *Le Programme de l'empire.* Mexico City, 1864.

Mercier de Lacombe, H. *Le Mexique, l'Amérique du Nord et l'Europe.* Paris, 1862.

    ——. *Le Mexique et les Etats-Unis.* Paris, 1863.

Moreau, Henry M. *La Politique française en Amérique.* Paris, 1864.

    The author was opposed to the occupation of Mexico; he wanted France to preserve the American Union as a counterbalance to England.

Porte, A. de la. *Maximilien d'Autriche: Empereur du Mexique.* Lille, 1867.

Prim, General Juan. *Le Sénat, les Cortes, et la presse espagnole.* Paris, 1863.

La Question mexicaine et la colonisation française. Paris, 1864.

    This anonymous author thought "Mexico can be to France what India is to England less the expenses of government." Semiofficial.

Rouher, Eugène. *Discours de Rouher.* Paris, 1864.

Sturm, Herman. *The Republic of Mexico and Its American Creditors.* Indianapolis, 1869.

Theodoros et Juárez. Paris, 1868.

    The anonymous author compared the French expedition to Mexico with the English expedition to Abyssinia for the exaction of reparations as compensation for the treatment of British subjects by Theodoros.

5. CONTEMPORARY PERIODICALS AND NEWSPAPERS

France

Le Charivari.

Le Constitutionnel; controlled by Persigny.

Le Correspondant.

Le Journal des débats; Edouard Laboulaye was a regular contributor.

La Liberté.

Le Mémorial diplomatique; Debranz de Saldapenha, editor.

Le Moniteur universel; official.

L'Opinion nationale; founded by Adolphe Gueroult, consul at Mazatlán, Mexico, in the 1840s and in 1863 a member of the Corps Législatif.

La Patrie; Felix Aucaigne, editor.

Le Pays; controlled by Granier de Cassagnac, influential member of the Corps Législatif.
La Presse; directed at one time by Gueroult.
Revue contemporaine.
Revue des deux mondes; Eugène Forcade, editor, approved the French invasion of Mexico as a check against the United States until 1866 when he opposed the policy of Napoleon III.
Le Siècle.
Le Temps.

Mexico

In 1946 the largest collection was in the Hemeroteca of the National Library. The language is indicated if not in Spanish.

El Cronista; Niceto de Zamacois, chief editor, was a Spanish Basque who later wrote an exhaustive history of Mexico.
El Diario del Imperio; official.
L'Ere nouvelle (French); edited by E. Masseras, former editor, *New York Courier des Etats-Unis*; established and subsidized by the French.
L'Estafette (French); Charles de Barrès, editor.
Mexican Times (English); edited by Henry W. Allen from September 1865 through March 1866; by John N. Edwards from March 1866 through November of that year at which time the subsidy from the empire was discontinued. Thereafter, the *Times* was independent and often critical of the empire. An almost complete file is in the Louisiana State University Library; several issues are in the library of the New-York Historical Society. Not a single issue was located in Mexico.
La Nación.
La Orquesta.
El Pájaro verde; organ of the ultra-clerical party; large circulation.
La Patria.
El Ranchero (Spanish and English); published at Matamoros and, according to the *New York Evening Post*, edited by "two fugitive rebels." Only a few issues were located; they were in enclosures in correspondence.
La Sociedad; organ of the moderate Clerical party.
La Sombra.
La Union.

United States

"The Napoleonic Idea in Mexico." *Blackwood's Edinburgh Magazine*, American edition (July 1864).

This accurate and exhaustive discussion of Napoleon III's Grand Design for the Americas is significant, particularly for the information given about Michel Chevalier and the definition of Napoleon III's "deepest thought of the Second Empire." This British periodical has enjoyed a worldwide reputation of more than 150 years for the high value of its contents.

New York Times, 1861–67.

6. PERIODICALS

Barker, Nancy Nichols. "Empress Eugénie and the Origin of the Mexican Venture." *Historian,* XXII, no. 7 (1960), 9–23.

————. "France, Austria, and the Mexican Venture, 1861–1864," *French Historical Studies,* III, no. 2 (Fall 1963), 224–45.

Bartlett, I. S. "President Juárez at Old El Paso," *Bulletin of the Pan-American Union,* XLI (November 5, 1915), 641–58.

Blumberg, Arnold. "A Swedish Diplomat in Mexico, 1864," *Hispanic American Historical Review,* XLV (1965), 275–86.

————. "United States and the Role of Belgium in Mexico, 1863–1867," *Historian,* XXVI (February 1964), 206–27.

————. "William Seward and Egyptian Intervention in Mexico," *Smithsonian Journal of History,* I, no. 4 (Winter 1966–67).

Cadenhead, Ivie E., Jr. "González Ortega and the Presidency of Mexico," *Hispanic American Historical Review,* XXXII (August 1952), 331–46.

Chapman, Mary P. "The Mission of Elisha Crosby to Guatemala, 1861–1864," *Pacific Historical Review,* XXIV (August 1955), 275–86.

Cleven, N. Andrew N. "The Ecclesiastical Policy of Maximilian of Mexico," *Hispanic American Historical Review,* IX (August 1929), 316–60.

Coleman, Evan J. "Senator Gwin's Plan for the Colonization of Sonora," *Overland Monthly,* XVII (May 1891), 497–519, and (June 1891), 593–607.

Crenshaw, Ollinger. "The Knights of the Golden Circle," *American Historical Review,* XLVII (October 1941), 23–50.

This filibustering group proposed to annex Mexico and add as many as twenty-five slave states to the Union.

Delaney, Robert W. "Matamoros, Port for Texas during the Civil War," *Southwestern Historical Quarterly,* LVIII (April 1955), 473–87.

Denton, Bernice Barnett. "Count Alphonso de Saligny and the Franco-Texienne Bill," *Southwestern Historical Quarterly,* XLIV (1941).

Duniway, Clyde A. "Reasons for the Withdrawal of the French from Mexico," *Annual Report of the American Historical Association for 1902* (1903), I, 315–28.

Ellison, Simon J. "An Anglo-American Plan for the Colonization of Mexico," *Southwestern Social Science Quarterly*, XVI (September 1935), 42–52.

Ferris, Nathan L. "The Relations of the United States with South America during the American Civil War," *Hispanic American Historical Review*, XXI (February 1941), 51–78.

Frazer, Robert W. "Latin American Projects to Aid Mexico during the French Intervention," *Hispanic American Historical Review*, XXVIII (August 1948), 377–88.

––––––––. "Maximilian's Propaganda Activities in the United States," *Hispanic American Historical Review*, XXIV (February 1944), 4–29.

––––––––. "Trade between California and the Belligerent Powers during the French Intervention in Mexico," *Pacific Historical Review*, XV (1946), 390–99.

Goldwert, Marvin. "Matías Romero and Congressional Opposition to Seward's Policy toward the French Intervention in Mexico," *Americas* (July 1965), 22–40.

Hall, Martin H. "The Campbell-Sherman Diplomatic Mission to Mexico," *Bulletin of the Historical and Philosophical Society of Ohio*, XIII (October 1955), 254–70.

Hanna, Alfred J. "A Confederate Newspaper in Mexico," *Journal of Southern History*, XII (February 1946), 67–83.

––––––––. "The Role of Matthew Fontaine Maury in the Mexican Empire," *Virginia Magazine of History and Biography*, LV (April 1947), 105–25.

Annual address before the Virginia Historical Society, 1947.

Hanna, Alfred J., and Hanna, Kathryn Abbey. "The Immigration Movement of the Intervention and Empire as Seen through the Mexican Press," *Hispanic American Historical Review*, XXVII (May 1947), 220–46.

Of this article the *Handbook of Latin American Studies*, 1947, made the following comment: "Very little attention has been given, to date, to studies of the Latin American press or of public opinion. It is to be hoped that this study will serve as a pilot project for similar enterprises in other areas and periods of time."

Hanna, Kathryn Abbey. "Incidents of the Confederate Blockade," *Journal of Southern History*, XI (May 1945), 214–29.

Delivered at the annual meeting of the Southern Historical Association, 1944.

Harmon, George D. "Confederate Migration to Mexico," *Hispanic*

American Historical Review, XVII (November 1937), 458–87.

Haskins, Ralph W. "Juan José Flores and the Proposed Expedition against Ecuador, 1846–1847," *Hispanic American Historical Review,* XXVII (August 1947) 467–95.

    Contains references, also, to various early attempts to establish a monarchy in Mexico.

Hauck, Charles C. "Attitude of Foreign Governments toward Spanish Re-occupation of the Dominican Republic," *Hispanic American Historical Review*, XXVII (May 1947), 247–68.

Hill, Lawrence F. "Confederate Exodus to Latin America," *Southwestern Historical Quarterly*, XXXIX (October 1935), 100–34, and XXXIX (January 1936), 161–99.

————. "The Confederates in Middle America," *Southwestern Historical Quarterly*, XXXIX (April 1936), 309–26.

Hoskins, Halford Lancaster. "French Views of the Monroe Doctrine and the Mexican Expedition," *Hispanic American Historical Review*, IV (1921), 677–89.

    This summary is of value but it is an example of the acceptance, without careful analysis, of inaccurate and misleading French sources and confusing conclusions.

McCornack, Richard B. "James Watson Webb and French Withdrawal from Mexico," *Hispanic American Historical Review,* XXXI (May 1951), 274–86.

————. "Maximilian's Relations with Brazil," *Hispanic American Historical Review*, XXXII (February 1952), 175–86.

McPherson, Hallie M. "The Plan of William McKendree Gwin for a Colony in North Mexico, 1863–1865," *Pacific Historical Review,* II (December 1933), 357–86.

Miller, Robert R. "The American Legion of Honor in Mexico," *Pacific Historical Review*, XXX (August 1961), 229–41.

————. "Californians against the Emperor," *California Historical Society Quarterly*, XXXVII (September 1958), 193–214.

————. "Gaspar Sánchez Ochoa: A Mexican Secret Agent in the United States," *Historian*, XXIII (May 1961), 316–29.

————. "Herman Sturm: Hoosier Secret Agent for Mexico," *Indiana Magazine of History*, LVIII (March 1962), 1–15.

————. "Lew Wallace and the French Intervention in Mexico," *Indiana Magazine of History*, LIX (March 1963), 31–50.

————. "Matías Romero: Mexican Minister to the United States during the Juárez-Maximilian Era," *Hispanic American Historical Review*, XLV (May 1965), 228–45.

————. "The Ochoa Bond Negotiations of 1865–1867," *Pacific Historical Review*, XI (December 1942), 397–414.

————. "Placido Vega: A Mexican Secret Agent in the United States, 1864–1866," *Americas*, XIX (October 1962), 137–48.

————. "The United States, European and West Virginia Land and Mining Company," *Pacific Historical Review*, XIII (March 1944), 28–40.

Nicolay, John G., and Hay, John. "Abraham Lincoln: A History," *Century Magazine*, XXXVIII (May 1889), 838–56.

Richards, Edward W. "Louis Napoleon and Central America," *Journal of Modern History*, XXXIV (June 1962), 178–84.

Rister, Carl C. "Carlota: A Confederate Colony in Mexico," *Journal of Southern History*, XI (February 1945), 33–50.

Robertson, William S. "The Tripartite Treaty of London," *Hispanic American Historical Review*, XX (May 1940), 167–89.

Salomon, Henry. "Prince Richard de Metternich et sa correspondance pendant son ambassade à Paris (1859–1871)," *La Revue de Paris*, XXXI (February 1, 1924), 507–41, and XXXI (February 15, 1924), 762–803.

Sears, Louis M. "A Confederate Diplomat at the Court of Napoleon III," *American Historical Review*, XXVI (January 1921), 255–81.

Shields, James C. "Sonora y los franceses," *Revista de historia de América*, no. 46 (December 1958), pp. 337–74.
    Treats of French-backed colonization projects in Sonora, primarily the one promoted by Gwin.

Smith, Justin H. "La República de Río Grande," *American Historical Review*, XXV (July 1920), 660–75.

Sonolet, Luis. "L'Agonie de l'empire du Mexique," *La Revue de Paris*, XXXIV, pt. 1 (August 1, 1927), 590–625, and pt. 2 (August 15, 1927), 862–98.
    Based on the papers of Castelnau who accused Bazaine of shameless duplicity.

Stevenson, Sara Yorke. "Prince Louis Napoleon and the Nicaraguan Canal," *Century Magazine*, LXIV, no. 3 (July 1902), 391–96.
    This important article has been supplemented by Edward W. Richards, "Louis Napoleon and Central America," *Journal of Modern History*, XXXIV (June 1962), 178–84. See note on Sara Yorke Stevenson under Contemporary Accounts.

Vasquez-Machicado, Humberto. "La Monarquía en Bolivia," *Revista de historia de América*, no. 32 (December 1951), pp. 21–82.

Vigness, David M. "Relations of the Republic of Texas and the Republic of the Rio Grande," *Southwestern Historical Quarterly*, LVII (January 1954), 312–21.

Wilgus, A. Curtis. "Official Expressions of Manifest Destiny Sentiments Concerning Hispanic America, 1848–1871." *Louisiana Historical Quarterly*, XVI (July 1932), 486–506.

Wilson, Howard L. "President Buchanan's Proposed Intervention in Mexico," *American Historical Review*, V (July 1900), 687–701.

7. BIOGRAPHIES AND MEMOIRS

Auer, John J. "Tom Corwin: King of the Stump." Ph.D. dissertation, University of Wisconsin, 1947.

    A study of one of the architects of Lincoln's Latin American policy.

Barker, Charles A., ed. *Memoirs: Reminiscences of California and Guatemala from 1849 to 1864.* San Marino, 1945.

Bigelow, John. *Retrospections of an Active Life.* 5 vols. New York, 1909–13.

    Volumes 2 and 3 include Bigelow's activities in France.

Díaz, Porfirio. *Memorias de Porfirio Díaz.* Mexico City, 1923.

    Probably the most important Juarista general and later long-time dictator of Mexico.

Fleury, Emile F. *Souvenirs du général Fleury.* 2 vols. Paris, 1897–98.

    An intimate friend and counselor of Napoleon III, Fleury claims he foresaw the failure of the Mexican expedition.

Grant, Ulysses S. *Personal Memoirs of U. S. Grant.* 2 vols. New York, 1885–86.

    Volume 2, pages 545–47, contains Grant's attitude toward France.

Guérard, Albert. *Napoleon III.* Cambridge, 1943.

Knapp, Frank A., Jr. *Life of Sebastian Lerdo de Tejada, 1823–1889: A Study of Influence and Obscurity.* Austin, 1951.

Leonardon, H. *Prim.* Paris, 1901.

McCormack, Thomas J., ed. *Memoirs of Gustav Koerner.* 2 vols. Cedar Rapids, Ia., 1909.

    A German refugee, Koerner's understanding of European conditions enabled him to render valuable services as U.S. minister to Spain.

McKee, Irving. *"Ben Hur" Wallace.* Berkeley, 1947.

McPherson, Hallie M. "William McKendree Gwin, Expansionist." Ph.D. dissertation, University of California, 1931.

    The most comprehensive, authoritative body of material about Gwin, this dissertation is an indispensable enlargement of other Gwin materials. The sketch in the *Dictionary of American Biography* is surprisingly inadequate, even inaccurate. McPherson's sources were drawn primarily from the extensive materials in the Bancroft Library. *Eclaircissement sur le projet de colonisation des etats de Sonora et de Chihuahua, Mars 1864* is the original which was submitted by Gwin to Napoleon III. The Bancroft Library also houses Gwin's *Memoirs*.

Metternich, Pauline de. *Souvenirs*. Paris, 1929.
> The author's husband was the Austrian ambassador to France.

Miguel Verges, Josef María. *El General Prim, en España y en México*. Mexico City, 1949.

O'Connor, Richard. *Sheridan the Inevitable*. Indianapolis, 1953.

Paléologues, Georges Maurice. *The Tragic Empress*. Translated by Hamish Miles. New York, 1928.
> Purportedly based in part on interviews with Eugénie; she allegedly told the author that the intervention idea was given her by Hidalgo at Biarritz in the fall of 1861 and that her husband chose Maximilian because of Leopold's political influence and to influence the cession of Venice to Italy.

Roeder, Ralph. *Juárez and His Mexico*. 2 vols. New York, 1947.
> Extremely valuable.

Romero, Emilia. *Corpancho: Un amigo de México*. Mexico City, 1949.

Salm Salm, Agnes. *Ten Years of My Life*. 2 vols. London, 1875.

Salm Salm, Prince Felix zu. *My Diary in Mexico*. 2 vols. London, 1868.

Sánchez-Navarro y Peón, Carlos. *Miramón: El Caudillo conservador*. Mexico City, 1945.

Schofield, John M. *Forty-six Years in the Army*. New York, 1897.

Sherman, William T. *Memoirs*. 2 vols. New York, 1891.
> Volume 2 treats the Campbell-Sherman mission to Mexico. Sherman believed that by allowing himself to be substituted for Grant on this mission, a serious quarrel between Grant and President Johnson was prevented.

Simpson, F. A. *The Rise of Louis Napoleon, 1808–1848*. London, 1909.
> Included in a review of this book in the Literary Section of the *New York Times*, February 5, 1910, is the following comment: "In its extensive bibliography, the most complete ever formed on the subject, an attempt has been made to denote the relative value of the authorities enumerated."

Thompson, James M. *Louis Napoleon and the Second Empire*. Oxford, 1954.
> See page 93 for some informative and incisive characterizations of Napoleon III by Madame Hortense Cornu. A lifelong friend of the French emperor, she was virtually a foster sister. Her husband, Dr. Cornu, attended Napoleon III during his imprisonment and helped him escape from France.

Van Deusen, Glyndon G. *William Henry Seward*. New York, 1967.

Wellesley, Victor, and Sencourt, Robert. *Conversations with Napoleon III*. London, 1934.
> Contains valuable quotations from Lord Cowley; Sencourt was the "official" biographer of Eugénie.

8. SECONDARY WORKS

Aronson, Theo. *The Fall of the Third Napoleon*. Indianapolis, 1970.
An excellent and dramatic account.

————. *The Golden Bees*. Greenwich, Conn., 1964.
A lively and informing story of the Bonaparte family.

Barker, Nancy Nichols. *Distaff Diplomacy: The Empress Eugénie and the Foreign Policy of the Second Empire*. Austin, 1967.

A scholarly analysis of diplomatic records, its findings indicate that Eugénie was extremely active in promoting the French expedition to Mexico. Her pro-Church, proclerical attitudes are made clear as is her erratic and emotional interference in foreign affairs. Such was Eugénie's ignorance about Latin America that she naïvely assumed that transforming American republics into American monarchies would "civilize" Spanish Americans. She deeply resented the Protestant influence of the United States.

Beyens, Napoleon Eugène. *Le Second Empire, vu par un diplomate belge*. . . . 2 vols. Lille-Bruges, 1924–26.

The author, son of a Belgian ambassador to France, contends the Mexican expedition was the most flagrant political error of Napoleon III.

Blumenthal, Henry. *France and the United States: Their Diplomatic Relations, 1789–1914*. Chapel Hill, N.C., 1970.

————. *A Reappraisal of Franco-American Relations, 1830–1871*. Chapel Hill, N.C., 1959.

Bock, Carl H. *Prelude to Tragedy: The Negotiation and Breakdown of the Tripartite Convention of London, October 31, 1861*. Philadelphia, 1966.

The most exhaustive compilation of the French expedition, this book traces the Grand Design throughout its preliminary development.

Brown, Robert B. "Guns over the Border." Ph.D. dissertation, University of Michigan, 1951.

A thorough study of United States military aid to Juárez. The author died so soon after the completion of this valuable work that it was never published.

Case, Lynn M., ed. *French Opinion on the United States and Mexico, 1860–1867*. New York, 1936.

————. *French Opinion on War and Diplomacy during the Second Empire*. Philadelphia, 1954.

Case, Lynn M., and Spencer, Warren F. *The United States and France: Civil War Diplomacy*. Philadelphia, 1970.

Corti, Count Egon Caesar. *Maximilian and Charlotte in Mexico*. Translated by Catherine Alison Phillips. 2 vols. New York, 1928.

See the prologue for a general evaluation of this work. The

surprisingly inaccurate assertion by Count Corti, the able Austrian historian, that the young Conservative Mexican émigré in Europe, José Manuel Hidalgo, was "chiefly responsible" for the concept of the French Intervention in Mexico has misguided other historians and writers. Numerous investigations have long since proved that Hidalgo was utterly unreliable and untruthful in the claims he made for directing French activities in Mexico. His influence was limited primarily to the gigolo-like attendance he danced upon the Empress Eugénie. See references to Corti in the annotation for Percy Martin's *Maximilian in Mexico* in this bibliography.

Dabbs, Jack Autrey. *The French Army in Mexico, 1861–1867.* The Hague, 1963.

Davis, Edwin A. *Fallen Guidon.* Santa Fe, N.M., 1962.

Account of the expedition of Shelby and his Confederate followers.

Dawson, Daniel. *The Mexican Adventure.* London, 1935.

One of the ablest interpretations based primarily on materials in the British and Austrian archives. Unfortunately there is limited use of American sources.

Delord, Taxile. *Histoire illustrée du Second Empire.* 6 vols. Paris, 1869–1875.

Anti-Bonapartist. Volumes 3 and 4 relate to Mexico.

Frazer, Robert W. "Matías Romero and the French Intervention in Mexico." Ph.D. dissertation, University of California, 1941.

Fuentes Mares, José. *. . . y México se refugió en el desierto: Luis Terrazas, historia y destino.* Mexico City, 1954.

Gorce, Pierre de la. *Histoire du Second Empire.* 7 vols. Paris, 1894–1905.

Volumes 4 and 5 relate to Mexico.

Hyde, H. Montgomery. *Mexican Empire: The History of Maximilian and Carlota.* New York, 1946.

The *American Historical Review,* in its issue of July 1947, explained, "This highly readable account of a fantastic episode in history won for its author a prize of £100 in the series of awards offered by Macmillan (London) to members of the forces of the British Empire under thirty-five for the celebration in 1943 of the centenary of this noted publishing house. . . . Colonel Hyde's treatment is the reverse of his title: it is primarily concerned with the lives of Maximilian and Carlota and, secondarily, with the Mexican Empire. . . . Its chief value to the scholar is the exhaustive listing of sources with explanatory notes."

Specifically, Colonel Hyde has not thoroughly used the sources he lists. For example, he asserts Percy F. Martin's *Maximilian in Mexico* has a superior treatment. A careful examination of the

Martin book reveals the unhappy truth that Martin did not use adequately the sources he lists.

Jordan, Donaldson, and Pratt, Edwin J. *Europe and the American Civil War*. Boston, 1931.

Kulstein, David I. *Napoleon III and the Working Class*. Los Angeles, 1969.

The following comment on this book is from the *American Historical Review*, 75, no. 5 (June 1970), 1466: "The Second Empire was hardly a democracy, but it was, after all, firmly based on public consent. This book amply demonstrates that Napoleon III and his officials not only never forgot the importance of public opinion but used surprisingly modern methods of persuasion to maintain their hold on public approval."

Lally, Frank E. *French Opposition to the Mexican Policy of the Second Empire*. Baltimore, 1931.

Lepidus, Henry. *History of Mexican Journalism*. Columbia, Mo., 1928.

Loliée, Frédéric. *Le Duc de Morny et la société du Second Empire*. Paris, 1901.

Lynch, M. Claire. *The Diplomatic Mission of John Lothrop Motley to Austria, 1861–1867*. Washington, D.C., 1944.

Martin, Percy F. *Maximilian in Mexico*. London, 1914.

This book appears to have been written with little consultation of official documents and from a subjective point of view. It is a conspicuous example of biased interpretations, replete with oft-repeated inaccuracies borrowed from uncritical authors. Count Corti reveals his lack of discrimination in praising Martin's work.

Montufar y Rivers Maestre, Lorenzo. *Reseña histórica de Centro-América*. 7 vols. Guatemala City, 1878–87.

Núñez Ortega, Angel. *Memorias sobre las relaciones diplomáticas de México con los estados libres y soberanos de la América del Sur*. Mexico City, 1878.

Included are treatments on Brazil, Chile, Ecuador, and Peru.

O'Connor, Richard. *The Cactus Throne*. New York, 1971.

Ollivier, Emile. *L'Empire libéral: Etudes, récits, souvenirs*. 17 vols. Paris, 1895–1915.

Volumes 5, 6, and 7 relate to Mexico.

Owsley, Frank L. *King Cotton Diplomacy*. Chicago, 1959.

Perkins, Dexter. *A History of the Monroe Doctrine*. Boston, 1955.

In his treatment of Napoleon III's scheme of interposing French power in the New World, Dr. Perkins asserts: ". . . no more sinister project, in terms of American interest, American influence, and American ideas, has ever been conceived in the history of the Monroe Doctrine." In this brief analysis (pp. 108–38) of the conspiracy for American monarchy, the conclusion is that the attitude of the United States was ". . . a major factor in the French withdrawal; it was distinctly not the only factor."

Rippy, J. Fred. *Latin America in World Politics*. New York, 1938.

_____. *South America and Hemisphere Defense*. Baton Rouge, La., 1941.

_____. *The United States and Mexico*. New York, 1931.

Roel, Santiago. *Nuevo León*. 2 vols. Monterrey, 1938.

Saldivar, Gabriel. *Historia compendiada de Tamaulipas*. Mexico City, 1945.

Salomon, Henry. *L'Ambassade de Richard de Metternich à Paris*. Paris, 1931.

Schéfer, Christian. *La Grande Pensée de Napoléon III*. Paris, 1939.

Schéfer wrote this book at the age of eighty-three, claiming he used documents "kept in official archives only recently come accessible." He refers to data on the Marquis de Radepont which he uses scantily but which have been available since 1927 in the French archives. Curiously Schéfer limits his work from the preliminary period of 1858 to the summer of 1862 and therefore ignores the actual implementation of the Grand Design.

The author claims that President James Buchanan of the United States provoked the intervention of England, France, and Spain by his expansionist proposals in 1859.

Shields, James C. "Inmigración y colonización durante el segundo imperio mexicano (under Maximilian)." Ph.D. dissertation, National University of Mexico, 1958.

This work is entirely unsatisfactory.

Sobarzo, Horacio. *Crónica de la aventura de Raousset-Boulbon en Sonora*. Mexico City, 1954.

Treats of Jecker concessions in Sonora.

Terrell, Alexander W. *From Texas to Mexico and the Court of Maximilian in 1865*. Dallas, 1933.

Tindall, George B., ed. *The Pursuit of Southern History*. Baton Rouge, La., 1964.

The annual addresses of presidents of the Southern Historical Association are reproduced in this publication. The subject of Kathryn Abbey Hanna's address as president of the Southern Historical Association in 1953 was "The Roles of the South in the French Intervention in Mexico."

West, W. Reed. *Contemporary French Opinion on the American Civil War*. Baltimore, 1924.

White, Elizabeth B. *American Opinion of France from Lafayette to Poincaré*. New York, 1927.

Wyllys, Rufus K., *The French in Sonora, 1850–1854*. Berkeley, 1932.

INDEX

A Note on the Book

Text set in Baskerville Linotype

Display lines set in Caslon Bold Condensed Monotype

Composition and printing by
The TJM Corporation, Baton Rouge, Louisiana

Binding by
Kingsport Press, Kingsport, Tennessee

Sixty-pound Olde Style wove paper by
S. D. Warren Company, Boston, Massachusetts

Designed and published by
The University of North Carolina Press, Chapel Hill,
North Carolina